# Advanced Principles in Environmental Policy

NEW HORIZONS IN ENVIRONMENTAL ECONOMICS

**General Editor:** Wallace E. Oates, *Professor of Economics, University of Maryland*

This important series is designed to make a significant contribution to the development of the principles and practices of environmental economics. It includes both theoretical and empirical work. International in scope, it addresses issues of current and future concern in both East and West and in developed and developing countries.

The main purpose of the series is to create a forum for the publication of high quality work and to show how economic analysis can make a contribution to understanding and resolving the environmental problems confronting the world in the late twentieth century.

Recent titles in the series include:

# Advanced Principles in Environmental Policy

Anastasios Xepapadeas

*Professor of Economics, University of Crete, Greece*

NEW HORIZONS IN ENVIRONMENTAL ECONOMICS

**Edward Elgar**
Cheltenham, UK • Northampton, MA, USA

363.7
X5a

Published by
Edward Elgar Publishing Limited
8 Lansdown Place
Cheltenham
Glos GL50 2HU
UK

Edward Elgar Publishing, Inc.
6 Market Street
Northampton
Massachusetts 01060
USA

A catalogue record for this book
is available from the British Library

**Library of Congress Cataloguing in Publication Data**

Xepapadeas, Anastasios.
    Advanced principles in environmental policy / Anastasios
Xepapadeas.
        (New horizons in environmental economics)
        Includes bibliographical references and index.
        1. Environmental economics. 2. Environmental policy—Economic
    aspects. I. Title. II. Series.
    HD75.6.X46   1997
    363.7—dc21                                              97–24220
                                                                CIP

ISBN 1 85898 332 0

Printed and bound in Great Britain by MPG Books Ltd, Bodmin, Cornwall

*To Joan, Petro and Dimi*

# Contents

# Figures

# Tables

# Preface

Environmental policy has become an issue of increasing importance at the levels of both applied policy and theory. At the theoretical level the 1990s can be regarded as a period of extensions of the basic theoretical policy framework developed in earlier decades. These extensions are an outcome of the evolution of the field, as environmental problems come under more detailed scientific scrutiny and environmental economics interacts with other branches of economics. This has improved our understanding of a number of basic issues, such as nonpoint source pollution, transboundary pollution and international environmental cooperation, and the impact of market imperfections on environmental policy instruments. This evolution has helped to modify existing policy tools or design new ones, in the constant pursuit of an efficient policy framework capable of providing answers to theoretical questions. Also, and perhaps more importantly, it has helped to provide policy-makers with more efficient tools in order to face the numerous and complex environmental problems.

This books presents these extensions and the policy rules which they imply in a systematic way, starting from a basic environmental policy framework, and extending along the issues that characterize the current evolution of the theory of environmental policy. The book does not examine issues of natural resource management; however, since the focus is on developing rather general models for policy design, resource management issues can be analysed with the help of concepts and models developed in this book.

The book is addressed to advanced undergraduate and graduate students in environmental economics, as well as to professionals, researchers and policy-makers seeking to understand some fundamentals of environmental policy.

Many thanks to Aart de Zeeuw, Eftichios Sartzetakis, Peter Kort and Carlo Carraro who read various chapters of the book and offered valuable comments. Special thanks to Joan Stefan for her invaluable contribution in preparing the book.

# 1. Introduction

The design and application of environmental policy is an issue of great importance, at both the level of applied research and the level of applied policy-making. It is well known that from the economists' point of view, environmental policy is a case of analysing externalities and market failure, issues thoroughly examined in microeconomic theory. As pointed out by William Baumol and Wallace Oates (1988 p.1) in their book *The Theory of Environmental Policy,* one of the most influential works in the field, 'When the "environmental revolution" arrived in the 1960s, economists were ready and waiting'. The economic literature contained an apparently coherent view of the pollution problem together with a compelling set of implications for public policy. Although the economists had a framework – at least in theory – for the design of environmental policy, it was not the economic instruments that were used first for applied policy purposes but rather command and control type policies that did not take into account economic considerations.[1] The recent experience, however, shows an increasing use of economic instruments – or, as they are commonly called, economic incentives or market-based instruments – in practice. These instruments tend to substitute or complement command and control issues (OECD 1989, 1991, 1994a,b).

The type and the structure of policy instruments used to design environmental policy in practice are founded on the theory of environmental policy developed mainly in the 1970s and the 1980s. However, the continuing in-depth analysis of the nature of specific environmental problems and the quest for ways to deal with important issues such as climate change or agricultural run-off, along with the continuous interactions of environmental economics with areas such as dynamic investment theory, industrial organization and international economics, has produced a number of important extensions to the basic environmental theory framework. These extensions have not only helped us to better understand existing environmental problems, but have also made it possible to analyse new

---

[1]See Cropper and Oates (1992) for a description of the first stages of environmental policy applications in the US.

1

problems and examine the design of environmental policy under various assumptions about issues such as the type of market structure, the distribution of information or the time horizon of the problem.

The purpose of this book is to present in a unifying way these recent extensions in the theory of environmental policy. Using as a foundation the basic framework of environmental policy theory – which has been well-developed in the recent decades – the book builds upon and extends the theory by paying special attention to the interrelationships between environmental economics and other areas of economics. Following this principle the book is organized in the following way. Chapter 2 presents a basic environmental policy framework, where policy instruments – both market based and command and control – are analysed. This chapter, which mainly reviews standard results in the theory of environmental policy, serves as a basis for the further development of environmental policy presented in the rest of the book. By relaxing standard assumptions underlying the basic model four main extensions are presented.

Chapter 3 relaxes the assumption of a static framework and analyses issues of stock pollution and environmental policy in a dynamic set-up. In particular the chapter examines issues of dynamic optimality in the design of environmental policy, the effect of environmental policy on investment decisions, strategic interactions among agents in a differential game framework, uncertainty, as well as the link between environmental pollution and economic development. The dynamic models developed at this stage are also used in the subsequent chapters since, they help analyse the specific extensions in a dynamic framework

Chapter 4 relaxes the assumption of a symmetric distribution of information between the environmental regulator and the polluting agents. By introducing asymmetric information in the analysis of environmental policy, it is possible to analyse the so-called nonpoint source pollution, a very important pollution problem in practice related to the agricultural run-off, and develop new types of policy instruments capable of addressing this issue.

In Chapter 5 the assumption of perfect competition is relaxed, and environmental policy is analysed in the context of oligopolistic markets. The introduction of market imperfections in the design of environmental policy necessitates the modification of standard instruments or the use of a combination of instruments in order to account for the complications arising from the introduction of market imperfections externalities in addition to environmental externalities.

Chapter 6 examines the international dimension of environmental policy, by considering the case of transboundary or global pollution, an issue related to environmental problems such as global warming, depletion of the ozone layer or acid rains. Issues related to the achievement of international environmental agreements are analysed and the basic instruments for designing international environmental policy are presented. This chapter also examines the link between international trade and environmental policy.

Chapter 7 reviews the basic mathematical tools which are necessary for the analysis of environmental policy. Static and dynamic optimization are presented. In the latter case the presentation includes calculus of variations, optimal control, comparative dynamics, stochastic control and differential games which are all mathematical tools with wide use in current research in environmental economics.

The issues examined in this book are mainly topics of current research in the theory of environmental policy. Furthermore, the analysis of the issues addressed is carried out to a level where it can be used as a starting point for supporting new research by extending existing results or by relaxing maintained assumptions. In this respect the present book could perhaps provide some stimulus for further research in the theory of environmental policy.

# 2. Basic Environmental Policy Framework

## 1 INTRODUCTION

The presence of detrimental environmental externalities, which take the form of environmental pollution generated by the industrial sector of the economy, calls for specific policy measures that could induce individual polluters (firms) to behave in a way that would result in the socially-desirable level of environmental pollution.

In this chapter we develop a basic framework for environmental policy design which is used for the derivation of alternative environmental policy instruments. The two major approaches to environmental policy – economic incentives, and command and control – are presented, and the alternative instruments corresponding to these approaches are analysed and evaluated. Environmental pollution in this framework is assumed to be of the flow or fund type. For this type of pollution the assimilating capacity of the environment is such that it does not allow the accumulation of pollutants. Thus pollution generates damages only in the period emitted and not in subsequent periods. Examples of fund or flow pollution include smoke; noise; organic pollutants that can be transformed by bacteria, in an oxygen-rich environment, into substances that are not harmful (Tietenberg 1996). Considering flow type pollution allows for the use of a static analytical framework that greatly simplifies exposition.

Another feature of this chapter is that the only distortion considered is the environmental externality. This implies that only one instrument is required to correct the distortion. As will be shown in subsequent chapters, when more distortions, such as informational asymmetries or market imperfections, are included along with the environmental externality, then more complex instruments become necessary.

The models and the policy instruments developed in this chapter, although relatively straightforward, provide the basis for the extensions necessary to analyse issues such as stock pollution and dynamics, informational constraints, market imperfections or international considerations.

## 2 INDUSTRIAL POLLUTION AND THE SOCIAL OPTIMUM

The development of policy instruments capable of securing the socially-desirable level of pollution implies that an environmental regulator, or more generally a social planner, chooses pollution levels by maximizing a criterion function. This is given by a social welfare function, defined on environmental variables along with the other relevant choice variables. The social optimum determines optimal pollution and provides the benchmark for comparisons with unregulated market equilibrium. These comparisons in turn determine the appropriate environmental policy instruments.

Three alternative approaches are used in this section to characterize the social optimum. All three are equivalent; each of them, however, highlights different aspects of the problem and allows an alternative interpretation of the optimality conditions. The alternative models developed in this section will also prove useful in the subsequent extensions, since these extensions can be presented more clearly by using alternative ways to model the problem of the social planner and the firms. The three models are: first, the social planner chooses emissions using derived damage and profit functions; second, the choice is over output production and pollution abatement; and third, the choice is strictly over inputs that can be used for either production or for pollution abatement.[1]

### 2.1 Descriptive Models of Industrial Pollution and Social Damages

We start the exposition by considering a market of $i=1,\ldots,n$ firms that behave competitively. The firms produce a homogeneous output $q_i$ and during production generate emissions $e_i$. Let $x_i=(x_{i1},\ldots,x_{iM})$ be a vector of $M$ inputs. Some of these inputs can be used for pollution abatement. Then the production possibility set is a set of all $(q_i,e_i,x_i)$ combinations that are technically feasible given the structure of the technology.

A derived profit or derived benefit function can be defined as:

$$B_i(e_i)=\max_{q_i\geq 0}\ \pi_i=\max_{q_i\geq 0}\ \left[pq_i-c_i(q_i,e_i)\right],\ B_i''(e_i)<0 \qquad\qquad \text{(B)}$$

---

[1] As it will become clear later on, when the objective is to explore pollution dynamics, an emission choice model could be used for a better exposition of the dynamic characteristics of the model. An output-abatement choice model is better suited to analysing the effects of market imperfections and strategic behavior among firms, while an input choice model is more useful when the impact of environmental policies on the input choices of the firms is examined.

where $p$ is the exogenously determined output price, and $c_i(q_i,e_i)$ is a convex cost function decreasing in $e_i$. A reduction in emissions will increase costs since this involves the use of resources for pollution abatement. The cost function is defined as:

$$c_i(q_i,e_i)=\min_{x_i\geq 0} \ w\cdot x_i$$

$$\text{s.t.} \quad G_i(q_i,e_i,x_i)\leq 0$$

where $w$ is the vector of competitive input prices and $G_i(\cdot,\cdot,\cdot)$ is a product transformation function of outputs and inputs.[2]

It will prove convenient in many cases to consider a specification of the production-emission technology in terms of an emission function, and abatement. Let $e_i=s_i(q_i,\alpha_i)$ be an emission function, where $\alpha_i$ denotes the level of abatement activity. This function is assumed to be increasing in output and convex for any given abatement activity level, and decreasing in abatement activity and convex for any given output level. Convexity with respect to abatement means that successive increases in this activity reduce emissions at a decreasing rate, reflecting diminishing returns in the pollution treatment process.

Let $c_i(q_i,\alpha_i)$ be a convex cost function defined as:

$$c_i(q_i,\alpha_i)=\min_{x_i\geq 0} \ w\cdot x_i$$

$$\text{s.t.} \ f(x_i)\geq q_i$$

$$h_i(x_i)\geq \alpha_i$$

where $f_i(x_i)$ is a twice-differentiable and strictly concave production function, while $h_i(x_i)$ is a twice-differentiable and strictly concave function indicating the efficient abatement level associated with any given input vector.[3] Given the emission and cost functions the firm's profit is defined in terms of output and abatement as:

$$\pi_i(q_i,\alpha_i)=pq_i-c_i(q_i,\alpha_i)-\tau(e_i) \tag{QA}$$

where $\tau(e_i)$ reflects private emission-related costs, which can be attributed to the existence of environmental policy.

A further specification of the technology can be made in terms of production, emission and abatement functions. Let there be a partition of the

---

[2] If $G(q,e,x)$ is convex in its arguments then $c_i(q_i,e_i)$ is convex in $(q_i,e_i)$. Since $\pi_i(q_i,e_i)$ is concave in $(q_i,e_i)$ the benefit function is concave in $e_i$ (see, for example, Beavis and Dobbs 1990, Chapter 4).

[3] The cost function is convex by the concavity of the production and the abatement functions.

inputs into a vector of $m$ productive and emission-generating inputs $x_i^P=(x_{1i}^P,...,x_{mi}^P)$, and a vector of $M-m$ abatement inputs $x_i^a=(x_{m+1}^a,...,x_{Mi}^a)$. Define the production and abatement functions as the twice-differentiable and strictly concave functions $q_i=f_i(x_i^P)$, $a_i=h_i(x_i^a)$ respectively and the twice-differentiable and strictly convex emission function $e_i^G=s_i(x_i^P)$.[4] Then net emissions released in the ambient environment are defined as $e_i^G-\alpha_i$. The firm's profit is defined in terms of inputs as:[5]

$$\pi_i(x_i^P,x_i^a)=p\,f_i(x_i^P)-w^P x_i^P-w^\alpha x_i^a-\tau\big(s_i(x_i^P)-h_i(x_i^a)\big) \qquad (I)$$

where $w^P$ and $w^\alpha$ are the competitive input prices, and as before $\tau(e_i^G-\alpha_i)$ reflects private emission-related costs.

Having described the production-emission structure of the technology the next step is to define social damages due to pollution. Since a nondepletable externality is considered, the consumers are affected by the total amount of emissions generated by the firms. Let $E=\sum_{i=1}^n e_i$ be total emissions generated. Assume that the utility function of the $j$th individual, $j=1,...,J$, is defined with respect to a vector of $N$ traded goods $c_j=(c_{1j},...,c_{Nj})$, and total emissions $E$. The derived utility function over total emissions, when a consumer with wealth $W_j$ maximizes his/her utility by purchasing the traded goods at a price $\varrho=(\varrho_1,...,\varrho_N)$, is defined as:

$$v_j(\varrho,W_j,E)=\max_{c_j\geq 0} u_j(c_j,E)$$

$$\text{s.t. } \varrho\cdot c_j\leq W_j$$

Assuming a quasi-linear utility function in a numeraire commodity the derived utility function can be written, following Mas-Colell et al. (1995), as:

$$v_j(\varrho,W_j,E)=\phi_j(E)$$

where we assume that $\phi_j$ is twice-differentiable with $\phi_j'<0$, and $\phi_j''<0$. Define the individual damage function for the $j$th consumer as $d_j(E)=-\phi_j(E)$. Social damages can then be defined as the sum of individual damages:

---

[4]The same symbol $s_i$ is used to denote the gross emissions function as well as emissions after abatement. This method of notation was adopted in order to have a uniform notation of marginal emissions since by the separability of net emissions in productive and abatement inputs, marginal gross emissions changes are also marginal net emissions changes. However, it is always indicated in the text whether the net (that is, after abatement) or gross emissions function is used.
[5]There are formulations where emissions are treated as an input in the production process. In this case the production function takes the form $q_i=f_i(x_i,e_i)$ (see Brock 1977, Cropper and Oates 1992).

$$D(E) = \sum_{j=1}^{J} d_j(E), \ E = \sum_{i=1}^{n} e_i \qquad \text{(D)}$$

The social damage function is a strictly increasing and strictly convex function.

## 2.2 Social Optimum and Suboptimality of Competitive Markets

The above framework, describing production-emission technology and social damages, can be used to analyse the problem of the social planner or environmental regulator. The social planner seeks to determine the levels of a set of choice variables such that social welfare, which includes environmental damages, is maximized. The problem of the social planner is solved for the three alternative models describing technology.

### 2.2.1 Emission choice model (ECM)
Social welfare is defined as total benefits from production less social damages from emissions. Using the derived profit function (B) and the social damage function (D) the social planner solves the problem:

$$\max_{(e_1,\ldots,e_n)\geq 0} \ \sum_{i=1}^{n} B_i(e_i) - D(E), \ E = \sum_{i=1}^{n} e_i \qquad \text{(ECM)}$$

which has necessary and sufficient first-order conditions for the socially-optimal emissions $e_i^*$ generated by the $i$th firm:

$$B_i'(e_i^*) - D'(E^*) \leq 0, \text{ with equality if } e_i^* > 0 \qquad (2.1)$$

Thus when positive emissions are generated marginal benefits equal marginal social damages. Since $D'(E^*) = \sum_{j=1}^{J} d_j'(E^*)$, which is the sum of the consumers' marginal damages from emissions, condition (2.1) is Samuelson's optimality condition for a public bad.

### 2.2.2 Output-abatement choice model (OACM)
In this model social welfare[6] is defined as the sum of consumers' and producers' surplus less environmental social damages. Let $p = P(Q)$, $Q = \sum_{i=1}^{n} q_i$

---

[6]The use of Marsahallian aggregate surplus as a measure of social welfare can be justified by the use of quasilinear individual utility functions and lump sum transfers of the numeraire commodity (see Mas-Colell et al. 1995, Chapter 10).

be the market inverse demand function.[7] Thus, the social planner (or regulator) solves the problem:

$$\max_{(q_i,\alpha_i)\geq 0} \int_0^{\Sigma_i q_i} P(Q)dQ - \sum_{i=1}^n c_i(q_i,\alpha_i) - D(E)$$

$$E = \sum_{i=1}^n e_i, \quad e_i = s_i(q_i,\alpha_i) \qquad \text{(OACM)}$$

The optimality conditions require:

$$P(Q^*) - \frac{\partial c_i(q_i^*,\alpha_i^*)}{\partial q_i} - D'(E^*)\frac{\partial s_i(q_i^*,\alpha_i^*)}{\partial q_i} \leq 0,$$

$$\text{with equality if } q_i^* > 0 \qquad (2.2.1)$$

$$-\frac{\partial c_i(q_i^*,\alpha_i^*)}{\partial \alpha_i} - D'(E^*)\frac{\partial s_i(q_i^*,\alpha_i^*)}{\partial \alpha_i} \leq 0, \quad \text{with equality if } \alpha_i^* > 0 \qquad (2.2.2)$$

For interior solutions, condition (2.2.1) indicates that at the social optimum output should be chosen so that marginal benefits equal marginal production costs plus marginal external damages, that is marginal social costs. From (2.2.2), at the optimal level of abatement, marginal abatement costs should be equal to marginal external damage savings due to abatement.

The same model can be used to analyse long-run considerations (Spulber 1985). Assume that firms are identical, that free entry exists, and that newly established firms incur positive fixed costs $F$. The social planner not only seeks the socially-optimal emission level in the short run, but also the optimal pollution in long-run equilibrium. This implies choice of the socially-optimal number of firms in long-run equilibrium. Under symmetry $Q=nq$ and the planner solves:

$$\max_{(q,\alpha,n)\geq 0} \int_0^{nq} P(Q)dQ - nc(q,\alpha) - nF - D(ne)$$

The optimality conditions for the output and abatement choice are similar to (2.2.1) and (2.2.2), with $q_i^* = q^*$, $\alpha_i^* = \alpha^*$ for all $i$, and $E^* = ne^*$. The condition for the optimal choice of the number of firms $n$, assuming an interior solution, is:

$$P(n^*q^*)q^* - c(q^*,\alpha^*) - F - D'(n^*e^*)e^* = 0 \qquad (2.3)$$

---

[7]The demand function is independent of emissions if it is assumed that the individual utility functions are quasilinear with respect to emissions.

This is the zero profit condition indicating that at the social optimum private revenues equal private costs plus social damages.

### 2.2.3 Input choice model (ICM)

In this model the planner chooses productive and abatement inputs to maximize social welfare defined as above by net surplus. The problem is:

$$\max_{(x_i^p, x_i^a) \geq 0} \int_0^{\Sigma_i f(x_i^p)} P(Q)dQ - \sum_{i=1}^n \left( w^p \cdot x_i^p + w^\alpha \cdot x_i^a \right) -$$

$$D \left( \sum_{i=1}^n \left[ s_i(x_i^p) - h_i(x_i^\alpha) \right] \right) \tag{ICM}$$

The optimality conditions imply that:

$$p \frac{\partial f_i(x_i^{*p})}{\partial x_i^p} - w_i^p - D' \frac{\partial s_i(x_i^{*p})}{\partial x_i^p} \leq 0, \text{ with equality if } x_i^{*p} > 0 \tag{2.4.1}$$

$$D' \frac{\partial h_i(x_i^{*\alpha})}{\partial x_i^\alpha} - w_i^p \leq 0, \text{ with equality if } x_i^{*\alpha} > 0 \tag{2.4.2}$$

Thus for interior solutions the marginal value product of the productive (and polluting) inputs equals marginal social costs, while marginal damage savings due to abatement inputs equal their competitive prices.

It is clear that all three models described above lead to equivalent results, implying always equality between marginal benefits and marginal social costs. Suppose that we are in an unregulated competitive equilibrium. It can easily be shown that this equilibrium is suboptimal in the sense that emissions exceed the socially-optimal emission level. Consider for example the ECM. The unregulated firm solves the problem $\max_{e_i} B(e_i)$ with necessary and sufficient first-order condition:

$$B_i'(e_i^o) \leq 0, \text{ with equality if } e_i^o > 0$$

Comparing this condition with (2.1) it is clear that for interior solutions, that is $e_i^o > 0$, we have $e_i^o > e_i^*$ for all $i$. The same result extends to the other two models. In fact with quasi-linear individual utilities in emissions, unregulated firms will do zero abatement, and thus maximize total emissions.

# 3 STANDARD ENVIRONMENTAL POLICY INSTRUMENTS

Given the suboptimality of the unregulated competitive markets, the social planner can correct this distortion in the full information competitive context using a number of environmental policy instruments which internalize external social damages.

Environmental policy instruments can be divided into two broad categories: economic incentives or market-based instruments, and direct regulation or command and control approaches. Following the OECD (1991, 1994b) classification, economic instruments include environmental or emission charges or taxes, marketable or tradeable emission permits, output taxes, deposit–refund systems, performance bonds and voluntary agreements. Along with taxes, the case of subsidies can also be included. On the other hand, command and control approaches include the use of limits on output, inputs, emissions or technology at the firm level. The polluting firms are required to set outputs, inputs or emissions at some prespecified level, or they are required not to exceed (or fall short of) certain predefined levels (Baumol and Oates 1988). This form of direct regulation is popular among decision-makers; however, since the early 1980s, economic instruments – which have been advocated by economists for a number of decades – have started gaining popularity in the management of environmental pollution.[8]

## 3.1 Emission Taxes

The polluting firms fully internalize external social damages if they are confronted with an emission tax per unit of waste released in the ambient environment, equal to marginal social damages. This price incentive for emission control is the well-known 'Pigouvian tax' or 'effluent fee'.

Let the emission tax $\tau$ be defined as $\tau = D'(\sum_{i=1}^{n} e_i^*)$ and consider the ECM model. The firm solves the problem:

---

[8]OECD has played an important role in advocating the use of economic instruments for environmental management (OECD 1989, 1991). For surveys and assessment of the use of economic instruments for environmental protection, see OECD (1989, 1994a,b). For a brief history of the evolution of economic instruments in policy making, see Cropper and Oates (1992). For a discussion of the reasons that direct regulation has been preferred, see Bohm and Russell (1985) and for an attempt to integrate theory and practice regarding economic incentives, see Hahn and Stavins (1992). Hahn (1989) provides a chronicle of the introduction of marketable permits and emission charges in the USA and Europe.

$$\max_{e_i \geq 0} B_i(e_i) - \tau e_i$$

with necessary and sufficient first-order conditions

$$B_i'(e_i^o) \leq \tau, \text{ with equality if } e_i^o > 0 \qquad (2.5)$$

Since $\tau = D'\left(\sum_i e_i^*\right)$, it can be seen by comparing (2.5) to (2.1) that the emission tax leads to the socially-optimal emissions for firm $i$, that is $e_i^o = e_i^*$.

This result can be formally proven in an optimal taxation set-up. The social planner or environmental regulator seeks to maximize social welfare by choosing emission levels and tax rates under the constraint that firms maximize profits under the given tax regime. The problem can be written as:

$$\max_{e_i, \tau \geq 0} \sum_i B_i(e_i) - D(\sum_i e_i)$$

subject to

$$e_i = \operatorname*{argmax}_{e_i} B_i(e_i) - \tau e_i \text{ for all } i$$

Since the optimization constraints correspond to strictly concave optimization problems, they can be replaced by the corresponding first-order conditions. Then the problem becomes:

$$\max_{e_i, \tau_i \geq 0} \sum_i B_i(e_i) - D(\sum_i e_i)$$

$$\text{s. t. } B'(e_i) - \tau \leq 0$$

The Lagrangean function for this problem is written as:

$$\mathcal{L} = \sum_i B_i(e_i) - D\left(\sum_i e_i\right) - \sum_i \lambda_i \left(B_i'(e_i) - \tau\right)$$

where $\lambda_i$ is the Lagrangean multiplier. The first-order condition implies that $(e_i^*, \tau^*, \lambda_i) \geq 0$ exists for all $i$ such that:

$$B'(e_t^*) - D'\left(\sum_i e_i^*\right) - \lambda_i B_i''(e_i^*) \leq 0, \text{ with equality if } e_i^* > 0 \qquad (2.5.1)$$

$$\lambda_i \leq 0, \text{ with equality if } \tau^* > 0 \qquad (2.5.2)$$

$$B_i'(e_i^*) - \tau^* \leq 0, \; \lambda_i\left(B_i'(e_i^*) - \tau^*\right) = 0, \; \lambda_i \geq 0 \qquad (2.5.3)$$

Thus from (2.5.2) and (2.5.3), $\lambda_i = 0$ for all $i$ and from (2.5.1) and (2.5.3) for firms with positive emissions we have $\tau^* = B_i'(e_i^*) = D'\left(\sum_i e_i^*\right)$.

The same result can be obtained by using the OACM or the ICM. In both of these models the firm solves:

$$\max_{(q_i,\alpha_i)\geq 0} pq_i - c(q_i,\alpha_i) - \tau e_i, \; e_i = s_i(q_i,\alpha_i) \tag{2.6.1}$$

$$\max_{(x_i^P,x_i^\alpha)\geq 0} pf(x_i^P) - w^P \cdot x_i^P - w^\alpha \cdot x_i^\alpha - \tau\left[s_i(x_i^P) - h_i(x_i^\alpha)\right] \tag{2.6.2}$$

By taking the first-order conditions it can be shown that for $\tau = D'$:

from (2.6.1) $\left\{q_i^o = q_i^*, \; \alpha_i^o = \alpha_i^*\right\} \Rightarrow e_i^o = e_i^*$

from (2.6.2) $\left\{x_i^{op} = x_i^{*P}, \; x_i^{o\alpha} = x_i^{*\alpha}\right\} \Rightarrow e_i^o = e_i^*$

Furthermore in the long run, the Pigouvian tax provides the correct incentives for entry assuming symmetric firms. The zero profit condition for long-run equilibrium using the OACM under the Pigouvian tax is:

$$P(nq)q - c(q,\alpha) - F - \tau s(q,\alpha) = 0$$

It is clear that by adding this constraint to the optimality conditions of problem (2.6.1) and setting $\tau = D'(n^*e^*)$, the optimal allocation under the regulated market equilibrium will reproduce the socially-optimal allocation, or $(q^o,\alpha^o,n^o) = (q^*,\alpha^*,n^*)$.

Regarding exit–entry conditions under Pigouvian taxes, there have been arguments starting with Rose-Ackerman (1973) suggesting that, given that marginal social pollution damages are an increasing function of emissions, the achievement of the long-run equilibrium optimal number of firms under free entry depends on the size of the firms. If firms are small so that the effect from the entry of an additional firm on marginal social damages is negligible, then the Pigouvian tax will lead to the socially-optimal number of firms in the long run. In this case, as shown by Spulber (1988), marginal social cost is equal to the minimum social average cost,[9] under the zero profit entry condition in the long run. If, on the other hand, firms are large so that entry increases marginal damages, then the total tax bill paid by the firm (defined as emissions times the Pigouvian tax) exceeds the social damages that the firm imposes on society (Baumol and Oates 1988). This excess tax burden may induce the firms to exit the industry, leaving as a result less than the socially-optimal number of firms in the long run. In such a case, the correct entry–exit decision requires that the firm pay both the cost corresponding to the marginal damage of its emissions, and the cost corresponding to the total damage of its emissions. However, as Kohn (1994) suggested regarding

---

[9]The same result holds if marginal damages are constant (Burrows 1979).

entry–exit decisions, the problem of a Pigouvian tax forcing a firm to shut down when its output has a net positive value to society appears in a partial equilibrium setup. In a general equilibrium context when competitive conditions are satisfied, economic efficiency does not require a specific entry–exit condition.

### 3.1.1 General equilibrium considerations

In the previous section the optimal emission tax was determined in the context of a partial equilibrium framework. However, environmental taxes when imposed will have to coexist with other taxes in the economy. When environmental taxes are considered in the broader framework of the economy as a whole, two interrelated issues arise. The first relates to determining the optimal emission tax in the presence of other distortionary taxes in the economy, including commodity and labour taxes. The second relates to whether the gross efficiency cost of emission taxes is reduced when tax revenues are used to lower existing distortionary taxes.[10]

Regarding the first issue, Bovenberg and Goulder (1996) consider a modelling framework incorporating as inputs labour, one 'dirty' and one 'clean' intermediate input, and one 'dirty' and one 'clean' consumption good, with individual utility depending on the consumption good, environmental quality and public consumption. They obtain optimal taxes on the 'dirty' intermediate input and consumption as marginal environmental damages divided by the marginal cost of public funds. This cost depends on the distortionary tax on labour and the uncompensated wage elasticity of labour supply, and is expected to exceed unity. Thus the optimal emission tax in the presence of distortionary labour taxes is less than marginal damages.

The choice of an optimal emission tax either equal to or less than environmental damages can be regarded as an efficient instrument for environmental protection. It has been argued, however, that in the presence of other distortionary taxes in the economy environmental taxes may result in benefits over and above benefits associated with environmental protection. These benefits are associated with the way in which tax revenues are recycled in the economy and in particular with the possibility of reducing distortionary taxation in the economy. As noted by Pearce (1991) the use of environmental taxes to reduce distortionary taxes in a revenue neutral way could result in two benefits. The first benefit relates to environmental protection while the

---

[10]Both issues are closely related. The results presented in this section follow Bovenberg and De Mooij (1994), Bovenberg and van der Ploeg (1994), Parry (1995), Goulder (1995a), Bovenberg and Goulder (1996).

second relates to the distortionary cost of the tax system.[11] Several meanings have been attached to the double dividend claim:

(i)     Benefits exist when tax revenues from environmental taxes are used to reduce distortionary taxation as compared to the case where tax revenues are returned to tax payers in a lump-sum fashion.

(ii)    There are zero costs or even benefits if tax revenues are used to reduce typical or representative distortionary taxes.[12]

(iii)   The revenue neutral swaps raise the welfare gains from environmental taxes (Parry 1995).

(iv)    The revenue neutral swap produces a second dividend in the form of higher employment or profits (Bovenberg and van der Ploeg 1994; Bovenberg 1995; Carraro, Galeolti and Gallo 1996).

The idea of a double dividend, especially in the strong form or in the form of an employment double dividend, is especially appealing to policy makers since it implies that environmental taxes could be introduced without any cost and therefore there is no need to justify them in terms of uncertain environmental benefits. Theoretical and empirical research does not seem however to support the idea of a double dividend in its strong form or in its employment form. In particular the double dividend hypothesis holds only in the weak form but not in general for the other forms. Two effects are present when a revenue neutral tax swap takes place. The first is the revenue effect which reflects welfare gains from reducing distortionary taxes, and the second is the interdependence effect which reflects the likely increase of preexisting tax distortions due to the introduction of environmental taxes that also create extra costs.[13] The extra costs are mainly due to losses of revenue and efficiency in labour and capital markets if environmental taxes discourage employment and investment. These two effects work in different directions with the interdependence effect exceeding the revenue effect under plausible parameters values.[14] Carraro, Galeolti and Gallo (1996), by simulating the recycling of carbon tax revenues to reduce employers' social security contributions in the EU, show that an employment double dividend may exist

---

[11]For earlier discussion on the same issue see also Repetto et al. (1992), Pezzey (1992), Oates (1991), Poterba (1993), Terkla (1984).

[12]The meanings (i) and (ii) above correspond to the weak and strong form of the double dividend hypothesis. See Goulder (1995b) where an additional intermediate form of double dividend is also defined.

[13]See Parry (1995) for detail definitions of these concepts.

[14]The double dividend hypothesis in the strong form is also not confirmed by empirical studies using computable general equilibrium models (Goulder 1995a, Shah and Larsen 1992).

in the short run. Bovenberg and van der Ploeg (1994, 1996), using analytical models where emission tax revenues are used to reduce labour taxes, show that greater environmental concern, that is a shift toward green preferences, may reduce rather than expand employment. In any case, more environmental concern may boost employment if initial concern is small. Similar results are obtained for the employment type of double dividend (Bovenberg and van der Ploeg 1994; Carraro, Galeolti and Gallo 1996).

Based on these results it seems that although the concept of a second dividend and the consequent 'no cost' introduction of environmental taxes is appealing to policy-makers, the difficulty in establishing the strong double dividend hypothesis – especially when the existing tax system is suboptimal – suggests that the environmental benefits of emission taxes is a crucial factor in justifying their introduction.

## 3.2  Subsidies

A subsidy scheme involves payments to the firm for reducing emissions below a given benchmark.[15] Denoting this benchmark by $\bar{e}_i$, a linear subsidy scheme is defined as $v(\bar{e}_i-e_i)$, where $v$ is the subsidy per unit reduction of emissions below the benchmark level. Under the subsidy scheme the firm solves the problem:

$$\max_{(q_i,\alpha_i)\geq 0} \ pq_i-c_i(q_i,\alpha_i)+v(\bar{e}_i-e_i), \ e_i=s_i(q_i,\alpha_i)$$

Since the firm's objective function under the subsidy scheme differs from the corresponding objective function under taxes only by the constant $v\bar{e}_i$, a subsidy equal to marginal social damages evaluated at the optimal emission level will induce firms to emit at the social optimum, $e_i^*$.

Although taxes and subsidies offer the same marginal incentives for emission reductions, they differ with respect to their effects on long-run pollution. This is because they affect the long-run entry–exit decisions of firms differently.

The long-run market equilibrium condition under the subsidy scheme, assuming again symmetric firms, is:

$$P(nq)q-c(q,\alpha)-F+v\bar{e}-ve=0$$

---

[15]For a detailed analysis of subsidies as an environmental policy instrument, see Baumol and Oates (1988).

If we set $v=D'(n^*e^*)$, it is clear that under the subsidy scheme a larger number of firms will enter the market than under the Pigouvian tax. Thus the Pigouvian tax leads to a reduction in the industry size relative to the unregulated equilibrium, while a subsidy leads to an increase in the industry size. It is possible that the increase in the industry size under the subsidy scheme could lead to an increase in total emissions in the long run (Baumol and Oates 1988).

## 3.3 Tradeable Emission Permits

Tradeable or marketable emission permits were first proposed by Crocker (1966) and Dales (1968) and represent a system of tradeable property rights for the management of environmental pollution. Tradeable permits involve the determination of a total level of allowable emissions and then distribution of these permits to the firms. After their initial distribution, permits can be traded subject to a set of prescribed rules.

Permits can be allocated by means of an auction or by initiating a 'grandfathering' system which allocates permits on the basis of the past emission records of firms. Let $e^*=\sum_i e_i^*$ be the total number of permits issued by the environmental regulator and let $\tilde{e}_i$ with $\sum_i \tilde{e}_i = e^*$ be the initial permits holding of firm $i$. After the initial distribution, firm $i$'s net demand for permits is $(e_i - \tilde{e}_i)$, $e_i = s_i(q_i, \alpha_i)$. Assuming competitive markets for permits, the firm is a price taker in the permits market and solves the problem:

$$\max_{(q_i, \alpha_i) \geq 0} pq_i - c_i(q_i, \alpha_i) - P^T \left[ s_i(q_i, \alpha_i) - \tilde{e}_i \right] \tag{2.7}$$

where $P^T$ is the equilibrium price for permits. The necessary and sufficient first-order conditions for the profit-maximizing choices $q_i^o, a_i^o$ imply:

$$p - \frac{\partial c_i}{\partial q_i} - P^T \frac{\partial s_i}{\partial q_i} \leq 0, \text{ with equality if } q_i^o > 0 \tag{2.8.1}$$

$$-\frac{\partial c_i}{\partial \alpha_i} - P^T \frac{\partial s_i}{\partial \alpha_i} \leq 0, \text{ with equality if } \alpha_i^o > 0 \tag{2.8.2}$$

The above conditions determine the profit-maximizing output, abatement and emissions as functions of the output and the permit prices, or $q_i^o = q_i^o(p, P^T)$ and $\alpha_i^o = \alpha_i^o(p, P^T)$, $e_i^o = s_i(q_i^o, a_i^o)$. The aggregate demand for permits is defined as $e^o(P^T) = \sum_i e_i^o(P^T)$, suppressing $p$.

The impact of changes in the price of permits on output, abatement and demand for permits can be obtained by comparative static analysis of system

(2.8) for interior solutions. The comparative static matrix is defined as:[16]

$$\begin{bmatrix} -c_{q_iq_i} & -P^Ts_{q_i\alpha_i} \\ -c_{\alpha_iq_i} & -P^Ts_{\alpha_i\alpha_i} \end{bmatrix} \begin{bmatrix} \dfrac{\partial q_i^o}{\partial P^T} \\ \dfrac{\partial \alpha_i^o}{\partial P^T} \end{bmatrix} = \begin{bmatrix} s_{q_i} \\ s_{\alpha_i} \end{bmatrix}$$

Thus

$$\frac{\partial q_i^o}{\partial P^T} = \frac{P^T(-s_{q_i}s_{\alpha_i\alpha_i} + s_{\alpha_i}s_{\alpha_iq_i})}{D} < 0$$

$$\frac{\partial \alpha_i^o}{\partial P^T} = \frac{-s_{\alpha_i}c_{q_iq_i} + s_{q_i}c_{\alpha_iq_i}}{D} > 0$$

where $D = P^T(c_{q_iq_i}s_{\alpha_i\alpha_i} - s_{\alpha_iq_i}c_{\alpha_iq_i}) > 0$, $c_{q_iq_i}$, $s_{a_ia_i} > 0$, $s_{\alpha_iq_i} > 0$, $c_{\alpha_iq_i} > 0$

Therefore an increase in the price of permits will reduce output and increase abatement. Furthermore both the individual demand for permits and the aggregate demand for permits are downward sloping, since the slope of the aggregate demand for permits is determined as:

$$\frac{\partial e^o}{\partial P^T} = \sum_{i=1}^{n} \left[ \frac{\partial s_i^o}{\partial q_i} \frac{\partial q_i^o}{\partial P^T} + \frac{\partial s_i^o}{\partial \alpha_i} \frac{\partial \alpha_i^o}{\partial P^T} \right] < 0$$

In equilibrium the price $P^T$ clears the permits market, that is:

$$\Sigma_i(e_i^o - \tilde{e}_i) = 0 \text{ or } \Sigma_i s_i^o(q_i^o(p, P^T), \alpha_i^o(p, P^T)) = \Sigma_i e_i^o = \Sigma_i \tilde{e}_i = e^*$$

It follows then by comparing (2.8.1) and (2.8.2) with the first-order conditions of problem (2.6.1) that the competitive equilibrium permit price is $P^T = D'(e^*)$. The market creates the correct incentive for firms which emit at the socially-optimum level $e_i^*$.

The equilibrium in the permit market is shown in Figure 2.1, where *BB* is the aggregate demand for permits. If the total issued number of permits is $e^*$ and the individual demands for permits are $B_1B_1$ and $B_2B_2$, for two firms, then permits are finally allocated to each firm according to $e_1^*, e_2^*$. If the total quantity of permits is chosen optimally, at the point where the marginal damage function $D'(e)$ intersects the demand for permits, then the social optimum is achieved. This solution is equivalent to the Pigouvian tax

---

[16]Subscripts denote partial derivatives.

solution, since problem (2.7) is equivalent to problem (2.6.1) because the objective functions differ only by a constant. Thus firms' emissions in the tax problem is a function of the tax rate in the same way as demand for permits is a function of the permit price, with both reflecting marginal benefits from emissions. So the Pigouvian tax determined at the intersection of the marginal damage function with the market demand for emissions equals the equilibrium permit price.

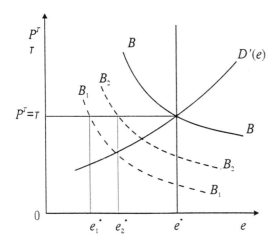

*Figure 2.1 Equilibrium in the permits market*

Assuming as before symmetric firms and positive fixed costs for the new entrants, the zero profit condition under permits can be written as:

$$P(nq)q - c(q,\alpha) - F - P^T s(q,\alpha)$$

for $P^T = D'(e^*) = \tau$, the socially-optimal long-run allocation is obtained.[17]

In the static framework considered throughout this section, the permits can be regarded as being of an exhaustive type. That is, once issued, permits are good for the prespecified amount of emissions after which the firm needs to buy more permits in order to realize more emissions. This is not, however, the case in practice; once issued, permits are good for more than one time period. So the firm can use the permit to emit for the period of time for

---

[17]A more detailed analysis of the optimality properties of a permit system in the long run can be found in Spulber (1988). The various permit systems applied in practice are discussed in Section 8 of this chapter. See also Tietenberg (1980) for a survey of the relatively early literature on permits.

which the permit is valid.[18] In order to examine the form of equivalence between taxes and permits in this context we assume that a permit, once issued, lasts forever.[19] The firm at an initial time $t=0$ obtains an initial amount of permits $e(0)$ which are worth $\tilde{P}^T e(0)$ to the firm. If the firm needs to increase emissions in any period, there could be a need for more permits since the banking of permits is not allowed. Thus $de(t)/dt = \dot{e}(t) > 0$, with $\dot{e}(t) < 0$ if the firm wants to reduce emissions and supply permits. The firm's expenses for permits will be $\tilde{P}^T \dot{e}(t)$ and the firm's profit at any instant of time will be, considering an ECM, $B_i(e_i(t)) - \tilde{P}^T \dot{e}_i(t)$. In an infinite time horizon the firm seeks time paths for emissions $\{e(t)\}$ and demand or supply of permits $\{\dot{e}(t)\}$ that maximize the present value of profits. The firm solves therefore the problem:

$$\max_{\{e_i(t), \dot{e}_i(t)\}} \int_0^\infty e^{-rt} \left[ B_i(e_i(t)) - \tilde{P}^T \dot{e}_i(t) - \tilde{P}^T e(0) \right] dt$$

where $r$ is the firm's discount rate. This is a problem of calculus of variations[20] and the necessary Euler condition implies:[21]

$$e^{-rt} \left[ B_i'(e_i^o(t)) - r\tilde{P}^T \right] = 0 \quad \text{or} \quad \frac{B_i'(e_i^o(t))}{r} = \tilde{P}^T$$

Thus the price that the firm is willing to pay for a permanent permit equals the present value of the extra benefits due to the emissions made possible by this permit, that will be realized in the future.[22] So the equivalence between the equilibrium permit price and the optimal tax rate can be stated as $\tilde{P}^T = \tau/r$. The equilibrium permit price equals the present value of the Pigouvian tax.

## 3.4 Deposit–Refund Systems

In a deposit–refund system the main target is the avoidance of pollution by returning potentially-polluting products or their residuals.    Under this

---

[18]For example in the Fox River case the permits issued were good for five years (Hahn 1989).

[19]This is equivalent to saying that the same number of permits is issued in each period and allocated in the same way under constant preferences and technology.

[20]See Chapter 7 for a presentation of this problem.

[21]By the concavity of the objective function in $e$ and $\dot{e}$ the sufficient condition for a maximum is also satisfied.

[22]For a similar result relating the permit price with the present value of marginal abatement savings see Howe (1994).

system[23] a deposit is paid on the potentially-polluting product and the refund follows upon the return of the product. There is considerable experience in market-generated deposit–refund systems mainly because of factors such as reuse value (beverage containers), recycle value (lead batteries), or more generally the avoidance of some charges imposed on the potential polluter's production.

The choices involved in a deposit–refund system can be described with the help of a simplified model. Let $B_i(e_i)$ be the derived benefit function for the $i$th firm with $e_i$ interpreted as pollution, or as the production of the polluting output that contains a fixed proportion of pollution. It is assumed that the firm pays a tax $\tau$ per unit of produced $e_i$ less the returned units. Following Bohm and Russell (1985) assume that the return rate is a function of the refund offer $R$, defined as $r(R)$ with $r \in [0,1]$, $r(0)=0$, $r'(R) \geq 0$, $r''(R) \leq 0$. Assume to simplify things that individuals who can return the polluting product have zero disposal and return costs, and finally assume that the returned product has a reuse value $v$. The firm chooses output $e_i$ and the refund offer $R$ to maximize profits, or:

$$\max_{(e_i, R) \geq 0} B_i(e_i) - \tau e_i [1 - r(R_i)] + r(R_i)(v - R_i)e_i$$

with necessary and sufficient first-order conditions:

$$B_i'(e_i^o) - \tau [1 - r(R_i^o)] + r(R_i^o)(v - R_i^o) \leq 0, \text{ with equality if } e_i^o > 0 \qquad (2.9.1)$$

$$r'(R_i^o)(\tau + v - R^o) - r(R_i^o) \leq 0, \text{ with equality if } R_i^o > 0 \qquad (2.9.2)$$

From (2.9.2) the firm will make a positive refund offer if tax savings plus the reuse value are sufficiently large. The optimal offer is determined at the point where marginal refund gains net of refund expenses equal the refund rate. Using the implicit function theorem in (2.9.1) and (2.9.2), comparative statics indicate that an increase in the tax rate will induce higher return rates, through the increase of the refund offer, or:

$$\frac{dR}{d\tau} = \frac{-r'}{r''(\tau + v - R) - 2r'} > 0$$

Consider now the case of a regulator who introduces a deposit–refund system. The regulator's problem is:

---

$$\max_{(e_i, R) \geq 0} \sum_{i=1}^{n} B_i(e_i) - D\big((1 - r(R_i))E\big) + r(R_i)(v - R_i)E, \quad E = \sum_i e_i$$

with necessary and sufficient first-order conditions

$$B_i'(e_i^*) - D'\big[(1 - r(R))\big] + r(R^*)(v - R^*) \leq 0, \text{ with equality if } e_i^* > 0$$

$$r'(R^*)(D' + v - R^*) - r(R^*) \leq 0, \text{ with equality if } R^* > 0$$

which have a similar interpretation as conditions (2.9). By comparing the optimality conditions for the regulator with the corresponding conditions for profit maximization, the optimal tax is defined as $\tau = D'$.

## 3.5 Output Taxes

Output or product taxes (or charges) are taxes levied on products that are environmentally harmful when used in production or consumption processes or when consumed. Output taxes are sometimes confused with Pigouvian taxes, although they are levied on the output in contrast to the Pigouvian taxes which are levied on emissions. As can be shown, the equivalence of the output and the Pigouvian taxes holds only in the special case of a single input production function (Spulber 1985).

Assume a single input production process, $q = f(x^P)$ where $e = s(x^P) = s(f^{-1}(q)) = z(q)$. The regulator, assuming identical firms, solves the problem:

$$\max_{x^P \geq 0} \int_0^{nf(x^P)} P(Q) dQ - nw^P x^P - D(ne)$$

with necessary and sufficient first-order conditions for interior solutions:

$$p \frac{\partial f(x^{*P})}{\partial x^P} - w^P - D' \frac{s'(x^{*P})}{f'(x^{*P})} f'(x^{*P}) = 0 \qquad (2.4.1.a)$$

On the other hand the firm solves the problem:

$$\max_{x^P \geq 0} pf(x^P) - w^P x^P - \tau f(x^P) \qquad (2.10)$$

with necessary and sufficient first-order condition for interior solution $(p - \tau)f'(x^{op}) = w^P$. If the output tax is set as $\tau = [D's'(x^{*P})]/[f'(x^{*P})]$, then the first-order condition for the firm implies $pf'(x^{op}) = w^P + D's'(x^{op})$, or that the marginal value product of the input equals the marginal social cost, which is the same as condition (2.4.1) or (2.4.1.a) for the social optimum. Thus the output tax is optimal.

However this optimality condition does not hold when the input space is increased. Consider the optimality conditions (2.4.1). The optimal input choice for any two inputs $i,j$ for the firm is determined as:

$$\frac{\partial f/\partial x_i^P}{\partial f/\partial x_j^P} = \frac{w_i^P + D'(\partial s/\partial x_i^P)}{w_j^P + D'(\partial s/\partial x_j^P)} \tag{2.11}$$

Under a Pigouvian tax the firm chooses inputs optimally according to optimality condition (2.11). Under the output tax the firm in the multi-input case solves the same problem as (2.10) with $x^P$ regarded now as the input vector. The optimality conditions for interior solutions imply:

$$\frac{\partial f/\partial x_i^P}{\partial f/\partial x_j^P} = \frac{w_i^P}{w_j^P} \tag{2.12}$$

In comparison to (2.11), relationship (2.12) implies suboptimal input choice. Furthermore if abatement inputs are separable then under the output tax the firm will not carry any abatement.

When entry incentives in the long run are examined, the output tax does not lead to the correct number of firms even in the single-input case. Following Spulber (1985) the entry condition in the long run under the output tax is:

$$P(nq)f(x^P) - w^P x^P - D'(ne)\frac{s'(x^P)}{f'(x^P)}f(x^P) - F = 0$$

while under the Pigouvian tax the third term of this condition should be replaced by $D'(ne)s(x^P)$. Therefore a lump-sum tax (or subsidy) is required in order to have the correct entry in the long run under the output tax.

## 3.6 Performance Bonds and Noncompliance Fees

Performance bonds are payments by potential polluters to authorities before an operation that could be harmful to the environment begins, in anticipation of compliance by the polluter to the environmental regulation associated with the activity. If compliance takes place, payments are refunded. Otherwise the initial payment (bond) is forfeited.[24] The limited use of performance bonds in environmental policy design can be attributed to imperfect monitoring of polluting activities, liquidity constraints, and legal restriction in contracting (Shogren et al. 1993).

---

[24]For a more detailed analysis see Hanley et al. (1997).

Noncompliance fees, on the other hand, are applied when polluters do not comply with the environmental regulation. The key issue here is that the rate of the fees is proportional to the benefits that the polluter achieves by not complying with the environmental regulation. The administering of noncompliance fees might be impeded by measurement problems and legal restrictions regarding profits from noncompliance.

### 3.7 Voluntary Agreements

Voluntary agreements are a relatively new instrument of environmental policy. A voluntary agreement is a result of negotiations between the government or an environmental regulator on the one hand, and potential polluters on the other. Reductions of emissions are obtained through an agreement that can take the form of a contract. In the contract, the firm agrees to achieve an environmental target such as emissions reduction through changes in investment patterns, technological change or waste treatment. In exchange the firm could receive subsidies in order to change its technology.

Carraro and Siniscalco (1996) in analysing voluntary agreements, suggest that their use can mainly be justified in cases in which the target is to obtain environmental protection through technological innovation, especially in cases where market imperfection exists, or when environmental innovation has positive spillovers.

### 3.8 Command and Control Regulation: Performance and Design Standards

Under command and control the regulator specifies an emission limit for the firm. The firm then adjusts output or abatement so that the standard is achieved. Let $\bar{e}_i$ be the maximum allowable emission for firm $i$. The firm chooses output and abatement to solve the problem:

$$\max_{(q_i, \alpha_i) \geq 0} pq_i - c_i(q_i, \alpha_i)$$

$$\text{s. t. } e_i \leq \bar{e}_i, \ e_i = s_i(q_i, \alpha_i)$$

(2.13)

The Lagrangean function for this problem is defined as:

$$\mathcal{L} = pq_i - c_i(q_i, \alpha_i) + \lambda_i \left[ \bar{e}_i - s_i(q_i, \alpha_i) \right]$$

The Kuhn-Tucker conditions imply that if $(q_i^o, a_i^o)$ solve the maximization problem (2.13), then a Lagrangean multiplier $\lambda_i \geq 0$ exists such that:[25]

$$p - \frac{\partial c_i(q_i^o, \alpha_i^o)}{\partial q_i} - \lambda_i \frac{\partial s_i(q_i^o, \alpha_i^o)}{\partial q_i} \leq 0, \text{ with equality if } q_i^o > 0 \qquad (2.14.1)$$

$$-\frac{\partial c_i(q_i^o, \alpha_i^o)}{\partial \alpha_i} - \lambda_i \frac{\partial s_i(q_i^o, \alpha_i^o)}{\partial \alpha_i} \leq 0, \text{ with equality if } \alpha_i^o > 0 \qquad (2.14.2)$$

$$\bar{e}_i - s_i(q_i^o, \alpha_i^o) \geq 0, \ \lambda_i \left[ \bar{e}_i - s_i(q_i^o, \alpha_i^o) \right] = 0, \ \lambda_i \geq 0 \qquad (2.14.3)$$

For strictly increasing cost function with respect to abatement and strictly decreasing emission function with respect to abatement, $\lambda_i > 0$ from (2.14.2). Thus the emission constraint is always satisfied as equality and it will be optimal for the firm to discharge up to the allowed emission limit. Using the envelope theorem, $\lambda$ can be interpreted as the shadow cost of the emission limit indicating the marginal change in profits from increasing the stringency of the emission standard. If the limit $\bar{e}_i$ is set at the welfare maximizing level $e_i^*$, the command and control approach is equivalent to emission charges.[26]

This type of regulation where the actual emissions are the objective of direct regulation is called performance standard. A performance standard leaves the firm maximum freedom to comply with the standard by either reducing output or by increasing abatement, but requires individual monitoring and knowledge of compliance costs. If emission monitoring is expensive or technically infeasible then the regulator could require the use of a specific technology. This type of regulation is called a design standard.[27]

Design standards can be specific or general. Following Besanko's (1987) example, a specific design standard for a firm manufacturing tyres and

---

[25]If there is an abatement output combination $(q_i, \alpha_i)$ that corresponds to emissions below the emission limit, or $\bar{e}_i - s_i(q_i, \alpha_i) > 0$, then the Slater condition for the nonlinear program (2.13) is satisfied. The Slater condition along with the convexity of the emission function implies that the constraint qualification is satisfied and, given the concavity of the objective function, the Kuhn-Tucker conditions are necessary and sufficient.

[26]The discussion about the comparison between charges and command and control is extensive; it will be analysed in more detail later in this chapter. One of the major difficulties with the application of charges is the size of the informational requirements necessary for its application. Although these requirements are inherent in any application of optimal policies, nevertheless they acquire important practical significance when the optimal policies need to be transformed into actual policies. In this respect emission permits may possess some informational advantages.

[27]For a more detailed analysis of performance and design standards, see Bohm and Russell (1985). For a comparison of performance and design standards under oligopolistic conditions, see Besanko (1987).

creating hazardous creosote in the process, could be the requirement that the firm use a specific procedure for disposing of or storing hazardous wastes. On the other hand a performance standard would require that the firm generate creosote below a prespecified level. More general design standards may require potential polluters to apply 'best practice' or 'best available' technology.

Let $\bar{\alpha}_i > 0$ be the minimum required abatement to use the specific design. The problem for the firm is:

$$\max_{q_i \geq 0, \alpha_i} pq_i - c_i(q_i, \alpha_i)$$

$$\text{s t. } \alpha_i \geq \bar{\alpha}_i$$

The necessary and sufficient conditions imply that $(q_i^o, \alpha_i^o, \mu_i) \geq 0$ exists such that:

$$p - \frac{\partial c_i(q_i^o, \alpha_i^o)}{\partial q_i} \leq 0, \text{ with equality if } q_i^o > 0 \tag{2.15.1}$$

$$-\frac{\partial c_i(q_i^o, \alpha_i^o)}{\partial \alpha_i} + \mu_i \leq 0, \text{ with equality if } \alpha_i^o > 0 \tag{2.15.2}$$

$$(\alpha_i^o - \bar{\alpha}_i) \geq 0, \ \mu_i(\alpha_i^o - \bar{\alpha}_i) = 0, \ \mu_i \geq 0 \tag{2.15.3}$$

From (2.15.2), $\mu_i > 0$ for interior solutions and thus the constraint is always binding, that is $\alpha_i^o = \bar{\alpha}_i$. From (2.15.1) output is determined as $q_i^o = q_i(\bar{\alpha}_i)$ and emissions under the standard are determined as $e_i = s_i(q_i(\bar{\alpha}_i), \bar{\alpha}_i) = s_i(\bar{\alpha}_i)$. Therefore there is a direct relationship between the design standard and emissions. If the regulator sets an emission target, $e_i^+$, then the optimal design standard for this target is defined as $\alpha_i^+ = s_i^{-1}(e_i^+)$.

Although by choosing the emission target and the abatement level a performance standard and a design standard both lead to the same emission level, the output abatement combinations are different in the two cases. By comparing (2.14.1) to (2.15.1) it can be seen that output under the performance standard is lower than output under the design standard since in the former case there is an extra implicit marginal output cost, $\lambda(\partial s / \partial q_i)$, that reduces output as compared to the design standard case. This discrepancy reveals the qualitative difference between the two regulatory approaches. The performance standard provides more flexibility for the firm since it can reduce output instead of increasing abatement to achieve the emission standard. This substitution is not however possible under the design standard.

# 4 ENVIRONMENTAL POLICY UNDER PRODUCTION EXTERNALITIES

The analysis in the previous sections focused mainly on cases in which emissions generated by firms during the output production process caused damages to individual consumers who have preferences defined over commodities and environmental quality.

There are, however, cases in which pollution generated by a firm negatively affects the production process of other firms, thereby creating a detrimental externality in production. This can be associated with the standard textbook case of an upstream pollution-generating firm and a downstream pollution-receiving firm, or a more general set-up where emissions generated by each producer adversely effect the production functions of all the producers in a given sector. This latter case can be associated for example with agricultural production, in which the use of polluting inputs such as fertilizers or pesticides creates agricultural run-off that pollutes surface or groundwater used for irrigation. This reduction in the quality of irrigation water adversely affects the production of each farmer.[28]

In the upstream–downstream case, let firm 1 be an upstream firm that uses input $x_1$ to produce output according to the production function $f_1(x_1)$.[29] The firm sells its output and buys an input at competitive prices, $p_1$ and $w_1$, respectively. The use of the input creates pollution according to the strictly increasing and convex emission function, $e_1 = s(x_1)$. Consider for example the case where the upstream firm is a factory that contaminates a river, while the downstream firm is a cattle breeder who uses the river to provide water to his animals. The downstream firm which suffers from the detrimental externality has a production function defined as $g(x_2, Q)$, where $Q$ is an index of water quality. Let $Q = Q(e_1)$ with $Q' < 0$. Then firm 2's production function can be written as $f_2(x_2, e_1)$ with $\partial f_2 / \partial e_1 < 0$.

In the unregulated equilibrium, firm 1 solves the problem:

$$\max_{x_1} \ p_1 f_1(x_1) - w_1 x_1$$

and chooses the optimal input[30] $x_1^o$ such that $p_1 f_1'(x_1^o) = w_1$ and thus $e_1^o = s(x_1^o)$. In maximizing its profits firm 2 treats the emissions of firm 1 as given, thus solving the problem $\max_{x_2} \ p_2 f_2(x_2, e_1^o) - w_2 x_2$. Optimal input is

---

[28]For an extensive analysis of this type of problem, see Dinar and Zilberman (1991).

[29]Since no abatement inputs are considered, $x$ refers to productive inputs only and the superscript $p$ is omitted to simplify the notation.

[30]Interior solutions are assumed throughout this problem.

chosen according to the first-order condition such that $p_2 f_2'(x_2^o, e_1^o) = w_2$, or $x_2^o = x_2^o(e_1^o)$.

When the regulator's problem is examined, the objective is to maximize social profits, that is, total profits less any other environmental damages from emissions, defined as $D(e_1)$.[31] Thus the regulator solves the problem:

$$\max_{x_1, x_2} \left[ p_1 f_1(x_1) - w_1 x_1 \right] + \left[ p_2 f_2(x_2, e_1) - w_2 x_2 \right] - D(e_1), \ e_1 = s(x_1)$$

The first-order conditions for an interior maximum are:[32]

$$p_1 f_1'(x_1^*) - p_2 \frac{\partial f_2}{\partial e_1} e_1'(x_1^*) - D' e_1'(x_1^*) = w_1 \qquad (2.16.1)$$

$$p_2 \frac{\partial f_2(x_2^*)}{\partial x_2} = w_2 \qquad (2.16.2)$$

By comparing the unregulated solution with the regulator's solution it is clear that in the latter case firm 1 uses less of the polluting input, since in choosing the optimal level for $x_1$ the regulator equates the input's marginal value product with the marginal social cost that includes private costs plus the cost imposed on firm 2 plus the other marginal environmental damages. The regulator's optimum can be achieved by introducing a Pigouvian tax equal to aggregate marginal external damages, or $\tau = p_2 (\partial f_2 / \partial e_1) e_1'(x_1^*) + D' e_1'(x_1^*)$. The same outcome can be achieved in a command and control framework using a performance standard such as firm 1's emissions that will not exceed $e_1(x_1^*)$.

The above production externality problem is a relatively simple one that does not allow some important aspects, mainly associated with interactions among firms, to be examined. Let us therefore consider the problem in which each firm generates pollution, as in the case of agriculture, with total pollution negatively affecting the production of each firm in the sector. The production function for each firm is specified as $f_i(x_i, e)$ where $e$ is the sum of individual emissions of all firms. That is:

$$e = \sum_i e_i, \ e_i = s_i(x_i) \text{ with } \frac{\partial f_i}{\partial e} < 0, \ \frac{\partial^2 f_i}{\partial x_i \partial e} < 0$$

---

[31]Environmental damages in addition to those suffered by firm 2 can be associated with the pollution of the river which is used by individuals for recreational purposes. However the presence of these costs is not essential to the rest of the argument.

[32]It assumed that the objective function is concave as a function of $(x_1, x_2)$. This need not however be the case since, as will be shown in Section 7, the presence of detrimental externalities in $f_2$ can cause nonconvexities in the social profit set.

Thus an increase in pollution reduces output; an increase in pollution also reduces the marginal product of inputs. Denote by $x_{-i}$ the vector $x_{-i}=(x_1,...,x_{i-1}, x_{i+1},...,x_n)$. Then firm $i$'s profits are defined as $\pi(x_i,x_{-i})=pf_i(x_i,e)-wx_i$.

In analysing market equilibrium the Nash assumption is used to model the behavior of the firms. It is assumed that each firm chooses profit-maximizing input levels by considering the actions of the other firms with respect to input choices as given. Thus a vector of input choices $x^o=(x_1^o,...,x_n^o)$ is a Nash equilibrium if $\pi_i(x_i^o,x_{-i}^o)\geq\pi(x_i',x_{-i}^o)$, $\forall\ x_i'\geq0$, for every $i=1,...,n$. The Nash equilibrium input choices are determined by the solution of the problem:[33]

$$\max_{x_i\geq0}\ pf_i(x_i,e)-wx_i,\ e_i=s_i(x_i)$$

If $(x_1^o,...,x_n^o)$ is a Nash equilibrium, the input choices should satisfy:

$$p\left[\frac{\partial f_i(x_i^o,e^o)}{\partial x_i}+\frac{\partial f_i}{\partial e_i}s_i'(x_i^o)\right]-w\leq0 \text{ with equality if } x_i^o>0 \tag{2.17}$$

$$\text{for all } i=1,...,n,\ e^o=\sum_{i=1}^n s_i(x_i^o)$$

The equilibrium described by (2.17) is a noncooperative equilibrium where each firm maximizes profits by using a pollution-generating input that affects its own production and by acting independently of the rest of the firms. In choosing inputs each firm – taking into account the adverse effects of its own actions on its own product as expressed by the term $(\partial f_i/\partial e_i)s_i'(x_i)$ – reduces its input use as compared to a naive equilibrium case where the firm ignores the effects of its own emissions on its own output. In the naive case the optimality condition would be $p[\partial f_i(x_i^n)/\partial x_i]-w=0$, $\forall i$. Thus $x_i^n>x_i^o$ and $e^n>e^o$, implying that naive behavior generates more pollution.

Consider now the problem of a regulator that seeks to maximize social welfare defined as the sum of consumer and producer surplus, and has perfect information about individual production functions, inputs used and emissions generated. The regulator's problem is:

$$\max_{x_i\geq0}\int_0^{\sum_i f_i(x_i,e)}P(Q)dQ-\sum_i w\cdot x_i,\ Q=\sum_i f_i(x_i,e)$$

The optimality condition requires

---

[33]It is assumed that the objective function is concave. See Section 7 for the relevant implications if this assumption is not satisfied.

$$p\left[\frac{\partial f_i(x_i^*,e^*)}{\partial x_i}+\frac{\partial f_i}{\partial e_i}s_i'(x_i^*)+\sum_{i\neq j}\frac{\partial f_j}{\partial e_i}s_i'(x_i^*)\right]-w\le 0,$$

with equality if $x_i^*>0$, for all $i=1,...,n$                    (2.18)

By comparing (2.17) to (2.18) it can be seen that at the social optimum the optimal input use is determined by taking into account the term $[\sum_{j\neq i}(\partial f_j/\partial e_i)s_i']$ which reflects the impact on the social welfare resulting from $i$'s emissions on the production of the rest of the firms. This effect is not taken into account at the Nash equilibrium and this is the reason why market equilibrium generates more emissions as compared to the social optimum. That is, $x_i^o>x_i^*$ and $e^o>e^*$.

To obtain the social optimum alternative instruments of the forms discussed above can be used.

*Emission taxes*    Consider the Pigouvian tax $\tau=[\sum_{j\neq i}(\partial f_j/\partial e_i)]$ evaluated at the socially-optimal input level $x_i^*$. In this case firm $i$ is charged with the adverse effects generated by itself which affect the other firms, $j\neq i$, and which are not taken into account when firm $i$ maximizes its profits. Under Pigouvian taxes the firms solve $\max_{x_i} pf_i(x_i,e_i,e_{-i})-wx_i-\tau s_i(x_i)\ \forall i$, and by fully internalizing the external effects choose the socially-optimal input levels. With heterogenous firms the Pigouvian tax is personalized in the sense that different rates apply to different firms. If, in addition to production damages, total emissions generate more general environmental damages such as damages to wildlife due to surface water pollution from agricultural run-off, which are expressed by the function $D(e)$, then the Pigouvian tax should be increased by adding the term $D'$. Thus $\tau=[\sum_{j\neq i}(\partial f_i/\partial e_i)+D']$. The first term internalizes the external effects of emissions on production while the second term internalizes environmental damages.

*Performance standards*    If the performance standard is set at the optimal emission level for each firm, then the constraint becomes $e_i\le e_i^*$, $e_i=s_i(x_i)$, $e_i^*=s_i(x_i^*)$. This type of standard implicitly defines a maximum allowable level of usage for input $x_i$. The Lagrangean function for the profit-maximizing firm is:

$$\mathcal{L}=pf_i(x_i,e_i,e_{-i})-wx_i+\lambda_i\left[e_i^*-s_i(x_i)\right]$$

The firm chooses the input so that the constraint is binding which implies that $s_i(x_i^o)=s_i(x_i^*)$, or $x_i^o=x_i^*$.

*Tradeable emission permits* The total amount of permits is defined as $e^* = \sum_i e_i^* = \sum_i s_i(x_i^*)$, with an initial distribution of permits $\sum_i \bar{e}_i = e^*$. Assuming as before a competitive permit market, the firm solves the problem:

$$\max_{x_i \geq 0} pf_i(x_i, e_i, e_{-i}) - wx_i - P^T[e_i(x_i) - \bar{e}_i]$$

By taking the first-order conditions of this problem it can be seen that $\sum_i e_i(x_i^o) = e^*$, implying that the permit system achieves the optimal emission level.

The above analysis suggests that under perfect information, production externalities, either in the simple form of the upstream–downstream firm or in a more complicated form where the detrimental externality affects all the firms – even the generator of the externality – can be optimally controlled by using standard environmental policy instruments.

## 5   BARGAINING SOLUTIONS FOR ENVIRONMENTAL EXTERNALITIES

In the previous sections a number of policy instruments were examined which, when applied, could lead to the socially-optimal pollution level. This approach can be regarded as the traditional one, stemming directly from Pigou's (1938) *The Economics of Welfare*. According to this approach the divergence between private and social costs can be breached by imposing a tax on the party that creates the environmental damage, or by imposing other equivalent measures. In the classical example of a factory generating smoke that has harmful effects on individuals living nearby, the Pigouvian tradition would support the decision to make the owner of the factory liable for the damages created by the smoke and impose a tax that varies with smoke or equivalent damages, or restrict the creation of smoke, or even exclude the factory from residential areas. This type of reasoning led to the development of the different policy instruments that were described in the previous sections.

This approach was challenged by Coase (1960, p.69) who argued that 'the suggested [by the Pigouvian tradition] courses of action are inappropriate, in that they lead to results which are not necessarily, or even usually, desirable.' Coase's criticism lies in the fact that if, given two parties – say 1 and 2 – party 1 inflicts harm on party 2 by generating a detrimental externality, the Pigouvian tradition focuses on deciding how much party 1 should be restrained. According to Coase, by restraining party 1 in order to avoid harming party 2, party 1 is also harmed. Thus the problem is to decide on a policy, by weighing both harms involved: the harm to 2 from 1's activities and the harm to 1 from the restriction of its activities in order to reduce the harm to 2.[34] As Coase suggests, the decision should be guided by comparing the value of what is obtained by restricting a certain activity with the value of what is sacrificed by the restriction of the activity. This approach leads to bargaining processes among the parties in order to reach an optimal agreement on the level of the environmental externality. This optimal agreement can secure, under certain circumstances, a Pareto optimal solution without any need for regulation.

In order for this private bargaining process – which has come to be known as the Coase theorem – to take place, a basic requirement is the existence of well-defined and enforceable property rights or, as is more suitable in our analysis, well-defined and enforceable environmental rights. Well-defined property rights means that party 1 has to obtain party 2's permission in order to generate the externality that affects party 2, or that party 2 has the right not to accept the imposition of the externality by party 1.[35] Enforceable rights mean that the level of the externality, that is emission of pollutants, can be measured; otherwise there is no incentive to bargain for the right to emit a certain level of pollutants. Coase's theorem ascertains that in the presence of well-defined and enforceable property rights, the optimal solution can be achieved through private negotiations, irrespective of who owns the property rights. Consider the problem in the framework of Section 4, in which party 1 is the upstream firm (the factory which pollutes the water), while party 2 is the downstream firm (the farmer who uses the polluted water for irrigation), and set more general environmental damages at zero, $D(e_1)=0$. Assume that the farmer has the right to clean water. In this case, the property rights are assigned to the farmer and the firm can not emit without the farmer's permission. The firm engages in negotiations and makes the farmer an offer of a payment $T$ in order to obtain permission to emit. Party 2 (the farmer) must decide how much pollution to accept in the water and how much payment to ask, while party 1 (the firm) will meet the farmer's demand as long as the firm is as well-off by paying $T$ for a certain allowable level of emissions as in the case in which no emissions would have been allowed, that is $e_1=0$. Since emissions are related to the use of the polluting input $x_1$, the

---

[34]In Coase's examples, the production of confectioneries creates noise and vibration that disturbs a nearby doctor, or cattle raising destroys crops on a neighbouring piece of land. The restriction, however, of the confectioner's activities or of cattle raising in the Pigouvian fashion will also harm the confectioner or the cattle raiser.

[35]The rights could also be the other way around.

firm will pay the farmer $T$ if and only if:

$$p_1 f_1(x_1) - w_1 x_1 - T \geq 0, \text{ since } e_1 = 0 \Rightarrow x_1 = 0 \text{ and } f_1(0) = 0$$

Under these circumstances, party 2 solves the problem:

$$\max_{(x_2, e_1) \geq 0, T} p_2 f_2(x_2, e_1) - w_2 x_2 + T, \ e_1 = s_1(x_1)$$

$$\text{s. t. } p_1 f_1(x_1) - w_1 x_1 - T \geq 0$$

In the above problem the constraint is binding at any solution, thus $T = p_1 f_1(x_1) - w_1 x_1$. By substituting for $T$ in the objective function, the problem for party 2 – the farmer – is to choose the levels of $(x_1, x_2)$ that solve:

$$\max_{x_1, x_2 \geq 0} p_2 f_2(x_2, e_1) - w_2 x_2 + p_1 f_1(x_1) - w_1 x_1 \qquad (2.19)$$

But as shown in the previous section the solution to this problem determines the socially-optimal levels of the two inputs for $D(e_1) = 0$.

Consider now the case where party 1 has the property rights, which means that there are no rights for clean water, and the factory can emit at the level that maximizes profits or at $x_1^o$ with $e_1^o = s_1(x_1^o)$ as determined in Section 4. Party 2 enters negotiations and offers $T$ to party 1 to reduce emissions below $e_1^o$. The offer of $T$ should be such that party 2 will be at least as well-off as in the case where profit-maximizing emissions $e^o$ were generated by party 1. Thus party 2 will pay party 1 the amount $T$ if and only if

$$p_2 f_2(x_2, e_1) - w_2 x_2 - T \geq p_2 f_2(x_2^o, e_1^o) - w_2 x_2^o \qquad (2.20)$$

Party 1, the factory, then solves the problem:

$$\max_{(x_1, x_2) \geq 0, T} p_1 f_1(x_1) - w_1 x_1 + T, \text{ subject to } (2.20)$$

Since the constraint is always binding at the solution, the above problem is equivalent to:

$$\max_{x_1, x_2 \geq 0} p_1 f_1(x_1) - w_1 x_1 + p_2 f_2(x_2, e_1) - w_2 x_2 + p_2 f_2(x_2^o, e_1^o) - w_2 x_2^o \qquad (2.19.\text{a})$$

which again leads to the socially-optimal input levels.

In both cases above, that is with property rights to either 1 or 2, the outcome of the bargaining is not affected by the initial allocation of the property rights. The initial allocation of the property rights affects the profits of the parties at the solution.

Coase's theorem can be shown diagrammatically in Figure 2.2 which draws on Takayama (1994). The $B'B'$ curve reflects marginal benefits to party 1 from using the pollution generating input $x_1$. Thus $B'B'$ is defined by $(p_1 f_1'(x_1) - w_1)$ and has a negative slope because of the assumptions about the production function. Damages to party 2 are determined by the marginal damage function $D\,'D\,'$, which is determined by the maximum profit function of party 2, as:

$$\pi_2(x_1)=\max_{x_2}\ [p_2 f_2(x_2,s_1(x_1))-w_2 x_2]$$  (2.21)

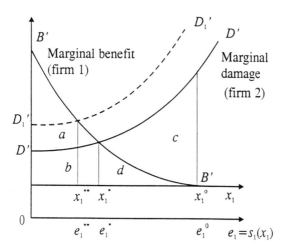

*Figure 2.2   Coase's theorem*

By the envelope theorem $\pi_2'(x_1)=p_2(\partial f/\partial s_1)s_1'(x_1)$. Assume also that $\pi_2''(x_1)<0$,[36] then the marginal damage curve $D\,'D\,'$ is determined by $-\pi_2'(x_1)$ and is upward sloping. Since emissions are determined by the strictly increasing emission function $e_1=s_1(x_1)$, equilibrium in Figure 2.2 can be defined either in terms of the input or in terms of emissions. If the property rights belong to party 2 then party 1 will be willing to pay up to $a+b$, which is the total benefit from using the input up to level $x_1^*$, in order to use this amount of input with corresponding emissions $e_1^*$. Party 2 will accept anything above $b$ in order to suffer damages implied by emissions at level $e_1^*$. On the other hand if party 1 has the property rights, then party 1 will be willing to accept anything above $d$ (which represents total losses from reducing the input use from $x_1^o$ to $x_1^*$) in order to reduce emissions from $e_1^o$ to $e_1^*$, while party 2 will be willing to pay up to the area $c+d$ (which represents total damage savings from reduced emissions) for these reduced

---

[36]This condition ensures that the second-order conditions for the maximization problem (2.21) are satisfied (Takayama 1994).

emissions. The socially-optimal emission level is obtained independently of the allocation of the property rights and no regulation is necessary.

Although Coase's theorem suggests that there is no need for intervention in the form of regulation to control environmental externalities, there are objections to the assumptions made in order to obtain the results, as pointed out by Fisher (1981). These assumptions reduce the importance of the theorem as a practical solution for controlling environmental problems.

In the example used above, as well as in Coase's examples, there are only two parties involved and no transaction costs. In the majority of environmental problems, however, more than two parties are involved. In our example pollution of the water by firm 1 can create more general environmental damages in the form, for example, of diminishing recreational opportunities or adversely-affected wildlife. These damages can be represented by the environmental damage function $D(e_1)$ which was assumed to be zero before. But when these damages are considered, the objective functions (2.19) or (2.19.a) are no longer the social welfare functions. Thus private negotiations between the two parties will not lead to the social optimum. In terms of Figure 2.2 general environmental damages mean that the marginal damage curve shifts upwards to $D_1'D_1'$. The social optimum is now at the point $x_1^{**} < x_1^*$. To reach the social optimum through negotiations, all the affected parties should be involved. This however definitely implies high transaction costs which have been assumed zero before. It can be shown that the existence of sufficiently high transaction costs may block private bargaining.[37] Suppose that the property rights belong to firm 1 and that total damages to firm 2 and general environmental damages exceed the benefits from emitting at the profit-maximizing level $x_1^o$ for firm 1. In order for the affected parties to make an offer to firm 1 to reduce pollution, these parties have to meet and agree upon the payment. If the transaction costs associated with the agreement among the affected parties are sufficiently high, the offer might not materialize. In this case there is excess pollution and the final outcome depends on the assignment of the property rights.

The existence of transaction costs implies some problems regarding the ability of bargaining to achieve an optimal solution. The same problem appears even in a bilateral case if another assumption underlying Coase's theorem – that of perfect knowledge – is relaxed. Assume that the degree to which each agent is affected by the externality is private information known only to the affected parties. The asymmetries in information can be modelled following Mas-Colell et al. (1995). In the two-firm context, let $\theta \in \Re$ and

---

[37]For further elaboration of these arguments, see Fisher (1981).

$\eta \in \Re$ be two parameters that denote the type of each firm and enter the production function of each firm. The value of these parameters are known only privately while their *ex ante* probability distributions are public knowledge. It is further assumed that $\theta$ and $\eta$ are independently distributed.

Consider the case in which firm 1 has the property rights and there are only two possible emission levels: the uncontrolled private optimum $e_1^o = s_1(x_1^o)$ and the social optimum $e_1^* = s_1(x_1^*)$. For any type $\theta$ the gain to firm 1 from emitting at the uncontrolled optimum compared to the social optimum is:

$$\pi_1(\theta) = \left[ p_1 f(x_1^o, \theta) - w_1 x_1^o \right] - \left[ p_1 f(x_1^*, \theta) - w_1 x_1^* \right] > 0$$

On the other hand the gain to firm 2 from restricting the emissions of firm 1 to the social optimum is:

$$\pi_2(\eta) = \left[ p_2 f_2(x_2^*, s_1(x_1^*), \eta) - w_2 x_2^* \right] - \left[ p_2 f_2(x_2^o, s_1(x_1^o), \eta) - w_2 x_2^o \right]$$

In this set-up only the possible values of $\pi_1$ and $\pi_2$ matter. Let $G(\pi_1)$, and $H(\pi_2)$ be the probability functions induced by the underlying probability distributions of $\theta$ and $\eta$ respectively. Since firm 1 has the property rights the firm will insist on producing at the uncontrolled private optimum $x_1^o$. However at a socially-optimal solution firm 1 should emit at $x_1^*$, whenever $\pi_2 > \pi_1$. Firm 2 will make an offer $T$ to firm 1 to reduce emissions if and only if $\pi_2 \geq T$. On the other hand firm 1 knows that the probability that firm 2 will agree to pay $T$ for reduced pollution is equal to the probability that $\pi_2 \geq T$, which is equal to $1 - H(T)$. So firm 1 will demand a payment in order to reduce emissions, determined by the solution of:

$$\max_{T} \ (1 - H(T))(T - \pi_1)$$

Since the objective function of the above problem is zero if $T = \pi_1$ and strictly positive for $T > \pi_1$, the solution to this maximization problem should be $T^*$ with $T^* > \pi_1$. But if $\pi_1 < \pi_2 < T^*$, then firm 2 can not meet the demand of firm 1. So, although it is socially desirable to reduce emissions to the socially-optimal level $x_1^*$, since $\pi_2 > \pi_1$, the demand made by firm 1 in order to reduce emissions exceeds – due to asymmetric information – the maximum amount that firm 2 is willing to pay. Thus emissions remain at the inefficient level $e_1^o$. If firm 2 has the property rights it can be shown in a similar way that the bargaining process could lead to an inefficient outcome at the level $e_1 = 0$ instead of the social optimum.

A deviation from the socially-optimal emissions level can also be the result of the bargaining process if one of the affected parties is a consumer, while the other is the polluting firm. In this case if the property rights belong to the firm, then the consumer's ability to make an offer is constrained by his or her income. This income constraint, if it is effective, could lead to a deviation from the social optimum. Assume that a firm with a reduced profit function $B(e)$ generates emissions that cause damages $d(e)$ to a consumer. If the property rights are assigned to the firm it will emit at a level $e^o$ that maximizes its benefit function or $e^o = \text{argmax}_e B(e)$. The consumer will make an offer $T$ to the firm to reduce emissions to some level $e$ if and only if $d(e) + T \leq d(e^o)$, and $T \leq M$, where $M$ is the consumer's income. The firm will choose the level of emissions and a payment to demand from the consumer, that solves the problem:

$$\max_{(e,T) \geq 0} B(e) + T$$

$$\text{s. t. } d(e) + T \leq d(e^o), \ T \leq M$$

The Lagrangean for the problem is:

$$\mathcal{L} = B(e) + T + \lambda[d(e^o) - T - d(e)] + \mu(M - T)$$

The first-order condition for the above problem implies that $(e^+, T^+, \lambda, \mu)$ exist such that:

$$B'(e^+) - \lambda d'(e^+) \leq 0, \text{ with equality if } e^+ > 0 \tag{2.22.1}$$

$$1 - \lambda - \mu \leq 0, \text{ with equality if } T^+ > 0 \tag{2.22.2}$$

$$d(e^o) - T - d(e^+) \geq 0, \ \lambda[d(e^o) - T - d(e^+)] = 0, \ \lambda \geq 0 \tag{2.22.3}$$

$$M - T^+ \geq 0, \ \mu(M - T^+) = 0, \ \mu \geq 0 \tag{2.22.4}$$

Suppose that at the solution $0 < T^+ < M$, then from (2.22.4) $\mu = 0$ and from (2.22.2) $\lambda = 1$, in which case (2.22.1) implies that $e^+ = e^*$. That is, the socially-optimal level of emissions is obtained at the point where marginal benefits equal marginal environmental damages. Suppose now that $T^+ = M$ and $0 < \mu < 1$, then from (2.22.2) $\lambda = (1 - \mu)$ and from (2.22.1) $B'(e^+) = (1 - \mu)d'(e^+)$, which implies that $e^+ > e^*$.[38] Thus when the consumer faces a binding income constraint regarding payment demanded by the firm, the outcome of the bargaining process is inefficient.

The above results seems to suggest that although Coase's theorem offers some important insights into dealing with externalities through negotiations

---

[38]Using the implicit function theorem in $B'(e^+) - (1 - \mu)d'(e^+) = 0$, we have that $de^+/d\mu > 0$. Thus an increase in $\mu$ from the value of zero will increase emissions.

of the affected parties and without the need for government regulation, the assumptions that are necessary for the validity of the theorem are not in general satisfied in the great majority of environmental problems. As a result Coase's theorem does not seem to offer a practical alternative to environmental policy based on Pigouvian tradition.

# 6   UNCERTAINTY AND THE CHOICE OF POLICY INSTRUMENTS

The previous section indicated that the presence of uncertainty impedes the achievement of the optimal outcome through a bargaining solution. In this section the impact of uncertainty is examined with respect to the traditional environmental policy instruments. As has already been shown, under certainty environmental policy instruments are equivalent irrespective of whether they take the form of price instruments such as emission taxes or quantity instruments such as emission limits or quotas related to tradeable permits. Weitzman (1974) showed however that the equivalence does not hold under conditions of uncertainty.

In our framework uncertainty takes in general two forms.[39] The first refers to uncertainty at the level of the firm that manifests itself through the firm's reduced profit or benefit function, emission function or abatement function. This is mainly technological uncertainty associated with uncertain pollutant content of inputs used in production (such as sulphur content of fuels), effects on abatement technology, learning effects in cleaning up procedures, price of abatement inputs and so on. The second refers to the social damage function and is associated with the inability to measure pollution damages with sufficient accuracy or with general uncertainties with respect to climatic conditions (for example, uncertainties regarding the increase in global temperature from the emissions of greenhouse gases) that affect social damages for any given level of emitted pollutants.

Considering these two types of uncertainty at the environmental regulator's level, the benefit function for the firm can be written as $B_i(e_i,\theta)$ where $\theta \in \Re$ has a distribution function $F(\theta)$ which is known to the regulator, while the damage function can be written as $D(e,\eta)$, $e=\Sigma_i e_i$ with $G(\eta)$, $\eta \in \Re$ being the

---

[39]See Adar and Griffin (1976) for details of the type and sources of uncertainty faced by firms and environmental agencies.

distribution function for $\eta$.[40] Thus $\theta$ denotes the first type of uncertainty while $\eta$ denotes the second type. Total welfare in this case depends on the values of $\theta$ and $\eta$ and can be written as $\Sigma_i B_i(e_i,\theta)+D(e,\eta)$. Thus the emission levels that maximize welfare can be defined as $e_i^*=e^*(\theta,\eta)$ where $B_i'(e^*(\theta,\eta),\theta)=D'(e^*(\theta,\eta),\eta)$. The optimal *ex ante* emission tax which is the price instrument will be contingent upon the realization of $(\theta,\eta)$ defined as $\tau(\theta,\eta)=D'(e^*(\theta,\eta),\eta)$. Using this tax, *ex ante* uncertainty is eliminated *ex post*. On the other hand the optimal *ex ante* quantity instrument, which could be either an emission limit or a quota related to marketable permits, is defined as $e^*=e^*(\theta,\eta)$, and again uncertainty is eliminated *ex post*.

However Weitzman (1974) shows that it is not feasible for the regulator to use contingent instruments since this may require the use of complicated and highly specialized contracts between the regulator and the firm which would be hard to understand and expensive to draw up. Second-best solutions are therefore considered in which the regulator does not use contingent instruments. Assume that a uniform emission tax, $t$, is used. The firm solves the problem $\max_{e_i} B_i(e_i,\theta)-te_i$ which yields $e_t^o=e_t^o(t,\theta)$ and implies that the firm's emissions are completely insensitive to changes in $\eta$. However, when the outcome is $(\eta,\theta)$ the optimal tax is $\tau(\eta,\theta)$. The loss in aggregate welfare from using tax $t$, that induces emissions $e_t^o=e_t^o(t,\theta)$ relative to the optimal tax $\tau(\eta,\theta)$ that induces emissions $e_i^*=e^*(\theta,\eta)$, is defined as:

$$\Delta W_t = \left[ \sum_i B_i(e_t^o,\theta)-D\left(\sum_i e_i^o,\eta\right) \right] - \left[ \sum_i B_i(e_i^*,\theta)-D\left(\sum_i e_i^*,\eta\right) \right]$$

This welfare loss is presented in Figure 2.3 under the assumption of a single polluting firm.[41]

Assume that the regulator calculates the emission tax $t$ on the basis of the mean values $(\bar{\theta},\bar{\eta})$ defined by the intersection of the marginal benefit function $B'(e,\bar{\theta})$ and the marginal damage function $D'(e,\bar{\eta})$. These functions can be regarded as the 'hypothesized' marginal curves. The realized marginal curves are however $B'(e,\theta)$ and $D'(e,\eta)$ which would have required an optimal tax, $\tau(\theta,\eta)$.

Consider now the case in which the regulator hypothesizes an emission limit $\bar{e}_i$ and sets a corresponding limit. The firm solves the problem $\max_{e_i} B_i(e_i)$ subject to $e_i \leq \bar{e}_i$. Under the quota system $e_q^o=e_q^o(\bar{e}_i,\theta)$. If

---

[40]This implies that all firms and all affected individuals are regarded by the environmental regulator as being of the same type.

[41]For this type of presentation, see for example Mas-Colell et al. (1995) or Pearce and Turner (1990) for a more environmentally-focused exposition.

$B'(e_i,\theta)>0$ for all $\theta$, then $e_q^o=\bar{e}_i$ for all $\theta$. The loss of aggregate surplus under the quota system is defined as:

$$\Delta W_q = \left[\sum_i B_i(\bar{e}_i,\theta) - D\left(\sum_i \bar{e}_i,\eta\right)\right] - \left[\sum_i B_i(e_i^*,\theta) - D\left(\sum_i e_i^*,\eta\right)\right]$$

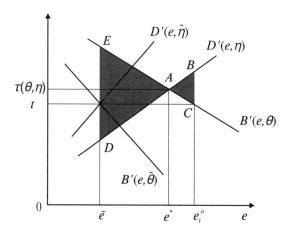

*Figure 2.3   Welfare loss under uncertainty*

The welfare loss for the quota case is represented in Figure 2.3 by area *EAD,* while the welfare loss from using the suboptimal tax *t* is equal to area *ABC.* The hypothesized marginal curve leads to the quota $\bar{e}_i$ instead of $e_i^*(\theta,\eta)$, which is the socially-optimal quota level. It is clear that the welfare loss differs in size in the two cases, implying that the two instruments are not equivalent. The specific circumstances determine which instrument results in the smaller welfare loss.

Let us consider now the case of Figure 2.4 in which $\theta$ is fixed at $\bar{\theta}$; uncertainty therefore exists only with respect to the damage function. On the basis of the hypothesized $D'(e,\bar{\eta})$ the quota is set at $\bar{e}$, while the tax is set at *t.* Welfare loss, when the realized marginal damage function is $D'(e,\eta)$, equals area *ABC,* which is the same for both instruments. This equivalence result holds because uncertainty in the damage function does not affect the firm's decisions. These decisions are sensitive only to uncertainty in the benefit function.

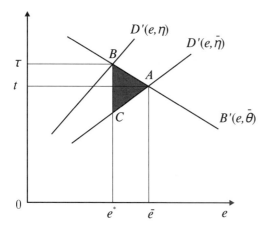

*Figure 2.4   Welfare loss under uncertainty in the damage function*

Alternatively consider the case of Figure 2.5, in which $\bar{\eta}$ is fixed and uncertainty affects only the benefit function. Taxes or quotas are set on the basis of the hypothesized marginal benefit function $B'(e,\bar{\theta})$, so the emission limit results in a loss of $ABC$, while the tax results in a loss of $ADE$. This asymmetry results because with the realized marginal benefit function above the hypothesized one, the quota restricts emissions at $\bar{e}$ (below the optimal level $e_i^*$) while the tax allows generations of emissions at $e^o$ (beyond the optimal level), since the firm equates marginal benefits with the tax rate which is fixed and does not reflect the increasing marginal emission costs.

Welfare losses under the quota system are defined as:

$$\Delta W_q = BCD - ACD = (1/2)(\Delta MB_q)(\Delta e_q) - ACD$$

where $(\Delta MB_q) = BC$, $(\Delta e_q) = \bar{e}e^*$. Denoting the elasticity of the marginal benefit function by $e_b = -(\Delta e/\Delta MB)(MB/e)$, we have:

$$BCD = -(1/2)(\Delta e_q)^2 (MB/e)(1/e_B), \quad MB = Ae_i^*, \quad e = e^*$$

On the other hand, the welfare loss under the tax is defined as:

$$\Delta W_t = EDC - ACD = (1/2)(\Delta MD_t)(\Delta e_t) - ACD, \quad \Delta MD_t = ED, \quad \Delta e_t = \bar{e}e^*$$

Using the definition for the elasticity of the marginal damage function, we have that $EDC = (1/2)(\Delta e_q)^2 (MB/e)(1/e_D)$. Thus

$$\Delta W_q - \Delta W_t = -\frac{1}{2}(\Delta e_q)^2 \frac{MB}{e}\left(\frac{1}{e_B} + \frac{1}{e_D}\right)$$

which implies that taxes and quotas have the same effect if the elasticity of the marginal damage and marginal benefit functions are equal in absolute values or if $\Delta e_q = 0$ which means that the realized outcome $\theta$ is the same as the hypothesized outcome $\bar{\theta}$. Thus depending on the relative magnitude of the elasticities one instrument can be superior to the other.

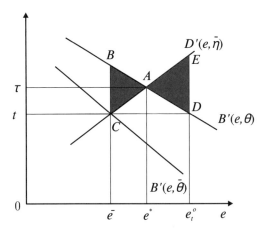

*Figure 2.5   Welfare loss under uncertainty in the benefit function*

The analysis associated with Figures 2.4 and 2.5 suggests that, while damage uncertainty is not relevant to the choice between price or quantity instruments, in the presence of benefit uncertainty the choice of instrument depends on the slopes of the marginal damage and marginal benefit functions. When uncertainty is present in both benefits and damages (as in the case of Figure 2.3) and there is statistical dependence between them, then as shown by Stavins (1996) a positive correlation tends to favour the quantity instrument while a negative correlation favours the price instrument, with positive correlation being more plausible in environmental problems.

There can also be cases in which for fixed $\bar{\eta}$, one instrument or the other can maximize aggregate surplus for every realization of $\theta$.[42] Consider the case of Figure 2.6 which draws on Mas-Colell et al. (1995) in which

---

[42]See Mas-Colell et al. (1995).

marginal damages are zero up to $e^*$ and infinite above $e^*$.

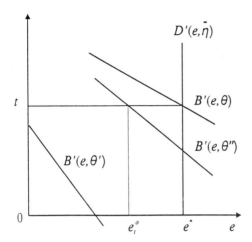

*Figure 2.6   Welfare maximization with a quota*

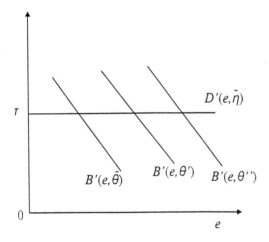

*Figure 2.7   Welfare maximization with a tax*

A quota set at level $e^*$ will maximize aggregate surplus for any realization of $\theta$. On the other hand, a tax set at a level high enough to restrict emissions to a level below $e^*$, like for example $t$, will result in low emissions, that is $e_t^o$ for the realization $\theta''$, or zero for the realization of $\theta'$.

When, on the other hand, marginal damages are constant – that is, independent of the level of the externality as shown in Figure 2.7 – a tax set at the level of the constant marginal damages will induce emissions that maximize aggregate surplus irrespective of the realization of $\theta$. In this case a quota cannot induce the correct amount of emissions, unless of course the hypothesized marginal benefit function is also the realized function.

## 7   NONCONVEXITIES AND ENVIRONMENTAL POLICY

The analysis of the social optimum and market equilibrium in Section 6 that served as the fundamental framework for the determination of policy instruments was carried out under the maintained assumption of convex preferences and production sets. This convexity assumption implies that all the maximization problems examined are well-behaved in the sense of being concave problems where second-order conditions are satisfied, and the solution of these problems are themselves continuous functions of the parameters of the problem.

It was demonstrated, however, starting in the 1970s,[43] that negative or detrimental externalities can cause nonconvexities in the social production set.

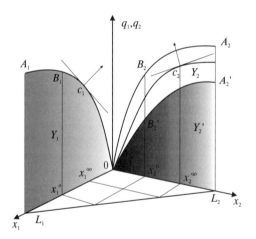

*Figure 2.8   Convex production sets for two firms*

The inducement of nonconvexities by a detrimental externality is shown in

---

[43]See Baumol and Bradford (1972), Starret (1972), Baumol and Oates (1988, Chapter 8).

Figure 2.8, which illustrates the production functions of two firms, 1 and 2. The production activities of firm 1 have an adverse effect on the output of firm 2.[44] Assume that both firms use a homogeneous primary input – say labour – that is in fixed supply. Thus $x_1 + x_2 = x$ is the available primary input. Let $Y_1$ and $Y_2$ be the convex production sets of the two firms with transformation or efficiency frontiers $0A_1$ and $0A_2$ respectively. The allocation of labour takes place along the line $L_1L_2$. So if all labour is allocated to firm 1, the efficient production is at $A_1$, while if all labour is allocated to firm 2, the efficient production is at $A_2$.

Assume for the moment that no externality exists. Then the social production possibility set is the convex set $Y$ shown in Figure 2.9.

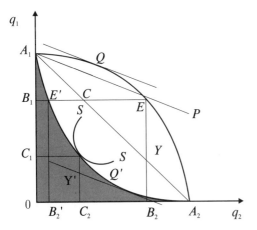

*Figure 2.9    Nonconvexities in the social production possibility set*

With labour allocated according to $(x_1^o, x_2^o)$, and without external effects on the output of firm 2, efficient production points for firms 1 and 2 are $B_1$ and $B_2$ which are equivalent to point $E$ on the social production possibility frontier in Figure 2.9. However, when the externality exists and firm 1 engages in production, then firm 2's production set is not $0A_2L_2$, which is the set contingent on firm 1 producing zero, but a set with transformation frontier below $0A_2L_2$, say $0A_2'L_2$, in Figure 2.8. The efficiency frontier $0A_2$, shifts downwards because of the externality. The firm produces at $B_2'$ and the

---

[44]Examples of a situation such as this can be the electricity–laundry case of Baumol and Oates (1988) or an upstream chemical plant and a downstream farmer, and so forth.

region $0A_2A_2'$ is not feasible. Consider now the social production possibility set.

The fact that production points on $B_2B_2'$ are not feasible implies that the point on the social production frontier that corresponds to $B_2'$, should be on the left of $E$ on the line $EB_1$ in Figure 2.9. If the externality is sufficiently strong to shift $B_2'$ to the left of point $C$, say $E'$, then the social production set is the nonconvex set $Y'$.

The implication of having a nonconvex social production set is that the problem of maximizing the value of output for any given possible output prices has a corner solution either on $A_1$, or $A_2$ depending on the price ratio. With a price ratio given by the slope of line $A_1P$ in Figure 2.9, point $A_2$ is a local maximum with a global maximum at $A_1$, indicating that the value of aggregate output is maximized if only firm 1 produces. It is important to notice that $Q'$, the point of tangency of the nonconvex social production set with the price line, is a point where the value of the output is minimized.

In contrast, without nonconvexities, the point of tangency, $Q$, maximizes the value of the output. From the policy point of view, the existence of multiple optima could create problems for a regulator which might choose a policy instrument that implements a local maximum instead of a global one. For example at point $A_2$, movement to the left reduces the value of total output until point $Q'$, which is the local minimum. Thus the regulator can be misled and choose a policy instrument to implement $A_2$ rather than $A_1$.

Related to the issue of implementing a certain policy is the issue of whether a price system can support a certain point on a nonconvex social possibility set. It has been demonstrated[45] that since the individual production sets are convex and the nonconvexities are induced by the detrimental externality, any desired point on the nonconvex social production possibility set can be supported by a price system that includes tax/subsidies for both firms. Assume that each firm solves the following maximization problem:

firm 1: $\max_{x_1} p_1 f_1(x_1) - (w + \tau_1)x_1$

firm 2: $\max_{x_2} p_2 f_2(x_2, x_1) - (w + \tau_2)x_2$

where $w$ is the competitive price of the input, $\tau_i, i = 1,2$ are taxes or subsidies imposed on firms 1 and 2, and firm 2 treats $x_1$ as fixed when solving its maximization problem. The objective function in each individual maximization problem is concave. Solving the first-order conditions

---

[45]See Baumol and Oates (1988, Appendix B to Chapter 8).

determines the profit-maximizing level of inputs as functions of the parameters $x_1^o = z_1^o(p_1, p_2, w, \tau_1, \tau_2)$, $x_2^o = z_2^o(p_1, p_2, w, \tau_1, \tau_2)$. Suppose that the regulator wants to achieve $(x_1^{oo}, x_2^{oo})$. The functions determining the profit-maximizing level of inputs for each firm can be inverted to yield the tax rates that can achieve the desired point as:

$$\tau_1^{oo} = z_1^{-1}(p_1, p_2, w, x_1^{oo}, x_2^{oo}), \quad \tau_2^{oo} = z_2^{-1}(p_1, p_2, w, x_1^{oo}, x_2^{oo})$$

The point $(x_1^{oo}, x_2^{oo})$ in Figure 2.8 that corresponds to the efficiency point $(C_1 C_2)$ on the social production possibility set in Figure 2.9 maximizes profits for each firm since individual production sets are convex. Thus the nonconvexity of the social production set does not prevent the regulator from using price incentives to achieve a designated point on the nonconvex production possibility set.[46]

The impact of nonconvexities can be mitigated if additional environmental damages caused to individuals increase at an increasing rate with the use of $x_1$. This can be examined by expressing the profit function of each firm in terms of input $x_1$ and examining the implications of nonconvexities. For firm 1 we have $\pi_1(x_1)$, with $\pi_1' > 0, \pi_1'' < 0$. For firm 2 we have $\pi_2(x_1) = \max_{x_2} \pi_2(x_2, x_1) - wx_2$, with $\pi_2' < 0$. If firm 2 has the possibility of shutting down, then the second derivative of $\pi_2$ can not be uniformly negative (Starret 1972). This is shown in Figure 2.10.

In Figure 2.10, $\pi_2''(x_1) < 0$ for $x_1 < \bar{x}_1$, but $\pi_2''(x_1) > 0$ for $x_1 > \bar{x}_1$. This implies that the social profit function defined as $\pi_1(x_1) + \pi_2(x_1)$ might not be a concave function for all $x_1 > 0$. The implication of this possible nonconcavity for the maximization of social profits is shown in Figure 2.11 in which the social profit-maximizing level of $x_1$ is defined by $\pi_1'(x_1^*) + \pi_2'(x_1^*) = 0$.

There could be two equilibria or no equilibrium at all. In the case of two equilibria (Figure 2.11), one is stable ($A$) and the other is unstable ($B$).[47] Furthermore following Mas-Colell et al. (1995) the social profit set defined by the maximum attainable profit by the two firms for each level of $x_1$, defined as $\Pi = \{(\pi_1, \pi_2): \pi_i \leq \pi_i(x_i), i = 1, 2\}$, is nonconvex.

---

[46]Of course point $C_1 C_2$ does not maximize the value of output but it can maximize social welfare as reflected by the tangency of the social indifference curve *SS* with the social production set. It is interesting to note that the point at which social welfare is maximized is different from the point at which the value of output is maximized.

[47]We consider only regular equilibria where the second derivative of the social profit function does not vanish at the equilibrium point.

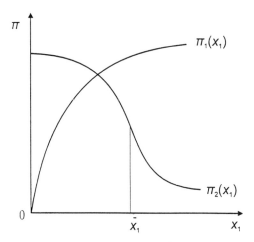

*Figure 2.10   Nonconcavity in the reduced profit function*

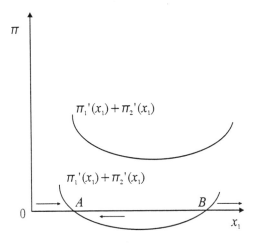

*Figure 2.11   Multiple equilibria with a convex social profit function*

This is shown in Figure 2.12. The problem max $\pi_1 + \pi_2$, s.t $\pi_1, \pi_2 \in \Pi$ has a global maximum at $A$ and a local maximum at $B$, which is a solution similar to the one obtained above.

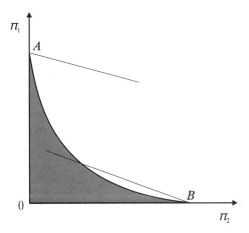

*Figure 2.12   Nonconvexity of the social profit set*

Having analysed some of the implications of the nonconvexities in terms of the social profits, assume now that the use of $x_1$ creates environmental damages to individuals. For example the upstream polluting plant not only affects the downstream farmer but also adversely affects recreational facilities (swimming, fishing) and the ecosystem itself. If these damages can be expressed by a convex damage function $D(x_1)$, then the social profit function can be defined as $\pi_1(x_1) + \pi_2(x_1) - D(x_1)$. Then even if $\pi_1''(x_1) + \pi_2''(x_1) > 0$ for some $x_1 > \bar{x}_1$, with sufficient convexity in the damage function we could have $\pi_1''(x_1) + \pi_2''(x_1) - D''(x_1) < 0$ for $x_1 > \bar{x}_1$. Hence the social profit function is concave and the maximization problem has a well-defined solution. In this case the convexity of the damage function dominates and the whole program is concave.[48]

The implications of the convexity of firm 2's profit function as a result of the detrimental externality generated by firm 1, can also be presented in terms of marginal benefit and marginal damage functions. Define the social marginal benefit function as $B'(x_1) = \pi_1'(x_1) + \pi_2'(x_1)$, with $B'(x_1) > 0$. If the second firm's profit function exhibits sufficiently strong convexity, this could imply that the social marginal benefits curve could be upward sloping after a certain level of $x_1$. With a normal upward-sloping marginal damage

---

[48]In a different context Repetto (1987) shows that a convex cost function, which plays the same role as the convex damage function, dominates the nonconvexities associated with a smog frontier.

function, there might be many or no equilibria at all, as shown in Figure 2.13.

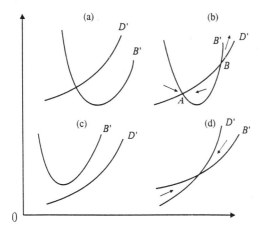

*Figure 2.13    Equilibrium with nonconcave benefit function*

Figure 2.13a shows a unique stable equilibrium. The pollution level $e^* = s(x_1^*)$ can be supported either by taxes or quotas. In Figure 2.13b, point $A$ is again a stable equilibrium, but $B$ is unstable since the marginal benefit function has the wrong curvature in the neighborhood of the equilibrium point. In Figure 2.13c there is no equilibrium while in 2.13d, although the benefit function is convex, $B'' > 0$, the damage function has sufficient convexity to make the whole optimization problem concave, $B'' - D'' < 0$, so that there is a unique stable equilibrium point.

In the previous examples, detrimental externalities caused a wrong curvature in the marginal benefit function, while the marginal damage function was normally upward sloping. There are however reasons that could cause a wrong curvature in the marginal damage function. For example, if faced with increased pollution individuals take 'averting behavior'[49] to protect themselves, say by not swimming in a polluted river, or even moving to another place. In this case marginal damages could decline at the relevant pollution levels. Also, as Pearce and Turner (1990) point out, in an area that has experienced environmental degradation, possibly from low income housing or industrial development, adding a few more houses or a few more

---

[49]See Fisher (1981).

plants might reduce marginal damages. In all these cases the marginal damage function could contain downward-sloping segments as marginal damages decline and then possibly increase as pollution accumulates and more individuals or areas are affected. This is shown in Figure 2.14, which draws on Fisher (1981), in which a normal downward-sloping marginal benefit function is combined with a nonconvex marginal damage function.

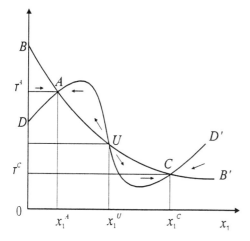

*Figure 2.14   Equilibrium with nonconvex damage function*

There are two stable equilibria at $A$ and $C$ and an unstable one at $U$. If *ex ante* pollution exceeds $e^U = s(x_1^U)$ then equilibrium is achieved at $C$ with the corresponding Pigouvian tax, $\tau^C$. Since there are two stable maxima the desired one should be the global maximum. This global maximum can be determined by comparing net benefits, defined as the difference between total benefits and total damages, for the two maxima. For point $A$, net benefits are defined as the area $0BAx_1^A$ less the area $0DAx_1^A$, while for point $C$ net benefits are defined as the area $0BCx_1^C$ less the area $0DAUCx_1^C$.

## 8   COST EFFECTIVENESS AND POLICY INSTRUMENTS

The analysis in the previous section indicated that in the presence of nonconvexities it might be difficult to determine the optimal policy, either because the regulator has to choose among many local optima, or the optimum is not well-defined either in the sense of unstable equilibria or no equilibrium at all. Apart from the possible nonconvexities a further problem in the pursuit of optimal policies relates to the informational requirements for the calculation of the optimal instruments,[50] and especially with the correct estimation of the damage function.[51] As an alternative to the pursuit of optimal policy, the approach of selecting a certain environmental standard[52] and then determining the instruments that could achieve this standard at a minimum cost has been proposed by Baumol and Oates (1971, 1988) and Baumol (1972). This approach, called the standards and charges approach by Baumol and Oates, demonstrates through a cost minimization theorem that the environmental quality standard can be achieved at a minimum cost.[53]

The cost minimization theorem can be presented in the following way. Consider the input selection model (I) of Section 2.1. The regulator's problem can be set as:

$$\min_{(x_i^p, x_i^a) \geq 0} \sum_{i=1}^{n} w^p \cdot x_i^p + \sum_{i=1}^{n} w^a \cdot x_i^a$$

$$\text{s.t.} \sum_{i=1}^{n} \left[ s_i(x_i^p) - h_i(x_i^a) \right] \leq \bar{e}$$

$$f_i(x_i^p) \geq q_i, \quad i=1,...,n$$

The Lagrangean function for this problem is defined as:

$$\mathcal{L} = \sum_{i=1}^{n} w^p \cdot x_i^p + \sum_{i=1}^{n} w^a \cdot x_i^a + \lambda \left[ \sum_{i=1}^{n} \left( s_i(x_i^p) - h_i(x_i^a) \right) - \bar{e} \right] + \sum_{i=1}^{n} \mu_i \left[ q_i - f_i(x_i^p) \right]$$

The Kuhn-Tucker conditions for this problem imply that if $(x_i^{*p}, x_i^{*a}) \geq 0$ solves the minimization problem then Lagrangean multipliers $(\lambda, \mu) \geq 0$ exist such that for all $i=1,...,n$:

---

[50]See Baumol and Oates (1988) and Fisher (1981) for a more detailed analysis of these issues.
[51]However significant advances have been made in this area. See for example Freeman (1985), Braden and Kolstad (1991).
[52]The environmental standard will reflect environmental quality at a given site. Standards for air can be set by using predetermined levels of concentration of certain pollutants in outdoor air, averaged over a certain period. Such pollutants, which have been called criteria pollutants, include sulphur dioxide ($SO_2$), total suspended particles (TSP), carbon monoxide (CO), nitrous oxides (NOX) and ozone (Tietenberg 1996). Standards for water can be set using predetermined levels of dissolved oxygen (DO) in the water body as a measure of ambient water quality or predetermined levels of biological oxygen demand (BOD) as a measure of emissions in the water body.
[53]For a similar cost minimization theorem, see Fisher (1981). The approach used here follows Fisher.

$$w^P + \lambda \frac{\partial s_i(x_i^{*P})}{\partial x_i^P} - \mu_i \frac{\partial f_i(x_i^{*P})}{\partial x_i^P} \geq 0, \text{ with equality if } x_i^{*P} > 0 \qquad (2.23.1)$$

$$w^a - \lambda \frac{\partial h_i(x_i^{*a})}{\partial x_i^a} \geq 0, \text{ with equality if } x_i^{*a} > 0 \qquad (2.23.2)$$

$$\lambda \left[ \sum_{i=1}^{n} \left( s_i(x_i^{*P}) - h_i(x_i^{*a}) \right) - \bar{e} \right] = 0, \ \lambda \geq 0 \qquad (2.23.3)$$

$$\mu_i \left[ q_i - f_i(x_i^{*P}) \right] = 0, \ \mu_i \geq 0, \ i = 1,...,n \qquad (2.23.4)$$

In this problem $\lambda$ can be interpreted as the shadow cost of emissions reflecting the increase in the firm's cost from making the emission standard more stringent.[54] Solving (2.23.1), (2.23.2) and (2.23.4) for interior solutions, the demand for input functions is obtained as $x_i^{*j} = x_i^{*j}(w^P, w^a, \lambda, q_i, \bar{e})$, $j = p, a$.

Consider now the problem of firm $i$ that is subject to an emission tax $t_i$ per unit of emissions and seeks to choose input levels that minimize total production costs plus tax payments. The firm's problem is:

$$\min_{(x_i^P, x_i^a) \geq 0} \quad w^P \cdot x_i^P + w^a \cdot x_i^a + t_i \left[ s_i(x_i^P) - h_i(x_i^a) \right]$$

$$\text{s.t. } f_i(x_i^P) \geq q_i$$

The Lagrangean for the problem is:

$$\mathcal{L} = w^P \cdot x_i^P + w^a \cdot x_i^a + t_i \left[ s_i(x_i^P) - h_i(x_i^a) \right] + \mu_i \left[ q_i - f_i(x_i^P) \right]$$

For the triplet $(x_i^{op}, x_i^{oa}, \mu_i) \geq 0$ that solves the above problem the Kuhn-Tucker conditions imply:

$$w^P + t_i \frac{\partial s_i(x_i^{op})}{\partial x_i^P} - \mu_i \frac{\partial f_i(x_i^{op})}{\partial x_i^P} \geq 0, \text{ with equality if } x_i^{op} > 0 \qquad (2.24.1)$$

$$w^a - t_i \frac{\partial h_i(x_i^{oa})}{\partial x_i^a} \geq 0, \text{ with equality if } x_i^{oa} > 0 \qquad (2.24.2)$$

---

[54] Let $C^*(w^P, w^a, q_1,..., q_n, \bar{e})$ be the minimum cost function. Then by the envelope theorem $\partial C^*/\partial \bar{e} = -\lambda$.

$$\mu_i\left[q_i - f_i(x_i^{op})\right] = 0, \ \mu_i \geq 0, \ i = 1,...,n \tag{2.24.3}$$

Solving (2.24.1) to (2.24.3) for interior solutions the demand functions for inputs are obtained as $x_i^{oj} = x_i^{oj}(w^P, w^a, t_i, q_i)$, $j=p,a$. It is clear that if the tax is set equal to $\lambda$, the shadow cost of the emission constraint, then $(x_i^{op}, x_i^{oa}) = (x_i^{*p}, x_i^{*a})$ and under the uniform emission tax $t_i = \lambda$, aggregate emissions equal the emission standard. If the emission standard is set at the welfare maximizing level in the sense of setting emissions at the point where marginal benefits equal marginal damages, then the emission tax will be equal to marginal damages calculated at the optimal emission level as derived in Section 3.1. If, however, the social welfare maximizing level of emissions can not be determined, either because the damage function is not known or because nonconvexities prevent the determination of a well-defined optimum, this approach can be said to achieve the standard at a minimum cost. It can easily be shown that the cost minimization theorem holds for other usual price incentive schemes.[55]

Suppose that the predetermined standard should be achieved by tradeable permits. For any initial allocation equal to the environmental standard, or $\bar{e}_i$ such that $\Sigma_i \bar{e}_i = \bar{e}$, firm $i$ solves the problem:

$$\min_{(x_i^p, x_i^a) \geq 0} w^P \cdot x_i^P + w^a \cdot x_i^a + P^T\left[s_i(x_i^P) - h(x_i^a) - \bar{e}\right]$$

$$\text{s.t. } f_i(x_i^P) \geq q_i$$

The Kuhn-Tucker conditions for this problem are identical to (2.24.1) – (2.24.3) with $t_i$ replaced by $P^T$. Demand functions for inputs depend on the price of permits or, $x_i^{oj} = x_i^{oj}(w^P, w^a, P^T, q_i) = x_i^{oj}(P^T)$, $j=p,a$. In equilibrium the price $P^T$ should clear the market or $\Sigma_i(e_i - \bar{e}_i) = 0$, which further implies $\Sigma_i[s_i(x_i^{op}(P^T)) - h_i(x_i^{oa}(P^T))] = \bar{e}$. Thus $P^T = \lambda$, that is, the equilibrium permit price equals the shadow cost of emissions.

---

[55]The case of subsidies is symmetric to the taxation case. The firm solves:

$$\min_{(x_i^p, x_i^a) \geq 0} w^P \cdot x_i^P + w^a \cdot x_i^a - v\left[\bar{e} - s_i(x_i^P) + h(x_i^a)\right]$$

$$\text{s.t. } f_i(x_i^P) \geq q_i$$

Of course, as was mentioned earlier, under free entry taxes or subsidies affect entry–exit decisions of the firm differently.

## 8.1 Spatial Considerations

The cost effectiveness of the policy instruments was demonstrated under the assumption that the emission standard is set with respect to a single location or site. The cost effectiveness can however be maintained in more complicated spatial models in which the target is to attain the environmental standard at different locations with diffusion of pollutants among regions.[56] In the following sections, emission taxes and tradeable permits which allow for spatial considerations are examined.

### 8.1.1 Regional tax systems

Following Xepapadeas (1992c) let an area be divided into $r=1,...,R$ regions with $i_r=1,...,n_r$ competing firms in each region. Net emissions of each firm in each region are defined as $e_{ri_r} = s_{ri_r}(x^p_{ri_r}) - h_{ri_r}(x^a_{ri_r})$ where the index $ri_r$ indicates firm $i_r$ in region $r$. Denote by $\delta_{ru}$ the amount from a unit of net emissions generated in region $r$ that is transported to region $u$. Thus aggregate emissions in region $r$ are defined as:

$$e_r = \left(1 - \sum_{\substack{r=1 \\ u \neq r}}^{R} \delta_{ru}\right) \sum_{i_r=1}^{n_r} e_{ri_r} + \sum_{\substack{m=1 \\ m \neq r}}^{R} \delta_{mr}\left(\sum_{i_m=1}^{n_m} e_{mi_m}\right), \quad r=1,...,R$$

The first term on the right-hand side represents emissions remaining in region $r$ after diffusion to other regions, while the second term represents emissions imported from other regions.

The regulator seeks to achieve given environmental standards in each region. Assuming perfect input mobility among regions the regulator seeks to solve the following problem:

$$\min_{\left(x^p_{n_r}, x^a_{n_r}\right) \geq 0} \sum_r \left[\sum_{i_r} \left(w^p \cdot x^p_{ri_r} + w^a \cdot x^a_{ri_r}\right)\right]$$

$$\text{s.t.} \sum_{i_r} e_{ri_r} \leq \bar{e}_r, \quad r=1,...,R \tag{2.25.1}$$

$$f_{ri_r}(x^p_{ri_r}) \geq q_{ri_r}, \quad i_r=1,...,n_r \tag{2.25.2}$$

Associating multipliers $\lambda_r, r=1,...,R$ with constraints (2.25.1) and multipliers $\mu_{ri_r}, i_r=1,...,n_r$, with constraints (2.25.2), the Kuhn-Tucker conditions imply for all $r, i_r$:

---

[56]For development of spatial models of environmental policy, see Siebert (1985).

*Advanced Principles in Environmental Policy*

$$w^P + \left[\lambda_r\left(1 - \sum_{u \neq r}\delta_{ru}\right) + \sum_{u \neq r}\delta_{ru}\lambda_u\right]\frac{\partial s_{ri_r}(x_{ri_r}^{*P})}{\partial x_{ri_r}^P} -$$

$$\mu_{ri_r}\frac{\partial f_{ri_r}(x_{ri_r}^{*P})}{\partial x_{ri_r}^P} \geq 0, \; x_{ri_r}^{*P} \geq 0 \tag{2.26.1}$$

$$w^a - \left[\lambda_r\left(1 - \sum_{u \neq r}\delta_{ru}\right) + \sum_{u \neq r}\delta_{ru}\lambda_u\right]\frac{\partial h_{ri_r}(x_{ri_r}^{*a})}{\partial x_{ri_r}^a} \geq 0, \tag{2.26.2}$$

$$x_{ri_r}^{*a} \geq 0$$

$$\lambda_r\left(\sum_{i_r}e_{ri_r}^* - \bar{e}_r\right) = 0, \; \lambda_r \geq 0 \tag{2.26.3}$$

$$\mu_{ri_r}\left(q_{ri_r} - f_{ri_r}(x_{ri_r}^{*P})\right) = 0, \; \mu_{ri_r} \geq 0 \tag{2.26.4}$$

where $\lambda_r$ is the shadow cost of the environmental constraint in region $r$. Assume that the regulator introduces regional taxes $t_r$ in each region $r = 1,\ldots,R$. Under the regional tax the firm solves the problem:

$$\min_{(x_{ri_r}^P, x_{ri_r}^a) \geq 0} \; w^P \cdot x_{ri_r}^P + w^a \cdot x_{ri_r}^a + t_r\left[s_{ri_r}(x_{ri_r}^P) - h_{ri_r}(x_{ri_r}^a)\right]$$

$$\text{s.t. } f_{ri_r}(x_{ri_r}^P) \geq q_{ri_r}$$

Following the same reasoning as in the case of a single location, the emission standard in each region can be achieved by a regional emission tax defined as:

$$t_r = \lambda_r\left(1 - \sum_{u \neq r}\delta_{ru}\right) + \sum_{u \neq r}\delta_{ru}\lambda_u$$

The first part of the tax corresponds to the shadow cost of emissions remaining in region $r$ while the second part reflects the shadow cost of the region that receives the pollutants generated in region $r$.[57] If emission standards in each region are chosen so that marginal benefits in each region equal marginal environmental damages, then regional taxes are optimal in the sense of achieving the social welfare maximizing emission level in each

---

[57]This regional differentiation of taxes might not be possible in practice due to legal restrictions. For the construction of uniform fee zones see Tietenberg (1978), Seskin et al. (1983) and Kolstad (1987).

region.[58]

## 8.1.2 Tradeable emission permits systems

In analysing spatial considerations in the context of tradeable permits, two major permit systems can be identified: single zone systems and ambient permit systems.

In a single zone system the location of each polluting source in the zone does not matter. One permit gives the potential polluter the right to emit and this permit can be traded on a one-to-one basis as long as the environmental standard is satisfied within the zone. In order to examine the permit system in more detail we consider the problem of the regulator which seeks to minimize costs within the zone subject to the achievement of the environmental standard. In order to facilitate the exposition, it is convenient to define a convex cost of abatement function in the following way:

$$C_i(a_i) = \max_{q_i} \ pq_i - c(q_i a_i)$$

Individual emissions are defined as usual by $e_i - a_i$ with $e_i$ interpreted as uncontrollable profit-maximizing emissions corresponding to the case in which no abatement is induced by environmental policy. Aggregate emissions are defined as $e = \Sigma_i(e_i - a_i)$. The regulator seeks to minimize costs in order to achieve the predetermined standard. That is:

$$\min_{a_i \geq 0} \ \sum_i C_i(a_i)$$
$$\text{s.t.} \ \sum_i (e_i - a_i) \leq \bar{e}$$

(2.27)

The first-order condition for an interior solution to the above problem is:

$$\frac{\partial C_i(a_i^*)}{\partial a_i} = \lambda, \ i = 1, \ldots, n$$

where $\lambda$ is the shadow cost of the emission constraint. It is clear that this is a condition similar to the one derived for the tax case.

---

[58]It can easily be shown by considering a static version of the model developed in Xepapadeas (1992c) that the optimal regional tax is defined as:

$$t_r = D_r'(e_r^*)\left(1 - \sum_{u \neq r} \delta_{ru}\right) + \sum_{u \neq r} \delta_{ru} D_u'(e_u^*)$$

where $D_r'(e_r^*)$, $r = 1, \ldots, R$ are marginal damages in region $r$ evaluated at the optimal emission level for the region.

There is an equivalence in principle between taxes and permits. Under the permit system, when the initial permit holding is $\tilde{e}_i$ and the competitive permit price is $P^T$, the quantity of permits traded is $e_i - a_i - \tilde{e}_i$ and the firm solves the problem:

$$\min_{a_i \geq 0} C_i(a_i) + P^T(e_i - a_i - \tilde{e}_i)$$

with first-order necessary and sufficient conditions for interior solution $[\partial C_i(a_i^o)/\partial a_i] = P^T$. Under the tax system the firm solves

$$\min_{a_i \geq 0} C_i(a_i) + t(e_i - a_i)$$

with first-order necessary and sufficient conditions for interior solution $[\partial C_i(a_i^o)/\partial a_i] = t$.[59]

However, the equivalence breaks if we take into account information requirements. In order to set the emission tax the regulator needs to know the abatement cost functions to determine the shadow cost of the emission standard which corresponds to the Lagrangean multiplier of problem (2.27) defined as $\mathcal{L} = \Sigma_i C_i(a_i) - \lambda(\bar{e} - e)$. Solving this problem the regulator can set $t = \lambda$. If, however, the abatement functions are not known, the tax should be determined iteratively. An initial tax is set that would probably result in violation of the standard, and then the rate is adjusted so that the standard is eventually achieved. Under the permit system, however, the regulator needs only to issue the correct number of permits in the zone, without needing to know abatement costs.

In order for the permit system to achieve the standard at the minimum cost and without welfare losses, the conditions for the existence of a competitive permit market should be satisfied. This requires a large number of potential polluters, independence of polluters in the product market, and differences in abatement cost functions to stimulate trading (Howe 1994, Lyon 1982, Hahn 1984). The method of allocating the permits initially is also of significance. While auctioning[60] of permits results in an efficient allocation, grandfathering requires trading in order to achieve the efficient allocation. Furthermore grandfathering could create barriers to the entry of new firms into the market.

---

[59]If the permit gives the firm the right to emit one unit forever then by an approach similar to the one used in Section 3.3 the competitive permit price is defined as:

$$P^T = \int_0^\infty e^{-rt} \left( \frac{\partial C_i(a_i^o)}{\partial a_i} \right) dt = \frac{\partial C_i(a_i^o)/\partial a_i}{r}$$

[60]For an evaluation of the Environmental Protection Agency's annual call auctions for permits to emit sulphur dioxide, see Cason and Plott (1996).

The single-zone system described above does not take into account the location characteristics of the polluting sources and the ambient concentration of the pollution. These spatial characteristics are taken into account by the ambient permit system (APS). In this system a number of emission locations or zones and a number of ambient standards at receptor points are defined. Emissions from the different zones affect concentrations at the receptor points differently. The objective is to obtain a given standard at each receptor point. Assume $i=1,...,n$ sources and $r=1,...,R$ receptor points. Let, as before, $\delta_{ir}$ denote the transportation coefficient reflecting the proportion of a unit of emissions generated by source $i$ that is transported in the ambient environment of receptor point $r$. As in the case of regional taxes, the ambient concentration at receptor point $r$ is defined as $e_r = \sum_{i=1}^{n} \delta_{ir}(e_i - a_i)$, $r=1,...,R$.[61] To determine standards at each receptor point the regulator solves the problem:

$$\min_{a_i \geq 0} \sum_{i=1}^{n} C_i(a_i)$$

$$\text{s.t.} \sum_{i=1}^{n} \delta_{ir}(e_i - a_i) \leq \bar{e}_r, \quad r=1,...,R$$

(2.28)

The first-order conditions for interior solutions imply:

$$\frac{\partial C_i(a_i^*)}{\partial a_i} = \sum_{r=1}^{R} \delta_{ri} \lambda_r$$

where $\lambda_r$ is the shadow cost of the emission standard at each receptor point. It is clear that the sum of the shadow cost weighted by the diffusion coefficients equals the emission tax on emission source $i$. To determine the tax without knowledge of the cost of abatement function but by using some iterative approach, the regulator should experiment on a large scale with the possibilities of realizing inefficient outcomes. On the other hand, the trading system requires only the setting of the standard at the receptor point with firms using knowledge of their own abatement characteristics to trade efficiently. As shown by Montgomery (1972), with a linear transport process there is a competitive equilibrium in the permit market that minimizes total abatement costs. Thus the regulator issues permits corresponding to allowable ambient concentration of emissions at each receptor point and the firms, through competitive bidding, achieve the least cost outcome. This least-cost outcome does not depend on initial allocation of permits.

---

[61]This notation is equivalent to the one used in the analysis of regional taxes. Since $\sum_i \delta_{ir} = 1$, then $\delta_{ir}$ can be replaced by $(1 - \sum_{i \neq r} \delta_{ir})$.

Although from the regulator's point of view the APS does not impose severe information requirements, it could involve high transaction costs for the emitting firms.[62] In the APS the permit is associated with the effects of the source's emissions on the ambient concentration at the receptor point. Under these circumstances the firms should hold a 'portfolio' of permits for each receptor point. There will be $r$ markets for permits and each firm will participate in each market to the extent that the firm's emissions reach the receptor point. This, however, requires knowledge of the diffusion process by each firm. Thus the APS could involve quite high transaction costs for the firms. Another problem is associated with the spatial application of the standard. If the standard is set at all points in the prespecified area, as in the case of the US Clean Air Act, while according to the APS the standards should be met only at the specific receptor points, there is a possibility that certain pollutants with localized effects will exceed the standard at points other than the receptor points. These points have been called 'hot spots'; in order to avoid them an extensive network of receptor points is required. This, however, will increase both market and transaction costs. Finally, as pointed out by Howe (1994), the existence of a competitive least-cost equilibrium for the APS has been proven only under a linear diffusion process. With a nonlinear diffusion process[63] where the ambient concentration at each point is determined by the nonlinear function $\delta_r(e_1-a_1,...,e_n-a_n)=e_r$, the linear constraint in problem (2.28) should be replaced by the nonlinear constraint $\delta_r(e_1-a_1,...,e_n-a_n)\leq\bar{e}_r$. In this case the permit market may not achieve the least-cost solution.

The difficulties associated with the APS can be reduced by using alternative systems, which – although they do not have the least-cost characteristics of the APS – represent improvements over the complications of the APS. These systems include the emission permit system (EPS), the zonal permit system and the trading rules and trading ratios (Tietenberg 1995). The EPS acts as a single zone system and ignores the spatial complexities of pollution control. As a result the system is suboptimal in reaching target concentrations of pollutants and 'hot spot' problems may appear. In a zonal permit system the area under consideration can be divided into different zones. Standards are set and permits are issued within each zone. This system facilitates trading among potential polluters and could avoid the hot spot problems of the EPS, but might impose severe

---

[62]See Baumol and Oates (1988, Chapter 12).
[63]The diffusion process can be nonlinear because the pollutant has nonlinear effects on the ambient concentration, such as the effect of BOD on dissolved oxygen.

informational requirements on the regulator. With many zones and pollutant diffusion among them, the regulator needs to determine the number of permits within each zone. This however implies the solution of the cost minimization problem. Furthermore the EPS will not achieve the least-cost solution in each zone if the pollution in each zone has different dispersion characteristics of the pollutants (Baumol and Oates 1988).

In systems associated with trading rules and trading ratios, some trades can be ruled out while others are allowed, and also permits need not be traded on a one-to-one basis. These systems include: (1) the pollution offset system (POS) (Krupnick et al. 1983); (2) the nondegradable offset (Atkinson and Tietenberg 1982), and (3) the modified pollution offset (McGartland and Oates 1985).[64]

According to the POS, permits correspond to the right to emit as with the EPS; however trading is not on a one-to-one basis but depends on the contribution of each polluter to the ambient concentration at a given receptor point. Suppose that polluters $i$ and $j$ contribute by their emissions to concentrations at the receptor point $r$. Let $\delta_{ir} = 2\delta_{jr}$. That is, the amount of polluter $i$'s emissions that is transported to receptor $r$ is twice the corresponding amount of polluter $j$. Thus if $i$ needs to increase emissions by one unit he or she should obtain two units of permits from $j$. The application of the POS requires the knowledge, from the point of view of the regulator, of the diffusion coefficients, $\delta$, so that the rate of substitution from one source to another is determined. It does not, however, require that the regulator solve the cost minimization problem to determine the permits in each zone. Any initial allocation will obtain a least-cost solution. Furthermore the POS does not require separate markets for each receptor point so it reduces the firm's transaction costs. The overall constraint in the POS is that the trading of permits does not violate the standard at any receptor point.

In order to allow trading of permits among sources, the nondegradable offset requires, in addition to the regular POS, that total emissions in the zone not increase.

Finally the modified pollution offset requires that neither the pretrade air quality nor the ambient concentration ratio target (which of the two is the most stringent) be exceeded at any receptor point.

In the USA practice, permit systems can be divided into inter-firm nonapproval trading and inter-firm, intra-firm approval trading. Approval trading refers to the intervention of the pollution control agency in the trade of permits. Inter-firm approval, in the case of trading air emission rights, has

---

[64]For more details and some comparisons, see Tietenberg (1995).

led to the following four different trading programs:[65]

(i)      Bubbles – In a bubble, more than one firm can be included. In determining allowable trades of emission permits in a bubble, emissions by different sources in the bubble are treated as if they were subject to a single aggregate emission limit.

(ii)     Offsets – Under the offset system, a new or a modified existing source of emissions can operate in an area where emissions are not allowed to increase, if they can obtain offsetting emission permits (or credits)[66] from other sources.

(iii)    Banking – Under banking a firm can save emission reductions credits for future use or sale.

(iv)     Netting – Under netting, a firm undergoing major modifications can avoid new source review if it can prove that aggregate emissions by all plants of the firm do not increase significantly.

Cost comparisons of different systems produce various results depending on the area and initial allocations (Atkinson and Tietenberg 1984). It is however indicated that the nondegradable system could be relatively more cost effective with a modified pollution offset being more expensive and all systems being cheaper than the pretrading command and control policy. In another simulation study that models the essential elements of trading processes under the bubble policy,[67] Atkinson and Tietenberg (1991) show that gaps between cost-minimizing emissions trading patterns and actual patterns are due to the sequential and bilateral character of trades. The sequence of bilateral trades produces less cost savings than those corresponding to the cost-minimizing allocation.

## 8.2 The Impact of Transaction Costs

As indicated in the previous section transaction costs could have a significant effect on the effectiveness of the APS system. However transaction costs are also present in the rest of the systems – single zone, EPS and OPS – and could reduce the volume of trading and the total effectiveness of the system. Even in the simplest case of a single-zone system with one-to-one trading,

---

[65]For detailed analysis, see EPA (1992).

[66]Emission credits are created when emissions are less than allowable limits, $e_i - a_i - \bar{e}_i < 0$.

[67]The bubble policy was initiated in 1979 by the Environmental Protection Agency. Under this policy existing sources could trade emissions among themselves. The bubble policy followed the offset policy introduced in 1976.

transactions costs are present and include consulting costs to identify potential permit sellers and more general financial costs of brokerage services.

Following Stavins (1995), transactions costs can be incorporated into the models of the previous section. Let transaction costs be captured by a function $T(z_i)$, where $z_i = [e_i - a_i - \bar{e}_i] \gtreqless 0$ is the number of permits traded with $T'(z_i) > 0$, that is an increase in the number of permits increases transaction costs. Under a competitive market for permits the firm solves the problem:

$$\min_{a_i \geq 0} C_i(a_i) + P^T(e_i - a_i - \bar{e}_i) + T(z_i)$$

The first-order necessary conditions imply:

$$\frac{\partial C_i(a_i^*)}{\partial a_i} + \frac{\partial T(z_i^*)}{\partial a_i} \leq P^T, \text{ with equality if } a_i^* > 0$$

Thus for interior solutions the firm equates marginal abatement costs plus marginal transaction costs with the permit price. In contrast to the case with zero transaction costs where marginal abatement costs are equated across sources, in the presence of transaction costs what is equated across sources is the sum of marginal abatement and transaction costs. The result of this discrepancy is that in general there could be a reduction in the number of tradings; furthermore if marginal transaction costs are not constant[68] then the initial allocation of permits affects trading and aggregate control costs.[69] Therefore Montgomery's (1972) result that the initial allocation of permits is not important to the achievement of the least-cost solution is not in general valid under nonconstant marginal transaction costs.

The policy implication associated with transaction costs is that there could be cases in which command and control approaches, especially when administrative costs are low, might be preferable to a permit system with high transaction costs.

# 9 CRITERIA FOR CHOICE OF ENVIRONMENTAL POLICY INSTRUMENTS

The discussion in the previous sections, while not exhaustive, covered to some extent the majority of the instruments which can potentially be used to

---

[68]Marginal transaction costs are increasing and sustainable if combined with sufficiently high fixed transaction costs, or decreasing if brokers offer quantity discounts or if an increase in the quantity of trading generates positive informational externalities.

[69]For a proof see Stavins (1995).

achieve specific environmental policy targets. Given, however, the division of instruments between economic-based and command and control, and the existence of different kinds of instruments among the two major categories, there is an important issue of specifying criteria for instrument choice. The need to specify criteria becomes more pressing since some fundamental equivalence conditions among the instruments hold only under simplifying assumptions. When these assumptions are removed, the instruments are no longer equivalent and the use of the 'wrong' instrument could result in undesirable effects.

The basic criteria for choosing among environmental policy instruments can be set out as follows:[70]

1. Environmental effectiveness – An instrument is effective if it can achieve specific policy objectives such as an ambient standard, an emission reduction, or a limit to the ambient concentration of a pollutant. The effectiveness of an instrument is mainly determined by the extent to which potential polluters react to its introduction. In this sense an instrument is more effective, the greater the incentive for pollution abatement and technical innovation which introduces environmentally-friendly processes.
2. Static efficiency – This refers to the achievement of the given environmental goal at a minimum cost given the level of technology and the location of the polluters.
3. Dynamic incentives – This concept refers to the incentives provided by the instrument in the long run. It includes incentives for the adoption of environmentally-friendly or 'clean' technologies, incentives for polluters to change location, or distortions in the relative price ratios of inputs that can make certain production methods relatively cheaper.
4. Flexibility – This refers to the ability of the instrument to adjust in order to maintain the environmental target where exogenous changes in technology or other types of economic activity take place. The crucial characteristic here is whether the adjustment takes place through a decentralized system of potential polluters or whether there is a need for new calculation by the regulating agency once an exogenous change has taken place.
5. Monitoring and enforcement – This is associated with the relative difficulty of obtaining measurements of emissions necessary to apply the specific instrument. The purpose of monitoring could be preparation of the tax bill,

---

[70]For more comprehensive coverage of the issue, see Bohm and Russell (1985) and OECD (1989, 1991).

verification that the standard is observed, or auditing of self-monitoring. In general the accuracy of monitoring is impeded by purely technical features such as malfunctions of equipment, inadequate operation of devices, or inability to obtain entry to premises, or by more fundamental problems such as diffusion of pollutants through the receiving body or changes in climatic conditions that affect concentration. These reasons make it very difficult, if not impossible, to identify and monitor individual emissions with sufficient accuracy.[71] Enforcement refers to actions to bring violators back into line. It includes mainly fines, court proceedings, penalties or indirect actions such as blacklisting. The relationship between accurate monitoring that determines the probability of detecting a violator and the application of penalties to the violator determines to a large extent the degree of compliance with a given instrument.

6. Equity – This criterion refers to the distributional effect of an instrument. For example charges imply payments for net emissions after abatement, that is, payment on residual pollution. The revenues from these taxes can be used in different ways with different distributional implications.[72] On the other hand, to the extent to which the initial allocation of permits is through grandfathering or through auction, there are different distributional consequences.

7. Acceptability – This refers to the degree to which the specific group of polluters affected by the instrument accepts the policy instrument. If the instrument is not acceptable on a long-run basis, then frequent changes of instruments could erode the objectives of environmental protection. Acceptability of the instrument could be increased by the provision of adequate information about the instrument, its consequences and its relationship with other policy instruments, by consulting with the target group before its introduction, by discussing the actual application of the instrument and by gradual implementation that will allow the target group to adjust to the change in environment.

There is a large body of literature which discusses specific policy instruments in terms of the above criteria. With respect to static efficiency, it has been shown through the cost minimization theorem in Section 8, that economic-based instruments minimize total cost. On the other hand, command and control approaches do not typically achieve cost-effective

---

[71]These complications create the so-called nonpoint-source pollution problems that will be analysed in detail in Chapter 4.

[72]The possibility of using the revenues from emission taxes to reduce distortionary taxation elsewhere in the economy was examined earlier in this chapter.

allocations (Baumol and Oates 1988). It has also been shown that the introduction of emission taxes or emission credit trading will increase consumer surplus and aggregate welfare as compared to command and control standards (Malueg 1990).

Another important comparison refers to the dynamic efficiency between economic-based instruments and command and control approaches. The general notion, derived from theoretical models, is that economic-based instruments provide more effective incentives in the long run for invention, innovation and diffusion of environmentally-clean technologies.[73] An economic instrument in the form of taxes, permits or subsidies creates continuous incentives for technical change since emission reductions realized through environmentally-superior technologies will reduce tax bills, or increase revenues from the sale of permits or increase subsidies.[74]

This is illustrated in Figure 2.15 which shows an increasing marginal cost function for a firm with the marginal cost curve $MC^o$.

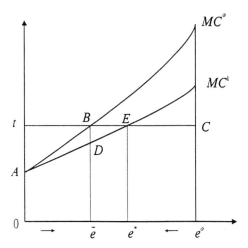

*Figure 2.15   Benefits of technical change*

With zero abatement, profit-maximizing emissions are $0e^o$. Suppose that a standard is set at $\bar{e}$. Then the firm engages in abatement $0\bar{e}$ and emissions

---

[73]Invention refers to the development of a new idea, innovation refers to the incorporation of this idea into a new product, while diffusion refers to the process by which the new product becomes used.

[74]See Tietenberg (1985), Downing and White (1986), Baumol and Oates (1988) and Milliman and Prince (1989).

$\bar{e}\,^o$. The total cost for the firm is the area $0AB\bar{e}$. If the standard is achieved with a tax then the cost to the firm is $0AB\bar{e}+\bar{e}BCe\,^o$, the last term being the tax bill on residual pollution. Suppose that due to the introduction of superior abatement technology, the marginal abatement cost curve shifts to $MC^1$. Under the standard, savings are $ABD$. Under the tax, however, superior technology makes it possible to increase abatement and reduce emissions to $e\,^oe\,^*$. Thus savings under the tax is $ABED$.[75] The same argument can, in principle, apply to the permits. With a quota of $\bar{e}$ the competitive permit price equals $t$. Reduction of emissions by $\bar{e}e\,^*$ allows the firm to sell an equal amount of permits at the competitive price with a profit equal to $BDE$.[76]

On the other hand there is no incentive for innovation or adoption of environmentally-friendly technologies once the standard has been satisfied. This applies especially to technology-based standards that do not leave any room for adoption of new technologies. Jaffe and Stavins (1995) provided an empirical test of the hypothesis that economic incentives performed better as compared to standards with respect to technology diffusion. Their findings suggest that *ad valorem* energy taxes and subsidies appear to be more effective in terms of technology diffusion, improving the efficiency of new homes (use of insulation) than conventional command and control instruments in the form of building codes.

Looking at the issue of flexibility it can be argued that a change in economic conditions will require, in a tax case, recalculation of taxes and changes in the tax rates. This, however, imposes severe informational requirements on the agency, while on the other hand it might cause acceptability problems. If the tax is adjusted by successive iterations then this might prevent the achievement of a cost-effective solution. Flexibility can be regarded as an advantage of permits. Once the appropriate number of permits is issued then exogenous changes that affect the demand for permits will be reflected in changes in the price of permits without any need, at least in principle, for intervention by the regulatory agency. Permits can also be preferable to taxes if nonconvexities in the production set determine the optimal solution to be a corner solution. If the problem is defined over two sites, a corner solution implies that pollution should be concentrated on one site only. In such a case it has been shown that a permit system could provide

---

[75]Of course if the regulator knows about the new technology a more stringent standard could be set at $e^*$.

[76]Malueg (1989) however points out that this might not always be the case. Depending on the firm's position in the emission trading market – buyer or seller – there might be decreasing incentives to adopt new technologies.

the necessary incentives for pollution concentration on one site, while this can not be achieved by a uniform tax (Helfland and Rubin 1994) .

When monitoring is not possible then conventional instruments, at least in their simple form, cannot be used for regulatory purposes. There are a number of new instruments that have been developed in the framework of asymmetric information resulting from the inability of the regulator to monitor individual emissions or observe the type of the polluter, which will be analysed in Chapter 4.

Regarding enforceability there are various results comparing instruments under imperfect enforceability. Harford (1978) compares imperfectly enforceable emission standards and imperfectly enforceable emission taxes.[77] Denote by $v = e - \bar{e}$ the size of the violation of a given standard by a polluter, $F(v)$ the fine as a function of the size of the violation $v$, and $p(v)$ the probability of detecting the violation. It can be shown that making the standard more stringent will reduce emissions if the fine function $F(v)$ is an increasing function of the size of the violation. On the other hand subsidies reduce the level of violation. In the case of taxes it has been found that an increase in the tax rate on reported emissions will reduce actual emissions but will reduce reported emissions even more, thus increasing tax evasion on emission charges. Harford (1978) suggests the use of emission taxes, in the presence of imperfect enforceability in water pollution, by reinterpreting the violation size as the difference between actual emissions and the standard, plus the reported emissions that go to a fee-charging treatment plant.

Incomplete enforceability under a permit system might alter the ability of the permits market to remain in equilibrium, especially if the number of firms is small (Malik 1990) or could increase pollution as compared to a standards system if the marginal fine for violation is either increasing or decreasing rapidly (Keeler 1991).

The issue of comparing different environmental policy instruments is not easily exhausted and requires careful examination of the general framework under which the comparison is made. Changing the basic assumptions could change the ranking of the instruments. Sometimes the situation calls for a combined use of more than one instrument. As Roberts and Spence (1976) show, if there is uncertainty with respect to the cleaning-up costs of the firm, the optimal policy consists of the combined use of permits, subsidies and penalties when emissions are different from the levels determined by the permit system.

---

[77]See also Russell et al. (1986) and Harford (1987).

# 10 LIABILITY

The environmental policy instruments examined up to this point can be regarded as *ex ante* instruments that affect the decision of polluters before emissions are generated. However, another way to approach the problem is to consider *ex post* policies. Under *ex post* policies, such as the strict liability or negligence rule,[78] emissions − or more generally the negative environmental externality − is regulated in a sense after it occurs.[79] The fact that the potential injurer is liable for the harm done causes an internalization of the expected damages and induces the exercise of optimal effort to prevent damages.[80]

Efficient liability rules for the case of groundwater contamination for pesticides have been developed by Segerson (1993). They are defined in terms of the part of the damage from the pesticides for which the farmers and the pesticides' manufacturers are liable. The rules take various forms of strict liability or negligence rule for a single party or a form jointly depending on the assumptions made about farmers' heterogeneity, attitudes of farmers and manufacturers toward risk, and the relevant control variables.

Inefficiencies with the *ex post* liability rule are associated with a number of factors including inability of the potential injurer to pay full damages to victims due to bankruptcy, uncertainty about a suit by the victims, uncertainty of the potential injurer about whether the court will find him or her liable, failure to impose liability due to uncertainty over the causation of the tort, and high transaction costs. It has been shown, in a general framework (Shavell 1984, Kolstad et al. 1990), that *ex ante* regulatory policies and *ex post* liability can be regarded as complementary policies in order to produce an efficient solution. An efficient joint policy requires that the regulatory standard be less than the socially-optimal level that would have been set if only *ex ante* regulation had been used.

Attention has also been given to *ex ante* liability regarding environmental

---

[78]Under strict liability the potential injurer is liable for the damage regardless of whether he or she exercised adequate care. Under negligence the potential injurer is liable if adequate care has not been exercised.

[79]In the liability literature the term tort is often used. This is a legal term referring to a detrimental or a negative externality.

[80]As Cropper and Oates (1992) point out, strict liability involves a payment to the victim. This might result in an inefficient outcome since it could distort the behavior of the victim. On the other hand a Pigouvian tax achieves the efficient outcome by charging the polluter. Perfect internalization through the Pigouvian tax and efficiency does not involve compensation of the victims.

damage accidents where inefficiencies in the liability rule can be brought about by bankruptcy constraints. In such cases extended liability rules have been analysed in which the liability of the firm responsible for the accident is extended to its lenders and financiers when the cost of liability is too high in relation to the firm's assets.[81] In such a case extended liability regimes that would overcome efficiencies of limited liabilities could have adverse effects on financial markets. In fact the optimal regime depends crucially on the structure of information with respect to a firm's profit potential and its accident-preventing activities,[82] between the lender and the firm and the insurance sector and the firm. Extending full liability to the lender when the firm goes bankrupt is optimal (Boyer and Laffont 1996), when there is complete information between the lender and the firm and incomplete information between the insurance sector and the firm. Under more severe informational asymmetries the results tend towards partial lender's liability regimes, but basically they depend on the specific case examined.

---

[81]See Pitchford (1995), Laffont (1995), Boyer and Laffont (1996), Boyd and Ingberman (1994).
[82]In general a firm will have better knowledge of this information than its lenders or the insurance sector.

# 3. Stock Externalities, Dynamics and the Design of Environmental Policy

## 1 INTRODUCTION

The analysis of the environmental policy developed in the previous chapter was based on the assumption that the pollutants emitted during the production activities were of the flow or fund type, and it was the flow of emissions released in the ambient environment at any point in time that created the damages.

A very important class of pollutants, however, are those for which the stock is built into the ambient environment as emissions accumulate at a rate exceeding the rate at which natural processes can absorb them. For a stock pollutant the damages are not caused by the flow of emissions per unit time but by the stock of the accumulated pollutants. In fact stock pollutants are associated with a number of very important environmental problems.

The anthropogenic emissions of the so-called greenhouse gases (GHGs) – carbon dioxide, chlorofluorocarbons (CFCs), methane, nitrous oxides, and ozone – resulting from the burning of fossil fuels increase the stock of carbon, as well as of the other gases, in the atmosphere. The increase of the atmospheric concentration of the GHGs is expected to increase the earth's average temperature through the trapping of the earth's outbound radiation. This is the so-called greenhouse effect. The climate change due to global warming is expected to cause serious damages in the long run.[1] The greenhouse problem is a very good example of a stock externality since it is not the emissions of the GHGs that cause the environmental damages but the accumulated stock of these gases in the atmosphere.

Other examples of stock externalities include the accumulation of heavy

---

[1] There is a large amount of literature on the "greenhouse effect" (see the discussion in Chapter 6). An idea about the damages associated with global warming can be obtained by considering the damage estimates from an increase in the mean temperature by 3°C. These estimates range from 0.25 per cent of the world product (Nordhaus 1991), to 2 per cent (Cline 1992) or even 2.5 per cent (Ayres and Walter 1991).

metals such as lead in the soil, the acid depositions in soil, or the uncontrollable accumulation of nondegradeable waste in landfills. In all these cases it is the accumulation of the pollutant that creates the environmental damages.

Once, however, the notion of the stock externality is introduced, time is also explicitly introduced into the analysis. Environmental pollution becomes a dynamic process of accumulated emissions generated by production or consumption activities, and depletion of the pollutants either by natural processes, reflecting the environment's self-cleaning or assimilating capacity,[2] or by anthropogenic abatement processes.[3]

Denoting by $S(t)$ the stock of pollution at time $t$ and by $e(t)$ the flow of emissions per unit time, the dynamic process of pollution accumulation can be described in a continuous time context by a first-order differential equation of the form:

$$\frac{dS(t)}{dt} \equiv \dot{S}(t) = e(t) - \beta(S(t)), \ \ S(0) = S_o \geq 0$$

The function $\beta(S(t))$ reflects the removal or the decay of the pollution by natural sources and $S_o$ is some initial accumulation of the pollutant. In most studies the rate at which pollution decays is considered constant so that $\beta(S(t)) = bS(t)$, where $b$ is a constant exponential decay rate.[4] Under this assumption the accumulation equation can be written as:[5]

$$\dot{S}(t) = e(t) - bS(t), \ \ S(0) = S_o \geq 0 \tag{3.1}$$

Since damages relate to stock the damage function is an increasing and convex function of the pollution stock:

---

[2]For example a large part of carbon dioxide emissions is removed from the atmosphere and is absorbed into the oceans.

[3]Dynamic models of pollution accumulation date back almost 25 years. See, for example, Forster (1973) Keeler at al. (1971), d'Arge and Kogiku (1973), Plourde (1972), Mäler (1974) and Brock (1977).

[4]This assumption is not free of criticism. It has been suggested (Forster 1975, Dasgupta 1982, Pethig 1993, Cesar 1994, Tahvonen and Withagen 1996, Tahvonen and Salo 1996) that if pollution is sufficiently high then the environment's self-cleaning capacity deteriorates and may eventually become zero. Thus the decay function may take an inverted U shape, in contrast to the exponential decay assumption where the decay function increases monotonically in the stock of the pollutant.

[5]In a discrete time formulation, pollution accumulation is described by the first-order difference equation $S_t = e_t - (1-b)S_{t-1}$.

$$D(S(t)), \, D'>0, \, D''\geq0 \tag{3.2}$$

The introduction of dynamics in this way gives a new dimension to the problem since current action creates damages in the future, therefore intertemporal trade-offs should be taken into account. This chapter will examine these trade-offs and their implication for resource allocation over time and for the structure of environmental policy.

## 2 SOCIAL OPTIMUM AND MARKET EQUILIBRIUM UNDER STOCK POLLUTION

In analysing the social optimum under stock pollution, a market consisting of a fixed number of $i=1,...,n$ firms is considered for the whole time horizon of the problem which is extended to infinity, $t\in[0,\infty)$.[6] Using the ECM model it is assumed that the social planner or the environmental regulator seeks to choose time paths $e_i(t)$, $i=1,...,n$ for the emissions of each firm in order to maximize the present value of aggregate benefits less environmental damages over an infinite time horizon.[7] The problem can be stated as:

$$\max_{\{e_1(t),...,e_n(t)\}} \int_0^{+\infty} e^{-rt}\left[\sum_{i=1}^n B_i(e_i(t))-D(S(t))\right]dt$$

$$\text{s. t. } \dot{S}(t)=\sum_{i=1}^n e_i(t)-bS(t), \, S(0)=S_o \tag{P1}$$

$$e_i(t)\geq0 \text{ for all } i \text{ and } t$$

where $r>0$ is the regulator's discount rate. Thus the regulator's problem is a formal optimal control problem with the stock of pollution $S(t)$ as state variable and the individual emissions $e_i(t)$ as control variables.[8] To solve this problem the current value Hamiltonian is defined as:

$$H(S(t),e_1(t),...,e_n(t),\lambda(t))=\sum_i[B_i(e_i(t))-D(S(t))]+\lambda(t)\left(\sum_i e_i(t)-bS(t)\right)$$

---

[6] The analysis can also be performed in a finite time horizon as shown later in this section. The infinite horizon assumption is maintained for most of this chapter since it allows us to study long-run equilibria.

[7] The analysis in this section is mainly based on Xepapadeas (1992a). For a similar approach see Ko et. al (1992).

[8] This is an autonomous control problem since the net benefit function is stationary, that is it does not depend explicitly on time. For a brief exposition of optimal control theory, see Chapter 7.

According to the maximum principle an optimal solution for the regulator's problem consists of time paths for emissions $\{e_1^*(t),...e_1^*(t)\}$ and an associated time path for the ambient stock of pollution $S^*(t)$, and a path for the costate variable $\lambda(t)$ that satisfy the following conditions:

(i)     $e_i^*(t)$ maximizes $H(S(t),e_1(t),...,e_n(t),\lambda(t))$ for all $i$, that is

$$\frac{\partial H}{\partial e_i}=B_i'(e_i^*(t))+\lambda(t)\leq 0, \text{ with equality if } e_i^*(t)>0, \forall i \qquad (3.3.1)$$

(ii)    $\dot{\lambda}(t)=r\lambda(t)-\dfrac{\partial H}{\partial S}$ or $\dot{\lambda}(t)=(r+b)\lambda(t)+D'(S^*(t))$ $\qquad (3.3.2)$

$$\dot{S}(t)=\sum_i e_i^*(t)-bS^*(t) \qquad (3.3.3)$$

(iii)   The Arrow type transversality conditions at infinity

$$\lim_{t\rightarrow+\infty} e^{-rt}\lambda(t)S^*(t)=0 \qquad (3.3.4)$$

Since the Hamiltonian function is jointly concave in the state and the costate variables, the necessary conditions of the maximum principle (i) and (ii) along with the transversality condition are also sufficient for the maximization.

The costate variable $\lambda(t)$ which is negative by (3.3.1) for any interior solution has a natural interpretation as the shadow cost of the pollutant's stock. To see this consider the maximum value function for the regulator's problem (P1) which reflects the maximum achievable social welfare:

$$W^*(S_o,0)=\max_{\{e_1(t),...e_n(t)\}} \int_0^{+\infty} e^{-rt}\left[\sum_{i=1}^n B_i(e_i(t))-D(S(t))\right]dt \qquad (3.4)$$

s. t. (3.1)

Then $\lambda(0)=\partial W^*/\partial S_o$ or the value of the costate variable measures the extra cost in terms of welfare from increasing the initial stock of pollution by a small amount. This result can be generalized for any instant of time along the optimal path. Thus the optimal value of the costate variable is the social shadow cost of the particular stock.

Conditions (3.3.1) describe short-run equilibrium conditions. These conditions can be solved for interior solutions to obtain a short-run demand function for emissions, or

$$e_i^*(t)=e_i(\lambda(t)) \text{ with } e_i'(\lambda(t))=-\frac{1}{B_i''(e_i^*(t))}>0, \forall i \text{ such that } e_i^*(t)>0$$

This function indicates the socially-optimal emission level at any instant of time as a function of the social shadow cost of the pollutant's stock. Since $\lambda(t) < 0$, a reduction in the absolute value of the social shadow cost of the pollutant will increase emissions.

Given the dynamic character of our model it is of interest to examine its long-run steady state equilibrium properties. By substituting the short-run demand functions for emissions into (3.3.2) and (3.3.3), we can obtain a dynamic system in the stock of the pollutant and its corresponding social shadow cost. This is the modified Hamiltonian dynamic system (MHDS), which is a system of differential equations defined as:

$$\dot{S}(t) = \sum_i e_i^*(\lambda(t)) - bS^*(t) \tag{3.5.1}$$

$$\dot{\lambda}(t) = (r+b)\lambda(t) + D'(S^*(t)) \tag{3.5.2}$$

with boundary conditions defined by $S(0) = S_o$ and the transversality condition (3.3.4). Solution of the above system will determine the socially-optimal path for the pollution stock $S^*(t) = S_S(t; r, b)$ and the corresponding social shadow cost $\lambda(t) = \lambda_S(t; r, b)$ as functions of the parameters $r$ and $b$. Given the path for the social shadow cost the optimal emission path is determined as $e_{iS}^*(t) = e_{iS}^*(\lambda_S(t; r, b)) = e_{iS}^*(t; r, b)$.

Given the MHDS the usual issues associated with the analysis of the long-run equilibrium are:

(i)      existence of solutions;
(ii)     existence and number of long-run equilibria; and
(iii)    stability of equilibria.

Since existence of solutions for $S_S$ and $\lambda_S$ can be shown on the basis of general results about differential equations,[9] we concentrate on the existence and stability of equilibrium. The long-run equilibrium or steady state for the stock of the pollutant and its corresponding shadow cost are defined as values $(S_\infty^*, \lambda_\infty^*)$ for which $S$ and $\lambda$ are stationary, or $\dot{S} = \dot{\lambda} = 0$. The characterization of equilibrium can be better presented with the help of the phase diagram in Figure 3.1.

The isocines for the MHDS are defined in the space $(S, \lambda)$ or phase space, as the loci for which $S$ and $\lambda$ do not change, that is $\dot{S} = \dot{\lambda} = 0$. The following system defines the isocines:

---

[9]See for example Varian (1981) or Brock and Malliaris (1989).

$$\phi_1(S,\lambda)=\sum_i e_i^*(\lambda)-bS^*=0 \qquad (3.6.1)$$

$$\phi_2(S,\lambda)=(r+b)\lambda+D'(S^*)=0 \qquad (3.6.2)$$

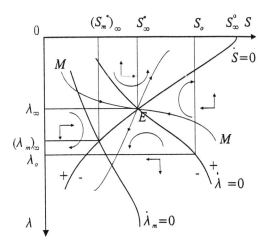

*Figure 3.1  Steady state equilibrium*

From $\phi_1$ and $\phi_2$ we have $d\lambda/dS=b/\sum_i e_i^{*'}(\lambda)>0$, $d\lambda/dS=-D''(S^*)/(r+b)<0$, respectively. The solution of the system (3.6.1), (3.6.2) which corresponds to the intersection of these two loci at $E$ determines the long-run equilibrium point $(S_\infty^*,\lambda_\infty)$. By the monotonicity of the loci the equilibrium is unique. Thus the steady state for the stock of the pollutant is determined as $S_\infty^*=\left[\sum_i e_i^*(\lambda_\infty)\right]/b$.

The local stability of the equilibrium can be analysed by using the Jacobian determinant of the MHDS around the equilibrium point. The Jacobian is determined as:

$$J_S=\begin{vmatrix} -b & \sum_i e_i^{*'}(\lambda) \\ D''(S^*) & (r+b) \end{vmatrix}<0$$

Since $J_S<0$ there are two characteristic roots of opposite sign. Therefore the equilibrium point has the saddle point property. The local saddle point property means that there is a one-dimensional manifold *MM* containing the equilibrium point $E$ such that if the system starts at the initial time on this manifold and at the neighbourhood of equilibrium, or to put it differently if the initial state of the system is at the neighbourhood of equilibrium, it will approach equilibrium as $t \to \infty$. In fact there are two solutions of the MHDS $(S_S^1(t), \lambda_S^1(t))$ and $(S_S^2(t), \lambda_S^2(t))$ that converge to the equilibrium point from different directions on *MM*.

The stability properties of the system can be extended to include the concept of the global asymptotic stability that characterizes convergence to equilibrium from any initial state of the system. It can be shown, using the Brock and Scheinkman (1976) approach, that the manifold *MM* is globally asymptotically stable in the sense that the system converges to equilibrium from any initial state. We consider solutions $S_S(t), \lambda_S(t)$ of the MHDS on *MM* which are bounded for $t \in [0, \infty)$.[10] The curvature matrix is defined as:

$$
Q = \begin{bmatrix} -H_{SS} & \dfrac{r}{2} \\[2ex] \dfrac{r}{2} & H_{\lambda\lambda} \end{bmatrix} = \begin{bmatrix} D'' & \dfrac{r}{2} \\[2ex] \dfrac{r}{2} & \sum_i \Sigma e_i^{*'} \end{bmatrix}
$$

This matrix is positive definite for sufficiently small $r$. It follows from the theorem by Brock and Scheinkman that the equilibrium point $(S_\infty^*, \lambda_\infty)$ is globally asymptotically stable for all bounded solutions. The significance of global stability is that for any initial pollution stock like $S_o$ in Figure 3.1 an initial social shadow cost $\lambda_o$ exists such that the system will be on the stable manifold *MM*. This property, as we will see later, is very useful for determining the optimal tax in the dynamic framework.

Both the time paths for the pollutant stock and its shadow cost, and the long-run steady state equilibrium depend on the parameters of the problem. The effects from changes in the fundamental parameters, the discount rate and the assimilating capacity of the environment, can be analysed with the help of comparative static analysis.

The issue of the choice of the discount rate for an environmental regulator or a social planner that seeks to solve the dynamic social optimization problem, has received a great deal of attention in both theoretical and applied environmental economics.[11] In general the greater the discount rate is, the less the weight given to the net benefits accruing to the future generations.[12]

---

[10]Technically a solution is bounded if it belongs to a compact set for $t \in [0, \infty)$. For details see Brock and Scheinkman (1976).

[11]See for example the special issue of the *Journal of Environmental Economics and Management* (1990) and Weitzman (1994).

[12]For a more detailed exposition of the intergenerational problems involved in environmental and resource economics, see Section 7 of this chapter.

The effects from changes in the discount rate $r$ on the steady state are obtained by comparative static analysis. By differentiating totally the system (3.6.1), (3.6.2) we obtain the comparative static system:

$$J_S \cdot \begin{bmatrix} \dfrac{\partial S_\infty^*}{\partial r} \\[2ex] \dfrac{\partial \lambda_\infty}{\partial r} \end{bmatrix} = \begin{bmatrix} 0 \\ -\lambda \end{bmatrix}$$

thus $\quad \dfrac{\partial S_\infty^*}{\partial r} = \dfrac{\lambda \Sigma_i e_i^{*\prime}}{J_S} > 0 \;$ and $\; \dfrac{\partial \lambda_\infty}{\partial r} = \dfrac{\lambda b}{J_S} > 0$

By giving less weight therefore to the net benefits accruing to future generations, the stock of the pollutant increases in the long-run equilibrium. The effects from a change in the discount rate on the entire optimal path can be analysed using comparative dynamics. Substitution of the solutions $S^*(t) = S_S(t;r,b)$ and $\lambda(t) = \lambda_S(t;r,b)$ in the optimal value function (3.4) determines this function as a function of the parameters $r$ and $b$:

$$W^*(r,b) = \int_0^\infty e^{-rt} \left[ \sum_i B_i(e_i^*(\lambda_S(t;r,b))) - D(S_S(t;r,b)) \right] dt$$

The change in the optimal value of the social welfare function from a change in the discount rate is obtained by using the dynamic envelop theorem as:[13]

$$\frac{\partial W^*(r,b)}{\partial r} \equiv \int_0^\infty \frac{\partial (e^{-rt} H^*)}{\partial r} dt = -\int_0^\infty t e^{-rt} \left[ \sum_i B_i(\cdot) - D(\cdot) \right] dt$$

where $H^*$ is the Hamiltonian function evaluated along the optimal path. Since the solutions are bounded as indicated by the stability analysis, the social net benefits $\pi_S(t;r,b) = \Sigma_i B_i(\cdot) - D(\cdot)$ are also bounded above, say by $\bar{\pi}_S$. Therefore:

$$\frac{\partial W^*(r,b)}{\partial r} = -\int_0^\infty t e^{-rt} \pi_S(t;r,b) dt \le -\bar{\pi}_S \int_0^\infty t e^{-rt} dt = \frac{-\bar{\pi}_S}{r^2} < 0$$

Thus an increase in the discount rate will reduce social benefits by an amount equal to the present value of the flow of net benefits weighted by the time they accrue.

---

[13] See Chapter 7 for the presentation of this theorem.

Considering the effects of a change in the environment's self-cleaning capacity reflected in $b$, the change in the optimal value function is defined as:

$$\frac{\partial W^*(r,b)}{\partial b} \equiv \int_0^\infty \frac{\partial(e^{-rt}H^*)}{\partial b}\,dt = -\int_0^\infty e^{-rt}[\lambda_S(t;r,b)S_S^*(t;r,b)]\,dt > 0$$

Thus a reduction in the assimilating capacity of the environment will reduce social welfare by an amount equal to the present value of the social cost of the accumulated stock of the pollutant.

In the uncontrolled market equilibrium each individual firm does not take into account environmental damages so it solves the static problem $\max_{e_i} B_i(e_i)$ and emits at the level $e_i^o$ which is determined, as in the second chapter, by $B_i'(e_i^o)=0$. As can be seen by comparing the market condition to (3.3.1), the uncontrolled emissions are determined by ignoring the social shadow cost of pollution, $\lambda(t)$. Therefore for all instances of time, $e_i^o(t) > e_i^*(t)$. The accumulation of the pollutant's stock is determined by (3.1) with emissions at the level $e_i^o$. Therefore the long-run equilibrium stock of the pollutant in the uncontrolled market equilibrium exceeds the socially-optimal long-run equilibrium pollution stock, and is determined as:

$$S_\infty^o = \frac{\sum_i e_i^o}{b} > S_\infty^*$$

In terms of Figure 3.1, $S_\infty^o$ is determined to the right of $S_\infty^*$ at $\lambda=0$.

## 2.1 Finite Time Horizon

The analysis up to this point was carried out in the context of an infinite time horizon since this framework allows for the analysis of the long-run equilibrium. There are, however, cases of empirical relevance where the regulator might seek to achieve some target pollution stock at the end of a finite time horizon or even to choose the optimal terminal time for achieving the target.

We start with the finite time horizon case $t \in [0,T]$ where the regulator's target is the pollutant stock at the end of the terminal time $T$, not to exceed a target level $S_T$. In this case the regulator's problem becomes:

$$\max_{\{e_1(t),\dots,e_n(t)\}} \int_0^T e^{-rt}\left[\sum_{i=1}^n B_i(e_i(t))-D(S(t))\right]dt$$

$$\text{s. t. } \dot{S}(t)=\sum_{i=1}^n e_i(t)-bS(t),\ S(0)=S_o,\ S(T)\leq S_T \qquad\text{(P1.a)}$$

$$e_i(t)\geq 0 \text{ for all } i \text{ and } t$$

The optimality conditions are the same as those for the infinite horizon problem $(3.3.1) - (3.3.3)$, with the exception of the transversality condition which is replaced by:

$$\lambda(T)\geq 0 \ (=0 \text{ if } S^*(T)<S_T) \qquad\text{(3.3.4a)}$$

$$\lambda(T) \text{ with no condition if } S^*(T)=S_T \qquad\text{(3.3.4b)}$$

Condition (3.3.4a) indicates that if at the end of the planning horizon the stock of the pollutant is less than the target stock, then its terminal shadow cost vanishes. On the other hand by (3.3.4b) if the target pollution stock is achieved at the end of the planning horizon then its cost is not relevant anymore. The solution of the fixed time horizon problem on the state space can be shown with the help of the phase diagram of Figure 3.2.

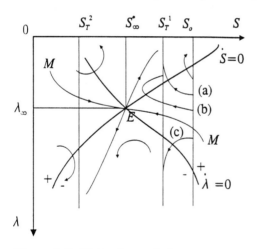

*Figure 3.2  Finite time solution*

Suppose that the initial stock is at $S_o$ and the target terminal stock is $S_T^1$. Optimal paths that could reach $S_T^1$ at finite time are paths like (a), (b) or (c). The actual path depends on the value of the terminal time since the target stock should be reached exactly at $T$. The smaller the terminal time to reach the target stock is, the further downwards the optimal path will be, like path (c). On paths like (c) the shadow cost is reduced in absolute value relatively fast, which means that emissions are reduced rapidly and the stock of the pollutant is reduced rapidly towards the target stock.

The regulator could also choose within the optimization process the terminal time to achieve the target stock of the pollution.[14] When the terminal time is open there is one condition in addition to those of the maximum principle which is required in order to determine the optimal terminal time. The regulator's problem is the same as (P1.a) with the exception that the terminal time $T$ is not specified *a priori*. The determination of the optimal terminal time $T^*$ is obtained by the additional condition which states that $T^*$ is determined such that:

$$H\left(S^*(T^*), e_1^*(T^*), ..., e_n^*(T^*), \lambda(T^*)\right) = 0 \tag{3.3.5}$$

which implies that the optimal time is determined such that the Hamiltonian at this time vanishes.

The results obtained above can be illustrated with the help of an example. Assume that the benefit function, dropping $t$ to simplify notation, is given by the quadratic function $B_i(e_i) = -(1/2)a_i e_i^2 + b_i e_i + c_i$, $(a_i, b_i, c_i) > 0$, with the damage function defined as $D(S) = (1/2)gS^2$, $g > 0$. Consider first the infinite horizon problem (P1). The current value Hamiltonian function is defined as:

$$H = \left[ \sum_i \left( -\frac{1}{2} a_i e_i^2 + b_i e_i + c_i \right) - \frac{1}{2} gS^2 \right] + \lambda \left( \sum_i e_i - bS \right)$$

By the maximum principle we have:

$$\frac{\partial H}{\partial e_i} = -a_i e_i^* + b_i \leq -\lambda, \ e_i^* \geq 0, \ e_i^* = \frac{b_i + \lambda}{a_i} \quad \text{for interior solutions} \tag{3.7.1}$$

$$\dot{\lambda} = (r+b)\lambda + gS^* \tag{3.7.2}$$

$$\dot{S} = \sum_i e_i^* - bS \tag{3.7.3}$$

$$\lim_{t \to \infty} e^{-rt} \lambda S^* = 0 \tag{3.7.4}$$

Substituting from (3.7.1) into (3.7.2) and (3.7.3) the MHDS is obtained as:

---

[14]One possible problem could be the minimum time problem where the objective is to reduce the stock of pollution to the target level in minimum time.

$$\dot{S} = B + A\lambda - bS^*, \quad B = \sum_i \frac{b_i}{a_i}, \quad A = \sum_i \frac{1}{a_i} \tag{3.8.1}$$

$$\dot{\lambda} = (r+b)\lambda + gS^* \tag{3.8.2}$$

The long-run equilibrium is obtained as the solution of the above system for $\dot{S} = \dot{\lambda} = 0$. Thus,

$$S_\infty^* = \frac{(r+b)B}{b(r+b) \cdot gA}, \quad \lambda_\infty = -\frac{gB}{b(r+b) + gA}$$

The long-run equilibrium point has the local saddle point property[15] since the Jacobian determinant of the MHDS, $J_S = -[b(r+b)+gA] < 0$. The optimal paths for $S$ and $\lambda$ are determined by the solution of the differential equation system (3.8.1) and (3.8.2). The roots of the characteristic equation are defined as:

$$m_{1,2} = \frac{r}{2} \mp \frac{1}{2}\sqrt{(-r)^2 + 4[b(r+b)+gA]}$$

The roots will be real and of opposite signs, say $m_1 < 0$, $m_2 > 0$, then the general solution is determined as:

$$S_S(t;r,b) = \Gamma_1 e^{m_1 t} + \Gamma_2 e^{m_2 t} + S_\infty^*, \quad S(0) = S_o \tag{3.9.1}$$

$$\lambda_S(t;r,b) = \Delta_1 e^{m_1 t} + \Delta_2 e^{m_2 t} + \lambda_\infty \tag{3.9.2}$$

We concentrate on the stable solution to obtain the converging manifold:

$$S_S(t;r,b) = \Gamma_1 e^{m_1 t} + S_\infty^* \tag{3.10.1}$$

$$\lambda_S(t;r,b) = \Delta_1 e^{m_1 t} + \lambda_\infty \tag{3.10.2}$$

The constants are determined as follows. In (3.10.1) $\Gamma_1$ is determined by the initial condition $S(0) = S_o$. Thus for $t=0$, $\Gamma_1 = S_o - S_\infty^*$. Furthermore in the solution (3.10.1) and (3.10.2), the constants $\Gamma_1$ and $\Delta_1$ are related as $\Delta_1 = (m_1 + b)\Gamma_1 / A$.[16] Therefore

$$\Delta_1 = \frac{(m_1 + b)(S_o - S_\infty^*)}{A} \quad \text{and} \quad \lambda_o = \Delta_1 + \lambda_\infty \tag{3.10.3}$$

---

[15]The equilibrium point is also globally asymptotically stable for small discount rate.
[16]This follows from the relation among the constants of the solution and the characteristic vector corresponding to the root $m_1$. See Chapter 7.

Thus for every initial value $S_o$ on the stable manifold an initial value $\lambda_o$ exists such that the system will converge to equilibrium. From (3.10.2) and (3.7.1) the optimal emission path is determined as:

$$e_i^* = \frac{b_i}{a_i} + \frac{1}{a_i}\left[\Delta_1 e^{m_1 t} + \lambda_\infty\right] \tag{3.11}$$

with the long-run equilibrium emission level determined as:

$$e_{i\infty}^* = \frac{b_i + \lambda_\infty}{a_i} \tag{3.12}$$

Consider now the case of the fixed time horizon with target pollution stock $S_T$. The solution of the problem is similar to the infinite horizon problem with substitution of the transversality condition by (3.3.4 a,b). Since a terminal condition for $S(t)$ or $\lambda(t)$ is determined by the transversality conditions we have to solve a two-boundary point problem. Assume first that $S(T)=S_T$ so that there are no conditions on $\lambda(T)$. From (3.9.1) the constants $\Gamma_1$ and $\Gamma_2$ can be determined by the initial and the terminal conditions, from the solution of the system:

$$S_o = \Gamma_1 + \Gamma_2 + S_\infty^* \tag{3.13.1}$$

$$S_T = \Gamma_1 e^{m_1 T} + \Gamma_2 e^{m_2 T} + S_\infty^* \tag{3.13.2}$$

Then $\Delta_1$ and $\Delta_2$ are determined by the relationships:

$$\Delta_1 = \frac{(m_1+b)\Gamma_1}{A}, \quad \Delta_2 = \frac{(m_2+b)\Gamma_2}{A} \tag{3.14}$$

Assuming that $S(T)<S_T$ then there is no terminal condition for $S(T)$, but there is a terminal condition on $\lambda(T)$, that is $\lambda(T)=0$. The constants $(\Gamma_1,\Gamma_2,\Delta_1,\Delta_2)$ are determined by:

$$S_o = \Gamma_1 + \Gamma_2 + S_\infty^* \tag{3.15.1}$$

$$0 = \Delta_1 e^{m_1 T} + \Delta_2 e^{m_2 T} + \lambda_\infty \tag{3.15.2}$$

and (3.14)

If the final time is free then it can be determined by substituting the solutions for the state, costate and control variables (3.10.1), (3.10.2) and (3.11) in the Hamiltonian function, set $t=T$, and then determine $T$ that solves equation (3.3.5).

The insights obtained by the above example suggest that the control problem can in principle be solved explicitly. The information requirements for this solution are associated with the knowledge of the benefit function, the damage function and the transition equation describing the accumulation of the pollutant. The benefit function can be estimated by econometric methods, by relating output in the sector to emissions, regarding emissions as a generalized index of the intensity of the production process, with the parameters of the function reflecting the status of the technology employed. In this case of course the type of emissions needs to be related to the specific production process (for example carbon dioxide emissions from the use of fossil fuels, or emissions of sulphur oxides). Since the regulator is interested in solving the problem over a long time horizon, the benefit function relevant for the problem corresponds to a long-run relationship and can be estimated using recently-developed cointegration techniques for the estimation of long-run equilibrium relationships.

The damage function can be estimated using environmental valuation techniques, something which of course is not an easy task, while the approximation of the transition equation requires the knowledge of the biophysical system that reflects the processes governing the accumulation of the pollutants in the ambient environment. Although the informational requirements are likely to be formidable, one might expect that at least for certain circumstances there will be enough information for the solution of the control problem.

Another complication that might arise in applied work relates to the possibilities of nonlinearities. In the example above the problem was of the linear-quadratic form, which in principle can be solved explicitly. However, empirical benefit functions are more likely to be of the Cobb-Douglas, or other nonquadratic type. This would induce nonlinearities in the MHDS. Numerical approximations can be pursued in these cases. For the fixed time problem and in cases where the transversality condition requires $\lambda(T) = 0$, nonlinearities in the MHDS may not allow the explicit determination of the initial value $\lambda(0)$. Then numerical techniques like multiple shooting can be used to determine $\lambda(0)$. That is, an initial value for $\lambda(0)$ is specified and the system is solved or shot forward. The initial value is chosen so that the terminal value $\lambda(T)$ is sufficiently close to zero.[17]

---

[17]For details of this method see Lipton et al. (1982). For an application to an environmental problem see Xepapadeas (1996b).

# 3  OPTIMAL ENVIRONMENTAL POLICY UNDER STOCK EXTERNALITY

Environmental policy instruments under stock externality are similar to those used for the control of flow pollution. A difference exists only in that the determination of the instruments' structure should take into account the dynamics of the problem.

## 3.1  Emission Taxes

The optimal emission tax should be determined such that the individual firm is induced to adopt an emission path that coincides with the socially-optimal emission path. By comparing the conditions for the social optimum given by (3.3.1) to the firm's profit-maximizing conditions it is clear that the optimal dynamic Pigouvian tax is time dependent and is equal to the social shadow cost of the pollutant's stock, or $\tau(t) = -\lambda(t)$. The profit-maximizing firm solves the problem:

$$\max_{e_i(t) \geq 0} B_i(e_i(t)) - [-\lambda(t)] e_i(t), \text{ for all } t$$

with first-order necessary and sufficient conditions for interior solution:

$$B_i'(e_i^o(t)) = -\lambda(t), \text{ for all } t$$

which of course implies $e_i^o(t) = e_i^*(t)$ for all $t$. Thus the regulator should set the path for the emission tax identical to the path of the social shadow cost of the pollutant's stock. In determining the time path for the optimal emission tax, the saddle point property of the long-run equilibrium is of great importance. In conjunction with the results of the previous section, the global saddle point property implies that for any initial stock of the pollutant an initial emission tax and a corresponding time path exist such that the system converges to long-run equilibrium. Using the example in the previous section for the infinite horizon case, the path for the dynamic Pigouvian tax is determined by (3.10.2) and (3.10.3). For the finite time horizon case the path for the emission tax is determined with respect to the path that leads to the terminal stock. In this case the tax is defined by (3.9.2), (3.13.1), (3.13.2) and (3.14) or (3.15.1) and (3.15.2).[18] The requirement that the optimal tax be time dependent, which requires constant changes of the tax rate, may not

----

[18] By the same argument it can be shown that the optimal time path for a subsidy on emission reductions is given by the social shadow cost of the pollutant's stock.

however be a feasible policy for practical purposes. A second-best Pigouvian tax which is time invariant has been proposed by Ko et al. (1992). Under this type of tax desired emissions are kept constant for the whole time horizon. Thus the regulator solves the problem:

$$\max_{e_i} \int_0^\infty e^{-rt} \left[ \sum_i B_i(e_i) - D(S) \right] dt$$

$$\text{s.t.} \quad \dot{S} = \sum_i e_i - bS, \text{ and } e_i \text{ constant for all } t$$

The first-order condition for an interior solution $i = 1, \ldots, n$ is:

$$\int_0^\infty e^{-rt} \left[ B_i'(\hat{e}_i(t)) - D'(S(t)) \frac{\partial S}{\partial e_i} \right] dt = 0$$

or, since $B_i'(\hat{e}_i)$ is constant over time for all $t$,

$$B_i'(\hat{e}_i) = r \int_0^{+\infty} e^{-rt} \left[ D'(S) \frac{\partial S}{\partial e_i} \right] dt$$

which implies that marginal benefits at the optimum should be equal to the interest corresponding to the discounted flow of marginal damages. Hence the optimal second-best time invariant emission tax is defined as:

$$\tau_S = r \int_0^{+\infty} e^{-rt} \left[ D'(S) \frac{\partial S}{\partial e_i} \right] dt$$

This tax scheme can be elaborated more to allow for discrete changes of the tax rate or phased-in policies. Such changes that can improve over the time invariant tax, are determined by the adjustment cost necessary to introduce the changes, such as costs of changing legislation, enforcement of new monitoring guidelines and so on.[19]

Farzin (1996) analyses a model in which a depletable resource[20] generates environmental externalities of both flow and stock type. That is, the damage function is defined as $D(e(t), S(t))$ where $e(t)$ is emissions flow and the stock externality exhibits threshold effects in the sense that its damages exist after a critical stock is reached. It is shown that the emission tax should take into account the stock damages even at the initial period where threshold effects have not yet been realized.

---

[19]For more details see Ko et al. (1992).
[20]Depletion effects are realized through resource exploitation costs that increase both with current exploitation (current resource extraction) and cumulative exploitation to date.

## 3.2  Tradeable Emission Permits

In cases in which the externality is of a stock type as discussed Chapter 2, the issuing of permits of an exhaustible type has been suggested (Tietenberg 1985). An exhaustible permit is used to emit the allowable amount once and cannot be used again. Thus the firm needs to buy new permits in the next period and the regulator needs to issue, for each time period, a number of permits equal to the optimal emissions for that period. Then the paths of the quantities of emission permits is determined as $e^*(t) = \Sigma_i e_{iS}^*(t;r,b)$.

   Let the initial allocation of permits at each point in time be $\tilde{e}_i(t)$ and the competitive permit price be $P^T(t)$. The firm solves the problem:

$$\max_{e_i} \ B_i(e_i(t)) - P^T(t)[e_i(t) - \tilde{e}_i(t)]$$

Since the permit market clears at each time period, the competitive permit price should be equal to the current social shadow cost of the pollutant, which establishes once again the equivalence between permits and taxes in this set up.

## 3.3  Emission Limits

When emission limits are considered the regulator needs to set the limit at each instant of time. To set the limits optimally their level should be equal to the optimal emission level, that is $\bar{e}_i(t) = e_{iS}^*(t;r,b)$. The firm solves the problem:

$$\max_{e_i(t)} \ B_i(e_i)$$

$$\text{s.t. } e_i(t) \le e_{iS}^*(t;r,b)$$

In the solution of this problem the constraint is binding and the firms emit at the predetermined levels. Since the limit has been set optimally, the Lagrangean multiplier of the constraint equals the current shadow cost of the pollutant.

   The analysis up to now has not taken into account the investment decisions of the firm or possible effects from the stock of the pollutant on the firm's benefit function. Thus the firm's problem was essentially static, since profits are maximized at each instant of time without any linkage between past decisions and the current state of the system. In this framework the policy analysis indicates that for the stock pollution case the shadow cost of the pollutant's stock should replace the concept of static marginal damages, used for the flow pollution case, in order to determine the structure of the policy instruments.

# 4   ENVIRONMENTAL POLICY AND INVESTMENT DECISIONS

As was pointed out above, the analysis in the previous section did not include firms' investment decisions. It is of interest, however, to gain some insight into how environmental policy affects firms' investment decisions. Firms' investment decisions which affect the environment, and can be influenced by a given environmental policy, include installation of new productive capacity which could generate emissions (a coal-fired power plant or a paper pulp plant), installation of new abatement capacity for the purpose of cleaning up wastes after they have been generated, installation of new clean production technologies, or substitution of less polluting inputs for more polluting inputs. Installation of abatement equipment mainly corresponds to end-of-pipe abatement, while input substitution, for example low sulphur coal for high sulphur coal, reflects changes in production processes which become relatively cleaner.

In this section we examine how firms react to environmental policies regarding these investment decisions. To keep the analysis simple two separate cases are considered. In the first, firms' decisions with respect to installation of productive or abatement capacity are examined, while in the second decisions regarding input substitution are analysed. The environmental policy which is considered includes emission taxes, marketable emission permits and emission limits. Since firms regard the environmental policy as exogenously given,[21] we consider the simplest possible case in which the externality is of flow type and the regulator determines a time independent instrument.

## 4.1  Decisions about Productive Abatement Investment

A standard neoclassical investment decision model is considered where firms accumulate productive and abatement capital.[22] Productive capital generates output and emissions, while on the other hand abatement capital will either

---

[21]There is no need to assume that the environmental policy instruments have been chosen optimally. If they have then the firms' decisions will be consistent with social welfare maximization.

[22]For details see Xepapadeas (1992a).

make it possible to keep emissions within specified limits, or will reduce the total cost of emissions to the firm. Abatement capital can therefore be regarded as a defensive expenditure. This expenditure can be differentiated from productive capital by differences in installation costs, training costs and so on. These differences mean that the firms face different adjustments costs when investing in productive or abatement capital. The neoclassical investment model with emissions and two types of capital – productive and abatement – is formulated in terms of the input selection model (ICM) defined in Chapter 2. The firm uses capital and labour in output production and emission generation activities or in emission-reducing abatement activities. Let $k(t)=(k_p(t),k_a(t))$ be a vector describing capital employed in output production and pollution abatement at time $t \in [0,\infty)$, and $l(t)=(l_p(t),l_a(t))$ the corresponding labour input in the two sectors.[23] Output is produced according to a standard neoclassical production function $f(k_p(t),l_p(t))$ while net emissions are defined as $e(t)=s(k_p(t),l_p(t))-h(k_a(t),l_a(t))$.[24] Net capital formation in each type of capital is defined as:

$$\dot{k}_j = I_j(t) - \delta_j k_j(t), \quad k_j(0) = k_{jo} > 0, \quad j = p, a \qquad (3.16)$$

where $I_j(t)$ is gross capital formation in the production and the abatement sector and $\delta_j$ is the exponential depreciation rate of the capital stock in each sector. It is further assumed that investment is irreversible, that is $I(t)=(I_p(t),I_a(t)) \geq 0$. In the production process labour is assumed to be the flexible input but capital, both in production and abatement processes, is assumed to be 'quasi-fixed'. Installation of capital at rates $I_p(t)$ or $I_a(t)$ results in costs $vI_j + C_j(I_j)$, $j=p,a$, where $v$ is a common purchase price of a unit of capital equipment and $C_j(I_j)$ is the full adjustment cost that includes installation costs, worker training and so on. Since it is more expensive to accelerate the increase in the capital stock, $C_j(0)=0$, $C_j'(I_j)>0$, $C_j''(I_j) \geq 0$. Differences in the two adjustment cost functions can be regarded as reflecting differences in installation or training costs corresponding to production or abatement capital.

Three different environmental policy instruments are considered:

---

[23]The time symbol $t$ will be omitted in order to simplify notation when it does not create confusion. Also, since we refer to the behavior of the representative firm, the firm index $i$ is dropped.

[24]A more general formulation would be to specify emissions as $e(t)=g(k_p(t),k_a(t))$, with $g(0,k_a)=0$ and $e(t)>0$ if $k_p(t)>0$. Different assumptions about the cross partial derivative of the function could reflect the impact of changes in one type of capital given the level of the other. We use, however, the separable form in order to simplify things.

(i)     *Emission taxes* – Assuming a constant tax rate per unit of emissions, the firm pays at any instant of time a tax bill

$$\tau e(t) = \tau\left[s(k_p,l_p) - h(k_a,l_a)\right] \tag{3.17}$$

(ii)    *Tradeable emission permits* – In the case of emission permits[25] it is assumed that, under a constant competitive emission price $P^T$, the firm receives an initial quantity of permits equal to $\bar{e}(0)=e_o$, whose worth to the firm is $P^T e_o$. The firm will demand more permits if there is a need to increase emissions and it is relatively more costly to increase abatement capital or reduce productive capital. In this case $\dot{e}(t)>0$. Alternatively the firm will supply permits if the initial allocation of permits exceeds the firm's needs, in which case $\dot{e}(t)<0$. Therefore, assuming that permits are valid forever, the firm's expenses or receipts in the permit market are defined as

$$P^T \dot{e}(t) \tag{3.18}$$

(iii)   *Emission limits* – Assuming a constant maximum permitted volume of emissions $\bar{e}$, the emission constraint at any instant of time is defined as

$$e(t) = s(k_p,l_p) - h(k_a,l_a) \le \bar{e} \tag{3.19}$$

The instantaneous cash flow for the firm under the three alternative environmental policy instruments takes the form:

*Emission taxes*

$$\pi_\tau = pf(k_p,l_p) - \sum_j \left[w_j l_j + vI_j + C_j(I_j)\right] - \tau\left[s(k_p,l_p) - h(k_a,l_a)\right] \tag{3.20}$$

*Tradeable emission permits*

$$\pi_{PT} = pf(k_p,l_p) - \sum_j \left[w_j l_j + vI_j + C_j(I_j)\right] - P^T \dot{e} - P^T e_o \tag{3.21}$$

*Emission limits*

$$\pi_{\bar{e}} = pf(k_p,l_p) - \sum_j \left[w_j l_j + vI_j + C_j(I_j)\right]$$
$$\text{with } s(k_p,l_p) - h(k_a,l_a) \le \bar{e} \tag{3.22}$$

---

[25]See Kort (1995) and Hartl and Kort (1996) for a more detailed analysis of firms' investment decisions under a tradeable permit system.

where $p$ is a stationary and exogenous output price and $w_j$ is the wage rate for each type of labour.

In the following we assume that the firm's objective is to maximize, over an infinite time horizon, the present value of its cash flow subject to the constraints imposed by environmental policy.

### 4.1.1 Investment decisions under emission taxes

Under emission taxes the firm solves the problem:

$$\max_{\{I(t),\,l(t)\geq 0\}} \int_0^{\infty} e^{-rt}\pi_{\tau}(t)\,dt$$

$$\text{s.t. (3.16) and } e(t) \geq 0$$

The current value Hamiltonian function for the problem is defined as:

$$H = pf(k_p,l_p) - \sum_j \left[w_j l_j + v I_j + C_j(I_j)\right] - \tau\left[s(k_p,l_p) - h(k_a,l_a)\right] + \sum_j \phi_j(I_j - \delta_j k_j)$$

Assuming interior solutions for the controls $I(t)$, $l(t)$ and $e(t) \geq 0$ for all $t$ at the solution, the maximum principle implies the following necessary and sufficient optimality conditions with all expressions evaluated at the optimal path $k^o(t)$, $l^o(t)$, $I^o(t)$:

$$\frac{\partial H}{\partial l_p} = 0 \text{ or } p\frac{\partial f(k_p^o,l_p^o)}{\partial l_p} - w_p - \tau\frac{\partial s(k_p^o,l_p^o)}{\partial l_p} = 0 \qquad (3.23.1)$$

$$\frac{\partial H}{\partial l_a} = 0 \text{ or } \tau\frac{\partial h(k_a^o,l_a^o)}{\partial l_a} - w_a = 0 \qquad (3.23.2)$$

$$\frac{\partial H}{\partial I_j} = 0 \text{ or } \phi_j = v + C_j'(I_j^o), \; j=p,a \qquad (3.24)$$

$$\dot{\phi}_p = (r+\delta_p)\phi_p - p\frac{\partial f(k_p^o,l_p^o)}{\partial k_p} + \tau\frac{\partial s(k_p^o,l_p^o)}{\partial k_p} \qquad (3.25.1)$$

$$\dot{\phi}_a = (r+\delta_a)\phi_a - \tau\frac{\partial h(k_a^o,l_a^o)}{\partial k_a} \qquad (3.25.2)$$

$$\dot{k}_j = I_j^o - \delta_j k_j^o, \; j=p,a \qquad (3.26)$$

and the transversality condition $\lim_{t\to\infty} e^{-rt}\phi_j(t)k_j^o(t) = 0$, $j=p,a$.

Using the implicit function theorem (3.23.1) and (3.23.2) can be solved to obtain the short-run demand functions for labour:

$$l_j^o(t) = l_j(k_j(t),w_j,\tau), \; j=p,a \qquad (3.27)$$

Short-run comparative statics indicate the effects on demand for labour in the short run, from changes in the capital stocks, the wage rate or the tax parameter, and can be obtained by totally differentiating (3.23.1) and (3.23.2). The results are presented in Table 3.1.

*Table 3.1 Short-run comparative statics for the case of emission taxes*

|           | $k_p$           | $k_a$         | $w_p$ | $w_a$ | $\tau$ |
|-----------|-----------------|---------------|-------|-------|--------|
| $l_p$     | + or 0 [*]      | NE[**]        | -     | NE    | -      |
| $l_a$     | NE              | +             | NE    | -     | +      |

[*] As long as $p \dfrac{\partial^2 f}{\partial k_p \partial l_p} \geq \tau \dfrac{\partial^2 s}{\partial k_p \partial l_p}$; [**]NE: no effect

As would be expected an increase in the tax rate will reduce labour input in production and increase labour input in abatement. An increase in abatement capital will increase labour input in the abatement sector, while an increase in the productive capital will not reduce labour in the productive sector, as long as the increase in the marginal value product of labour resulting from adding one more unit in the stock of productive capital, is no less than the increase in the marginal emission costs associated with the same change in the productive capital.[26]

The short-run demand for investment is obtained by (3.24) as:

$$I_j^o = g(\phi_j - v) \ , \quad \frac{\partial I_j}{\partial \phi_j} = \frac{1}{C_j''} > 0, \ j = p, a \tag{3.28}$$

By differentiating (3.24) with respect to time we obtain $\dot{\phi}_j = C_j''(I_j^o)\dot{I}_j$. Substituting into (3.25.1) and (3.25.2) and using (3.24), we obtain two differential equations describing the evolution of gross investment in the productive and abatement sectors:

$$\dot{I}_p = \frac{1}{C_p''(I_p^o)} \left[ (r + \delta_p)\left[ v + C_p'(I_p^o) \right] - p \frac{\partial f}{\partial k_p} + \tau \frac{\partial s}{\partial k_p} \right] \tag{3.29.1}$$

---

[26]The no effect result from changes in the productive capital on abatement labour and vice versa is a result of the separability assumption of the productive and abatement inputs.

$$\dot{I}_a = \frac{1}{C_a''(I_a^o)}\left[(r+\delta_a)\left[v+C_a'(I_a^o)\right]-\tau\frac{\partial h}{\partial k_a}\right] \tag{3.29.2}$$

Alternatively it is possible to derive:

$$\int_t^\infty \left(p\frac{\partial f}{\partial k_p}-\tau\frac{\partial s}{\partial k_p}\right)e^{-(r+\delta_p)(\omega-t)}d\omega - v - C_p'(I_p)=0$$

$$\int_t^\infty \left(\tau\frac{\partial h}{\partial k_a}\right)e^{-(r+\delta_a)(\omega-t)}d\omega - v - C_a'(I_a)=0$$

which implies that discounted net cash inflow streams, corrected for depreciation, equal cash outflow for the marginal unit of investment. That is, the net present value of marginal investment equals zero.

Short-run demand functions (3.27) and (3.28) can be substituted into (3.29.1), (3.29.2) and (3.26) to obtain the MHDS that determines the dynamic behaviour of the system. The steady state long-run equilibrium is defined as the point $(I_{p\infty}^o, I_{a\infty}^o, k_{p\infty}^o, k_{a\infty}^o):\dot{I}_p=\dot{I}_a=\dot{k}_p=\dot{k}_a=0$. It can be shown (Xepapadeas 1992a) that the long-run equilibrium point has the local saddle point property. Comparative statics of the steady state allow us to determine the long-run effects on capital stocks and investment from changes in the tax policy. The steady state comparative static results are presented in Table 3.2.

*Table 3.2 Steady state comparative statics*

|   | $k_{p\infty}$ | $k_{a\infty}$ | $I_{p\infty}$ | $I_{a\infty}$ | $l_{p\infty}$ (*) | $l_{a\infty}$ |
|---|---|---|---|---|---|---|
| $\tau$ | - | + | - | + | - | + |

(*) As long as $p\dfrac{\partial^2 f}{\partial k_p \partial l_p} > \tau\dfrac{\partial^2 s}{\partial k_p \partial l_p}$.

Thus an increase in the tax rate will produce 'normal effects' in the long run, in the sense of reducing productive emission-generating inputs. By calculating explicitly the derivatives it can be seen that the higher the adjustment costs, in the sense of being relatively more expensive to accelerate increases in the capital stock (that is $C_j''$ is relatively high), the less potent the environmental policy. Less potent here means that a given tax change produces relatively smaller changes in the capital stocks.

Comparative dynamic results can be obtained by using the dynamic envelope theorem. Denoting by $J^o(t)$ the optimal value function as a function of the tax rate, that is:

$$J^o(\tau) = \max_{\{I(t),l(t)\}} \int_0^{+\infty} e^{-rt}\pi_\tau \, dt$$

we have

$$\frac{\partial J^o(\tau)}{\partial \tau} = \int_0^\infty \frac{\partial\left(e^{-rt}H^o\right)}{\partial \tau} \, dt =$$

$$-\int_o^\infty e^{-rt}\left[s\left(k_p^o(t;\tau),l_p^o(t;\tau)\right) - h\left(k_a^o(t;\tau),l_a^o(t;\tau)\right)\right]dt < 0$$

This derivative defines the cumulative discounted emission function. Furthermore the slope of the cumulative emission function can be determined as:

$$\frac{\partial^2 J^o(\tau)}{\partial \tau^2} = -\int_o^\infty e^{-rt}\frac{\partial}{\partial \tau}\left[s\left(k_p^o(t;\tau),l_p^o(t;\tau)\right) - h\left(k_a^o(t;\tau),l_a^o(t;\tau)\right)\right]dt \le 0$$

which implies that cumulative discounted emissions for the firm over the entire planning horizon never increase when the tax rate increases.

### 4.1.2 Investment decisions under tradeable emission permits
In the case of emission permits it is assumed, in order to simplify the presentation, that the emission function does not depend on labour, that is $e(t) = s(k_p(t)) - h(k_a(t))$. Thus $\dot{e}(t) = s\,'\dot{k}_p - h\,'\dot{k}_a$. Then the firm solves the problem:

$$\max_{\{I(t),l_p(t)\ge 0\}} \int_0^\infty e^{-rt}\pi_P \tau(t)\, dt$$

s.t. (3.16) and $e(t) \ge 0$

The current value Hamiltonian function for the problem is defined as:

$$H = pf(k_p,l_p) - w_p l_p - \sum_j \left[vI_j + C_j(I_j)\right] -$$

$$P^T\left[s\,'(k_p)(I_p - \delta_p k_p) - h\,'(k_a)(I_a - \delta_a k_a)\right] - P^T e_o + \sum_j \phi_j(I_j - \delta_j k_j)$$

Assuming as before interior solutions, the necessary and sufficient conditions implied by the maximum principle are:

$$\frac{\partial H}{\partial l_p}=0 \text{ or } p\frac{\partial f}{\partial l_p}-w_p=0 \tag{3.30}$$

$$\frac{\partial H}{\partial I_p}=0 \text{ or } v+C_p'(I_p^o)+P^Ts'(k_p^o)=\phi_p \tag{3.30.1}$$

$$\frac{\partial H}{\partial I_a}=0 \text{ or } v+C_a'(I_a^o)-P^Th'(k_a^o)=\phi_a \tag{3.30.2}$$

$$\dot{\phi}_p=(r+\delta_p)\phi_p-p\frac{\partial f(k_p^o)}{\partial k_p}+P^Ts''(k_p^o)\dot{k}_p-P^Ts'(k_p^o)\delta_p \tag{3.31.1}$$

$$\dot{\phi}_a=(r+\delta_a)\phi_a-P^Th''(k_a^o)\dot{k}_a+P^Ts'(k_a^o)\delta_a \tag{3.31.2}$$

along with (3.16) and the transversality conditions at infinity.

From (3.30.1) and (3.30.2) the short-run demand function for investment is defined as:

$$I_j^o=I_j(\phi_j-v,P^T,k_j), \ j=p,a$$

By comparing the above expression to (3.28) it can be seen that the short-run investment demand depends on the permit price and the capital stock, in addition to the net value of one unit of investment, $\phi_j-v$, while for the tax case the short-run investment demand depends solely on $\phi_j-v$. This result implies that the short-run investment behaviour would be different under the tax or the tradeable permit regimes. By totally differentiating (3.30.1) and (3.30.2) we obtain:

$$\frac{\partial I_p^o}{\partial P^T}=-\frac{s'(k_p)}{C_p''(I_p^o)}<0, \quad \frac{\partial I_a^o}{\partial P^T}=\frac{h'(k_a)}{C_a''(I_a^o)}>0$$

Thus an increase in the permits price, resulting for example from an upsurge in the demand for emissions under constant overall quantity of permits, will stimulate abatement investment in the short run, and discourage productive investment. As in the case of emission taxes, the higher the adjustment costs the less potent the environmental policy is. In order to examine the steady state and compare it to the tax case we differentiate (3.30.1) and (3.30.2) with respect to time and then substitute for $\dot{\phi}_j$ and $\phi_j$ in (3.31.1) and (3.31.2) respectively to obtain:

$$\dot{I}_p=\frac{1}{C_p''(I_p^o)}\left[(r+\delta_p)\left[v+C_p'(I_p^o)\right]-p\frac{\partial f}{\partial k_p}+rP^Ts'(k_p^o)\right] \tag{3.33.1}$$

$$\dot{I}_a = \frac{1}{C_a''(I_a^o)} \left[ (r+\delta_a) \left[ v + C_a'(I_a^o) \right] - rP^T h'(k_p^o) \right] \tag{3.33.2}$$

At the long-run equilibrium where $\dot{I}_p = \dot{I}_a = \dot{k}_p = \dot{k}_a = 0$ it can be deduced by comparing (3.33.1) and (3.33.2) to (3.29.1) and (3.29.2) that the emission tax and the tradeable permit regulation lead to the same long-run equilibrium level for investment and capital stocks in the productive and abatement sectors when $P^T = \tau/r$.[27] This result is similar to the one obtained in Chapter 2. In order to buy a unit permit that saves an infinite stream of tax payments, the firm will pay an amount equal to the present value of the tax payments.

### 4.1.3 Investment decisions under emission limits

Under a fixed and time invariant emission limit the firm solves the problem:

$$\max_{\{I(t), l_p(t) \geq 0\}} \int_0^\infty e^{-rt} \pi_{\bar{e}}(t) dt$$

s.t. (3.16), (3.19) and $e(t) \geq 0$

The current value Lagrangean for the problem is defined as:

$$\mathcal{L} = H + \mu(t) \left[ \bar{e} - s(k_p, l_p) + h(k_a, l_a) \right] \tag{3.34}$$

with $H$ being the Hamiltonian function

$$H = pf(k_p, l_p) - \sum_j \left[ w_j l_j + v I_j + C_j(I_j) \right] + \sum_j \phi_j(I_j - \delta_j k_j)$$

In the Lagrangean function (3.34) the dynamic multiplier $\mu(t)$ should be interpreted as the current-value shadow cost to the firm of an increase in the stringency of the emission standard. Assuming interior solution the optimality conditions imply:

$$\frac{\partial H}{\partial l_p} = 0 \text{ or } p \frac{\partial f(k_p^o, l_p^o)}{\partial l_p} - w_p - \mu \frac{\partial s(k_p^o, l_p^o)}{\partial l_p} = 0 \tag{3.34.1}$$

$$\frac{\partial H}{\partial l_a} = 0 \text{ or } \mu \frac{\partial h(k_a^o, l_a^o)}{\partial l_a} - w_a = 0 \tag{3.34.2}$$

$$\frac{\partial H}{\partial I_j} = 0 \text{ or } \phi_j = v + C_j'(I_j^o), \ j = p, a \tag{3.34.3}$$

---

[27]The stability properties of the steady state and the steady state comparative statics are the same as in the tax case.

$$\frac{\partial \mathcal{L}}{\partial \mu} \geq 0, \quad \mu\left[\bar{e} - s(k_p^o, l_p^o) + h(k_p^o, l_p^o)\right] = 0, \quad \mu \geq 0 \quad \forall t \tag{3.34.4}$$

$$\dot{\phi}_p = (r + \delta_p)\phi_p - p\frac{\partial f(k_p^o, l_p^o)}{\partial k_p} + \mu\frac{\partial s(k_p^o, l_p^o)}{\partial k_p} \tag{3.35.1}$$

$$\dot{\phi}_a = (r + \delta_a)\phi_a - \mu\frac{\partial h(k_a^o, l_a^o)}{\partial k_a} \tag{3.35.2}$$

$$\dot{k}_j = I_j^o - \delta_j k_j^o, \quad j = p, a \tag{3.35.3}$$

along with the transversality condition at infinity. From (3.34.2), $\mu(t) > 0$, so the emission constraint is always satisfied as equality. That is, the emission limit is binding. Thus along the optimal path the firm will adjust inputs in order to discharge up to the allowed limit, without any other incentive for emission reduction.[28] From (3.34.1), (3.34.2) and the emission constraint (3.19), short-run demand for labour functions and the shadow cost of the emission limit are defined as functions of the capital stocks, the wage rates and the emission limit. The short-run comparative statics are presented in Table 3.3.

*Table 3.3  Short-run comparative statics for the case of emission limits*

|       | $k_p$    | $k_a$ | $w_p$ | $w_a$ | $\bar{e}$ |
|-------|----------|-------|-------|-------|-----------|
| $l_p$ | ?        | +     | -     | -     | +         |
| $l_a$ | +        | ?     | -     | -     | -         |
| $\mu$ | +$^{(*)}$ | -    | -     | +     | -         |

(*) As $p\dfrac{\partial^2 f}{\partial k_p \partial l_p} > \mu\dfrac{\partial^2 s}{\partial k_p \partial l_p}$

These results can be compared to the tax case. An increase in the capital

---

[28]It should be noted that constraints of the type $k_a \geq 0$, $l_a \geq 0$ are not considered. If these constraints were allowed, it could be possible to have $k_a = 0$ and $l_a = 0$, if the constraint is not binding, or $e^o < \bar{e}$. Cases when the constraint is not binding and the transitions from binding to nonbinding emission limits are analysed in Kort (1995). Cases of nonbinding emission limits can be encountered if, for example, the firm is relatively small so it is not optimal to have $e^o = \bar{e}$.

stock will unambiguously increase the demand for labour in the other sector (production or abatement), while the results in its own sector are ambiguous. These positive cross effects are due to the fact that an increase in abatement capital will make it possible to increase labour in the productive sector without exceeding the emission limit. On the other hand an increase in the productive capital makes necessary an increase in the labour input used in the abatement sector so that the limit is not exceeded. It should also be noted that there is no incentive to reduce emissions under the emission limits, a result related to the dynamic efficiency of the instrument discussed in Chapter 2.

An increase in wages will reduce labour input in both sectors. Under emission limits labour is a substitute factor in the two processes. Another result of the short-run comparative static analysis is that the current value shadow cost of emission limits $\mu(t)$ will be higher, the higher the productive capital is. In this case it is relatively more costly to obey the limit, while on the other hand it is relatively cheaper to obey the limit, the higher the abatement capital is. Finally, as expected, an increase in the emission limit will reduce the limit's shadow cost.

The dynamics of the system are determined by the MHDS defined by (3.35.1), (3.35.2) and (3.35.3) after substituting the short-run solutions for labour, investment and the shadow cost of the emission limit. The steady state equilibrium under emission limits has the local saddle point property as in the tax case, provided that the emission limit is not 'very stringent'. Furthermore steady state comparative statics produce ambiguous results concerning the effects of changes of the emission limit on steady state investment and capital.[29]

Comparative dynamic analysis can reveal the effects of changes in the emission limits on the entire optimal path. By the dynamic envelope theorem:

$$\frac{\partial J^o(\bar{e})}{\partial \bar{e}} = \int_o^\infty \frac{\partial (e^{-rt}\mathcal{L})}{\partial \bar{e}} dt = \int_o^\infty e^{-rt} \mu(t;\bar{e}) dt > 0$$

Thus an increase in the emission limit will increase the firm's net present value by an amount equal to the cumulative discounted shadow cost of emissions limits. Furthermore, by the concavity of the value function,

$$\frac{\partial^2 J^o(\bar{e})}{\partial \bar{e}^2} = \int_o^\infty e^{-rt} \frac{\partial \mu(t;\bar{e})}{\partial \bar{e}} dt \leq 0$$

Thus an increase in the emission limit will not increase the cumulative

---

[29]For details see Xepapadeas (1992a).

present value of the limit's shadow cost.

The comparison of both the short-run and the steady state comparative statics, as well as the stability properties of the long-run steady state equilibrium for the tax and the emission limit cases, indicate significant differences regarding the effects of the two policy instruments. These differences acquire some empirical relevance for an environmental regulator that seeks to trace the consequences of changes from a given environmental policy, or seeks to obtain specific targets by changing from one policy instrument to the other.

## 4.2 Decisions about Input Substitution

The previous section examined decisions related to investment in productive emission-generating capital or investment in abatement emission-reducing capital. In this section we examine input substitution in the production process, where the relatively more expensive input is the 'clean' input generating less emissions per unit used, as compared to a less expensive 'dirty' input. An example of such an input substitution is the substitution of low sulphur coal for high sulphur coal in electricity generation.

The production function for a firm facing input substitution possibilities can be defined[30] as $f(x,k)$ with $x = x_d + x_c$, where $x_d$ is the dirty input, $x_c$ is the clean input and $k$ is the stock of capital used in production and accumulated according to $\dot{k} = I - \delta k$. The emission function is defined as the convex function $s(x_d, x_c)$ with $\partial s/\partial x_d > \partial s/\partial x_c$, that is the marginal emission coefficient of the dirty input exceeds that of the clean input. Furthermore the clean input is more expensive, or $w_c > w_d$.

The firm chooses under any given environmental policy the time paths for investment, assuming as before convex adjustment costs, and the use of dirty and clean inputs to maximize the net present value of the firm's cash flow. As before the three main policy instruments are examined.

### 4.2.1 Emission taxes
Under the emission tax the firm solves

$$\max_{\{(I(t), x_d(t), x_c(t)) \geq 0\}} \int_0^\infty e^{-rt} \left[ pf(x_d + x_c, k) - w_d x_d - w_c x_c - v - C(I) - \tau s(x_d + x_c) \right] dt$$

$$\text{s. t. } \dot{k} = I - \delta k, \quad k(0) = k_o > 0$$

---

[30]The model presented here is a simplified version of the model developed by Hartl and Kort (1994).

The current value Lagrangean for the problem is defined as:

$$\mathcal{L} = pf(x_d + x_c, k) - w_d x_d - w_c x_c - vI - C(I) - \tau s(x_d + x_c)$$
$$+ \phi(I - \delta k) - \mu_d(t)x_d - \mu_c(t)x_c$$

where $\mu_d(t)$, $\mu_c(t)$ are the Lagrangean multipliers associated with the nonnegativity constraints on the substitute inputs.[31] By the maximum principle the necessary and sufficient conditions for interior solutions imply:

$$\frac{\partial \mathcal{L}}{\partial x_d} = 0 \text{ or } p\frac{\partial f(x_d^o + x_c^o, k)}{\partial x_d} - w_d - \tau \frac{\partial s(x_d^o + x_c^o)}{\partial x_d} - \mu_d = 0 \qquad (3.36.1)$$

$$\frac{\partial \mathcal{L}}{\partial x_c} = 0 \text{ or } p\frac{\partial f(x_d^o + x_c^o, k)}{\partial x_c} - w_c - \tau \frac{\partial s(x_d^o + x_c^o)}{\partial x_c} - \mu_c = 0 \qquad (3.36.2)$$

$$\mu_d \geq 0 (= 0 \text{ if } x_d^o > 0), \ \mu_c \geq 0 (= 0 \text{ if } x_c^o > 0) \qquad (3.37)$$

$$\phi = v + C'(I^o) \qquad (3.38)$$

$$\dot{k} = I^o - \delta k^o \qquad (3.39.1)$$

$$\dot{\phi} = (r + \delta)\phi - p\frac{\partial f(x_d^o + x_c^o, k^o)}{\partial k} \qquad (3.39.2)$$

along with the transversality condition at infinity.

From (3.36.1) and (3.36.2) when both inputs are in use, so that $\mu_d(t) = \mu_c(t) = 0$, we obtain:

$$w_c - w_d = \tau \left( \frac{\partial s}{\partial x_d} - \frac{\partial s}{\partial x_c} \right)$$

That is, the optimal input combination is obtained at the point where the extra cost from using the clean input equals the marginal tax savings.

The dynamic behavior of the system is obtained by using the MHDS defined by (3.39.1) and (3.39.2). By the concavity of the production function and the convexity of the adjustment cost function, the steady state equilibrium can be described as a standard adjustment cost equilibrium with local saddle point characteristics.[32]

---

[31]To simplify things we disregard the multiplier associated with the irreversibility of investment constraint.

[32]See for example Takayama (1985, 1994).

## 4.2.2 Tradeable emission permits

It is assumed as earlier that the permits last forever and that the firms are given an initial allocation $\bar{e}_o$ that is worth $P^T\bar{e}_o$ where $P^T$ is as usual the competitive stationary permit price. A firm's expenses or receipts from changing the number of initial permits are $P^T\dot{e}(t)$ with $e(t)=s(x_d(t),x_c(t))$. Under these assumptions, with gross investment defined as $I=\dot{k}+\delta k$, the firm solves the problem:

$$\max_{\{k(t),\dot{k}(t),x_d(t),x_c(t),\dot{x}_d(t),\dot{x}_c(t)\}} \int_o^\infty e^{-rt}[pf(x_d+x_c,k)-w_dx_d-w_cx_c-$$

$$(v(\dot{k}+\delta k)+C(\dot{k}+\delta k))-P^T\left(\frac{\partial s}{\partial x_d}\dot{x}_d+\frac{\partial s}{\partial x_c}\dot{x}_c\right)]dt$$

The Euler conditions for the problem imply:

$$p\frac{\partial f}{\partial x_d}-w_d-P^T\frac{\partial^2 s}{\partial x_d^2}\dot{x}_d-P^T\frac{\partial^2 s}{\partial x_d\partial x_c}\dot{x}_c-rP^T\frac{\partial s}{\partial x_d}=0 \qquad (3.40.1)$$

$$p\frac{\partial f}{\partial x_c}-w_c-P^T\frac{\partial^2 s}{\partial x_c^2}\dot{x}_c-P^T\frac{\partial^2 s}{\partial x_c\partial x_d}\dot{x}_d-rP^T\frac{\partial s}{\partial x_c}=0 \qquad (3.40.2)$$

$$p\frac{\partial f}{\partial k}-(r+\delta)[C'(I)+v]-C''(I)(\dot{k}+\delta\dot{k})=0 \qquad (3.41)$$

At the steady state $\dot{x}_d=\dot{x}_c=0$, and for $P^T=\tau/r$, the combination of the two inputs under the permit system is the same as under the tax system, as can be easily seen by comparing (3.36.1) and (3.36.2) to (3.40.1) and (3.40.2).[33]

## 4.2.3 Emission limits

Under an emission limit of the form $s(x_d,x_c)\leq\bar{e}$ the firm solves the following problem, formulated in optimal control terms:

$$\max_{\{(I(t),x_d(t),x_c(t))\geq 0\}} \int_o^\infty e^{-rt}[pf(x_d+x_c,k)-w_dx_d-w_cx_c-(v+C(I))]dt$$

$$\text{s. t. } \dot{k}=I-\delta k,\ k(0)=k_o>0$$

$$s(x_d,x_c)\leq\bar{e}$$

The current value Lagrangean for the problem is:

---

[33] It should be noted that the necessary condition (3.41) implied by the Euler equation is equivalent to condition (3.39.2) obtained by the optimal control formulation, since if we set $\phi=C'(I)+v$ as in (3.38) we have $\dot{k}+\delta\dot{k}=\dot{I}=\dot{\phi}/C''$.

$$\mathcal{L} = pf(x_d + x_c, k) - w_d x_d - w_c x_c - (vI + C(I)) + \phi(I - \delta k)$$
$$+ \mu[\bar{e} - s(x_d + x_c)] - \mu_d(t)x_d - \mu_c(t)x_c$$

The optimality conditions are the same as (3.36.1) to (3.39.2) with $\tau$ replaced by $\mu$, the dynamic shadow cost of the emission limit in (3.36.1) and (3.36.2), along with

$$\frac{\partial \mathcal{L}}{\partial \mu} \geq 0, \quad \mu[\bar{e} - s(x_d^o, x_c^o)] = 0, \quad \mu \geq 0, \quad \forall\, t \qquad (3.42)$$

By subtracting (3.36.1) from (3.36.2) with $\tau$ replaced by $\mu$ we obtain:

$$w_c - w_d = \mu\left(\frac{\partial s}{\partial x_d} - \frac{\partial s}{\partial x_c}\right) + (\mu_c - \mu_d) \qquad (3.43)$$

It can be seen from (3.43) that it is not possible to have an ineffective constraint, that is $\bar{e} > s(x_d^o, x_c^o)$, and at the same time positive use of the clean input. If that were possible we would have $\mu = 0$, $\mu_c = 0$, in which case $w_c - w_d = -\mu_d \leq 0$ which contradicts the assumption that $w_c - w_d > 0$. Thus the firm uses a positive amount of the clean input only if the constraint is binding. This result is in accordance with results obtained earlier when comparing emission taxes to emission limits. Emission limits do not offer any dynamic incentives to reduce emissions.

# 5 STRATEGIC INTERACTIONS AND POLLUTION DYNAMICS

The analysis up to this point was carried out under the assumption that each firm's benefits are not affected directly by the stock of pollution. In such a case once the policy instrument is chosen the firm reacts at each instant of time to the specific instrument. This implies that in each time period the firm solves an investment problem without considering the pollution dynamics.

Pollution dynamics can however enter the firm's problem directly if the net benefit function is affected by the stock of the pollutant. This situation can be considered in the context of an agricultural example. Pollutants accumulated in a water body as a result of agricultural run-off negatively affect the firm's production function, which can be written as

$f(x,S)$ with $f_x>0$ , $f_S<0$ , $f_{xS}<0$,[34] where $x$ is a vector of inputs. The benefit function for the firm can be written as:

$$B_i(e_i,S), \text{ with } \dot{S}=\sum_{i=1}^{n} e_i-bS, \ S(0)=S_o\geq 0$$

where $p$ and $w$ have the usual interpretation as output price and vector of input prices respectively, and $e_i$ is emissions generated by firm $i$.

In this formulation pollution dynamics enter the firm's problem directly, and since the emissions of each individual firm affect the accumulation of the pollutant's stock, these emissions also affect the actions of the rest of the firms. For the sake of simplicity, we do not consider capital accumulation dynamics.

To derive the optimal policy rules we again solve the regulator's problem on the one hand and the firm's problem on the other, and then determine policy instruments that will induce firms to choose emissions policies consistent with the social optimum. In analyzing the problem it is convenient to assume that the individual firm's net benefit function takes the separable form $B_i(e_i)-d_i(S_i)$ with $d_i>0$, $d_i''\geq 0$. The regulator's objective function, the social welfare function, can be written in the context of the ECM model defined in Section 2 as $\Sigma_i[B_i(e_i)-d_i(S)]-D(S)$, where $d_i(S)$ reflects production damages to the firms by the externality and $D(S)$ reflects general environmental damages, like for example negative effects on recreational activities due to surface water pollution from agricultural run-off. In order to more clearly show the effects from the presence of the stock externality on the individual benefit function, it will be assumed that $D(S)\equiv0$.[35] Thus the regulator solves the problem:

$$\max_{\{e_i(t)\geq 0\}} \int_0^{\infty} e^{-rt}\left[\sum_i (B_i(e_i)-d_i(S))\right]dt \tag{P.2}$$

$$\text{s. t. } \dot{S}=\sum_i e_i-bS, \ S(0)=S_0\geq 0$$

The current value Hamiltonian for the problem can be written as:

$$H=\sum_i (B_i(e_i)-d_i(S)) + \lambda\left(\sum_i e_i-bS\right)$$

By the maximum principle the necessary and sufficient optimality conditions

---

[34]For a similar formulation see Section 4 of Chapter 2.
[35]This assumption does not change the nature of the results regarding the effects of the stock externality.

imply, along the optimal path $e_i^*(t)$, $S^*(t)$,

$$B_i'(e_i^*) \leq \lambda \text{ with equality if } e_i^* > 0 \,\, \forall \,\, i \text{ and } t \qquad (3.44)$$

$$\dot{\lambda} = (r+b)\lambda + \sum_i d_i'(S^*) \qquad (3.45.1)$$

$$\dot{S} = \sum_i e_i^* - bS^* \qquad (3.45.2)$$

and the usual transversality condition.

As in the previous sections short-run demand for emissions is defined as $e_i^* = e_i(\lambda)$, $e_i' > 0$, and pollution dynamics are determined by the MHDS:

$$\dot{S} = \sum_i e_i^*(\lambda) - bS^* \qquad (3.46.1)$$

$$\dot{\lambda} = (r+b)\lambda + \sum_i d_i'(S^*) \qquad (3.46.2)$$

The dynamic properties of the system are similar to those of the system (3.5.1) and (3.5.2). The long-run equilibrium for the pollutant stock and its social shadow cost are defined as:

$$S_\infty^* = \frac{\Sigma_i e_i^*(\lambda)}{b}, \quad \lambda_\infty = \frac{-\Sigma_i d_i'(S^*)}{r+b} \qquad (3.47)$$

It should be noted from (3.47) that the long-run equilibrium social shadow cost depends on the sum of individual marginal damages in the long run.

In the uncontrolled market equilibrium each firm maximizes individual benefits, $B_i(e_i) - d_i(S)$, which implies that both the firm's own emissions and the emissions of the rest of the firms enter the individual firm benefit function through the accumulation of the pollutant $S$. The analysis of this type of market equilibrium should be carried out in the context of an $n$-player noncooperative differential game, where each player chooses strategies consisting of emission time paths $\{e_i(t)\}$. In analyzing noncooperative differential games the information structure of the game determines the choice of the strategy spaces for the players.[36] Two of the most commonly used information structures are the open-loop (OL) and the feedback (FB).[37] Under an OL information structure the strategy of each player depends only on the initial state of the system, that is the initial stock of the pollutant $S_o$ and time.

---

[36]A strategy space is the space of all the possible strategies that can be followed by the players.
[37]For detailed definitions of the information structures see Basar and Olsder (1982).

Therefore under an OL information structure, individual emissions are determined as:

$$(OL): \quad e_i(t) = \theta_i(S_o, t), \quad i = 1, \ldots, n \tag{3.48}$$

Under the FB information structure the strategy depends on the current state of the system, that is the current stock of the pollutant $S(t)$ and time. Therefore with an FB information structure individual emissions are defined as:

$$(FB): \quad e_i(t) = \theta_i(S(t), t), \quad i = 1, \ldots, n \tag{3.49}$$

The FB strategy described by (3.49) is often referred to as a Markov perfect strategy in which the stock of the pollutant is a 'sufficient statistic' for the history of the game.

Given the strategy spaces determined by OL or FB information structures, the open-loop Nash equilibrium (OLNE) and the feedback Nash equilibrium (FBNE) are defined. An important feature of these two Nash equilibrium solutions relates to the concept of time consistency. A dynamic policy is time consistent if, at any point in time, a decision-maker looking into the future should have no reason to revise the future portion of his/her policy, provided that the truncated version of the policy is subject to the same criteria as the original version (Basar 1989). Both OLNE and FBNE are time consistent in this sense. The OLNE however corresponds to an infinite period of commitment. Players, that is polluting firms, commit themselves to a particular emission path at the outset of the game and do not respond to observed variation in the stock of the pollution. Thus if there is a small deviation from the optimal path, the policy that was optimal at the outset of the game will not necessarily be optimal for the remaining part of the game. In this sense OLNE is referred to as weakly time consistent. On the other hand the FBNE is a strongly time consistent solution in the sense of possessing the property of subgame perfectness (Fershtman 1987, Basar 1989) which implies that the equilibrium strategies constitute an equilibrium for all subgames along the equilibrium path.

The payoff for firm $i$ can be defined as:

$$J^i(e_1(t), \ldots, e_n(t)) = \int_0^\infty e^{-rt} [B_i(e_i) - d_i(S)] dt$$

Each firm seeks to maximize its payoff subject to $\dot{S} = \Sigma_i e_i(t) - bS$. The OLNE (or FBNE) equilibrium is defined as an $n$-tuple of OL (or FB) strategies $(e_1^o(t), \ldots, e_n^o(t))$ where $e_i(t)$ is defined by (3.48) or (3.49) such that:

$$J^i(e_1^o(t), \ldots, e_n^o(t)) \geq J^i(e_1^o(t), \ldots, e_{i-1}^o, e_i(t), e_{i+1}^o, \ldots, e_n^o(t)) \text{ for all } i$$

*Open-loop Nash equilibrium*
With an OL information structure the current value Hamiltonian for the problem is defined as:

$$H^i = B_i(e_i) - d_i(S) + \lambda_i^{OL}\left[e_i + \sum_{j \neq i} e_j^o - bS\right]$$

where $e_{-i}^o = (e_1^o,...,e_{i-1}^o,e_{i+1}^o,...,e_n^o)$ is the vector of the optimal responses for the rest of the firms, and $\lambda_i^{OL}$ is the private shadow cost of the pollutant's stock for firm $i$. The presence of this cost in the firm's problem is due to the fact that the externality affects the firm's benefits, so the firm's own emissions have a negative effect on the firm's own benefits and this cost is captured by $\lambda_i^{OL}$. In a sense there is a partial internalization of the environmental damages. The necessary and sufficient optimality conditions along the optimal OLNE path imply:

$$B_i'(e_i^o) \le \lambda^{OL} \text{ with equality if } e_i^o > 0 \; \forall \; i \text{ and } t \tag{3.50}$$

$$\dot{\lambda}_i^{OL} = (r+b)\lambda_i^{OL} + d_i'(S) \tag{3.51}$$

From (3.50) the short-run demand for emissions for the $i$th firm under an OL information structure is defined as $e_i^o(\lambda_i^{OL})$, $e_i^{o'} > 0$ and depends on the private shadow cost of the pollutant stock for firm $i$.

From (3.50) the pollutant accumulates in the ambient environment according to:

$$\dot{S} = \sum_i e_i^o\left(\lambda_i^{OL}\right) - bS, \; S(0) = S_o \tag{3.52}$$

The $n+1$ differential equations (3.51) and (3.52) describe the dynamic behaviour of the system. The steady state long-run equilibrium under OLNE is defined as the point:

$$\left(\lambda_{1\infty}^{OL},...,\lambda_{n\infty}^{OL}, S_\infty^{OL}\right) : \dot{\lambda}_1^{OL} = ... = \dot{\lambda}_n^{OL} = \dot{S} = 0$$

From (3.51) we obtain:

$$\lambda_{i\infty}^{OL} = -\frac{d_i'(S)}{r+b}, \text{ while } \lambda_\infty^* = -\frac{\sum_i d_i'(S)}{r+b} \text{ where } |\lambda_{i\infty}^{OL}| < |\lambda_\infty^*|$$

Thus for any level of the pollutant stock the long-run equilibrium private shadow cost of the pollutant is less than the corresponding social cost. This is due to the fact that in the market equilibrium each firm takes into account only its own contribution to the stock of pollution and ignores the effects of its own pollution on the rest of the firms. On the other hand at the social optimum the regulator takes into account the contribution of all the firms to the pollution stock. Thus $e_i^o(\lambda_{i\infty}^{OL}) > e_\infty^*(\lambda_\infty^*) \ \forall \ i$; since $e_i'(\lambda) > 0$ it follows therefore that $S_\infty^{OL} = \left(\sum_i e_{i\infty}^o\right)/b > S_\infty^* = \left(\sum_i e_{i\infty}^*\right)/b$. This result implies that uncontrolled market equilibrium under OL information structure leads to excess accumulation of the pollutant, because firms undervalue the shadow cost of the pollutant's stock.[38]

*Feedback Nash equilibrium*
To analyse the feedback equilibrium a specification of the state dependent Markov strategy is required. In particular it is assumed that the firm follows linear Markov strategies where the emission rate of the firm is a linear function of the pollutant's stock. It is therefore assumed that

$$e_i(t) = \bar{e}_i + \beta S(t), \quad \beta < 0, \quad i = 1,...,n \tag{3.53}$$

The linear Markov strategy (3.53) indicates that each firm will reduce its emissions if the pollutant stock increases.[39] This is a plausible assumption given that each firm realizes the effects of its own actions on the accumulation of the pollutant. The common slope of the function (3.53) reflects the assumption of similar beliefs of the firms about the impact of their own emissions on the stock of the pollutant.

Under linear Markov strategies the current value Hamiltonian for firm $i$ is defined as:

$$H^i = B_i(e_i) - d_i(S) + \lambda_i^{FB}\left[e_i + \sum_{j \neq i} (\bar{e}_j + \beta S) - bS\right]$$

---

[38]Regarding the properties of the long-run equilibrium the Jacobian determinant of the system of the $n+1$ differential equations (3.51) and (3.52) is defined as:

$$J^o = \begin{vmatrix} -b & e_1^{o\prime} & e_2^{o\prime} & \cdots & e_i^{o\prime} \\ -d_1' & (r+b) & 0 & \cdots & 0 \\ \cdot & \cdot & \cdot & \cdot & \cdot \\ -d_n' & 0 & 0 & \cdots & (r+b) \end{vmatrix}$$

with tr($J^o$) > 0. Thus, provided a long-run equilibrium exists, the equilibrium has the local saddle point property. However, the dimension of the stable manifold cannot be determined.

[39]For the use of linear Markov strategies in related problems of environmental and resource management, see for example Provencher and Burt (1993), Dockner and Van Long (1993), Xepapadeas (1992a, 1995b). The use of linear Markov strategies makes the analysis more tractable. Similar results can be obtained under the more general specification $e_i(t) = \bar{e}_i + \beta(S(t))$, $\beta' < 0$.

The optimality conditions imply:

$$B_i'(e_i^o) \leq \lambda^{FB} \text{ with equality if } e_i^o > 0 \ \forall \ i \text{ and } t \tag{3.54}$$

$$\dot{\lambda}_i^{FB} = [(r + b - (n-1)\beta]\lambda_i^{FB} + d_i'(S) \tag{3.55}$$

From (3.54) the demand for emissions depends on the private shadow cost of the pollutant stock, $e_i^o(\lambda_i^{FB})$, $e_i^{o'} > 0$, and the stock of the pollutant accumulates according to

$$\dot{S} = \sum_i e_i^o(\lambda_i^{FB}) - bS, \ S(0) = S_o \tag{3.56}$$

The steady state long-run equilibrium is determined and characterized as in the open-loop case. There is however an important difference between the two types of information structures. From (3.55) we have at the steady state

$$\lambda_{i\infty}^{FB} = -\frac{d_i'(S)}{r + n - (n-1)\beta}, \ i = 1,...,n$$

Since $\beta < 0$ we have $|\lambda_{i\infty}^{FB}| < |\lambda_{i\infty}^{OL}| < |\lambda_\infty^*|$. Thus the private shadow cost under the linear Markov strategy is less than the private shadow cost under the OL information structure. Therefore for the steady state emission and pollutant stock it holds that:

$$e_i^o(\lambda_{i\infty}^{FB}) > e_i^o(\lambda_{i\infty}^{OL}) > e_i^*(\lambda_\infty^*)$$

$$S_\infty^{FB} > S_\infty^{OL} > S_\infty^* \tag{3.57}$$

The fact that linear Markov strategies result in overemissions as compared to the open-loop case can be explained as follows.[40] Each firm chooses to emit more as compared to the open-loop case because it believes that the effects of its own overemissions will be partly offset by the other firms' lower emissions as they respond in this way to the increase in the pollution stock according to (3.53). Therefore in equilibrium all firms have an incentive to overemit when linear Markov strategies are followed as compared to the case in which firms follow open-loop strategies with an infinite period of commitment.

---

[40]For analysis of similar cases where Markov strategies lead to overemissions, see van der Ploeg and de Zeeuw (1992), Xepapadeas (1992b, 1995b). The overemission result holds under the more general Markov strategy defined in footnote 35.

## 5.1 Optimal Environmental Policy

Since the unregulated market equilibrium leads to a suboptimal outcome, that is excess accumulation of the pollutant, the regulator needs to adopt a certain environmental policy in order to induce the desirable emission paths from the firms.

In this section we examine only the case of emission taxes but the approach can easily be extended, following the general framework of the previous section, to cover both the cases of tradeable emission permits of the exhaustible type and emission limits. Assume that the regulator is committed to a path of emission taxes, $\{\tau(t)\}$, and that the firms use linear Markov strategies.[41] Then each firm $i=1,\ldots,n$ solves the problem:

$$\max_{\{e_i(t) \geq 0\}} \int_0^\infty e^{-rt}[B_i(e_i) - d_i(S) - \tau(t)e_i]dt$$

$$\text{s. t. } \dot{S} = \sum_i e_i - bS, \quad S(0) = S_o \tag{P.3}$$

$$e_i = \bar{e}_i + \beta S$$

The current value Hamiltonian for the problem is defined as:

$$H^i = B_i(e_i) - d_i(S) - \tau e_i + \lambda_i^{FB}\left[e_i + \sum_{j \neq i}(\bar{e}_j + \beta S) - bS\right]$$

The optimality conditions imply

$$B_i'(e_i^o) - \tau \leq \lambda_i^{FB} \text{ with equality if } e_i^o > 0 \; \forall \; i \text{ and } t \tag{3.58}$$

$$\dot{\lambda}_i^{FB} = [r + b - (n-1)\beta]\lambda_i^{FB} + d_i'(S) \tag{3.59}$$

From (3.58) the demand for emissions is now a function of both the private shadow cost of the pollutant's stock and the tax rate, or $e_i^o = e_i^o(\tau, \lambda_i^{FB})$.

Comparing (3.58) to (3.44) it is clear that the tax scheme that will induce the socially-optimal behavior should take the form:

$$\tau_i(t) = \left|\lambda(t) - \lambda_i^{FB}(t)\right| \tag{3.60}$$

Thus the tax is firm specific and is equal to the difference between the social shadow cost of the pollutant's stock, $\lambda(t)$, and the private shadow cost of the

---

[41]We use the assumption of linear Markov strategies because the infinite period of commitment implied by the open-loop strategies is somehow unrealistic. In the problem analysed here the open-loop case can be regarded as a special case of the feedback solution for $\beta = 0$.

pollutant's stock, $\lambda_i^{FB}(t)$, at each instant of time. This is due to the fact that overemissions occur because in the unregulated market equilibrium the shadow cost of the pollutant is undervalued, $\left|\lambda_i^{FB}\right| < |\lambda|$ for all $i$. Thus the purpose of the tax is to bridge the gap between the social and the private costs of the pollutant. Since the private cost of the pollutant is not the same across the firms, the tax needs to be firm specific.[42]

The tax rate determined by (3.60) is however only implicitly defined since $\lambda_i^{FB}$ is a function of the tax rate. To see this consider the dynamic system of the $n+1$ differential equations determining the paths of $\lambda_i^{FB}$ and $S$. Using the short-run demand for emissions function this system is determined as:

$$\dot{S} = \sum_i e_i^o(\lambda_i^{FB}, \tau_i) - bS \qquad (3.60.1)$$

$$\dot{\lambda}_i^{FB} = [r + b - (n-1)\beta]\lambda_i^{FB} + d_i'(S) \qquad (3.60.2)$$

The solution of the above system will determine the paths

$$\lambda_i^{FB}(t) = \hat{\lambda}_i^{FB}(t; \tau_1, ..., \tau_n, r, b, \beta, n) \ , \ i = 1, ..., n \qquad (3.61.1)$$

$$S^{FB}(t) = \hat{S}^{FB}(t; \tau_1, ..., \tau_n, r, b, \beta, n) \qquad (3.61.2)$$

Thus the private shadow cost depends on the tax rates. Therefore a simultaneity problem exists that precludes the direct estimation of the tax rates. The simultaneity problem can be handled in the following way. In the firm's problem define the tax rate at any instant of time as $\tau_i(t) = \lambda(t) - \xi_i(t)$ where $\xi_i$ is a parameter which is unspecified. Then the firm's short-run demand for emissions is a function of $\lambda_i^{FB}$, $\lambda$ and $\xi_i$ or $e_i^o = e_i^o(\lambda_i^{FB}, \lambda, \xi_i)$. Substituting in (3.60.1), the solution for $\lambda_i^{FB}(t)$ and $S^{FB}(t)$ defined by (3.61.1) and (3.61.2) can be written as:

$$\lambda_i^{FB}(t) = \tilde{\lambda}_i^{FB}(t; \xi_1, ..., \xi_n, r, b, \beta, n), \ i = 1, ..., n \qquad (3.62.1)$$

$$S^{FB}(t) = \tilde{S}^{FB}(t; \xi_1, ..., \xi_n, r, b, \beta, n) \qquad (3.62.2)$$

In (3.62.1) make the substitution $\xi_i = \lambda_i^{FB}$, $i = 1, ..., n$, then the fixed point of the system[43] will determine the private shadow costs which are independent

---

[42]The tax would be uniform if the firms were symmetric. In this case the private shadow costs would have been the same across firms and the emission tax would have been uniform.

[43]The system of differential equations (3.60.1) and (3.60.2) is continuous in the parameters $\xi_i$. Then by the properties of the solutions of differential equations to be continuous in the parameters, (3.62.1) is continuous in $\xi_i$. The private shadow values defined in (3.62.1) should

of the tax rates. Then,

$$\lim_{\xi_i \to \lambda_i^{FB}} B_i'(e_i) + \lambda_i^{FB} - \tau_i = B_i(e_i) - \lambda \text{ for } \tau_i = \lambda - \xi_i$$

and the individual emissions coincide with the socially-desirable emissions.[44]

# 6   UNCERTAINTY AND STOCK EXTERNALITY

The analysis in the previous sections was carried out in a deterministic framework. However, the accumulation of pollutants in the environment is affected by many stochastic factors. Stochastic effects can be associated with pollution-generating output production processes and pollution abatement processes, as well as general environmental conditions that affect factors like the pollution natural decay process or the transportation of pollutants from one region to the other. Production uncertainty results mainly from the uncertain pollution content of fuels or from uncertainties in the efficiency of the production process or the end-of-pipe abatement process. For example uncertainties about the emissions of a coal-fired power plant can be attributed to the composition of the coal, the effectiveness of the burners or the effectiveness of the electrostatic filters. Environmental uncertainty relates to climatic or topographic conditions. Factors such as temperature, air or sea currents and humidity affect both the rate at which waste biodegrades or is assimilated in the environment and the processes of interregional waste diffusion. These types of uncertainty result in pollution accumulation processes which are of a stochastic nature.

In this section we examine the implications of uncertainty in the formulation of environmental policy. To keep the analysis relatively simple, only environmental uncertainty related to the environment's assimilating

---

belong to a bounded set for stability. If furthermore this set is closed and convex, then a fixed point exists by Brower's fixed point theorem.

[44]For computational purposes the fixed point approach is cumbersome. A less demanding approximate approach would be to define the tax as $\bar{\tau}_i = \lambda_i - \lambda_i^{FB}$ where $\lambda_i^{FB}$ corresponds to the solution of the unregulated problem for the FBNE and can be treated as an exogenous parameter eliminating the simultaneity problem. However the tax defined in this way does not exactly achieve the social optimum. A correction is possible by considering the deviation between the estimated $\lambda_i^{FB}$ when $\tau_i = \bar{\tau}_i$ in the problem (P.3) and the $\lambda_i^{FB}$ in the original unregulated FBNE equilibrium and then calculating an additional correction in the tax (for details see Xepapadeas 1996a).

capacity is examined.[45] As an example of such uncertainty we can consider the stochastic uptake by the oceans of the carbon dioxide accumulated in the atmosphere. In an uncertain environment the evolution of the pollutant's stock can be described by the stochastic differential equation:

$$dS(t) = \left[ \sum_i e_i(t) - bS(t) \right] dt + \omega(S(t)) d\zeta, \; S(0) = S_o \text{ nonrandom} \qquad (3.63)$$

where $\{\zeta(t)\}$ is a Wiener process[46] and $\omega^2(S) = \sigma S$, $0 < \sigma < b$. By (3.63) $\sum_i e_i - bS$ is the instantaneous expected change of the pollutant's stock $S$ per unit time, with $-bS$ being the mean of the pollution removal process and $\sigma S$ the instantaneous variance. Hence the accumulation of the pollutant follows a diffusion process. In this stochastic environment the regulator seeks to maximize expected welfare by choosing time paths for the emissions. Therefore the regulator solves the problem:[47]

$$\max_{\{e_i(t) \geq 0\}} \mathscr{E}_0 \int_0^\infty e^{-rt} \left[ \sum_i B_i(e_i) - D(S) \right] dt$$

s. t. (3.63)

Applying the stochastic maximum principle[48], the generalized current value Hamiltonian is defined as:

$$H = \sum_i B_i(e_i) - D(S) + \lambda \left( \sum_i e_i - bS \right) + \frac{1}{2} (\sigma S) \lambda_S$$

where $\{\lambda(t)\}$ is a random process reflecting the social shadow cost of the pollutant accumulation. The nature of $\lambda(t)$ can be better analysed by defining the maximum value function:[49]

$$W = \max_{e_i(t)} \mathscr{E}_0 \int_0^\infty e^{-rt} \left[ \sum_i B_i(e_i) - D(S) \right] dt, \text{ s. t. (3.63)}$$

---

[45]For a model with production and environmental uncertainty see Plourde and Yeung (1989); for a model that also incorporates uncertainty regarding interregional diffusion of the pollutant see Xepapadeas (1992c).

[46]For definitions see Malliaris and Brock (1982).

[47]In solving the stochastic model no strategic interactions are considered. The development of a model with strategic effects such as the one developed in Section 5 requires the use of stochastic differential games (see Basar and Oldser 1982).

[48]See Malliaris and Brock (1982) and Chapter 7.

[49]The maximum value function solves the Hamilton-Bellman-Jacobi equation:

$$rW = \max_{e_i} \left[ \Sigma_i B_i(e_i) - D(S) + W_S(\Sigma_i e_i - bS) + \frac{1}{2}(\sigma S) W_{SS} \right]$$

Then,

$$\lambda = \frac{\partial W(S)}{\partial S} = W_S, \quad \lambda_S = \frac{\partial^2 W(S)}{\partial S^2} = W_{SS}$$

Since the Hamiltonian is concave in $(S, e_i)$, the maximum value function $W$ is concave in $S$, hence $W_{SS} < 0$ reflects the regulator's risk aversion. Assuming a quadratic maximum value function, $W_{SS}$ is independent of $S$. Then the optimality conditions can be written as:

$$B_i'(e_i^*) \le \lambda \quad \text{with equality if } e_i^* > 0 \ \forall \ i \text{ and } t \tag{3.64}$$

$$d\lambda = \left[(r+b)\lambda + D'(S) - \frac{1}{2}\sigma\lambda_S\right]dt + \omega(S)\lambda_S d\zeta \tag{3.65}$$

along with (3.63) and a transversality condition at infinity that can be stated as $\lim_{t \to \infty} \mathscr{E}_o[e^{-rt}\lambda(t)S^*(t)] = 0$, where $\{S^*(t)\}$ is the optimal random process that solves the problem.[50] From (3.64) the short-run demand for emissions is defined as $e_i^* = e_i^*(\lambda)$. The system of (3.63), (3.65) with $e_i^* = e_i^*(\lambda)$ determines a stochastic MHDS for $S(t)$ and $\lambda(t)$.[51] In this stochastic environment the expected long-run steady state of the stock of the pollutant exceeds the corresponding level for the deterministic case. To see this clearly consider the following differential system in expected values,[52] where $\mathscr{E}(S) = S_m$ and $\mathscr{E}(\lambda) = \lambda_m$:

$$\dot{\lambda}_m = (r+b)\lambda_m + \mathscr{E}[D'(S)] - \frac{1}{2}\sigma\lambda_S \tag{3.66.1}$$

$$\dot{S}_m = \sum_i e_i^*(\lambda_m) - bS_m \tag{3.66.2}$$

By the convexity of the damage function and using Jensen's inequality, it follows that the locus $\dot{\lambda}_m = 0$ lies everywhere below the locus $\dot{\lambda} = 0$ for the deterministic case and is relatively steeper, as shown in Figure 3.1. Thus $\mathscr{E}(S_\infty^*) = (S_m^*)_\infty < S_\infty^*$. The regulator's risk aversion, as reflected in the risk premium $(-1/2)\sigma\lambda_S$, causes the expected socially-optimal long-run steady state pollutant's stock to be lower than the corresponding level for the

---

[50]For a detailed statement of the transversality condition see Brock and Magill (1979).

[51]The solution of the stochastic MHDS provided it exists has the diffusion property. This means that given a pollutant stock $S$ at time $t$, the probability that in some future time the accumulation of the pollutant will fall within the interval $(\alpha_1, \alpha_2)$ with $0 < \alpha_1 < \alpha_2 < \infty$ can be determined. Furthermore it can be shown following Brock and Magill (1979) that all bounded solutions converge to the optimal stochastic process $S^*(t)$ and $\lambda(t)$, and that a steady state distribution for the stock of the pollutant exists.

[52]For the derivation of such a system see Gard (1988).

deterministic case.

In the unregulated market equilibrium each firm solves the problem $\max_{e_i} B_i(e_i)$ emitting at $e_i^o : B_i'(e_i^o) = 0$. In this equilibrium the stock of the pollutant evolves according to (3.63) with $e_i = e_i^o$. Since the firms' objective functions are independent of $S$, the profit-maximizing emission level for each firm is independent of the pollutant's shadow cost. Then the expected long-rum equilibrium pollutant stock in the unregulated equilibrium equals the stock level in the unregulated deterministic equilibrium. Denoting by $\mathscr{E}(S_\infty^o) = (S_m^o)_\infty$ we have $(S_m^o)_\infty = \left(\sum_i e_i^o\right)/b = S_\infty^o$.

If under these circumstances the regulator's objective is to induce firms to emit at levels such that the socially-optimal expected path of the pollutant's stock is achieved, then the optimal tax should be determined so that it is equal to the expected social shadow cost of the pollutant's stock at each instant of time, or $\tau_m(t) = -\lambda_m(t)$. To see the difference between this tax and the deterministic tax consider the tax at the steady state, defined as:

$$\tau_\infty = \frac{D'(S_\infty^*)}{r+b} = -\lambda_\infty \;,\; (\tau_m)_\infty = \frac{\mathscr{E}[D'(S)] - (1/2)\sigma\lambda_S}{r+b} = -(\lambda_m)_\infty$$

As can also be seen from Figure 3.1, $(\tau_m)_\infty > \tau_\infty$. Thus risk aversion on the regulator's part results in higher emission taxes.


# 7   ENVIRONMENTAL POLLUTION AND ECONOMIC GROWTH

The discussion in the previous sections of this chapter examined the issues of the dynamic externality and the implications of moving from a static to a dynamic framework mainly from a micro point of view. It is of great interest, however, to examine the implications of conducting the analysis in a dynamic framework on a macro level. Examining the implications of environmental pollution at a macro level in this context brings up the issue of environmental pollution and economic growth. The relationship between these two issues has been a subject of great controversy since the 1960s. Ideas have been put forward suggesting that economic growth will come to a halt owing to the finiteness of the natural resource base, or that continuous growth will cause serious and possibly irreversible damage to the environment. This controversy stresses the need for the adoption of environmental policies that would secure sustainable growth. Closely related to the above argument are issues referring to the impeding of growth due to environmental policies, or in contrast, to the alleviation of the pressure on the environment and the use of natural resources from technical change.

Clearly the linking of environmental pollution and economic growth creates the need to clarify a number of concepts and issues. They include the concept of sustainability, the measurement of economic welfare in such a way that the resource base and the natural environment are taken into account, the qualitative results derived from formal growth models augmented by environmental and natural resource considerations, and finally empirical results referring to the relationship between economic development and environmental pollution.

## 7.1 Sustainability

Sustainable development can be regarded as a response to the excessive use of the natural resource and the environmental base of the economy.[53] In fact the term has become increasingly popular, being part of the agendas of international organizations such as the UN, the EU and the OECD, and also of national governments.

The definition of sustainable development proposed by the Brundtland Commission (1987, p. 43), which has become widely accepted, defines sustainable development as: 'development that meets the needs of the present without compromising the ability of future generations to meet their own needs'. Other definitions close in spirit to the above can be found in Mäler (1991, p. 11) who states that: 'Economic development is sustainable if and only if utility is non-decreasing over time', and Solow (1992, p. 15) who writes that 'the duty imposed by sustainability is to bequeath to posterity not any particular thing ... but rather to endow them with whatever it takes to achieve a standard of living at least as good as our own...'.

The need to make the above definitions operational leads to a number of interpretations of sustainability. These include the Rawlsian interpretation, the Hicksian interpretation and the discounted utilitarian interpretation (Nordhaus 1994, Heal 1995).[54]

The Rawlsian interpretation is based on the Rawlsian principle (Rawls 1971) that welfare is maximized by maximizing the welfare of the worst-off

---

[53]Natural resources are mainly used as factors of production and can be distinguished into depletable or exhaustible resources and renewable resources (see Dasgupta and Heal [1979] for a theoretical treatment). On the other hand environmental resources refer to the resources desirable for their amenity values (clean air, clean water, forest amenities and so on). Of course natural resources also have amenity values.

[54]For a detailed analysis of the interrelated issues of sustainablility and intergenerational equity see Beltratti (1996).

generation. Thus sustainability in the above sense requires determining the welfare of the worst-off generation corresponding to all feasible consumption paths and then determining a feasible path that maximizes this minimal value (Heal 1995).[55]

The concept of the Hicksian income as a measure of sustainability has been proposed by Daly and Cobb (1989). In this approach a sustainable path should leave income intact, with income defined as consumption plus capital accumulation, less the value of resource depletion and environmental degradation. In defining Hicksian income in a way that is compatible with sustainability, the net national product is adjusted in order to account for both the depreciation of natural capital depleted in the production processes and defensive expenditures necessary to keep the environmental quality from deteriorating.

According to the discounted utilitarian interpretation (Mäler 1991, Heal 1995, Chichilnisky 1993), sustainable growth policies are those for which future generations can enjoy nondeclining consumption (utility) paths. This interpretation implies a premium on the consumption of future generations and in particular that:

(i)     The present and the long-term future are treated symmetrically with a positive value of welfare in the very long run; and

(ii)    The intrinsic value of the environmental assets is explicitly recognized.

The sustainability path can then be obtained by maximizing a criterion function defined over the discounted utilities over an infinite time horizon, where utility depends on the flow of consumption and the level of environmental pollution.[56]

Denoting by $c(t)$ the consumption flow and by $S(t)$ the stock of the environmental asset, or equivalently the stock of the accumulated pollutant at time $t$, the instantaneous valuation of the economy's state can be obtained

---

[55]As noted by Heal (1995) a basic problem with the application of the Rawlsian principle in the developing countries in which the present generation is the poorest, is that the principle would imply a transfer from the poor present to the presumably richer future. For a critique of the Rawlsian principle see also Dasgupta and Heal (1979) and Solow (1974).

[56]There is a well-known controversy about the legitimacy of discounting future utilities at a positive discount rate (see for example Arrow and Kurz [1970, p. 12]). Cline (1992) suggests zero discounting in global warming problems. For a discussion about the choice of the discount rate in environmental problems see the special issue of the *Journal of Environmental Economics and Management* (1990) and also Weitzman (1994) for the adjustments necessary to the discount rate in order to account for environmental considerations (the so-called environmental drag).

by the utility function of the representative individual $U(c(t),S(t))$.[57] Then, consumption paths can be ranked according to the value of the following objective functional (Heal 1995):[58]

$$\theta \int_0^\infty e^{-rt} U(c(t),S(t))\, dt + (1-\theta) \lim_{t\to\infty} U(c(t),S(t)) \tag{3.67}$$

where the second term reflects the valuation in the very long run. For $\theta = 1$ the above criterion results in the usual utilitarian objective function that can be used to incorporate environmental or natural resource considerations into optimal growth models.[59]

A criterion for sustainable development compatible with the nondeclining utility approach has been proposed by Pearce et al. (1990). According to this criterion a vector of social goals is defined. These social goals include real per capita income, health and nutrition, education, access to resources, fair income distribution and democracy. Sustainability is then defined as a state in which the development vector does not decrease over time. In attempting to derive practical policy rules for sustainability in the context of the above definition, attention was given to the management of natural environments so that a nondeclining standard of living is attained. Thus the 'capital intact' concept has been introduced as an operational sustainability criterion (Pearce et al. 1990, Pearce and Turner 1990). This criterion however is not free from difficulties and conceptual problems (Nordhaus 1994). Concentrating on natural capital the capital intact definition implies that renewable resources substitute exhaustible resources, man-made capital substitutes natural capital, and technical change increases the efficiency in the use of natural resources and the environment. The constancy of the capital stock can be defined, in physical terms, with resulting aggregation problems, or in value terms. In the latter case intact natural capital implies constancy in the real value of the stock of natural assets.[60]

The above discussion suggests that defining rigorous and operational

---

[57]The utility function has the usual properties. That is:

$$\frac{\partial U}{\partial c} > 0, \quad \frac{\partial^2 U}{\partial c^2} < 0, \quad \frac{\partial U}{\partial S} \gtrless 0, \quad \frac{\partial^2 U}{\partial S^2} \lessgtr 0, \quad \frac{\partial^2 U}{\partial c \partial S} \gtrless 0$$

according to whether $S$ is treated as an environmental asset that is beneficial or as a stock of pollution that is harmful.

[58]The definition of the criterion (3.67) requires the satisfaction of two added axioms defined by Chichilnisky (1993): namely the axioms of no dictatorship of the present over the future and vice versa.

[59]For results where $\theta$ is not restricted to unity see Beltratti et al. (1993).

[60]For other interpretations of the natural capital constancy, see Pearce and Turner (1990).

criteria for sustainability is not an easy task. The main approaches require nondeclining capital stock or net income or consumption (utility). In the next section some welfare measures that can be used to give operational meaning to these criteria are discussed.

## 7.2  Welfare Measures

As noted by Solow (1992) a central role in a logically-sound approach to the issue of sustainability is played by the way in which the economy will be charged for the consumption of its resource endowments and for the degradation or improvement of the environmental assets. Thus measurement of growth implies that the measurement of a country's income should take into account natural and environmental resources as a distinct capital stock.

Traditionally growth is measured by the rate of growth of per capita GDP.[61] The GDP in a closed economy is defined as the sum of consumption and investment. Consumption reflects current welfare while investment reflects future welfare, since current investment determines future consumption opportunities. GDP is not however an appropriate measure of economic welfare since it is not a net concept and does not include depreciation in the resource base of the economy and environmental degradation (Mäler 1994b). The correct concept is the net national product (NNP) adjusted for the consumption of natural resources and environmental damages.

In a dynamic framework the NNP concept can be determined with the help of a Hamiltonian representation. The concept of the current value Hamiltonian introduced by Arrow and Kurz (1970) can be used to express the value of the NNP (Cass and Shell 1976). In a standard optimal-growth model with one all-purpose commodity that can either be invested or consumed, the current value Hamiltonian is the sum of the current utility from consumption and the shadow value of the current net investment. The NNP is the linear support of the current value Hamiltonian that values consumption and investment at their respective shadow values. To see this consider the standard one-sector optimal growth model (Arrow and Kurz 1970):

---

[61]The problems associated with the use of GDP per capita as an indicator of the success of development are well-known (see for example Sen 1988). On the other hand, however, there is a positive correlation between the GDP and some important development indicators, such as daily calorie intake, life expectancy, infant mortality or enrolment in education, suggesting that per capita GDP can be used as an approximate index of the developmental stage of a country.

$$\max_{\{c(t) \geq 0\}} \int_o^\infty e^{-rt}[N(t)U(c(t))]dt \qquad (3.68)$$

$$\text{s. t. } \dot{k} = f(k) - c - \delta k, \ k(0) = k_o > 0$$

where $c(t)$ is per capita consumption, $N(t) = N(0)e^{\pi t}$ is population at time $t$, $U(c(t))$ is utility from current consumption, $f(k)$ is a standard concave neoclassical production function with $k$ indicating capital per worker (and per capita) and $\delta$ is the rate of depreciation of the capital stock.

The current value Hamiltonian for the problem is defined as:

$$H = U(c(t)) + p(t)[f(k) - c - \delta k] \qquad (3.69)$$

Assuming as usual $U'(0) = +\infty$, the maximum principle requires choosing the consumption path $c(t)$ to maximize the current value Hamiltonian at each instant of time, or $U'(c(t)) = p(t)$, where $p(t)$ is the shadow value of current investment. Taking a Taylor expansion of (3.69) the linear support of the Hamiltonian function along the optimal path is:

$$NNP = U'c^*(t) + p(t)\dot{k}(t) = p(t)\left[c^*(t) + \dot{k}(t)\right]$$

That is, the value of NNP equals current consumption plus the net change in the value of the capital stock valued at the shadow or social price $p(t)$. The NNP can also be expressed in terms of aggregate consumption by dividing throughout by $U'$. Since the utility function does not depend explicitly on time, the problem is stationary and, for given values of the capital stock $k$ and the social price $p$, the Hamiltonian function is independent of $t$ (Arrow and Kurz 1970). Denoting by $H^*$ the value of the Hamiltonian along the optimal path, its time derivative is:

$$\frac{\partial H^*}{\partial t} = \frac{\partial H^*}{\partial k}\frac{\partial k}{\partial t} + \frac{\partial H^*}{\partial p}\frac{\partial p}{\partial t}$$

but from the auxiliary conditions we have

$$\dot{p}(t) = \rho p(t) - \frac{\partial H}{\partial k}, \quad \rho = (r - \pi)$$

Thus,

$$\frac{\partial H^*}{\partial t} = \left(\rho p - \frac{\partial p}{\partial t}\right)\frac{\partial k^*}{\partial t} + \frac{\partial k^*}{\partial t}\frac{\partial p}{\partial t} =$$

$$\rho p\frac{\partial k^*}{\partial t} = \rho(H^* - U(c^*)) \text{ since } H^* = U(c^*) + p\frac{\partial k^*}{\partial t}$$

(3.70)

Solving the differential equation $\dot{H}^* = \rho(H^* - U(c^*))$ defined above, we obtain

$$\int_t^\infty H^*(t)e^{-\rho(\tau-t)}d\tau = \int_t^\infty U(c^*(\tau))e^{-\rho(\tau-t)}dt$$

(3.71)

where $U(c^*)$ is the maximum utility along the optimal path. Relation (3.71) implies that $H^*(t)$ is the maximum current utility that can be sustained forever. Thus $H^*(t)$ is a measure of sustainable well-being or welfare. The NNP, defined as the linearized Hamiltonian along the optimal path, reflects the maximum consumption that the economy can enjoy at any date under the assumption that consumption is not allowed to fall. Equivalently the NNP along the optimal path is the maximum sustainable consumption at that date (Dasgupta and Mäler 1991).[62] Therefore the current value Hamiltonian along the optimal path is a net welfare measure (NWM) reflecting sustainable income in utility terms. This result can be further extended to take into account issues like renewable resources, environmental pollution and abatement expenses.[63]

A one-sector economy is considered in which total output $y(t)$ at each instant of time $t$, regarded as an all-purpose commodity, is produced by using produced capital $k(t)$ and the current flow $u(t)$ of an exhaustible resource extracted from a stock $R(t)$, that is coal reserves or oil reserves. The 'manufactured' output of the economy at time $t$ is produced according to a neoclassical production function, $y(t) = f(k(t), u(t), t)$.[64] The extraction of the natural resource has the following effects on the economy. The economy incurs extraction costs $E(t)$, in terms of the composite produced good. The use of the resources in the production process at time $t$ generates emissions $\beta u$. The accumulation of the pollutant creates environmental damages (the use of coal will generate carbon dioxide or sulphur dioxide emissions).

---

[62]This result is due to Weitzman (1976), and was later extended by Dasgupta and Heal (1979) and Solow (1986) to take into account exhaustible resources.

[63]See for example Hartwick (1990), Mäler (1991, 1994b), Dasgupta and Mäler (1991).

[64]Labour input is assumed fixed and is suppressed in order to simplify the exposition and exemplify the role of produced and natural capital. When labour is introduced and wages equal the disutility of the work effort, then the wage bill valued at the appropriate shadow price should not be included in the NNP definition (Dasgupta and Mäler 1991, Mäler 1991).

Furthermore it reduces the stock of the resource, that is $R(t+1)=R(t)-u(t)$. Assume that the pollution can be reduced by abatement and the resource stock can be augmented by new discoveries. Let $a(t)$ denote abatement expenses and $D(t)$ discovery expenses in terms of the composite good. The total manufactured output in the economy is allocated among consumption $c(t)$; gross investment in produced capital; and extraction, abatement and discovery expenses, as:

$$f(k(t),u(t),t)=y(t)=c(t)+I(t)+E(t)+a(t)+D(t) \tag{3.72}$$

In the framework of an aggregate optimal growth model the welfare of the society at any point in time is a function of the flow of consumption and the stock of the pollutant $S(t)$. A stationary time invariant utility function for the representative individual can be written as:[65]

$$U=U(c(t),S(t)), \quad \frac{\partial U}{\partial c}>0, \quad \frac{\partial U}{\partial S}<0, \quad \frac{\partial^2 U}{\partial c^2}<0, \quad \frac{\partial^2 U}{\partial S^2}<0, \quad \frac{\partial^2 U}{\partial c\partial S}<0$$

The objective is the maximization of the usual social welfare functional:

$$\int_o^\infty e^{-\rho t}U(c,S)dt \tag{3.73}$$

where $\rho$ is the discount rate for future utilities as defined earlier in this section.

The objective is to maximize (3.73) subject to a capital accumulation constraint, and a resource depletion constraint. Let $E=q(u,R)$ be the current cost of the exhaustible resource extraction from stock $S$, and $D=h(Z,R)$ be the current cost of discovering an amount of resource $Z$.[66] Then the capital accumulation constraint can be written as:

$$\dot{k}=f(k,u)-c-q(u,R)-a-h(Z,R)-\delta k, \quad k(0)=k_o>0 \tag{3.74}$$

Let abatement expenses result in pollution reduction determined by the abatement function $g(a)$, $g'>0$, $g''<0$. Then pollution accumulation is defined as:

$$\dot{S}=\beta u-bS-g(a), \quad S(0)=S_o\geq0 \tag{3.75}$$

Finally the exhaustible resource accumulation is determined as:

---

[65] See for example Keeler et al. (1971). The appropriate shape for the indifference curves is guaranteed if $U_{cc}U_{SS}-U_{cS}^2>0$, with subscripts indicating second-order partial derivatives.

[66] $q_u>0$, $q_{uu}>0$, $q_R<0$, $q_{RR}>0$, $h_Z>0$, $h_{ZZ}>0$, $h_R<0$, $h_{RR}<0$, that is, there are negative stock effects: the lower the stock, the higher the extraction cost.

$$\dot{R} = -u + Z, \ R(0) = R_o > 0 \tag{3.76}$$

The welfare maximization problem becomes:

$$\max_{\{(c(t),\, u(t),\, a(t),\, Z(t)) \geq 0\}} \int_o^\infty e^{-\rho t} U(c,S)\, dt$$

s. t. (3.74), (3.75), (3.76)

The current value Hamiltonian for this optimization is:

$$H = U(c,S) + p(t)[f(k,u) - c - q(u,R) - a - h(Z,R) - \delta k] + \\ \mu(t)[\beta u - bS - g(a)] + v(t)[-u + Z] \tag{3.77}$$

where the costate variables $p(t)$, $\mu(t)$ and $v(t)$ can be interpreted as the dynamic social values of the produced capital stock, the stock of pollution and the resource stock respectively. The optimality conditions for interior solutions can be written as:

$$\frac{\partial H}{\partial c} = 0 \ \text{ or } \ \frac{\partial U}{\partial c} = p \tag{3.78.1}$$

$$\frac{\partial H}{\partial u} = 0 \ \text{ or } \ p\left(\frac{\partial f}{\partial u} - \frac{\partial q}{\partial u}\right) + \mu\beta - v = 0 \tag{3.78.2}$$

$$\frac{\partial H}{\partial Z} = 0 \ \text{ or } \ -p\frac{\partial h}{\partial Z} + v = 0 \tag{3.78.3}$$

$$\frac{\partial H}{\partial a} = 0 \ \text{ or } \ -p - \mu g\,'(a) = 0 \tag{3.78.4}$$

$$\dot{p} = \rho p - \frac{\partial H}{\partial k} = \left(\rho + \delta - \frac{\partial f}{\partial k}\right)p \tag{3.79.1}$$

$$\dot{\mu} = \rho\mu - \frac{\partial H}{\partial S} = (\rho + b)\mu - \frac{\partial U}{\partial S} \tag{3.79.2}$$

$$\dot{v} = \rho v - \frac{\partial H}{\partial R} = \rho v + p\left(\frac{\partial q}{\partial R} + \frac{\partial h}{\partial R}\right) \tag{3.79.3}$$

along with

$$\dot{k} = \frac{\partial H}{\partial p}, \ \dot{S} = \frac{\partial H}{\partial \mu}, \ \dot{R} = \frac{\partial H}{\partial v} \tag{3.79.4}$$

and the transversality conditions at infinity.

Consider the linear approximation of the utility function $U_c c + U_S S$,[67] and then divide the linear support of the Hamiltonian by $p(t) = U_c$. The NNP is defined as:

$$\frac{NNP}{p} = c + \frac{\partial U / \partial S}{p} S + \dot{k} + \frac{\mu}{p} \dot{S} + \frac{v}{p} \dot{R}$$

Using conditions (3.78.1) to (3.78.3) we obtain:

$$\frac{NNP}{p} = c + \frac{\partial U / \partial S}{\partial U / \partial c} S + \dot{k} - \frac{1}{g'(a)} \dot{S} + \left[ \left( \frac{\partial f}{\partial u} - \frac{\partial q}{\partial u} \right) - \frac{\beta}{g'(a)} \right] \dot{R} \qquad (3.80)$$

The NNP definition (3.80) indicates that the value of the NNP in the economy consists of consumption plus net capital formation $(c + \dot{k})$ which is a conventional measure, less the cost of the pollution stock valued at the marginal rate of substitution between pollution and consumption $(U_S / U_c)$, less the cost from any increase in pollution $\dot{S}$ valued at the inverse of the marginal abatement costs $(1 / g'(a))$, less the current 'Hotelling rents', as the net resource stock diminishes, adjusted for the environmental impact of the resource $[(f_u - c_u) - \beta / g'(a)] \dot{R}$. Note that $f_u$ is the market value of the resource flow and $c_u$ is its marginal extraction cost. This 'accounting rule' represents a synthesis of Hartwick's (1990) rule and Mäler's (1991) rule by accounting for both the exhaustibility and the effects from pollution.[68]

Denote as before the current value Hamiltonian by $H^*$, defined by (3.77) along the optimal path $\{k^*(t), S^*(t), R^*(t), c^*(t), u^*(t), a^*(t), Z^*(t)\}$. Since the problem is autonomous the time derivative of $H^*$ is given by:

$$\frac{dH^*}{dt} = \frac{\partial H^*}{\partial k} \dot{k} + \frac{\partial H^*}{\partial S} \dot{S} + \frac{\partial H^*}{\partial R} \dot{R} + \frac{\partial H^*}{\partial p} \dot{p} + \frac{\partial H^*}{\partial \mu} \dot{\mu} + \frac{\partial H^*}{\partial v} \dot{v}$$

Using the auxiliary conditions (3.79.1) to (3.79.4) we obtain:

$$\frac{dH^*}{dt} = \rho \left( p\dot{k} + \mu \dot{S} + v \dot{R} \right) = \rho \left( H^* - U^* \right) \qquad (3.81)$$

where $U^*$ is the maximum utility along the optimal path. The differential equation (3.81) can be solved to obtain:

---

[67]Subscripts are used to denote partial derivatives.
[68]The idea that current Hotelling rents should be netted out of the GNP in order to arrive at NNP can be found in Solow (1986) and Hartwick (1989).

$$H^* = \rho(pk^* + \mu S^* + vR^*) \text{ or} \tag{3.82.1}$$

$$\int_t^\infty H^*(t) e^{-\rho(\tau - t)} d\tau = \int_t^\infty U^*(\tau) e^{-\rho(\tau - t)} d\tau \tag{3.82.2}$$

$H^*$ again defines, through (3.81) and (3.82), the net welfare measure which should be nondeclining for sustainability. Relationship (3.82.1) indicates that the current value Hamiltonian is a measure of the sum of the social returns of all types of capital in the economy, along the optimal path. That is, the produced capital, the pollution stock (negative stock externality) and the natural capital. Relationship (3.82) on the other hand indicates that the current value Hamiltonian is a sustainability measure in utility terms. From (3.81) it can be seen that the net welfare measure remains constant if the value of the total capital stock in the economy defined as $pk + \mu S + vR$ remains constant. Thus sustainability requires that the value of the total capital in the economy be nondecreasing.[69]

The analysis above suggests therefore that the sustainability concept can be formally defined in the context of an optimal growth model which incorporates resource exhaustibility and/or accumulation of environmental pollution. These models are analysed in the following sections.

## 7.3 Optimal Growth and Environmental Pollution

The development of optimal growth models which incorporate environmental considerations has been marked by recent advances in growth theory which have come to be known under the name of 'endogenous growth'. Thus two types of models can in general be distinguished: those based on standard neoclassical growth models, which represent the great majority; and those that have recently emerged and which have been developed in an endogenous growth framework.

---

[69]This concept was introduced by Solow (1986) and can be related to the 'capital intact' interpretation of sustainability in value terms introduced by Pearce et al. (1990). The feasibility of sustainable development is not guaranteed but rather depends on the parameters of the model such as the elasticity of substitution between the natural and the produced capital and the rate of technical change (see also Dasgupta and Heal 1979). In a similar context Hartwick's (1977) rule states that sustainability is feasible if the Hotelling rents of the exhaustible resource are invested in the produced capital. Pezzey (1995), by defining sustainability as a situation of nondeclining utility, introduces the additional constraint, $\dot{U} \geq 0$ or $U_c \dot{c} + U_S \dot{S} \geq 0$, to the welfare-maximization problem.

### 7.3.1 Neoclassical growth models

Neoclassical models of pollution and growth have been developed since the early 1970s.[70] In this section we follow the Brock (1977) model which has recently been extended by Tahvonen and Kuuluvainen (1993). The utility function is defined in the same way as before as $U(c,S)$. The basic assumption of Brock's model is that emissions are an input in the production process so that the production function can be written as $y=f(k,e)$, where $k$ is as usual capital stock and $e$ is aggregate emissions. This formulation allows the substitution between capital and emissions and is closer to a representation of technology that includes inputs which generate pollution in the production process. The production function has the standard neoclassical characteristics. Emissions and capital are assumed to be substitutes (that is, $f_{ke}>0$) and furthermore a level of emissions $\bar{e}$ exists, such that the marginal product of emissions with a given level of capital is zero. That is, at this emission level, production cannot increase without further increasing the capital stock. The capital stock accumulates according to:

$$\dot{k}=f(k,e)-c-\delta k, \; k(0)=k_o>0 \tag{3.83}$$

while pollution accumulates in the ambient environment as:

$$\dot{S}=e-bS, \; S(0)=S_o\geq 0 \tag{3.84}$$

In order to determine the social optimum the problem of the social planner is to choose non-negative consumption and emission paths that solve the infinite-horizon optimal-control problem:

$$\max_{\{(c(t),e(t))\geq 0\}}\int_o^\infty e^{-\rho t}U(c,S)dt \tag{3.85}$$

s. t. (3.83), (3.84)

The current value Hamiltonian for the above problem can be written as:

$$H(k,S,c,e)=U(c,S)+p(t)[f(k,e)-c-\delta k]+\lambda(t)(e-bS)$$

with $p(t)$ being the shadow or social value of net capital formation and $\lambda(t)$ the shadow cost of the pollutant. The necessary and sufficient optimality

---

[70]The first of such models was developed by Forster (1973). The analysis of environmental pollution in the context of neoclassical optimal growth under a variety of assumptions include, among others, models developed by Keeler et al. (1971), Brock (1977), Gruver (1976), Becker (1982), Siebert (1992), Heal (1982) and Kamien and Schwartz (1982). See also van der Ploeg and Withagen (1991) for the analysis of the Ramsey problem under environmental pollution.

*Advanced Principles in Environmental Policy*

conditions for the optimal choices $C^*(t)$, $e^*(t)$ can be written as:[71]

$$\frac{\partial U}{\partial c} = p \tag{3.85.1}$$

$$p\frac{\partial f}{\partial e} + \lambda \leq 0 \text{ with equality if } e^*(t) > 0 \tag{3.85.2}$$

$$\dot{p} = \left(\rho + \delta - \frac{\partial f}{\partial k}\right)p \tag{3.86.1}$$

$$\dot{\lambda} = (\rho + b)\lambda - \frac{\partial U}{\partial S} \tag{3.86.2}$$

along with the differential equations (3.83), (3.84) and the transversality conditions at infinity, which can be written as:

$$\lim_{t \to \infty} e^{-rt} p(t) = \lim_{t \to \infty} e^{-rt} \lambda(t) = \lim_{t \to \infty} e^{-rt} k(t) = \lim_{t \to \infty} e^{-rt} S(t) = 0$$

implying that the present value of capital and pollution becomes negligible at infinity.

As analysed earlier in the chapter, the short-run equilibrium conditions (3.85.1) and (3.85.2) determine consumption and emissions as functions of the capital stock and the stock of pollution as well as their respective shadow values, or $c^* = c(k,S,p,\lambda)$, $e^* = e(k,S,p,\lambda)$. The concavity of the production and the utility functions ensure that these maximizing values are unique. Substituting the optimal short-run choices for consumption and emissions, $c^*$ and $e^*$ respectively, into (3.83), (3.84), (3.86.1) and (3.86.2) we obtain the MHDS that determines the evolution of the capital stock, the pollution stock and their respective shadow prices along the optimal path. The NNP in this problem is defined by using consumption as the numeraire as follows:

$$\frac{NNP}{p} = c + \dot{k} + \frac{\partial U/\partial S}{p}S + \frac{\lambda}{p}\dot{S}$$

That is, NNP is the sum of consumption and net investment less the disutility from the existing pollution stock and its net changes.

The long-run socially-optimal steady state equilibrium is defined as $k_\infty^*$, $S_\infty^*$, $p_\infty^*$, $\lambda_\infty^*$, : $\dot{k} = \dot{S} = \dot{p} = \dot{\lambda} = 0$. Tahvonen and Kuuluvainen (1993) showed that if the marginal product of capital exceeds its shadow value at very low capital levels and the marginal utility of consumption is reduced at high

---

[71]It is assumed that $\lim_{c \to 0} U_c(c,S) = \infty$, $\lim_{S \to \bar{S}} U_S(c,S) = -\infty$, $\lim_{S \to 0} U_S(c,S) = 0$.

pollution levels, then the steady state exists and is unique.[72] Furthermore under these two assumptions the steady state has the local saddle point property.

It can also be shown that when pollution is not controlled then the steady state values of consumption and capital are comparatively greater. To see this consider the case where $\lambda = 0$, which implies that the accumulation of pollution has no social cost. In this case emissions will be increased up to the point where there marginal product is zero, or $\bar{e} : p(\partial f(k, \bar{e})/\partial e) = 0$. Thus $\bar{e} > e^*$, and steady state capital and consumption are determined by the system

$$\frac{\partial f(k_\infty, e)}{\partial k} = \rho + \delta$$

$$f(k_\infty, e) - \delta k_\infty - c_\infty = 0$$

Under the assumptions made above about the production function and the substitutability between capital and emissions, the comparative statics of the steady state indicate:

$$\frac{\partial k_\infty}{\partial e} = \frac{f_{ke}}{-f_{kk}} > 0 \text{ and } \frac{\partial c_\infty}{\partial e} = \frac{-f_e f_{kk} + f_{ke}(f_k - \delta)}{-f_{kk}} > 0$$

with subscripts denoting partial derivatives. Thus an increase in emissions at the unregulated state will increase capital stock and consumption.

Results of this type underlie most of the discussion about the link between pollution control and growth, the idea being that stricter pollution control will reduce consumption and standards of living determined solely by consumption levels.

Environmental policy can be introduced into this context by considering instruments under which competitive markets can be controlled in such a way as to attain the socially-optimal paths $k^*(t)$ and $S^*(t)$ as outcomes of a decentralized system subject to a given environmental policy.

In a competitive framework the representative consumer takes as given time paths $\{w(t), r_m(t), \pi(t)\}$ for $t \in [0, \infty)$, of wages, market rates of interest and profits. The instantaneous utility of the consumer is defined by $U(c, S)$ as before. The consumer sells fixed labour input normalized to unity, to the representative firm at a given wage, and rents capital, $k(t)$, at the market rate of interest to the firm which maximizes profits under perfectly competitive

---

[72]These two assumptions can be stated as $\lim_{k \to 0} \dfrac{\partial f(k, e)}{\partial k} > p$, $\dfrac{\partial^2 U}{\partial c \, \partial S} \leq 0$, for $S$ sufficiently large.

conditions. The firm generates emissions $e(t)$ per unit time and pays a tax $\tau(t)$ on these emissions. Total tax proceeds collected by the government are redistributed to the consumer. The objective of the consumer is to choose a consumption path which achieves the maximum value of utility, consistent with his/her expectations on all prices, dividends, externality taxes and the initial stock of capital. The consumer's problem is to:

$$\max_{\{c(t) \geq 0\}} \int_0^\infty e^{-\rho t} U(c(t), S(t)) dt \qquad \text{(CO)}$$

$$\text{s. t. } \dot{k} = \pi(t) + r_m k(t) + \tau e(t) - c(t) - \delta k(t)$$

where $\rho$ is the consumer's discount rate and $\delta$ is the depreciation rate of capital.

The representative firm takes as given time paths of emission taxes $\{\tau(t)\}$, $t \in [0, \infty)$ along with the time paths of wages and interest rates, to produce the all-purpose commodity. The firm can reduce its tax payments on emissions by reducing output. Output is produced according to a standard neoclassical production function $q = f(k, e, l)$, where $l = 1$ is labor input. Thus the firm solves the problem:

$$\max_{\{(k(t), e(t)) \geq 0\}} \pi(t) = f(k(t), e(t)) - r_m(t) k(t) - \tau(t) e(t) \qquad \text{(FO)}$$

Assume that the consumer perfectly predicts the time paths $\{w(t), r_m(t), \pi(t)\}$ and the firm predicts the time paths $\{w(t), r_m(t), \tau(t)\}$. Then the solution of the consumer's problem determines consumption demand, $c^d$, and the supply of the capital stock, $k^s$, while solution of the firm's problem determines the supply of consumption, $c^s$, the demand for capital, $k^d$, and the emissions, $e$. The paths $\{w^c(t), r_m^c(t), \pi^c(t), \tau(t)\}$ are a perfect foresight competitive equilibrium with emissions taxes if the solution $\{c^s(t), k^d(t), e(t)\}$ of the (FO) problem is such that if profits are defined by $\pi = f(k^d, e) - r_m k^d - \tau e$, for each $t$, and if $\{c^d(t), k^s(t)\}$ solves the (CO) problem then for all $t \in [0, \infty)$ we have:

$c^d(t) = c^s(t)$: flow market equilibrium,

$k^d(t) = k^s(t)$: stock market equilibrium,

$e^c(t)$: competitive emissions,

$\dot{S}(t) = e^c(t) - bS(t)$, $S(0) = S_o$: evolution of the pollution stock.

Given the structure of the economy defined above the problem of the social planner is defined in (3.85). Let $p, \lambda$ denote the shadow prices of capital and pollution respectively along the socially-optimal path. Then if the emission tax is defined as $\tau(t) = -\lambda(t)/p(t)$, the competitive equilibrium solution for the consumer's problem (CO) and the firm's problem (FO) is identical to the solution of the social optimization problem.[73] To show that, assume interior solutions for the firm's problem (FO). Then the first-order conditions require that:

$$\frac{\partial f}{\partial k} = r_m \tag{3.87.1}$$

$$\frac{\partial f}{\partial e} = \tau \tag{3.87.2}$$

which determine the instantaneous demand for capital and competitive emissions.

The consumer solves the problem (CO). The current value Hamiltonian for this problem is defined as:

$$H = U(c,S) + \mu(t)\left(\pi + r_m k + \tau e - c - \delta k\right)$$

The necessary conditions for optimality are:

$$\frac{\partial U}{\partial c} = \mu \tag{3.88.1}$$

$$\dot{\mu} = (\rho + \delta - r_m)\mu \tag{3.88.2}$$

$$\dot{k} = \pi + r_m k + \tau e - c - \delta k, \ k(0) = k_o \tag{3.88.3}$$

and the transversality conditions as $t \to \infty$, $e^{-\rho t}\mu(t) = 0$, $e^{-\rho t}\mu(t)k(t) = 0$.

From (3.85.1) and (3.88.1) it is clear that $\mu = p$. For $\tau = -\lambda/p$, comparing (3.87.2) to (3.85.2), competitive emissions and socially-optimal emissions coincide. Finally by substituting $r_m$ in (3.88.2) from (3.87.1) and using $\mu = p$, (3.88.2) becomes identical to (3.86.1). The evolution of the optimal tax $\tau(t)$ is determined by (3.86.1) and (3.86.2). Therefore the optimality conditions for the consumer's and the firm's problems are identical to those for the social optimum.

Therefore by solving the social planner's problem, the government can impose flexible emission taxes, inducing profit-maximizing firms to follow the socially-desirable production and emission policy. In this sense the time path and the steady state equilibrium corresponding to the optimally-controlled competitive equilibrium will be identical to those for the social

---

[73]See also Tahvonen and Kuuluvainen (1993). In their model a renewable resource is also included which is an input in the production function along with emissions, and the growth function of the resource is adversely affected by the pollution stock. The optimal policy in this case consists of an emission tax and a tax on the harvesting rate of the renewable resource.

optimization problem.[74]

### 7.3.2  Endogenous growth models

Growth theorists have concentrated on a number of facts characterizing economic growth that Romer (1994) summarizes as:

(i)      A large number of firms in the market economy;

(ii)     Information in technical knowledge is a nonrival input in the sense that it is technologically possible to use knowledge at the same time;

(iii)    Physical activities can be replicated. That is, the aggregate production function in the rival input is homogeneous of degree one;

(iv)    Technological advances in the aggregate relate positively to the aggregate number of researchers involved in research and development activities; and

(v)     Individuals and firms have market power and can earn monopoly rents on discoveries.

Although the first three facts are incorporated in the traditional neoclassical growth theory (Solow 1956, 1957), it was not until recently that endogenous growth models[75] explicitly introduced fact (iv) (Romer 1986, Lucas 1988), and fact (v) (Romer 1987, 1990).[76]

Given this new analytical framework, relatively recent attempts have been undertaken towards the introduction of environmental considerations into endogenous growth models.

Bovenberg and Smulders (1995) extend the models of Lucas (1988) and Rebello (1991). They consider a process of technical knowledge development that enables production to take place in a less polluting way and use renewable resources more efficiently. A two-sector model is developed with one sector producing a final employment good and the other sector generating

---

[74]The problem of the trade-off between capital accumulation and environmental quality in the context of Brock's model presented above has been examined by Becker (1982), with the aim of determining intergenerational equitable programs according to the Rawlsian maximum criterion. The regulator's maximin paths correspond to a competitive equilibrium controlled by a system of emission taxes, environmental rental charges and lump-sum transfers. The resulting equilibrium path keeps utility constant for all generations over time. The maximin path also satisfies a generalized Hartwick rule stating that at each time invest all emission taxes revenues associated with net changes in environmental quality in reproducible capital.

[75]Endogenous growth models emphasize that economic growth is the endogenous outcome of the economic system.

[76]For a more detailed presentation of these arguments see the special issues of the *Journal of Political Economy* (1990), *Quarterly Journal of Economics* (1991) and *Journal of Economic Perspectives* (1994).

knowledge in pollution reduction which is a public good. Production and pollution are modelled by a Brock-type model where output is produced according to the production function, $Y = F(N, K_Y, Z_Y)$, where $N$ is the stock of the environmental capital, $K_Y$ is 'man-made' capital used in the production of the final good and $Z_Y$ is effective input of the harvested environmental capital interpreted as pollution. The knowledge sector generates knowledge of stock $h$ according to $\dot{h} = H = H(K_H, Z_H)$, where $K_H$, $Z_H$ are man-made capital and pollution input in the technology sector respectively. The total effective level of pollution is $Z = Z_Y + Z_H$ with the economy-wide level of pollution $P$ determined as $Z \equiv hP$, thus $Z_Y = \alpha hP$ and $Z_H = (1 - \alpha)hP$. Man-made capital stock accumulates according to $\dot{K} = Y - c$ with $K = K_Y + K_H$. Finally the environmental stock has a renewable resource characteristic evolving according to a growth function $\dot{N} = E(N, P)$.[77] The social optimum is determined by maximizing the usual functional:

$$\max_{\{K_Y, K_H, Z_H, Z_H\}} \int_o^\infty e^{-\rho t} U(c(t), N(t)) dt$$

subject to the constraints defined above. The problem is solved to derive conditions for optimal sustainable balanced growth where consumption knowledge and man-made capital grows while the flow of pollution and the stock of environmental capital remain constant. The attainment of the social optimum requires government intervention in the form of taxes and pollution. Since knowledge is a public good governments should earmark part of the revenues for investment in the knowledge sector. The optimal size of the government's budget tends to increase with environmental concerns.

In a similar context Xepapadeas (1997a) uses Romer's (1986) model to introduce two types of knowledge accumulation: one in output production and the other in emission reductions. Production functions exhibit increasing returns in the aggregate knowledge and can be written suppressing labour input as $Y = F(k_q, K_q)$, where $k_q$ is knowledge in the production sector by a single firm and $K_q = nk_q$ is aggregate knowledge for $n$ symmetric firms. Emissions are generated according to $e = vF(k_q, K_q)$, with the output emission coefficient defined as $v = v(k_a, K_a, K_q)$, where $k_a$ is knowledge devoted to pollution abatement and $K_a$ is aggregate abatement knowledge. The unit emission coefficient is reduced at an increasing rate in absolute value for a certain range of aggregate knowledge. Knowledge in each sector accumulates according to $\dot{k}_j = k_j g_j (I_j / k_j)$, $j = q, a$, where $I_j$ is investment in each sector,

---

while output is distributed among consumption and knowledge investment as $Y=F(k_q,K_q)=c+I_q+I_a$. Environmental pollution accumulates according to the transition equation $\dot{S}=nv(k_a,K_a,K_q)F(k_q,K_q)-bS$, $S(0)=S_o$. The social optimum is obtained by maximizing the welfare functional

$$\max_{\{c,I_q,I_a\}} \int_0^\infty e^{-\rho t}[U(c(t))-D(S(t))]dt$$

Solution of the social optimization problem indicates that if the range of increasing returns in pollution abatement is sufficiently large and can be exploited then sustained growth is possible with pollution accumulation being kept at the socially-desirable level.[78] This result however depends on the initial value of knowledge in the two sectors, which exhibits threshold characteristics. Thus a country with low initial stock of knowledge in the abatement sector can be trapped in low growth regions. Environmental concern in this case impedes sustained growth. The attainment of the social optimum requires government intervention in the form of emission taxes and subsidies to induce research and development in the knowledge sectors.

Elbasha and Roe (1996) follow Romer (1990) to introduce imperfect competition in the growth model along with international trade considerations along the lines of Grossman and Helpman (1991) and Rivera-Batiz and Romer (1991). An open economy with two traded goods, $Y$ and $Z$, is considered. The production functions for the two goods are given by:

$$Y=A_y K_y^{a_1} L_y^{a_2} D_y^{a_3}, \quad Z=A_z K_z^{\beta_1} L_z^{\beta_2} D_z^{\beta_3}, \quad \Sigma a_i=\Sigma \beta_i=1$$

where $K_i$ and $L_i$ ($i=y,z$) denote capital and labor inputs respectively and $D_i$ is an index of differentiated inputs defined as:

$$D_i=\left(\int_o^{M(t)} X_i(j)^\delta dj\right)^{\frac{1}{\delta}}, \quad i=y,z, \quad \delta>0$$

where $M(t)$ is the number of differentiated inputs available at time $t$ and $X(t)$ is the amount of differentiated input $j$. Each type (brand) of input $j$ can be produced once a license is obtained from the research and development (R&D) sector of the economy, according to the production function:

$$X(j)=A_x[K_x(j)]^\eta [L_x(j)]^{1-\eta}, \quad 0<\eta<1, \quad j\in[0,M]$$

where $K_x$ and $L_x$ are capital and labour inputs respectively in the production

---

[78]This result can be compared with the 'ecological paradise' considered by Michel (1993).

of differentiated products. The R&D sector produces new blueprints to increase the number of brands, by using capital, labour and knowledge capital which is a public good, according to:

$$\dot{M} = A_m K_m^\theta L_m^{1-\theta} M, \ 0 < \theta < 1$$

where $M$ is the number of brands assumed proportional to the knowledge capital. In this model all markets are competitive with the exception of the differentiated input market, where producers sell their product in an imperfectly competitive market.

In the above described framework environmental quality is considered as a flow variable related either to the production of the two consumption goods or as a stock variable related to the use of the differentiated intermediate inputs. In the first case environmental quality is defined as:

$$Q = A_\alpha E_y^{\varepsilon_y} E_z^{\varepsilon_z}, \ \varepsilon_y, \varepsilon_z < 0$$

where $E_y$ and $E_z$ are emissions from the production of the traded goods $Y$ and $Z$ respectively. In the second case pollution is defined as:

$$S = \left( \int_0^{M(t)} (X(j))^\epsilon dj \right)^{-\frac{1}{\epsilon}}, \ \epsilon > 0$$

The model is solved for the market equilibrium and the social optimum and the two solutions are compared. The results indicate that if the elasticity of the intertemporal substitution of consumption is less than one then environmental concerns increase growth, while the opposite happens if the elasticity is greater than one. On the other hand the effects of trade on environment and welfare depend mainly on price elasticities, the terms of trade effects on growth and pollution intensities. Numerical simulations show that trade improves welfare but might worsen environmental quality.

The discussion above seems to indicate that the endogenous growth type models which include environmental considerations suggest that deceleration of growth because of environmental concerns can be overcome under specific circumstances.[79]

### 7.3.3 Some empirical evidence

Assessing the relationship between economic growth and environmental pollution on empirical grounds presents a number of difficulties, mainly in

---

[79]Endogenous growth models developed in a similar context include Musu (1995), Gradus and Smulders (1993), Michel (1993), Michel and Rotillon (1992), Beltratti (1992) and Barbier (1996). For a survey see Beltratti (1996).

terms of availability of appropriate data. The existing evidence, although perhaps not 'stylized facts', provides an idea about the movements of some key variables. Some recent results suggest that a break exists in the link between growth and pollution, at least for OECD countries (World Bank 1992). This break seems to be associated more with local pollutants (e.g., lead) than with global pollutants (e.g.,$CO_2$). At the same time, there is no indication that this link is breaking for lower income countries. Also as found by Hettige et al. (1992), there is an upward long-term trend in industrial emissions relative to both GDP and manufacturing output, with emissions growing faster in low income countries than in high income countries.

Research based on the estimation of empirical relationships between environmental and development variables also seems to suggest the de-linking of environmental pollution with economic growth. Grossman and Krueger (1993, 1995) and Selden and Song (1994) suggest that an inverted U relationship exists between the emissions of certain types of environmental pollutants and per capita GDP, the so-called environmental Kuznets curve,[80] wherein after a turning point emissions decline despite economic development. The results obtained by de Bruyn et al. (1995) also seem to indicate some kind of de-linking between environmental pressure and growth in some specific cases of emissions of air pollutants and countries. However they stress the point that in order to obtain more substantiated results the dynamic effects of structural and technology factors on pollution should be taken into account. Finally, Xepapadeas and Amri (1997) obtain results suggesting that a negative relationship exists between the probability of a country having unacceptable environmental quality, measured in terms of concentrations of certain pollutants in air and water, and the stage of the country's economic development.

In general the results, especially those related to the inverted U curve, seem to indicate that economic growth may not cause harm to the environment, at least with regard to the pollutants examined.[81] Grossman and Krueger (1995) calculate that the turn of the inverted U curve is around $8,000 (1985 dollars). Thus for countries with income above $10,000 the hypothesis that further growth will be associated with environmental degradation can be rejected at the 5 per cent significance level for most of the

---

[80]See also Selden and Song (1995) for a theoretical derivation of the inverted U curve in the context of a neoclassical growth model.

[81]In the empirical studies the range of the pollutants related to per capita GDP include sulphur dioxide, smoke, heavy particles, dissolved oxygen, BOD, COP, nitrates, fecal and total coliform, lead, cadmium, arsenic, mercury, and nickel (Grossman and Krueger 1995).

pollutants examined.

Environmental quality can be preserved or improved by restructuring production towards cleaner activities and by adopting environmental regulations. By simulating the US economy with and without environmental regulation, Jorgenson and Wilcoxen (1990) found that regulations associated with investment in pollution control equipment, motor vehicle emissions as well as operating costs in pollution abatement, are responsible for a drop in the growth of GDP by 0.191 percentage points. On the other hand, the results found by Hettige et al. (1992) suggest an industrial displacement effect, as a result of stricter regulations in developed countries, with dirtier industries moving towards low-income counties. This industrial displacement positively affects the environmental quality of the developed countries.

# 4.  Informational Constraints and Nonpoint Source Pollution

## 1   INTRODUCTION

The analysis of environmental policy presented in the previous chapters was developed under the basic assumption that the regulator has perfect information regarding the emissions generated by each potential polluter. That is, the source, the size and the distinctive characteristics of the emissions can be identified with sufficient accuracy at a nonprohibitive cost. A situation like this can be identified with pollution associated with large industrial or municipal emissions and is referred to in the literature as point source (PS) pollution.

In contrast to a PS pollution problem, in a nonpoint source (NPS) pollution problem neither the source nor the size of the individual emissions can be observed by an environmental regulator which seeks to implement a given environmental policy. NPS pollution problems relate mostly to emissions by small sources like farmers or households, or mobile sources such as vehicles. The pollution that these sources generate mainly includes nutrient pollution, pesticide pollution, sedimentation, vehicle pollution, and hazardous and solid wastes.

The significance of NPS type pollution is indicated by the fact that part of the degradation of many of the world's lakes and reservoirs can be traced to this type of pollution. Degradation is due to a number of factors including eutrophication which results from accelerated nutrient loading due to expanded farming practices; toxic substances entering the water bodies as agricultural run-off, along with forestry drainage which contains a range of toxic pesticides and herbicides; accelerated sedimentation caused by farming on fragile soils and steep slopes, forestry activities, construction activities and urban drainage; acidification of aquatic systems from emissions of sulphur dioxide and nitrous oxides which occurs due to acid rain or through leaching from affected land. In all of these cases monitoring of the individual emissions which are associated with farming or forestry activities, with acid rain, or with urban drainage, and which are responsible for environmental degradation, is not possible due to the number of sources and the diffused character of the pollution. In many cases critical pollution-generating inputs are not always observable and weather introduces stochastic elements into the pollution process, making identification of the polluting source and its contribution to the ambient pollution in the specific receiving body practically impossible. Thus in an NPS problem an environmental regulator can measure the ambient pollution at specific 'receptor points', but cannot attribute any specific portion of the pollutant's concentration to a specific discharger.

The problems that characterize NPS pollution are mainly informational, and have been distinguished by Braden and Segerson (1993) into two broad classes: problems related to monitoring and measurement, and problems related to natural variability. Monitoring problems are associated with the inability to directly observe individual emissions or to infer them from observable inputs or from the ambient concentration of the pollutant. Then the pollution control agency cannot efficiently monitor emissions or abatement efforts by an individual polluter. This is due to a number of factors such as equipment and personnel limitations, or inability to enter the polluter's premises. On the other hand, while it is relatively easy to determine whether the polluter has installed adequate abatement capacity, it is difficult to make sure that this capacity is being operated at the desired level. As a result the development of efficient and relatively accurate measurement methods could be costly. Therefore the environmental regulator faces a situation in which it could be prohibitively costly to measure with sufficient accuracy the emissions of potential polluters as well as the pollution abatement efforts. The regulator can only measure ambient pollutant concentration at prespecified receptor points. It is not however possible to attribute any specified portion of the accumulation of the pollutant to a specific polluter in the case of many polluters of the same pollutant. Natural variability is associated mainly with weather or topographical conditions or technological uncertainty and results in stochastic pollution processes.

The informational asymmetries between the regulator and individual dischargers in an NPS problem could take the form of moral hazard characterized by hidden actions or/and adverse selection. A situation where the emissions of each potential polluter or his/her abatement efforts are not observable while the outcome of all polluters' actions – that is, the ambient concentration of the pollutant at the receptor point – is observed, implies moral hazard. The individual polluter can increase profits by choosing lower emission levels since his/her actions are not observable. On the other hand the inability to know the specific characteristics or type of each potential polluter – which is private information known only to the polluter and affects the polluter's emissions – is associated with adverse selection. In a situation which is characterized by these informational asymmetries, the environmental regulator cannot use the standard instruments of environmental policy – Pigouvian taxes, tradeable emission permits, emission standards – discussed above, as a means of inducing dischargers to follow socially-desirable policies. The potential polluters will choose higher than socially-desirable emission levels if by doing so they can increase their profits. Since their emissions cannot be observed the standard environmental policy instruments cannot be used to internalize external damages and to obtain the Pareto optimal outcome.

The inadequacy of the standard instruments of environmental policy to deal with NPS problems has resulted, in recent years, in increasing attention being given to the development of policy schemes appropriate for such problems. These schemes can be divided into two broad categories or types: first ambient taxes where the scheme is based on the observed ambient pollution or menus of ambient taxes and effluent fees, which are based on incomplete observability of individual emissions and self-reporting by potential polluters; and second input-based schemes, where the policy scheme is applied to observable polluting inputs. Policy schemes of both types capable of dealing with NPS pollution are presented in the rest of this chapter.

## 2    IMPERFECT OBSERVABILITY AND OPTIMAL TAXATION

To analyse the impact of imperfect observability on environmental policy we consider the ECM of Chapter 2, Section 3.1, which was used to determine the optimal emission tax. We relax, however, the assumption that the individual emissions $e_i$ are fully observable by the regulator, that is, $e_i$ is the moral hazard variable.

As we already saw in Chapter 2, a social planner seeking to maximize total benefit less environmental damages will choose the socially-optimum emission level for each firm, such that marginal benefit equals marginal damages for all $i=1,...,n$, or $B_i'(e_i^*)=D'$. Then the optimal level of ambient pollution is $e^*=\sum_i e_i^*$.

Let $s_i$ represent the observed part of emissions by firm $i$, that is, $s_i \in [0,e_i]$.[1] It is assumed that firm $i$'s observed emissions depend on a

---

[1]This section follows Xepapadeas (1995c, 1997b).

parameter $m_i$.[2] Thus observed emissions are assumed to be determined according to an at least twice differentiable nondecreasing function $s_i = f_i(m_i)$.

The parameter $m_i$ can be interpreted in different ways. It can be regarded as reflecting monitoring effort to determine physical characteristics of the polluter (e.g., location, types of inputs used, production practices) that permit the quantification of emissions, or as information provided by the polluting firm itself that can lead to a quantification of a certain part of its own emissions, or as the amount of installed monitoring equipment. The following assumptions are made about $f_i$, where for clarity we choose to interpret $m_i$ as monitoring effort:

(i)    $f_i(0) = 0$. That is, there is no observability without monitoring effort.
(ii)   A level of monitoring effort exists at which perfect observability can be obtained, or $\exists \bar{m}_i : f_i(m_i) = e_i, \ \forall \ m_i \geq \bar{m}_i$. The regulator will know that perfect individual monitoring has been achieved if $\sum_i s_i = e$, the observed ambient level of pollution.
(iii)  $f_i''(m) < 0$ reflecting diminishing returns in monitoring.

Assume that the environmental regulator tries to formulate a policy that will induce firms to emit at the socially-desirable level, $e_i^*$. Consider two possible policy instruments:

(a)   An effluent fee or emission tax, $\tau_i$, that is imposed on firm $i$ per unit of observed emissions.
(b)   An ambient tax which firms are liable to pay if measured total ambient emissions, $e$, at some receptor point exceed the desired cut-off level, $e^*$. The ambient tax is specified as a function of the observed emissions of each firm. That is, for firm $i$, the ambient tax is defined as $g(s_i) \equiv g_i(f_i(m_i)) \equiv h_i(m_i)$.

The following assumptions are made about the ambient tax function:

(i)    When observability is complete, the ambient tax is zero. That is, $g_i(s_i)$ or equivalently $h_i(m_i) = 0 \ \forall \ m_i \geq \bar{m}_i$.
(ii)   When firms' emissions cannot be observed, the ambient tax rate takes its maximum value. That is, $g_i(0)$ or equivalently $h_i(0) = \gamma_i$, $\gamma_i = \max\{h_i(m_i)\} \ \forall \ m_i \in M_i$.
(iii)  The more emissions are observed, the less the ambient tax. That is, $g_i'(s_i) < 0$ or equivalently $h_i'(m_i) < 0$.
(iv)   The ambient tax function is convex in monitoring effort. That is,

---

[2] $m_i$ is assumed to belong to a compact and convex set $M_i$.

$g_i''(s_i)>0$, which combined with $g''[f_i']^2+g_i'f_i''>0$ implies $h_i''(m_i)>0$.

If the firm faces a tax scheme consisting of both ambient and effluent taxes, its profit function will be:

$$\pi(e_i,m_i)=B_i(e_i)-h_i(m_i)(e-e^*)-\tau_if_i(m_i) \qquad (4.1)$$

The environmental regulator must choose the tax parameters $h_i(m_i)$ and $\tau_i$ to maximize total benefits less total damages. Furthermore, if firms follow its instructions about the environmental policy to be adopted, they should maximize their profits. The last requirement implies that in the regulator's problem the constraint that (4.1) is maximized for $e_i=e_i^o$, given the emission policies of the rest of the firms, should be imposed. This means that the regulator's problem takes the form:

$$\max_{\begin{cases}(e_1,...,e_n)\geq 0\\(m_1,...,m_n)\geq 0\\(\tau_1,...,\tau_n)\geq 0\end{cases}} \sum_{i=1}^{n}B(e_i)-D(e) \qquad (4.2.1)$$

$$e=\sum_{i=1}^{n}e_i,\; m_i\in M_i \qquad (4.2.2)$$

$$e_i\in \text{argmax}_{e_i}\; B_i(e_i)-h_i(m_i)(e_i+\sum_{j\neq i}e_j^o-e^*)-\tau_if_i(m_i)\forall\; i \qquad (4.2.3)$$

$$\text{s. t}\; f_i(m_i)\leq e_i \qquad (4.2.4)$$

In this problem $e^*$ is not fixed in advance, as it appears in constraint (4.2.3), but it indicates the value of the optimal ambient pollutant concentration which is the solution to the regulator's problem (4.2.1). Thus the constraint is defined implicitly by the solution of the problem itself.[3] The optimal ambient and effluent fees in the two polar cases of nonobservability and complete observability are determined as solutions of the regulator's problem in the following way:

(i)     If firms' emissions can not be observed at all – or equivalently for all $i$, $m_i=0$ – then the optimal ambient tax equals marginal damages at the optimum, $\gamma_i=D'(\sum e_i^*)$, and the optimal emission tax is zero, $\tau_i=0$.

(ii)    If firms' emissions are perfectly observable for all $i$, that is $m_i\geq \bar{m}_i$,

---

[3]This problem has been called an implicit programming problem by Feinstein and Luenberger (1981), and represents a well-defined mathematical programming problem.

then the optimal ambient tax is zero, $\gamma_i=0$, while the optimal emission tax is equal to marginal damages as in the perfect observability models, $\tau_i=D'$.

To show this result consider the regulator's problem (4.2.1). In this mathematical program constraints (4.2.3) and (4.2.4) represent firms' optimal choices. Since the firm's profit function is concave in $e$, and constraint (4.2.4) is linear in $e$, the problem (4.2.3, 4.2.4) has a global maximum.[4] This means that the constraint (4.2.3, 4.2.4) can be replaced by the corresponding first-order conditions. Cases (i) and (ii) above can be examined.

(i)      Since $m_i=0$, it follows that $f_i(m_i)=0$ and $h_i(0)=\gamma_i$. The Lagrangean for this problem is:

$$\mathcal{L}=\sum_{i=1}^{n} B_i(e_i)-D(e)+\sum_{i=1}^{n}\lambda_i\left[B'(e_i)-\gamma_i\right]$$

with first-order conditions

$$B_i'-D'+\lambda_i B_i''\leq 0,\ e_i\geq 0$$

$$-\gamma_i\lambda_i\leq 0,\ \gamma_i\geq 0$$

$$B_i'-\gamma_i=0$$

For interior solutions, we have $\lambda_i=0$ and $\gamma_i=D'$.

(ii)     Since $m_i\geq\bar{m}_i$, it follows that $h_i(m_i)=0$, $f_i(m_i)=e_i$. The Lagrangean for the problem is:

$$\mathcal{L}=\sum_{i=1}^{n} B_i(e_i)-D(e)+\sum_{i=1}^{n}\lambda_i\left[B_i'(e_i)-\tau_i\right]$$

The first-order conditions are the same as before with $\gamma_i$ replaced by $\tau_i$. Therefore for interior solutions, $\lambda_i=0$ and $\tau_i=D'$.

When there is no observability, the producers are liable for an ambient tax equal to marginal damages per unit deviation from the cut-off level. The producer facing this scheme will adjust its production and abatement process such that marginal benefits from emissions equal marginal damages, adopting therefore the socially-desirable emission levels. Under full observability the polluter discharges the socially-desired emissions when the tax per unit of its

---

[4]A global maximum further requires that the sets where individual emissions $e_i$ are defined be compact and convex.

own emissions is equal to marginal damages.

In this type of NPS pollution problem the regulator has no incentive to increase observability by increasing $m_i$ since it can achieve the social optimum by setting the ambient tax to the optimal level. Furthermore there is no incentive from the firm's point of view to reveal information about its emissions and as a result of this pay an effluent fee in exchange for a low ambient tax rate. This can be demonstrated as follows.

The maximum profit of the firm is defined, as a function of $m_i$ and for an optimal choice $e_i^{\,o} < f_i(m_i)$, by the concave function:

$$\pi_i(m_i) = \max_{e_i} \left[ B_i(e_i) - h_i(m_i)(e - e^*) - \tau_i f_i(m_i) \right]$$

The optimal choice of $m_i \geq 0$, can be determined by the envelope theorem. The optimality condition requires that:

$$-h_i'(m_i^{\,o})(e - e^*) - \tau_i f_i'(m_i^{\,o}) \leq 0, \ m^{\,o} \geq 0$$

If $e_i^{\,o} = e_i^*$ for all $i$, then $e = e^*$ and we have

$$-\tau_i f_i'(m_i^{\,o}) < 0 \text{ therefore } m_i^{\,o} = 0$$

Thus the firm will not reveal any information about its emissions; furthermore if the regulator's choice is $m_i = 0$, this value is optimal from the firm's point of view.

This result means that if the ambient tax is set at the level of marginal damages and there is no uncertainty, the firms that have adjusted their emissions to the desirable emission level are not willing to pay any effluent fee, by having their emissions measured or by revealing some information to the regulator, in order to be liable for a lower ambient tax rate. Since neither the regulator nor the firm have any incentive to increase $m_i$ from zero, it is socially optimal to have individual emissions remain unmonitored (or unobserved) in an NPS pollution problem, and use ambient taxes alone.

## 2.1 Ambient Taxes under Stock Externalities

Ambient taxes for an NPS pollution problem can also be defined in the context of stock pollution, using the dynamic models that were developed in Chapter 3.

In particular let $S^*(t)$, $\lambda(t)$, and $e_i^*(t)$, be the socially-optimal path for the stock of the pollutant, its shadow cost and the individual emissions for firm $i = 1, \dots n$, respectively with corresponding long-run equilibrium levels $S_\infty^*$, $\lambda_\infty$, $e_{i\infty}^*$ for $t \to \infty$, as derived by the solution of the social optimization problem in Chapter 3, Section 2. Under an NPS pollution problem the regulator cannot observe individual emissions but only the ambient stock $S(t)$. The objective of the regulator is to develop an incentive scheme based on the deviations between the observed ambient pollutant's stock and the socially-optimal stock of the pollutant, $z(t) \equiv S(t) - S^*(t)$. Following Xepapadeas (1992b) let $\phi(z(t))$ be a function with the following properties:

$$\phi(z) \gtreqless 0 \text{ as } z \gtreqless 0, \text{ with } \phi' > 0, \ \phi'' \geq 0$$

Let $S(\phi, t)$ be the path of pollution accumulation when profit-maximizing firms are subject to the incentive scheme $\phi$. The scheme will be efficient if $S(\phi, t) \to S_\infty^*$ as $t \to \infty$. It should be noted that the comparison is between the steady state corresponding to the social optimum and the regulated equilibrium under the incentive scheme and not along the entire optimal path.[5] So under the efficient scheme the observed steady state for the stock of the pollutant coincides with the socially-optimal steady state.[6]

The fact that the scheme depends on the observed stock $S(t)$ which in turn is determined by individual emissions implies that each potential polluter's benefit function is affected by the actions of the rest of the firms. This implies strategic interactions among firms of a type similar to that described in Chapter 3, Section 5. Thus the incentive scheme needs to be analysed in the context of an $n$-player noncooperative dynamic game. We concentrate on feedback information structures with linear Markov strategies.[7] Therefore it is assumed that:

$$e_i(t) = \bar{e}_i + \beta S(t), \ \beta < 0 \tag{4.3}$$

The pay-off for a potential polluter $i$ under the incentive scheme is defined as:

$$J_i(e_1(t), ..., e_n(t)) = \int_o^\infty e^{-rt} \big[ B_i(e_i) - \phi(z) \big] dt, \ i = 1, ..., n$$

The feedback Nash equilibrium (FBNE) will be an $n$-tuple of feedback strategies $(e_1^o(t), ..., e_n^o(t))$, with $e_i$ defined by (4.3) such that:

---

[5]For a similar approach for the case of public goods provisions, see Fershtman and Nitzan (1991).

[6]For the development of an incentive scheme, which is, however, considerably more complicated in its definition, such that the whole path under the scheme coincides with the socially-optimal path, see Xepapadeas (1994).

[7]For the analysis of open-loop information structures and nonlinear Markov strategies, see Xepapadeas (1992b).

$$J_i(e_1^o,...,e_n^o) \geq J_i(e_1^o,...,e_{i-1}^o,e_i,e_{i+1}^o,...,e_n^o)$$

Thus polluter $i$ solves the problem:

$$\max_{\{e_i(t)\}} J_i(e_1(t),...,e_n(t))$$

$$\text{s. t. } \dot{S}(t) = \sum_{i=1}^{n} e_i(t) - bS(t), \quad S(0) = S_o > 0, \text{ and } (4.3)$$

(4.4)

If we assume symmetric polluters the efficient incentive scheme is defined as:

$$\phi(z(t)) = -\lambda^*(t)[(r+b)-(n-1)\beta]z(t)$$

To show the efficiency of the scheme consider the current value Hamiltonian for the firm under the scheme, defined as:

$$H_i = B_i(e_i) + \lambda^*[(r+b)-(n-1)\beta]z + \lambda_i^{FB}\left[e_i + \sum_{j \neq i}(\bar{e}_j + \beta S) - bS\right]$$

The optimality conditions for interior solutions are:

$$B_i'(e_i^o) = -\lambda_i^{FB}$$ (4.5.1)

$$\dot{\lambda}_i^{FB} = [(r+b)-(n-1)\beta](\lambda_i^{FB} - \lambda^*)$$ (4.5.2)

$$\dot{S} = \sum_{i=1}^{n} e_i^o - bS$$ (4.5.3)

In equilibrium $\dot{\lambda}_i^{FB} = 0$, therefore $\lambda_\infty = \lambda_{i\infty}^{FB}$ for all $i$. Then it follows from (4.5.1) that $e_{i\infty}^* = e_{i\infty}^o$, and from (4.5.3) that $S_\infty^o = \left(\sum_i e_{i\infty}^o\right)/b = S_\infty^*$. Therefore the incentive scheme reproduces the social optimum.

The incentive scheme defined above is a dynamic ambient tax determined as $\gamma(t) = -\lambda^*(t)[(r+b)-(n-1)\beta]$. The tax is applied at each point in time on the deviation between the observed stock $S(t)$ and the socially-optimal stock of the pollutant $S^*(t)$. It should be noted that, if past overemissions have caused deviations from the optimal path, then the firms will pay the charge during the period of adjustment to the optimal path even if they currently follow optimal environmental policies.

To compare the outcome in terms of pollution accumulation, if a static ambient tax is used when the pollution problem has stock characteristics, the following comparison can take place. Let the static ambient tax be defined as $\gamma(t) = -\lambda(t)z(t)$, $z(t) = S(t) - S^*(t)$. When this tax is applied to the stock pollution problem the firm solves:

$$\max_{\{e_i(t)\}} \int_o^\infty e^{-rt}\left[B_i(e_i(t)) + \lambda z\right]dt$$

subject to

$$\dot{S} = \sum_{i=1}^n e_i - bS, \quad S(0) = S_o$$

$$e_i = \bar{e}_i + \beta S, \quad \beta < 0$$

The current value Hamiltonian for the problem is defined as:

$$H_i = B_i(e_i) + \lambda z + \mu_i^{FB}\left[e_i + \sum_{j \neq i}(\bar{e}_j + \beta S) - \beta S\right]$$

From the optimality conditions we have:

$$\dot{\mu}_i^{FB} = \left[(r+b) - (n-1)\beta\right]\mu_i^{FB} - \lambda, \quad \forall i$$

or in the long-run steady state equilibrium, $\mu_{i\infty}^{FB} = \lambda_\infty / \left[(r+b)-(n-1)\beta\right]$. Thus

$$\mu_\infty^{FB} \gtreqless \lambda_\infty, \quad e_i^o(\mu_\infty^{FB}) \gtreqless e_i^*(\lambda_\infty), \quad \text{and} \quad S_\infty^o \gtreqless S_\infty^*, \quad \mu_\infty^{FB}, \lambda_\infty < 0$$

$$\text{as} \quad \left[(r+b)-(n-1)\beta\right] \gtreqless 1$$

This result implies that in general the application of static ambient tax schemes to stock pollution problems when there are strategic interactions on the polluters' part will in general lead to suboptimal results. If $\beta$ is sufficiently high in absolute value and/or the number of potential polluters is sufficiently large so that $(r+b)-(n-1)\beta > 1$, then the static scheme will lead to overemisssions as compared to the social optimum.

## 2.2 The Impact of Uncertainty

The analysis in the previous sections was based on the assumption that the observed ambient level of pollution was deterministic. This of course need not be the case in a real NPS pollution problem, since the pollution process that determines the ambient pollutant level depends on factors with stochastic characteristics. Having a stochastic ambient level does not change the nature of the ambient tax incentive scheme. As has been shown by Segerson (1988) ambient taxes can be defined in terms of expected marginal abatement benefits or equivalently expected marginal damages.

The NPS pollution model can be extended to include spatial considerations by examining a multiple-zone system with stochastic transport of pollutants across zones and with ambient measurement in specific zones (Cabe and

Herriges 1992). Again the ambient tax, which is zone specific, depends on expected marginal damages as well as the possible discrepancies between the *a priori* beliefs of the regulator and the polluters about the probability distribution of factors influencing the ambient pollution level in each zone.

In the context of a dynamic model, uncertainty can be introduced by having the ambient pollution determined by the stochastic differential equation introduced in Chapter 3, Section 6:[8]

$$dS(t) = \left[ \sum_{i=1}^{n} e_i(t) - bS(t) \right] dt + \omega(S(t)) d\zeta, \quad S(0) = S_o \text{ nonrandom}$$

Using the linear Markov strategy (4.3) and following the same line of approach as in the deterministic dynamic case of the previous section, the optimal ambient tax for each polluter is determined according to the incentive scheme:

$$\phi_i(z(t)) = -\mathscr{E}(\lambda(t))[(r+b) - (n-1)\beta]z(t) + \frac{1}{2}\sigma \mu_{iS}^{FB}(t)z(t)$$

$$z(t) = S(t) - \mathscr{E}(S^*(t))$$

where $\mathscr{E}(S^*(t))$, $\mathscr{E}(\lambda(t))$ are the socially-optimal expected values of the ambient pollution stock and its shadow cost, and $\mu_{iS}^{FB}$ reflects the risk aversion of the $i$th polluter. Triggering of ambient taxes due to small fluctuations around the socially-optimal expected value of the ambient pollution stock can be avoided if a confidence belt is added to the scheme. Observed values outside the belt are not to be regarded as resulting from random fluctuations and charges would be imposed.[9]

### 2.2.1 Uncertainty and combined instrument use

In the context described above the effects of uncertainty were to basically redefine the incentive scheme in terms of expected values and to take into account risk premia.

However in an NPS pollution problem uncertainty may have a different effect stemming from the fact that ambient taxes have a collective penalty character that makes the payment of each polluter dependent on the behaviour of the rest of the polluters along with the existing stochastic factors. Thus, although an ambient tax can in principle solve the NPS pollution problem, it

---

[8]See also Plourde and Yeung (1989) and Xepapadeas (1992b, 1992c).

[9]This is similar to the safety rule approach of Lichtenberg and Zilberman (1988) where the regulation of environmental risk is obtained by using the concepts of maximum allowable risk and margin of safety.

is very likely that the introduction and implementation of ambient taxes will be difficult. While individual dischargers might accept the idea of paying an effluent fee based on their own emissions, they may very well resent the idea of being liable for a tax which will strongly depend on other dischargers' actions, along with random factors, after they have internalized the social costs by adjusting their emissions to the socially-desirable level.

These factors suggest that any increase in observability of individual emissions in an NPS pollution problem, through for example investment in pollution monitoring equipment, that will lead to a reduction or even abolition of ambient taxes, might be desirable. The argument can be made more precise under uncertainty. In this case, the polluting firm might be liable for the payment of the ambient tax, even if it has adjusted its emissions to the optimal level, because the measured ambient pollutant level could exceed the expected cut-off level due to random shocks.

On the other hand, the ambient tax liability would have been zero if individual emissions had been observed. So observability of individual emissions might be regarded as some type of insurance for individual dischargers when the ambient pollutant level is stochastic. Of course, observability, especially in an NPS pollution case, might never be complete. But even in the incomplete case, individual polluters which are risk averters might be willing to pay an effluent fee on some observed part of their emissions after having internalized social costs, along with accepting liability for an ambient tax, if the introduction of an effluent fee meant a reduction in the ambient tax rate. In this way the polluter would be partly insured against the possibility of being liable for an ambient tax due to random effects.

In this context it could be socially desirable to introduce an instrument scheme consisting of an ambient tax and a Pigouvian tax, even if society has to incur the extra cost of monitoring individual emissions. Of course society need not incur any monitoring costs if polluters consider it optimal to reveal some part of their emissions in order to insure against random effects.

Using the analytical framework of Section 2 and following Xepapadeas (1995c), let the observed ambient concentration of the pollutant be a stochastic variable $\tilde{e} = \bar{e} + \epsilon$ where the stochastic element can be attributed to weather conditions. Expected total emissions are equal to the sum of individual emissions $\mathscr{E}(\tilde{e}) = \bar{e} = \Sigma_i \bar{e}_i$, while variance is denoted by $\sigma_\epsilon^2$. It is further assumed that the higher moments of $\tilde{e}$ are negligible compared to $\sigma_\epsilon^2$ ($\epsilon$ is small). Under uncertainty the social planner will choose an emission level such that marginal benefit equals expected marginal cost or $B'(e_i^*) = \mathscr{E}(D')$.

Denote the expected socially-optimal level of pollutant concentration as

$\mathcal{E}(e^*) \equiv e_m^*,$[10] and assume that firms are risk averters. Then their profit function can be written as:

$$\pi_i(e_i, m_i) = B_i(e_i) - h_i(m_i)\phi_i(\bar{e} - e_m^*) - \tau_i f_i(m_i)$$

where $\phi(.)$ is a smooth function with $\phi(0) = 0$, $\phi' > 0$, $\phi'' > 0$, $\phi''' \geq 0$. Using the assumption of small $\epsilon$, $\phi$ can be approximated as:

$$\phi_i(\bar{e} + \epsilon - e_m^*) \approx \phi_i(\bar{e} - e_m^*) + \epsilon \phi_i'(\bar{e} - e_m^*) + \frac{\epsilon^2}{2}\phi_i''(\bar{e} - e_m^*)$$

It follows, since $\mathcal{E}(\epsilon) = 0$, that:

$$\mathcal{E}[\phi_i(\bar{e} - e_m^*)] \approx \phi_i(\bar{e} - e_m^*) + \frac{\sigma_\epsilon^2}{2}\phi_i''(\bar{e} - e_m^*)$$

Substituting this expression into the profit function, we obtain expected profits as:

$$\mathcal{E}[\pi_i(e_i, m_i)] = B_i(e_i) - h_i(m_i)\left[\phi_i + \frac{\sigma_\epsilon^2}{2}\phi_i''\right] - \tau_i f_i(m_i) \tag{4.6}$$

Using the above definition of expected profits, it can be shown that if:

(i)      firms are risk averse,
(ii)     $\sigma_\epsilon^2$ is sufficiently large, and
(iii)    $\tau \in (0, [-g_i'(0)/f_i'(0)](\sigma_\epsilon^2/2)\phi_i''(0))$,

then the value of $m_i$ consistent with private optimum in an NPS pollution problem is positive.[11]

This result means that, although the environmental regulator can choose not to exercise any monitoring effort and to rely on an ambient tax to achieve the optimum, the choice of no monitoring is not always optimal from the firm's point of view if the variance of the observed ambient pollutant is large. Thus the firm will be willing to adjust its emissions so that the expected optimal ambient pollutant is achieved and in addition to pay an effluent fee on some observed part of its socially-optimal emissions in exchange for a low ambient tax rate. In this way, the firm reduces its ambient tax liability if random effects cause observed ambient pollutant to exceed the corresponding expected levels. Under these conditions, the profit-maximizing tax scheme for the firm is not $(h_i(0), \tau_i = 0)$ but the combination

---

[10]It can easily be shown by using Jensen's inequality that since $(-D)$ is concave, the social planner is risk averse and $e_m^* < e^*$.

[11]For the proof see Xepapadeas (1995c).

of $(h_i(\hat{m}), \hat{\tau})$ that satisfies:

$$h_i'(\hat{m}_i) \frac{\sigma_\epsilon^2}{2} \phi_i''(0) + \hat{\tau}_i f_i'(\hat{m}) = 0 \tag{4.7}$$

Thus the optimal level of parameter $m$ as defined in (4.7) is such that the extra cost that firms pay for the effluent fee equals the ambient tax liability savings. In other words, by revealing for example information about their own emissions and choosing $\hat{m}_i > 0$ as an optimal value, the firms are insured against the possibility of paying high ambient taxes due to random shocks.

From (4.7) we can also obtain:

$$\frac{dm_i}{\partial \sigma_\epsilon^2} = -\frac{h_i' \phi_i''}{2\left(h_i'' \frac{\sigma_\epsilon^2}{2} + \tau_i f_i''\right)} > 0$$

Thus an increase in variance will increase the optimal value of $m_i$. This implies that for some sufficiently large $\sigma_\epsilon^2$, the optimal $m_i$ could be equal to $\bar{m}_i$ which means that the firm is willing to reveal all its emissions in order to be fully insured against the possibility of paying a high ambient tax due to random fluctuations.[12]

Equation (4.7) cannot be used, however, for policy purposes since $\hat{\tau}_i$ is not defined. The problem of the environmental regulator, therefore, is to choose the optimal tax scheme $(h_i(m_i^*), \tau_i^*)$, with $m_i^*, \tau_i^* \geq 0$.

The scheme will be optimal if private emissions result in the socially-desirable ambient pollution and if the tax parameters are consistent with the private profit maximization. The regulator's problem can be stated in terms of the implicit programming problem:

$$\max_{(e,m,\tau) \geq 0} \sum_{i=1}^n B_i(e_i) - \mathscr{E}[D(\tilde{e})] - \sum_{i=1}^n c_i(m_i) \tag{4.8}$$

$$\text{s. t. } \tilde{e} = \bar{e} + \epsilon, \ \bar{e} = \sum_{i=1}^n e_i \tag{4.8.1}$$

---

[12]If firms are risk lovers, that is, $\phi'' < 0$, then $m_i^o = 0$. In this case, firms would rather gamble on weather conditions than pay an effluent fee once they have adjusted their emissions to the optimal level.

$$(e_i, m_i) \in \underset{e_i, m_i}{\text{argmax}} \ \{B_i(e_i) - h_i(m_i)[\phi_i(\bar{e} - e_m^*) +$$

$$\frac{\sigma_\epsilon^2}{2} \phi_i''(\bar{e} - e_m^*)] - \tau_i f_i(m_i)\} \tag{4.8.2}$$

$$\text{s. t. } f_i(m_i) \le e_i \tag{4.8.3}$$

In this problem the term $c_i(m_i)$ is assumed to reflect cost associated with the choice of a positive $m_i$. It can be interpreted as the monitoring cost of the regulator if it decides to commence individual monitoring. The optimality conditions for this problem imply that optimal emissions, in the case where the regulator is involved in costly individual monitoring, are less than the optimal emissions in the case of no individual monitoring. No monitoring corresponds to the case in which only monitoring at the ambient receptor point takes place.[13] This, however, might not be entirely satisfactory from society's point of view, since the reduction in the desired emission level is a result not of environmental damages caused by these emissions, but rather of increased monitoring costs associated with them. But the monitoring aims at insuring firms against uncertainties, and as has been shown above, firms are willing to reveal a positive $m_i$. Thus it might not be desirable from the society's point of view to incur monitoring costs in order to determine the tax parameters. The alternative would be to choose the effluent tax parameter $\tau_i$ in a way that would induce individual firms to reveal the socially-optimal $m_i$.

As shown by Xepapadeas (1995c), if firms can reveal information about their own emissions without cost, then a tax scheme consisting of a menu of an ambient tax and an emission tax determined as:

$$h_i(m_i^*) = \frac{B_i'(e_i^*)}{\phi_i'(0) + \frac{\sigma_\epsilon^2}{2} \phi_i'''(0)}, \quad \tau_i^* = -\frac{h_i'(m_i^*) \frac{\sigma_\epsilon^2}{2} \phi_i''(0)}{f_i'(m_i^*)}$$

where $e_i^*$ is the solution of $B_i'(e_i^*) = \mathscr{E}(D')$ for all $i$, is socially optimal in the sense that: (i) the triple $(e_i^*, m_i^*, \tau_i^*)$ maximizes the social welfare indicator (4.8) for $c_i(m_i) \equiv 0$, and (ii) firms are induced to reveal to the regulator $m_i^*$. This result indicates that by solving a welfare maximization problem under the assumptions of zero individual monitoring cost, the regulator can choose

---

[13]The optimality conditions are derived by substituting the optimizing constraint with the corresponding first-order conditions (Xepapadeas 1995c).

a menu of instruments that includes an appropriate emission tax, that will induce risk-averse polluters to reveal the socially-optimal information about their own emissions. If uncertainties are large, the NPS pollution problem might be transformed into a PS pollution problem since the firms themselves reveal all their emissions in order to insure against the possibility of paying the ambient tax.

Thus when the measured ambient concentration of a pollutant is stochastic and firms are risk averters, profit-maximizing firms are willing, after internalizing social costs, to pay an effluent fee on an observed part of their emissions, which they reveal themselves, in exchange for a lower ambient tax rate. In this way firms are insured against the possibility of paying ambient taxes because of random shocks. By contrast, under certainty there is no incentive either for firms to reveal emissions or for the regulator to incur monitoring costs, and thus it is optimal to leave individual emissions completely unmonitored. This leads to the basic result that under uncertainty, the efficient policy scheme consists of a mix of effluent taxes and ambient taxes. Since the firms reveal their own emissions, the regulator need not incur any monitoring costs.[14]

Under the mixed regulatory scheme the ambient tax serves two purposes. First it internalizes the social cost, and second it transforms, at least partially, an NPS into a PS pollution problem. Even if firms do not reveal all their emissions, the regulator can accumulate information revealed by the firms and gradually form an accurate picture of individual emissions. In this sense an NPS pollution situation can be regarded, not as an entirely new problem, but as a special case of the PS pollution situation into which it can be transformed by an appropriate policy.

It should be noticed that even without uncertainty a mixed scheme might be desirable. If the benefits from reducing ambient taxes, which can be related to political economy issues – acceptability of ambient taxes by groups of potential polluters – are taken into account, then it might be socially desirable for the government to undertake an investment program in monitoring equipment. In this case the optimal policy will consist of a triplet of ambient taxes, emission taxes on the observed part of emissions and a path of investment for the accumulation of capital in monitoring.[15]

---

[14]In the context of an agricultural NPS pollution problem it should be noted that, even when farmers cannot quantify emissions themselves, they can reveal information about their emissions, by revealing rates of inputs used and the method of application, to a regulator who can use this information to infer their contribution to ambient pollution.

[15]For a detailed analysis of this problem in a dynamic context, see Xepapadeas (1994).

## 3   COLLECTIVE PENALTIES AND BUDGET-BALANCING SCHEMES

As the analysis of ambient taxes suggests, payments by all potential polluters are triggered when measured ambient pollutant levels at receptor points exceed some desired cut-off level. This of course gives the ambient tax incentive scheme the character of a collective penalty. The collective penalty character can be further intensified by adding to the scheme a fixed penalty that is independent of the size of deviations between observed and desired ambient pollution levels.[16] The structure of the collective penalty scheme can be described as follows.

Consider the output-abatement choice model (OACM) developed in Chapter 2. The optimal output and abatement levels, $(q_i^*, a_i^*)$, $i=1,...,n$, determine the optimal ambient pollution level as $e^* = \Sigma_i e_i^*$, $e_i^* = s_i(q_i^*, a_i^*)$. The social value of abatement can then be defined as:

$$SB = D'(e^*) \sum_{i=1}^{n} a_i^*$$

Consider now the case in which the environmental regulator cannot observe individual emissions or abatement efforts but only ambient pollution $e$ at some receptor point. This is again an NPS pollution problem characterized by moral hazard with hidden actions. Each individual polluter would choose, for any given level of (optimal) output, lower abatement levels since by doing so private profits can be increased. The regulator seeks to subsidize[17] optimal abatement for any given (optimal) output,[18] by offering specific subsidy contracts to the potential polluters.

Let $b_i$ be the subsidy received by discharger $i$ and let $TR$ be the exogenously given transaction cost associated with opening negotiations between the agency and the dischargers, and enforcing the contracts. Since optimal abatement is pursued, total subsidy, assuming $TR < SB$, must be $\Sigma_i b_i = SB - TR = RSB$. The discharger's profit for any given (optimal) output is:[19]

$$\pi_i(b_i, a_i) = \pi_i^o + b_i - c_i(a_i) \tag{4.9}$$

---

[16]See Meran and Schwalbe (1987) and Segerson (1988).

[17]The tax case can be treated symmetrically.

[18]This can be thought of as a two-stage process. In the first stage abatement is selected optimally, while in the second stage output is selected.

[19]$q$ is dropped from the definition of functions in order to simplify notation.

where $\pi_i^o$ is profit corresponding to given output without any subsidy or abatement and $c_i(a_i)$ is the minimal cost of abatement function.

A contract will be efficient if it satisfies the following Pareto optimality condition.[20] The vector of subsidies $b^* = (b_1^*,...,b_n^*)$ is Pareto optimal if subsidies $b_i^o$ and abatement levels $a_i^o$ do not exist such that:

(i)      $\pi_i(b_i^o,a_i^o) \geq \pi_i(b_i^*,a_i^*)$

(ii)     for some $i$, $\pi_i^o(b_i^o,a_i^o) > \pi_i(b_i^*,a_i^*)$

Let $a_i^o \in [0,a_i^*)$ denote the suboptimal 'cheating' abatement of polluter $i$, and let $a_{-i}^* = (a_1^*,...,a_{i-1}^*,a_{i+1}^*,...,a_n^*)$ be the vector of optimal abatement levels of the rest of the dischargers. Pareto optimality implies that polluter $i$ will never follow cheating abatement given that the rest of the polluters follow optimal abatement policies if profits under optimal abatement exceed profits under 'cheating abatement' or,

$$\Omega_i = \pi_i(b_i^o,a_i^o,a_{i-1}^*) - \pi_i(b_i^*,a_i^*,a_{i-1}^*) < 0, \ \forall \ a_i^o \in [0,a_i^*) \qquad (4.10)$$

When the optimal abatement levels are chosen then the marginal benefits from abatement equal the marginal abatement costs for every polluter $i$. Then the Pareto optimality condition using relationship (2.2.2) of Chapter 2, Section (2.2.2) implies that:

$$-D'(e^*)\frac{\partial s_i(q_i^*,a_i^*)}{\partial a_i} = \frac{\partial c_i(q_i^*,a_i^*)}{\partial a_i}, \ \forall \ a_i^* > 0 \qquad (4.11)$$

Using this framework the design of some efficient contracts of a collective penalty type can be examined.

In general we can distinguish between two types of contracts: non-budget-balancing (NBB) contracts, and budget-balancing (BB) contracts.[21]

## 3.1 NBB Contracts

An NBB contract implies that the total payment to the polluters, which is positive in the case of a subsidy, or negative in the case of a tax, exceeds the social value of abatement or emissions. It can easily be seen that an ambient tax is an NBB type contract since each polluter pays the whole social value of deviation between the desired and the observed ambient pollution level.

---

[20]See Holmstrom (1982) and Rasmusen (1987).
[21]NBB contracts were introduced by Holmstrom (1982), while BB contracts in the context of the theory of teams were introduced by Rasmusen (1987).

From the analysis of the ambient taxes in Section 2 it is clear that the sum of payments, if the ambient tax is triggered, $\Sigma_i D'(e^*)(e-e^*)$, exceeds the social cost of the deviation from the cut-off rate which is $D'(e^*)(e-e^*)$.

Alternative collective penalty NBB contracts can be defined as follows. Let $\phi_i = a_i^*/\Sigma a_i^*$ be polluter $i$'s share of total optimal abatement and let $\Gamma(e)$ be the social cost of excess pollution over the desired level $e^*$, that is, $\Gamma(e) = \Gamma(a_i, a_{-i}) = -D'(e^*)(e-e^*)$, when one or more polluters do not follow the optimal abatement policy. The following contract can be defined as:

$$b_i = \begin{cases} b_i^* = \phi_i RSB, & \text{if } \Gamma(e) = 0 \\ \phi_i RSB + k_i \Gamma(e) - \delta_i, & k_i, \delta_i \geq 0, \text{ if } \Gamma(e) < 0 \end{cases}$$

Thus if there is no deviation from the desired level of pollution, each firm receives a share of social benefits equal to its abatement share of total optimal abatement. If, however, deviations are observed then the terms $k_i\Gamma(e)$ and $\delta_i k_i$ can be adjusted in order to act as a collective penalty producing the desired outcome. The following cases can be distinguished depending on the choices of $k_i$ and $\delta_i$.

(i)      $k_i = 0$

In this case the contract is efficient if $\delta_i$ is chosen such that:

$$\delta_i > c_i(a_i^*) - c_i(a_i^o), \ \forall \ a_i^o \in [0, a_i^*)$$

This is a penalty scheme similar to the one proposed by Meran and Schwalbe (1987) for the case of taxation. The penalty is chosen in such a way as to eliminate any benefits in terms of cost savings from shrinking comparative to the optimal abatement effort.

(ii)     $k_i = 1, \ \delta_i = 0$

Under this scheme the optimal abatement is determined as the solution of the maximization problem:

$$\max_{a_i \geq 0} \pi_i^o + \phi_i RSB - D'(e^*)(e-e^*) - c_i(a_i)$$

with first-order conditions for interior solution:

$$-D'(e^*)\frac{\partial s_i(a_i^*)}{\partial a_i} = \frac{\partial c_i(a_i^*)}{\partial a_i}$$

This is however the Pareto optimality condition (4.11) which means that under the above scheme the optimal abatement effort is undertaken. If ambient pollution standards are exceeded then each polluter's subsidy is reduced by the full social cost of the reduced abatement. Thus the total reduction in the subsidies exceeds the social cost of excess pollution, which indicates the collective penalty character of the contract. The individual polluter chooses, however, the optimal abatement effort by comparing marginal cost savings from reduced abatement to the full marginal cost due to reduced abatement. Thus the optimal abatement level is chosen. This contract is similar to a deterministic equivalent of the scheme proposed by Segerson (1988). Moral hazard is prevented without distorting marginal incentives.

(iii) $k_i = \phi_i$

From (4.10) the contract is efficient if $\delta_i$ is chosen such that

$$\delta_i > c_i(a_i^*) - c(a_i^o) + \phi_i \Gamma(a_i^o, a_{-i}^*), \ \forall \ a_i^o \in [0, a_i^*)$$

In this case each polluter pays the share of the social cost that he/she creates plus a fixed penalty. The penalty $\delta_i$ is chosen to offset any benefits to a single polluter from the distribution of the 'cost of cheating' among all polluters while keeping the whole benefits from cheating.

(iv) $\delta_i$ is chosen arbitrarily

From (4.10) the value of $k_i$ for the efficient contract is defined as:

$$k_i D'(e^*) > \frac{c_i(a_i^*) - c_i(a_i^o) - \delta_i}{(e - e^*)}, \ \forall \ a_i^o \in [0, a_i^*)$$

In a sense the above contract has the characteristics of a modified ambient tax $a_i^+ = k_i D'(e^*)$, for a given choice of a fixed fine $\delta_i > 0$. Since, as shown in case (ii) above, $k_i = 1$ when $\delta_i = 0$, the scheme defined in this case is an ambient tax lower than the optimal ambient tax combined with a fixed fine.

The analysis of the NBB contracts indicate therefore that appropriate collective penalty schemes exist either of an ambient tax type or of a fixed fine type or of some combination of the two that can achieve the socially-desired solution.

The common characteristic of these contracts is that the amount paid by the polluters once the penalty is triggered exceeds the social cost of the excess pollution that causes the triggering of the penalty. This, however, might not be a satisfactory solution; collective penalties might place a financial strain on the whole group of firms, especially if the abatement efforts are close to the desired levels, and any gains from free riding are not likely to be substantial. In this case a balanced-budgeting approach might produce a more acceptable form of regulation.

## 3.2  BB Contracts

Under a BB contract, in the context of the NPS pollution problem discussed here, the polluters as a group are subsidized for abating pollution. The amount of subsidy to be distributed among polluters depends on the deviations between the observed level of ambient pollution and the desired or cut-off level at the receptor point. The smaller the deviation is, the larger the amount of subsidy to be distributed. When the desired ambient standards are exceeded one or more polluters are liable for a fine, while the rest of the polluters still receive some subsidies. The fines, along with the initial subsidy, are distributed back among the remaining firms that have not been fined. Thus the BB contract allocates to polluters in the group the total amount of subsidy that corresponds to any deviation between measured and desired ambient pollution levels.

Contracts of a BB type introduced by Xepapadeas (1991) in the area of environmental policy for NPS pollution problems can be defined as follows, keeping the same notation as in the case of NBB contracts above. If no deviations between measured and desired ambient pollution levels are observed, that is, $\Gamma(e)=0$, then each polluter receives the optimal subsidy $b_i^* = \phi_i RSB$. If, however, a deviation is observed, $\Gamma(e)<0$, then one polluter is selected randomly, say polluter $m$, and pays a fine $F_m$ with probability $\xi_m$, losing at the same time his/her subsidy. The rest of the polluters receive a subsidy plus a share of the fine paid by the polluter that was fined in the first place. The random penalty BB scheme takes the form:

$$b_i = \begin{cases} b_i^* = \phi_i RSB, & \text{if } \Gamma(e)=0 \\ -F_i, & \text{if } \Gamma(e)<0, \text{ with probability } \xi_i \in (0,1) \\ b_i^* + \phi_{im}\left[b_m^* + F_m + \Gamma(e)\right], & \text{if } \Gamma(e)<0, \text{ with probability } 1-\xi_i \end{cases}$$

where

$$\phi_{im} = \frac{\phi_i}{\sum\limits_{i \neq m} \phi_i}$$

It can be seen that the above contract balances the budget, since for $\Gamma(e)<0$

$$\sum_{i=1}^{n} b_i = -F_m + \sum_i b_i^* + \sum_i \phi_{im}\left[b_m^* + F_m + \Gamma(e)\right] = RSB + \Gamma(e), \ i \neq m$$

That is, total distributed subsidy equals the social value of the abatement reduced by the excess pollution cost due to the deviations from the desired ambient pollution level. Thus the contract balances the budget in the sense of distributing the total net social benefits from pollution reduction, without penalizing in excess of the pollution costs which are created by emissions causing deviations between measured and desired ambient pollution levels.

As shown by Herriges et al. (1994),[22] if polluters maximize the expected utility from profits and they are sufficiently risk averse in the sense of having sufficiently high constant absolute risk aversion, then the parameters of the contract can be determined in such a way that polluters choose the optimal abatement levels. In this sense the BB contract is efficient.

The BB contracts can be regarded as having certain informational advantages over the more conventional policy instruments. As noted by Herriges et al. (1994) the random fine mechanism underlying the BB contracts does not require knowledge of individual abatement efforts of each potential polluter but rather monitoring at the receptor point. Furthermore the BB character of the contract implies that no additional revenues are required beyond the welfare gains generated by abatement, and that in the case of taxes and not subsidies for pollution reduction, the total amount collected does not exceed the social cost of excess pollution.

On the other hand there could be problems associated with the acceptability of the instrument by the group of potential polluters, since the idea of the random fine might not be readily acceptable or there might be legal problems associated with the enforcement of random fine mechanisms. Finally it should be noted that for the successful application of the contract all potential polluters should participate. When uncontrolled potential polluters exist the enforceability of the contract cannot be guaranteed.

## 4  INPUT-BASED INCENTIVE SCHEMES

Input-based incentive schemes, also called indirect schemes, were first suggested by Griffin and Bromley (1982). In its simplest form this approach states that if unobservable emissions are perfectly correlated with an observed input and if there are no informational problems associated with the type of the potential polluters, then the first-best policy can be obtained by appropriately taxing the observed input.

However, the implementation of such input taxes is most likely to be impeded by informational asymmetries due to imperfect correlation between individual emissions and the observed variables. In such a case the approach is basically to build models describing the interactions between production technologies and environmental pollution. These combined economic-

---

[22]See also Hanley et al. (1997).

biophysical models can then be used to estimate individual emissions, by relating observable inputs used by the potential polluters and measured ambient concentration of pollutants. Provided that the models can be granted 'political legitimacy' they can be used as a basis for designing incentive schemes, such as economic instruments based on the individual emissions estimated by the biophysical models, or on the use of observed polluting inputs or management practice standards.

Input-based incentive schemes can easily be derived under perfect information in the context of the input choice model of Chapter 2, Section 2.2.3. Assume that the producer faces an input tax $\tau_i^p$ on polluting inputs and receives a subsidy $\tau_i^a$ on abatement inputs. The producer solves the problem:

$$\max_{\left(x_i^p, x_i^a\right) \geq 0} pf(x_i^p) - w_i^p x_i^p - w_i^a x_i^a - \tau_i^p x_i^p + \tau_i^a x_i^a$$

By combining the first-order conditions for interior solutions of the above problem with those of the ICM of Chapter 2 (2.4.1, 2.4.2), it is clear that input taxes and subsidies are defined as:

$$\tau_i^p = D' \frac{\partial s_i(x_i^{p*})}{\partial x_i^p}, \quad \tau_i^a = D' \frac{\partial h_i(x_i^{a*})}{\partial x_i^a}$$

It should be clear that the tax/subsidy scheme on inputs can be applied only when the biophysical emission process defined for the case as $e_i = s_i(x_i^p) - h_i(x_i^a)$ is known, that is when there is a perfect correlation between observed inputs and emissions. If the process is known and the model can be granted 'political legitimacy', then the regulator can use either input-based taxes/subsidies or emission taxes, since the observed input allows exact inference of the emissions, to achieve the social optimum.[23]

The complexity of the problem increases however if informational asymmetries or other uncertainties preclude the direct use of input taxes.

---

[23]The use of biophysical models underlies the work of Griffin and Bromley (1982), Shortle and Dunn (1986) and Dosi and Moretto (1992). Biophysical models for NPS pollution estimation in watersheds are more complicated than the simple one presented here, and include factors such as farm characteristics, agricultural practices, soil, hydrological and climatic conditions. For example, in Weaver (1996), the economic biophysical system can be described as:

$$f(q_i, x_i, \theta_i) = 0, \quad s(e_i, z, a_i, x_i, \theta_i) = 0$$

where $f$ describes production for producer $i$, and $s$ describes the emission process. $q_i$ is private output, $x_i$, $\theta_i$ are variable and quasi-variable inputs respectively, $e_i$ is emissions, $a_i$ denotes environmental effort or abatement, and $z$ denotes a public good input in the emission process. For a more detailed description of such models and empirical applications, see for example DeCoursey (1985), Vatn et al. (1996), Weaver et al. (1996).

These asymmetries relate to uncertainties about physical characteristics, farmers' abilities to follow practices and so on.[24] When in addition to the nonobservability of individual emissions – the moral hazard problem – the regulator has no specific information about the private characteristics of the potential polluter (such as ability, site quality) which are, however, private information for the discharger, there is an additional adverse selection problem.

Input-based incentive schemes in a case where moral hazard and adverse selection exist simultaneously, can be developed using recent advances in the theory of regulation under asymmetric information (Laffont 1994a).[25]

## 4.1 Input Taxes under Asymmetric Information

To make the discussion more relevant to a realistic NPS pollution problem we specify the problem to be one of agricultural pollution. Of course the model can be equally applied to other types of NPS pollution problems with similar characteristics. Thus we consider a region consisting of farmers that produce a homogeneous product. A continuum of farmers is further considered, with each farmer distinguished by his/her characteristic, or type, denoted by $\beta$. This characteristic could embody the farmer's ability, soil composition, or proximity to a receiving body. It is assumed that the types for all farmers belong to a certain interval $[\underline{\beta}, \bar{\beta}]$. The distribution of the farmers' types is characterized by the distribution function $F(\beta)$ with a strictly positive density $f(\beta)$. The price of the agricultural product is assumed to be

---

[24]See Dosi and Moretto (1994) for a model of regulation where the site quality of the potential polluter that affects emissions is uncertain and the regulator subsidizes improvements in site quality.

[25]The model presented here is based on Xepapadeas (1997c). A similar approach can be found in Shortle and Abler (1994), where individual emissions are stochastic and unobservable and the polluters' profits depend on private information. In this model input taxes and mixed schemes, consisting of input-based taxes/subsidies and permits for the use of polluting inputs, are used to control NPS pollution. Weaver and Thomas (1996) derive an input-based tax when the regulator cannot observe private characteristics associated with efficiency in the use of polluting inputs. Thomas (1995) estimates an emission tax based on an asymmetric information model where the efficiency of polluters in abatement is private knowledge. Laffont (1994b) also examines the regulation of pollution under asymmetric information. Laffont's model considers several cases such as monopoly regulation, regulation of industry, location issues and also examines one case of NPS pollution. In general, regulation is achieved by several schemes that include linear or nonlinear transfers, and Pigouvian taxes, personalized or uniform. In the same spirit, but using emission taxes instead of input taxes, Spulber (1988) derives an incentive scheme wherein the effluent tax and the effluent level depend on the combined announcement cost parameters of the firm.

determined exogenously. The production of output generates pollution that can be reduced if the farmer takes certain actions which imply monetary costs. The benefit function for any farmer of type $\beta$ can be defined as a function of his/her emissions as:

$$B(\beta) = B(e(\beta)) = \max_{q(\beta) \geq 0} \pi(q(\beta), e(\beta)) = \max_{q(\beta) \geq 0} [pq(\beta) - c((q(\beta), e(\beta)))]$$

where as usual $B(e(\beta))$ is a concave benefit function, $q$ is output, $e$ is emissions, $p$ is output price, and $c(\cdot, \cdot)$ is a strictly convex cost function. Since $\pi(q, e)$ is concave in $(q, e)$, $\max_q \pi(q, e)$ is concave in $e$.

The emissions generated by each farmer are defined as a function of an input $x$ used in the production process and the type $\beta$ of the farmer as:

$$e(\beta) = h(x(\beta)) - \beta + \epsilon, \ h_x > 0, \ h_{xx} < 0 \tag{4.12}$$

where $\epsilon$ is a random variable with zero mean that can be interpreted as an observational error of individual emissions. Thus farmers with relatively higher $\beta$ are regarded as having better characteristics with respect to pollution generation. Thus a high $\beta$ indicates that the farmer is relatively more efficient in pollution generation, emitting less than low $\beta$ farmers for given input $x$. Total emissions in the region are then defined as:

$$E = \int_{\underline{\beta}}^{\bar{\beta}} e(\beta) f(\beta) d\beta$$

Assuming furthermore a linear damage function, total damages from emissions are defined as $D = \alpha E$ with $\alpha$ being the constant marginal damages.

### 4.1.1 Regulation under complete information

Consider the problem of an environmental regulator that seeks to regulate pollution in the region, by maximizing regional welfare defined as the total value of the benefits generated by the farmers, less environmental damages. It is assumed that the regulator has complete information, that is, it can observe emissions $e$, and knows the type $\beta$ of each farmer.

It is furthermore assumed that public funds have a social price equal to $1 + \lambda$, with $\lambda > 0$.[26] Thus if the regulator collects total taxes, $t$, then these collected taxes have a value in terms of welfare of $\lambda t$. Under these assumptions regional welfare can be defined as follows.

---

[26] The positive social value of the collected environmental taxes could be justified both by standard arguments regarding the social cost of public funds and by more specific double dividend arguments.

The profits or rent of a farmer of type $\beta$ are defined as:

$$\pi(\beta) = B(e(\beta)) - t(\beta) \tag{4.13}$$

Then regional welfare is:

$$W = \int_{\underline{\beta}}^{\bar{\beta}} [B(e(\beta)) - \alpha e(\beta) + \lambda t(\beta)] f(\beta) d\beta$$

or, after substituting from (4.13):

$$W = \int_{\underline{\beta}}^{\bar{\beta}} [(1+\lambda) B(e(\beta)) - \alpha e(\beta) - \lambda \pi(\beta)] f(\beta) d\beta$$

This definition of welfare indicates that the environmental regulator does not want to leave a rent to the farmer, since rents reduce regional welfare. The objective of the regulator is to choose, under complete information, emissions $e$, and rents to be left to farmers $\pi$, so that regional welfare (4.14) is maximized subject to a participation constraint, which requires that regulation not drive farmers out of business. That is, $\pi(\beta) \geq 0$.

The first-order conditions for this maximization problem are:

$$B'(e^*) = \frac{\alpha}{1+\lambda} \tag{4.15.1}$$

$$\pi^* = 0, \text{ or } t = B(e^*) \tag{4.15.2}$$

It should be noticed in (4.15.1) that the marginal value product of emissions is less than marginal damages, since the social price of public funds exceeds unity ($\lambda > 0$). Furthermore by (4.15.2) the farmer receives no rent. The optimal regulatory scheme defined by (4.15.1) and (4.15.2) can be implemented in two ways:

(i)      The usual Pigouvian tax on emissions defined as $\tau_e = \alpha/(1+\lambda)$. The farmer then solves the problem $\max_{e \geq 0} B(e) - [\alpha/(1+\lambda)]e$ choosing thus emissions according to (4.15.1). In this case the Pigouvian tax is set below marginal damages, since the extra emissions that result from such a lower tax create tax revenue whose value balances on the margin the environmental cost of the extra emissions. This result can be compared to the one obtained in Chapter 2, Section 3.1.1 in which the optimal tax is less than marginal damages when the rest of the distorting taxes in the economy are taken into account.

(ii)     A tax on input $x$ defined as $\tau_x = (\alpha h_x(x^*))/(1+\lambda)$, where $x^*$ is defined by the relationship $e^* = h(x^*) - \beta$. In this case the farmer solves the problem:

$$\max_{x \geq 0} B(h(x) - \beta) - \left( \frac{\alpha h_x(x^*)}{1+\lambda} \right) x$$

choosing again emissions according to (4.15.1).

### 4.1.2 Regulation under incomplete information

In order to develop an asymmetric information framework it is assumed that the parameter $\beta$ is private information, known only to the specific farmer. Thus $\beta$ is the adverse selection parameter. On the other hand individual emissions are not observed outside the specific farm. Thus $e$ is the moral hazard parameter. The environmental regulator observes only the observed input $x$, and total emissions $E$, while for the moment the random variable $\epsilon$ is ignored.[27] Furthermore the regulator has a prior distribution function $F(\beta)$ on $[\underline{\beta}, \bar{\beta}]$ that satisfies the monotonous hazard rate assumption:[28]

$$\frac{d}{d\beta} \left( \frac{F(\beta)}{f(\beta)} \right) \geq 0$$

From the revelation principle any regulation mechanism is equivalent to a revelation mechanism $\{t(\hat{\beta}), x(\hat{\beta})\}$ that specifies for any announcement $\hat{\beta} \in [\underline{\beta}, \bar{\beta}]$ an aggregate tax $t$, and an input level $x$ to be realized by the farmer, that induces truthful revelation of the private information. Strictly speaking the scheme that each farmer faces should depend on the responses of the other farmers. Neglecting this possibility we are restricted to incentive schemes that depend only on the farmers' responses (Laffont 1989).

Let $\pi(\beta, \hat{\beta})$ be the profits for the specific farmer when his/her type is $\beta$ but he/she announces that his type is $\hat{\beta}$. Then profits are defined as:

$$\pi(\beta, \hat{\beta}) = B(h(x(\hat{\beta})) - \beta) - t(\hat{\beta}) \tag{4.16}$$

The regulation mechanism will induce truthful behavior if $\beta \in \text{argmax}_{\hat{\beta}} \pi(\beta, \hat{\beta})$. Thus truthtelling from the farmer's point of view with respect to his type requires that the announcement $\hat{\beta} = \beta$ maximize $\pi(\beta, \hat{\beta})$. Then the first-order condition for incentive compatibility is:

---

[27]It could be argued that if benefits can be observed then knowledge of the benefit function allows the inference of emissions. However, the inability to base a tax scheme on emissions inferred in such a way can be justified on technological or political grounds.
[28]See for example Laffont and Tirole (1993).

$$\frac{dt}{d\beta} = B'h_x \frac{dx}{d\beta} \qquad (4.17)$$

The local second-order condition requires $\partial^2\pi/\partial\beta\partial\hat{\beta} \geq 0$ (Guesnerie and Laffont 1984). This second-order condition is satisfied if:

$$-B''h_x\dot{x} \geq 0, \text{ or } \dot{x} \geq 0 \qquad (4.18)$$

By using $e = h(x) - \beta$, the second-order condition is satisfied if:

$$\dot{x} = \frac{\dot{e}+1}{h_x} \geq 0, \text{ or } \dot{e} \geq -1 \qquad (4.18.1)$$

Let $\pi(\beta) = B(h(x(\beta)) - \beta) - t(\beta)$ be the profits (rents) captured by a specific farmer when he is truth telling. The first-order condition for incentive compatibility can be written using the envelope theorem on the maximization of (4.16) with respect to $\hat{\beta}$ in a simpler form as:

$$\dot{\pi}(\beta) = -B'(h(x(\beta)) - \beta) \qquad (4.19)$$

Thus rents tend to increase for the less efficient types.

The participation constraint indicating that farmers' profits will not become negative[29] under the mechanism, which is equivalent to $\pi(\beta) \geq 0$ for any $\beta$, can be substituted by:

$$\pi(\bar{\beta}) \geq 0 \qquad (4.20)$$

since rents become smaller the more efficient the farmer is with respect to emissions. That is, the participation constraint is satisfied if at least the farmer with the best type with respect to emissions does not have losses under the mechanism.

In this context the regulator seeks to maximize regional social welfare subject to the incentive compatibility and participation constraints. The regulator's program is:

$$\max_{\{e(\beta) \geq 0\}} W = \int_{\underline{\beta}}^{\bar{\beta}} [(1+\lambda)B(e(\beta)) - \alpha e(\beta) - \lambda\pi(\beta)]f(\beta)d\beta$$

$$\text{subject to} \qquad (4.21)$$

$$\dot{\pi}(\beta) = -B'(e(\beta))$$

$$\dot{e}(\beta) \geq -1$$

$$\pi(\bar{\beta}) \geq 0$$

---

[29]The participation constraint could also be thought of as a limited liability constraint by requiring profits to exceed some negative number.

The Hamiltonian function for this problem is defined as:

$$H = [(1+\lambda)B(e(\beta)) - \alpha e - \lambda \pi] f(\beta) - \mu B'(e(\beta))$$

where $\mu(\beta)$ is the costate variable. By the maximum principle the optimality conditions require that:

$$\frac{\partial H}{\partial e} = 0 \qquad\qquad (4.22.1)$$

and

$$\dot{\mu}(\beta) = -\frac{\partial H}{\partial \pi} = \lambda f(\beta) \qquad\qquad (4.22.2)$$

Since $\pi(\beta)$ is unconstrained the transversality condition at $\beta = \bar{\beta}$ implies $\mu(\bar{\beta}) = 0$. Thus integrating (4.22.2) we obtain:

$$\mu(\beta) = \lambda F(\beta) \qquad\qquad (4.22.3)$$

Using the optimality conditions (4.22.1)-(4.22.3), the optimal regulatory mechanism, which characterizes the social optimum, can be described as follows:

$$B'(e^*(\beta)) = \frac{\alpha}{1+\lambda} + \frac{\lambda}{1+\lambda} \frac{F(\beta)}{f(\beta)} B''(e^*(\beta)) \qquad\qquad \text{(i)}$$

$$\pi^*(\beta) = \int_\beta^{\bar{\beta}} B'(e^*(\tilde{\beta})) d\tilde{\beta} \qquad\qquad \text{(ii)}$$

$$t^*(\beta) = B(e^*(\beta)) - \pi^*(\beta) \qquad\qquad \text{(iii)}$$

$$x^*(\beta) : e^*(\beta) = h(x^*(\beta)) - \beta \qquad\qquad \text{(iv)}$$

Relationship (i) defines optimal emissions. It can be seen that only for the less efficient farmer with respect to pollution $(F(\beta) = 0)$ is there no incentive correction and the emissions are the same as optimal emissions under complete information. Since the incentive correction is a negative number $(B'' < 0)$ all farmers except those who are less pollution efficient emit more as compared to the complete information allocation. This is shown in Figure 4.1.

The most efficient farmer obtains a rent equal to zero while the least efficient farmer receives a rent equal to $\pi^*(\beta)$. Rents are left to less efficient farmers in order to secure truthful revelation of their type. By (ii) rents increase with emissions, but so do taxes and therefore double dividend extraction increases with emissions. Thus the optimal regulation tends to increase relatively more the emissions of the farmers who are more efficient with respect to pollution and reduce their rents in order to extract double dividends from environmental taxation. In a sense the optimal regulation increases relatively more the emissions of the most efficient farmers, whose informational rents can be suppressed, and reduces the emissions of the less efficient farmers to whom informational rents need to be given in order for them to reveal their types.

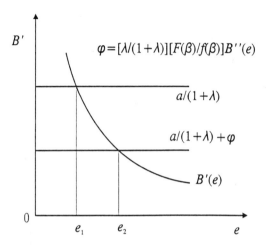

*Figure 4.1  Optimal emissions under complete and incomplete information*

Differentiating (i) with respect to $\beta$ we obtain:

$$\dot{e}(\beta) = \frac{\frac{\lambda}{1+\lambda} \frac{d}{d\beta} \left( \frac{F(\beta)}{f(\beta)} \right) B''(e(\beta))}{B'' - \frac{\lambda}{1+\lambda} \frac{F(\beta)}{f(\beta)} B'''(e(\beta))} \qquad (4.23)$$

Assume that $B''' \geq 0$, then from (4.23), we have that $\dot{e}(\beta) \geq 0$.[30] This means that farmers with better characteristics with respect to pollution emit more under the optimal regulatory scheme. This result can be related to the optimal regulatory mechanism defined above. The less efficient farmers with respect to pollution want to mimic the most efficient farmers so that they will be allowed to emit more and receive higher informational rents. But (4.23) implies that only the relatively more efficient farmers, with respect to

---

[30]The second-order condition for incentive compatibility is satisfied as $\dot{e}(\beta) \geq 0$ satisfies (4.18.1).

pollution, are allowed to emit more at the optimal regulation.

The regulatory scheme determined above is implemented by a tax on the observable input $x$. From part (iv) of the regulatory mechanism, the optimal level of the observable input is defined as $x^*(\beta) = H(e^*(\beta), \beta)$. Since $x^*(\beta)$ is monotonic in $\beta$ it can be inverted to define $\beta = \beta^*(x)$. Substituting in (iii) of the mechanism we obtain the tax as a function of the observable input:

$$t^*(\beta^*(x)) = T^*(x) = B(e^*(\beta^*(x)) - \pi^*(\beta^*(x)) \tag{4.24}$$

which is a nonlinear tax on observable input. The tax function $T^*(x)$ can be shown to be a concave function as follows:

$$\frac{dT}{dx} = \frac{dt}{d\beta}\frac{1}{dx/d\beta} = B'(h(x) - \beta^*(x))h_x$$

since  $\dfrac{dt}{d\beta} = B'(\dot{e}+1), \quad \dfrac{dx}{d\beta} = \dfrac{\dot{e}+1}{h_x}$

Then,

$$\frac{d^2T}{dx^2} = B''\left(\frac{h_x\dot{x}-1}{\dot{x}}\right)h_x + B'h_{xx} \le 0$$

since $h_x\dot{x} - 1 = \dot{e} \ge 0$. Thus $T(x^*)$ is a concave function. Because of its concavity the tax function can be replaced by the family of its tangents. These tangents represent linear tax schedules that can be used to implement the optimal regulatory mechanism. The linear input-based tax schedule takes the form:

$$t(\hat{\beta}, x) = t^*(\hat{\beta}) + \left[B'(e^*(\hat{\beta}))h_x(x^*(\hat{\beta}))\right](x - x^*(\hat{\beta})) \tag{4.25}$$

The linear tax schedule (4.25) induces: (i) truthtelling $\beta = \hat{\beta}$, (ii) the optimal emissions $e = e^*(\beta)$, and (iii) the optimal use of the observable input, $x = x^*(\beta)$. These properties of the linear tax can be shown by considering the farmer's program under the linear tax schedule:

$$\max_{(x,\hat{\beta})\ge 0} \ B(e) - \left[t^*(\hat{\beta}) + \left[B'(e^*(\hat{\beta}))h_x(x^*(\hat{\beta}))\right](x - x^*(\hat{\beta}))\right]$$

The first-order conditions for this problem, assuming interior solutions, are:

$$B'(e)h_x(x) - B'(e^*(\hat{\beta}))h_x(x^*(\hat{\beta})) = 0 \tag{4.26.1}$$

$$-B'(\dot{e}+1) + B'h_x\dot{x} - (x - x^*(\hat{\beta}))(-B''\dot{e}h_x - B'h_{xx}\dot{x}) = 0 \tag{4.26.2}$$

Since $\dot{e} + 1 = h_x\dot{x}$, (4.26.2) is satisfied if $x = x^*(\hat{\beta})$; thus we have optimal input choice. Then from (4.26.1), $e = e^*(\hat{\beta})$, so the optimal emission level is chosen. Furthermore, $e = h(x) - \beta$ and $e^*(\hat{\beta}) = h(x^*(\hat{\beta})) - \hat{\beta}$. Thus $\beta = \hat{\beta}$, and the tax schedule induces truthtelling. The linear tax schedules are presented in Figure 4.2.

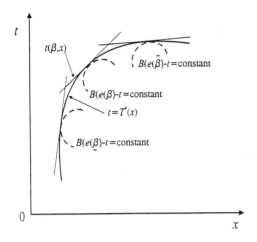

*Figure 4.2  Implementation with linear tax schedules*

The bold curve represents the function $t=T^*(x)$, which is concave in $x$. The dashed lines represent the farmer's isoprofit curves. The farmer has the same behavior whether he/she faces $T^*(x)$ or the linear tangents that correspond to the tax schedule (4.25).

The linear tax schedules can be administered using two approaches:

(i)     The farmers choose their own tax from a menu of linear tax schedules. The menu is defined as:

$$t = \Gamma + \Delta x \qquad \text{(M)}$$

The parameters $\Gamma, \Delta$ are defined for each type $\beta$ as:

$$\Gamma(\beta) = t^*(\beta) - B'(e^*(\beta))h_x(x^*(\beta))x^*(\beta) \qquad (4.27.1)$$

$$\Delta(\beta) = B'((e^*(\beta))h_x(x^*(\beta)) \qquad (4.27.2)$$

Then the farmer chooses the tax schedule that fits his/her type.

(ii)    The environmental regulator can recommend that the farmer use observable input $x^*(\beta)$ if he/she is type $\beta$, and then charge him/her a tax schedule:

$$t(x,x^*) = \gamma + \delta(x-x^*) \qquad \text{(R)}$$

Thus the farmer incurs extra cost for using more than the recommended amount of the observable input.

Since the implementation is achieved via linear taxes and farmers are assumed to be risk neutral, the error term $\epsilon$, which has a probability distribution independent of $\beta$ and $x$, does not affect incentives. Thus observational errors in the input use, which is the action variable, do not affect the input taxes.

At this point it would be worthwhile to compare allocations corresponding to the revelation mechanism, with allocations corresponding to the application of ambient taxes that do not account for differences in the types of farmers.

Assume that the regulator imposes an ambient tax, $\tau$, on the deviations between the desired and the observed ambient concentration of pollution. This deviation is defined as:

$$\int_{\underline{\beta}}^{\bar{\beta}} (e(\beta) - e^*(\beta))f(\beta)d\beta, \text{ where } \int_{\underline{\beta}}^{\bar{\beta}} e^*(\beta)f(\beta)d\beta$$

is the optimal level of ambient concentration of pollution. The optimal ambient tax is determined by the solution of the implicit programming problem defined earlier, as $\tau^* = \alpha/(1+\lambda)$. Therefore the optimal ambient tax is equal to the complete information Pigouvian tax. Thus, as has already been shown, the ambient taxes can solve the moral hazard problem associated with the nonobservability of individual emissions. On the other hand an ambient tax does not take into account the private characteristics of each farmer. Under the ambient tax the farmer solves the problem:

$$\max_{e \geq 0} B(e) - \left(\frac{\alpha}{1+\lambda}\right)\int_{\underline{\beta}}^{\bar{\beta}} (e(\beta) - e^*(\beta))f(\beta)d\beta$$

with first-order condition:

$$B'(e) - \left(\frac{\alpha}{1+\lambda}\right)\int_{\underline{\beta}}^{\bar{\beta}} f(\beta)d\beta = 0, \text{ or } B'(e) = \left(\frac{\alpha}{1+\lambda}\right) \tag{4.28}$$

By comparing this condition with (i) of the regulatory mechanism it can be seen that under the ambient tax only the farmer with the worst characteristics with respect to pollution emits at the same level as with the ambient tax. The rest of the farmers emit, under the ambient tax, less as compared to the case of the linear input tax with adverse selection. Thus it can be said that, when farmers differ with respect to their pollution characteristics (which are private information), then ambient taxes could lead to underemissions as compared to the socially-optimal regulatory scheme.

The input-based policy schemes discussed in this section, although complicated in their structure, overcome the problem of ambient taxes – the relation of the tax to a variable that is not totally under the control of the individual taxpayer – and allow the use of observed variables as yardsticks for tax determination. Furthermore, as shown, the use of ambient taxes that ignore the adverse selection problem leads to underemissions and underproduction relative to the social optimum; thus they can be regarded as an unduly restrictive instrument.

However this input-based incentive scheme imposes some extra informational requirements on the regulator, in addition to the usual information required about the benefit function and marginal damages for the design of ambient taxes. In particular the regulator needs to know the link between emissions and the use of polluting inputs as well as farming practices, the distribution of farmers according to their practices, and the social value of public funds. These informational requirements indicate that in order to obtain a sound basis for the design of input-based incentive schemes for NPS pollution problems, increasing attention should be given to the modelling of the production processes in general in conjunction with the emission process, as well as to the valuation of the damages from pollution, in combined economic-biophysical models.

# 5. Environmental Policy and Market Structure

## 1 INTRODUCTION

The analysis of environmental policy developed in the last two chapters focused on two departures from the basic model: first the introduction of the concept of stock externality that gives rise to dynamic considerations, and second the introduction of informational constraints which make necessary the use of alternative policy instruments. In both cases, however, the analysis was carried out under the explicit assumption of perfect competition in the product market.

Indeed the assumption of competitive product markets has been the most common one in the analysis of environmental policy during the last decades,[1] while some notable exceptions refer to the use of the monopoly assumption in the product market.[2] Much less attention, at least until recently,[3] has been given, however, to the analysis of environmental policy under the assumption of oligopolistic product markets, although this assumption could be regarded as the more realistic one for describing modern industrial societies.

The purpose of this chapter is to provide some insights into the structure of environmental policy when the product market is no longer competitive. The basic implications of the departure from the competitive market assumption is that more externalities in addition to environmental pollution enter the analysis, with the presence of these new externalities affecting – sometimes significantly – the effectiveness of the environmental policy instruments.

In particular when a second externality related to the structure of the product market is considered, this second externality affects the product side

---

[1]See for example Baumol and Oates (1988).

[2]It was Buchanan (1969) who first considered the implications of a monopolistic product market for environmental policy.

[3]See for example Levin (1985), Ebert (1991/2), Requate (1993), Conrad and Wang (1993) and the collected volume by Carraro, Katsoulacos and Xepapadeas (1996).

and relates to underproduction due to excessive monopoly power, as compared to the competitive case. In the case of two distortions, standard arguments suggest the use of two instruments in order to correct the two externalities: one instrument to correct for environmental pollution and another to correct for market imperfections. In most of the analysis that follows it will be assumed that the regulator cannot affect the firm's pricing policies, that is, the distortion in the product side cannot be corrected. In this case optimal second-best environmental policy instruments are developed. First-best instruments, that is instruments capable of correcting both externalities, are also derived in the context of optimal regulation of a natural monopoly.

The analysis in this chapter basically considers environmental policy under Cournot competition with homogeneous product. Further analysis of environmental policy in cases such as Bertrand competition or vertical product differentiation will undoubtedly be an important research area in the future.

## 2  ENVIRONMENTAL REGULATION UNDER MONOPOLY

When the output that generates environmental degradation is produced by a monopolist, there are two possible ways of considering environmental regulation. The first is to consider the pricing policy of the firm as given, that is not affected by the regulator, and then to determine a second-best emission tax as the only instrument available to the regulator, which is the traditional approach. The second is to consider the problem explicitly as a problem of optimal monopoly regulation. In this second case the emission tax is one element of the set of instruments that is used to achieve optimal regulation.

### 2.1  Emission Taxes under Monopoly

As shown earlier, emission taxes internalize the external damages associated with pollution-generating activities. The internalization is complete when the emission tax is equal to the marginal external damages of pollution, such as in the case of Pigouvian taxes. The socially-optimal degree of internalization depends however on the market structure. Under perfect competition, the desired internalization is complete (e.g., Baumol and Oates 1988), while under imperfectly competitive conditions, optimal taxes deviate from external damages, as was first noted by Buchanan (1969) for the case of monopoly.

Buchanan (1969) pointed out, in analysing the case of a polluting monopolist, that the use of effluent fees equal to marginal external damages of pollution, as in the case of competitive markets, will not lead to optimality and can even reduce social welfare. This is because the emission tax will reduce the already suboptimal monopoly output. Thus any gain in welfare due to reduced pollution might be outweighed by the welfare loss due to reduced output. This implies that complete internalization of the external pollution damages caused by a monopolist might not be desirable, but rather that the optimal policy requires underinternalization reflected in an emission tax less than marginal damages.

The optimal emission tax for the case of a monopolist can be derived as follows. Consider the output abatement choice model (OACM) presented in Section 2.2.2 of Chapter 2, but restrict the number of firms to $n=1$ and set $Q \equiv q$. In such a case the regulator's problem is to choose output and abatement expenses to maximize social welfare defined as usual as the sum of consumer and producer surplus by:

$$\max_{(q,a) \geq 0} \quad W = \int_0^q P(u)du - c(q,a) - D(e), \quad e = s(q,a) \qquad (5.1)$$

The first-order necessary conditions for the optimal allocation $(q^*, a^*)$ assuming interior solutions, can be written as:

$$\frac{\partial W}{\partial q} = 0 \text{ or } P(q^*) - \frac{\partial c(q^*, a^*)}{\partial q} - D'(e^*) \frac{\partial s(q^*, a^*)}{\partial q} = 0 \qquad (5.2.1)$$

$$\frac{\partial W}{\partial a} = 0 \text{ or } -\frac{\partial c(q^*, a^*)}{\partial a} - D'(e^*) \frac{\partial s(q^*, a^*)}{\partial a} = 0 \qquad (5.2.2)$$

The above conditions have a similar interpretation as conditions (2.2.1) and (2.2.2) in Chapter 2, and determine optimal emissions by the monopolist as $e^* = s(q^*, a^*)$. The monopolist facing an emission tax $t$ solves the problem:

$$\max_{(q,w) \geq 0} \quad \pi = P(q)q - c(q,a) - ts(q,a)$$

The first-order necessary conditions for the allocation $(q^m, a^m)$ which maximizes the monopolist's profit, assuming again interior solutions, are:

$$P + q^m \frac{dP}{dq} - \frac{\partial c(q^m, a^m)}{\partial q} - t \frac{\partial s(q^m, a^m)}{\partial q} = 0 \qquad (5.3.1)$$

$$-\frac{\partial c(q^m, a^m)}{\partial a} - t \frac{\partial s(q^m, a^m)}{\partial a} = 0 \qquad (5.3.2)$$

Condition (5.3.1) implies that the monopolist equates marginal revenue with marginal production plus marginal emission costs. On the other hand, (5.3.2) implies that in choosing profit-maximizing abatement, the monopolist equates marginal abatement costs with marginal emission tax savings due to abatement. Combining (5.2.1) with (5.3.1), the following monopoly tax is obtained:

$$t^m = D'(e^*) - \frac{P}{|\epsilon|} \frac{\partial q}{\partial e}$$

(5.4)

with $\quad P + q \frac{dP}{dq} = P\left(1 - \frac{1}{\epsilon}\right) = MR$

where $\epsilon$ is the elasticity of demand. Using the definition for marginal revenue and the fact that under profit maximization, marginal revenue equals marginal cost ($MR = MC$), relation (5.4) becomes:

$$t^m = D'(e^*) - \left|(P-MR)\frac{\partial q}{\partial e}\right| = D'(e^*) - \left|(P-MC)\frac{\partial q}{\partial e}\right|$$

(5.5)

By either (5.4) or (5.5), the second-best emission tax for the monopolist is less than marginal external damages. The deviation between tax and marginal damages is equal to the welfare losses from reduced output. This loss is expressed as the value of the marginal output unit less its marginal cost, or $P - MC$, times the reduction in output associated with a unit decrease in emissions, ($\partial q / \partial e$). By comparing (5.2.2) to (5.3.2), it can be seen that $t^m$ does not lead to the socially-optimal amount of abatement. That is, a trade-off exists between increasing abatement by using a higher emission tax and reducing output.

The monopoly tax $t^m$ is a second-best optimal tax, as can be seen by examining the optimal taxation problem formally. Solving the first-order conditions (5.3.1) and (5.3.2), assuming that the appropriate second-order conditions are satisfied, optimal output and abatement expenses are defined as functions of the tax rate, as:

$$q^m = q^m(t), \quad \frac{\partial q^m}{\partial t} < 0, \quad a^m = a^m(t), \quad \frac{\partial a^m}{\partial t} > 0$$

Substituting these values into (5.1), social welfare is defined as a function of $t$. The optimal second-best tax for the monopolist is defined as:

$$t^m = \operatorname*{argmax}_t W(t)$$

The first-order condition for maximization is defined as:

$$\frac{\partial W}{\partial q}\frac{\partial q^{m}}{\partial t}+\frac{\partial W}{\partial a}\frac{\partial a^{m}}{\partial t}=0$$

Using the derivatives of (5.1) and the derivatives $\partial c/\partial q$, $\partial c/\partial a$ from the first-order conditions (5.3.1) and (5.3.2) of the monopolist's profit-maximization problem, the optimal second-best emission tax is obtained as:

$$t^{m}=D'(e^{*})+\frac{\dfrac{\partial P}{\partial q}\dfrac{\partial q}{\partial t}q}{\dfrac{\partial e}{\partial q}\dfrac{\partial q}{\partial t}+\dfrac{\partial e}{\partial a}\dfrac{\partial a}{\partial t}}=D'(e^{*})-\frac{P}{|\epsilon|}\frac{\partial q}{\partial e} \qquad (5.6)$$

since the denominator of the second part of (5.6) is $\partial e/\partial t$.

The above results imply therefore that in a monopolistic market, the second-best optimal emission tax is less than marginal external damages of pollution.[4] This tax balances welfare losses from restricting the already suboptimal monopolist's output with welfare gains due to emission reductions.[5]

## 2.2  Optimal Regulation of Polluting Monopolies

We consider the case of a natural monopoly producing a single output and generating pollution during the production activities. The objective of the regulator is to maximize social welfare by inducing the monopoly to produce at the socially-optimal production and emission levels.

In developing the regulatory mechanism the Laffont-Tirole approach to regulation is used.[6] This approach has the advantage of incorporating readily into the model issues of incomplete information, and in particular, moral hazard and adverse selection.

Consider a natural monopoly producing a single output and generating

---

[4]For these derivations see also Barnett (1980), Misiolek (1980) and Baumol and Oates (1988).
[5]The efficiency properties of Pigouvian taxes have been further examined under various organizational forms and under alternative assumptions about conditions prevailing in monopolistic markets. Oates and Strassmann (1984) examine the properties of a system of effluent fees when the polluter takes the form of a private monopoly, managerial firm, regulated firm or public bureau. They tentatively conclude that the efficiency of a fee system which is invariant to the organizational form, is not seriously compromised by deviations from competitive conditions. Misiolek (1988) demonstrates that when rent-seeking costs are present, the optimal Pigouvian tax for a monopolist could exceed marginal external damages.
[6]See Laffont and Tirole (1993), Laffont (1994a). The approach in this section follows Laffont (1994b).

pollution as a byproduct, with a cost function defined as $C=C(q,z,e,\beta)$ where $q$ denotes output produced, $z$ denotes the level of effort undertaken by the firm (or more precisely the management of the firm) which reduces costs but creates disutility described by a function $\psi(z)$ with $\psi'>0$, $\psi''>0$, $\psi'''\geq0$, $e$ denotes generated emissions, and finally $\beta$ is a productivity parameter. For the partial derivatives of the cost function it is assumed that $C_q>0$, $C_z<0$, $C_e<0$, $C_\beta>0$ and that $C$ is strictly convex in $(q,z,e)$. Thus a reduction in emissions and an increase in the productivity parameter $\beta$ increase costs.

Let $p=P(q)$ be the demand function (inverse) for the monopolists's product and make the accounting convention that the regulator receives the proceeds from the sales of the firm's output defined as $R(q)=qP(q)$ and pays the firm total costs $C$ plus a transfer $T$ as compensation for the disutility of engaging in production. Thus the monopolist's utility or rent is defined as:

$$U=T-\psi(z)$$

As usual the regulator tries to maximize consumer and producer surplus; assume also that public funds have a social price of $(1+\lambda)$ with $\lambda>0$ because of distortionary taxation. Then social welfare is defined as:

$$W=\left[\int_0^q P(u)\,du-qP(q)\right]+ \tag{5.7}$$
$$(1+\lambda)qP(q)-(1+\lambda)(C+T)+U-D(e)$$

where as before $D(e)$ denotes environmental damages.

The first term on the right-hand side denotes net consumer surplus, the second term reflects the regulator's revenue evaluated at the social price of the public funds (because the revenues reduce the need for distortionary taxation), the third term reflects the total amount paid to the firm by the regulator valued again at the social price of public funds, the fourth term reflects producer's net rents, and the last term reflects environmental damages. After some rearrangement and writing $S(q)\equiv\int_0^q P(u)\,d(u)$, $T=U+\psi(z)$, (5.7) becomes:

$$W=S(q)+\lambda qP(q)-(1+\lambda)(C+\psi(z))-\lambda U-D(e) \tag{5.7.1}$$

It can be seen from the above definition of social welfare that rents left to the monopolist reduce social welfare since the social price of the public funds exceed unity, or $\lambda>0$.

The objective of optimal regulation under complete information, that is knowledge of $\beta$ and $z$, is to choose the triplet $(q^*,z^*,e^*)$ to maximize (5.7.1) subject to the participation constraint $U\geq0$. Assuming interior solution the optimal regulation is characterized as:

(i)      $$\frac{p^*-MC}{p^*} = \frac{\lambda}{1+\lambda}\frac{1}{\epsilon_p}, \quad p* = P^*(q^*), \quad MC = C_q$$

where $\epsilon_p$ is the elasticity of demand. The above condition is a form of Ramsey pricing for the regulated utility.

(ii)     $$\psi'(z^*) = -C_z$$

The marginal disutility of effort is equal to the marginal cost savings due to increased effort.

(iii)    $$D'(e^*) = -(1+\lambda)C_e$$

Marginal damages from pollution equal the marginal cost of pollution reduction evaluated at the social price for public funds.

(iv)     $$U^* = 0$$

No rents are left to the monopolists at the optimal regulation.

The above-defined optimal regulation can be implemented by the following mix of instruments (Laffont 1994b):

(a)      A subsidy per unit of commodity sold

$$s^* = \frac{p^*}{(1+\lambda)\epsilon_p} \tag{5.8.1}$$

(b)      An emission (Pigouvian) tax

$$\tau^* = \frac{D'(e^*)}{1+\lambda} \tag{5.8.2}$$

(c)      A lump-sum tax on profits

$$T^* = (P(q^*)+s^*)q^* - C(q^*,z^*,e^*,\beta) - \tau^*e^* - \psi(z^*) \tag{5.8.3}$$

The three instruments solve the three externality-related problems. The subsidy ensures that the monopoly will not underproduce, the Pigouvian tax fully internalizes environmental marginal damages scaled by the social value of public funds, while the lump-sum tax on profits solves the distribution problem by not leaving any rents to the monopoly.[7]

It is interesting to note that in the context of a more general optimal

---

[7]The optimality of the instrument mix can easily be seen by considering the monopolist's problem under the incentive scheme which is:

$$\max_{q,z,e} [P(q)+s^*]q - \tau^*e - C(q,z,e,\beta) - \psi(z)$$

The optimality conditions under the incentive scheme reproduce the optimal regulations (i) to (iv).

regulatory scheme there is no need for a second-best emission tax. The optimal tax under the optimal regulation fully internalizes marginal external damages after scaling down for the social cost of distortionary taxation.[8]

Optimal regulation of the monopoly can be extended to take into account the possibility of incomplete information, that is, unobservable effort, $z$ (moral hazard), and the unobservable productivity parameter, $\beta$ (adverse selection). The optimal scheme can be implemented again by a mix of subsidies, emission taxes and transfers. The emission taxes are however modified compared to (5.8.2) in order to take into account the need for incentive correction.[9]

# 3   ENVIRONMENTAL REGULATION IN OLIGOPOLISTIC MARKETS

As mentioned earlier, the framework of oligopolistic product markets has been disregarded in the majority of cases in the development of environmental policies. One reason for this could be the complications involved when one departs from the simplifying assumption of perfect competition or monopoly. According to Baumol and Oates (1988, p. 84), '... the rules for other market forms [oligopolists, monopolistic competitors] may be yet more complicated' [than for competitive firms or monopolists].

Under conditions of oligopoly, more externalities, in addition to output distortion and pollution, may be present. This could result both in drastic changes in the qualitative characteristics of the traditional environmental policy instruments used for the cases of perfect competition and monopoly,[10] and also in a need for additional instruments.

## 3.1  Emission Taxes in Fixed Number Oligopolies

In this section we examine, following Katsoulacos and Xepapadeas (1996a), optimal emission taxes for the case of an $n$-firm homogeneous product

---

[8]This result is compatible with the results obtained in Section 3.1.1 of Chapter 2 under general equilibrium considerations, where again the optimal tax is less than marginal damages due to distortionary taxation.

[9]For a detailed analysis of regulation under incomplete information see Laffont (1994b) in which additional issues such as nonverifiable pollution level, nonpoint source pollution and location choice are discussed.

[10]See also Levin (1985) for some counterintuitive results in the case of taxation under oligopoly.

oligopoly with fixed entry costs $F$, using the OACM framework.

The standard Cournot-Nash solution obtained when firms maximize their profits with respect to output $q$ and abatement $a$, taking the actions of their rivals as given, is considered, for any emission tax $t$. Denoting the inverse demand function by $p=P(Q)$, as before, with $Q$ denoting now total output produced by the $i=1,\ldots,n$ firms, or $Q=\Sigma_i q_i$, the problem for the firm is:

$$\max_{q_i,w_i} \pi_i = P(Q)q_i - c(q_i,a_i) - F - ts(q_i,a_i) \tag{5.9}$$

The first-order necessary conditions for a symmetric Cournot-Nash equilibrium choice of output and abatement $(q^N, a^N)$ can be written as:

$$P(nq^N) + q^N P'(nq^N) = \frac{\partial c(q^N,a^N)}{\partial q} + t\frac{\partial s(q^N,a^N)}{\partial q} \tag{5.9.1}$$

$$\frac{\partial c(q^N,w^N)}{\partial a} = -t\frac{\partial s(q^N,a^N)}{\partial a} \tag{5.9.2}$$

Conditions (5.9.1) and (5.9.2) have the same interpretation as the first-order conditions for profit maximization of a monopoly derived earlier in this chapter. Solving the system of first-order conditions, by assuming that the second-order conditions are satisfied, the Nash equilibrium values of $q$ and $a$ are defined as functions of the tax rate, $t$, and the number of firms, $n$, as:

$$q^N = q^N(t,n), \quad \frac{\partial q^N}{\partial t} < 0, \quad a^N(t,n), \quad \frac{\partial a^N}{\partial t} > 0$$

Thus an increase in the emission tax decreases the Nash equilibrium values of output and increases the Nash equilibrium value of abatement expenses.

The environmental regulator chooses the optimal second-best emission tax, $t^N$, by maximizing the usual welfare indicator defined as consumer and producer surplus. In this welfare function output and abatement are functions of the tax $t$ and the number of firms $n$ since output and abatement are substituted by their Nash equilibrium values defined above.

$$\max_t W = \int_0^{nq^N} P(u)du - nc(q^N,a^N) - D(ne^N) - nF, \tag{5.10}$$

where       $e^N = s(q^N, a^N)$

The first-order necessary condition for maximum implies:

$$\frac{\partial W}{\partial q}\frac{\partial q^N}{\partial t} + \frac{\partial W}{\partial a}\frac{\partial a^N}{\partial t} = 0$$

After some manipulations similar to those in Section 2.1 of this chapter, the second-best emission tax is defined as:

$$t^N = D'(ne^*) - \frac{P}{n|\epsilon|}\frac{\partial q}{\partial e} = D'(ne^*) - \left|(P-MC)\frac{\partial q}{\partial e}\right| \qquad (5.11)$$

In the above formulation the level of optimal emissions $e^*$ is defined from the solution of the welfare maximization problem for the $n$-firms market where the regulator is not constrained by the pricing policy of the firms. Thus $e^*$ is the first-best emission level derived by the solution of the problem:

$$\max_{q,a} W = \int_0^{nq} P(u)\,du - nc(q,a) - D(ne) - nF, \quad e = s(q,a)$$

The second-best tax defined in (5.11) generalizes the optimal emission tax obtained for monopoly (Barnett 1980, Misiolek 1980) for the case of oligopoly. The fixed number oligopoly emission tax is identical to the monopoly tax when $n=1$.[11] Thus, as in the case of monopoly, in a fixed number homogeneous product oligopoly, the second-best optimal emission tax is less than marginal external damages of pollution.

### 3.1.1 The case of product diversity

The results obtained in the previous section can be extended in a straightforward way to the case of product diversity. Following Spence (1976), the gross consumer benefit can be specified as:

$$B = G\left[\sum_{i=1}^{\infty} f(q_i)\right] \qquad (5.12)$$

where $f(0) = 0$, $f'>0$, $f''\leq 0$ for all $q \geq 0$ and $G'(z)>0$, $G''(z)<0$ for all $z \geq 0$. These assumptions imply that consumers prefer variety and that the outputs from various firms are substitutes for one another.

When the market has $n$ firms, consumer maximization implies that each firm's equilibrium price is $G'(\Sigma_i f(q_i)) f'(q_i)$. The problem for firm $i$ when it faces an emission tax $t$ is:

$$\max_{(q_i, a_i) \geq 0} \pi_i = G'\left[\sum_i^{\infty} f(q_i)\right] f'(q_i)q_i - c(q_i, a_i) - ts(q_i, a_i) - F \qquad (5.13)$$

---

[11]For a similar result see Ebert (1991/92). For the effects of the emission tax on the output of an oligopolistic industry see Conrad and Wang (1993).

The first-order conditions, after imposing symmetry, omitting arguments of functions to simplify notation, and assuming interior solutions, are derived as:

$$\frac{\partial \pi_i}{\partial q_i}=0 \text{ or } G'f'+G'f''q^N+G''n[f']^2q^N = \frac{\partial c}{\partial q}+t\frac{\partial s}{\partial q} \qquad (5.14.1)$$

$$\frac{\partial \pi_i}{\partial a_i}=0 \text{ or } \frac{\partial c}{\partial a}=-t\frac{\partial s}{\partial a} \qquad (5.14.2)$$

Substituting the Nash equilibrium values of $q$ and $a$ into the social welfare function, the optimal emission tax under product diversity is determined as:

$$t_d^N=\operatorname*{argmax}_t W(t)=G(nf(q^N))-nc(q^N,a^N)-D(ne^N)-nF \qquad (5.15)$$

The first-order condition for maximum implies:

$$\left(G'f'-\frac{\partial c}{\partial q}\right)\frac{\partial q^N}{\partial t}-\frac{\partial c}{\partial a}\frac{\partial a^N}{\partial t}-D'\left(\frac{\partial s}{\partial q}\frac{\partial q^N}{\partial t}+\frac{\partial s}{\partial a}\frac{\partial a^N}{\partial t}\right)=0 \qquad (5.16)$$

After substituting $\partial c/\partial q$ and $\partial c/\partial a$ from (5.14.1) and (5.14.2), we obtain the optimal emission tax under product diversity as:

$$t_d^N=D'(ne^*)+\frac{(G'f''+nG''(f')^2)\dfrac{\partial q^N}{\partial t}q^N}{\dfrac{\partial s}{\partial q}\dfrac{\partial q^N}{\partial t}+\dfrac{\partial s}{\partial a}\dfrac{\partial a^N}{\partial t}} \qquad (5.17)$$

Under the assumptions made about the $G$ and $f$ functions, the optimal tax is again less than marginal damages.

Therefore under a fixed number oligopoly, the result that the optimal Pigouvian tax is less than marginal damages holds both under the assumptions of product homogeneity and product diversity.

## 3.2 Emission Taxes under Endogenous Market Structure

The results obtained above should be interpreted as applying to a case where $n$, the number of firms in the market, can be thought of as reasonably stable at least in the short and medium run. This could be the case if firms in a given market are protected by significant barriers to entry. More generally, however, the number of firms in the market should be determined endogenously.

Following Katsoulacos and Xepapadeas (1995) the case is considered in which the equilibrium number of firms in the market is endogenously determined by the zero profit condition. Once the number of firms is allowed to vary, the environmental regulator in choosing the second-best optimal emission tax will have to take into account the effect of the emission tax on the entry decision of firms. In particular, the number of firms that satisfies the zero profit condition $\pi = 0$ can be written as $n = n(t)$. Thus the welfare function (5.10) is defined as $W = W(t, n(t))$, so that the optimal emission tax in the endogenous market structure case is determined as:

$$t_e^N = \operatorname*{argmax}_t W(t, n(t)) \tag{5.18}$$

Therefore the optimal tax must now satisfy:

$$\frac{\partial W}{\partial t} + \frac{\partial W}{\partial n} \frac{\partial n}{\partial t} = 0 \tag{5.19}$$

It can be shown using assumptions (i) to (iv) that the optimal second-best emission tax $t_e^N$ will in general lie in the range $\underline{t} < t_e^N < \bar{t}$, where $\bar{t} > 1$.[12] Since by assumption (iv) marginal damages are equal to 1, this result implies that in a homogeneous product oligopoly with free entry, the optimal emission tax may exceed marginal environmental damages.

The intuition behind this overinternalization result is the following. By imposing a positive emission tax, the environmental regulator should take into account three effects. The first two are the usual ones: (i) the beneficial effect of reducing pollution; and (ii) the negative effect of reducing output, the value of which is already distorted because of imperfect competition. There is a third effect however related to the fact that with endogenous market structure the equilibrium number of firms exceeds the second-best socially-optimal number of firms.[13] Thus when a positive emission tax is imposed the number of firms in the free-entry equilibrium is reduced and a beneficial effect exists in addition to (i) and (ii) above, from bringing the number of firms closer to the second-best social optimum. When the third effect is not taken into account, the optimal effluent fee is less than marginal external damages, in order to compensate for the negative effect of the tax on output. But if the third effect is taken into account, and is sufficiently strong, it is clear that the optimal tax may very well exceed marginal external damages (unity, in our example).

This overinternalization result is an example of the kind of distortions introduced into standard policy instruments when more externalities, which are present in oligopolistic markets, are considered.

---

[12]For the proof see Katsoulacos and Xepapadeas (1995).
[13]For this result see Mankiw and Whinston (1986).

The presence of the additional externalities can be handled of course with the introduction of more instruments.[14] For the endogenous market case a lump-sum licence fee can be introduced that will restrict the number of firms to the socially-optimal level along with the Pigouvian tax. The Pigouvian tax is now below marginal damages and corresponds to the second-best emission tax for a fixed number oligopoly with the socially-optimal number of firms.

### 3.3 Impacts of Emission Taxes and Market Structure

The previous sections focused on the determination of the emission taxes, first- or second-best, defined by maximizing the appropriate social welfare indicator. As shown, given the new type of externalities entering the model, underinternalization or overinternalization may occur. The derivation of these optimal taxes means that the environmental regulator knows society's valuations of environmental pollution and therefore can form the appropriate welfare function to be maximized. In the absence of such knowledge an approach is for the regulator to impose an environmental standard and then use the emission taxes to achieve this standard.[15]

In the analysis in Chapter 2 of the effects from a given environmental policy on the firms' decisions, under perfectly competitive conditions, it was found that firms' reactions are straightforward. This is not however the case for oligopolistic markets, since the number of externalities present can produce sometimes even counterintuitive results. Given the complexity of the analysis under oligopolistic markets it is virtually impossible for a single model to capture most of the possible effects. So most of the results are derived by using specific models that incorporate the structure necessary for the analysis of the particular problem.

Carraro and Soubeyran (1996a,b) explore models of an *n* firms homogeneous product oligopoly where firms, which could be heterogeneous, compete à la Cournot. Firms are also subject to an emission tax, and market demand depends on an index of environmental quality. Four main results are obtained in the context of this model.

(i)        Under increased environmental taxation a firm's profits could

---

[14]Brock and Evans (1985) develop a three-instrument scheme for the case of environmental regulation tiering where the regulation for the smaller firm is lighter than the regulation for the larger firm. This scheme consists of: (a) a licence fee that discourages entry of inefficient firms, (b) an emission tax that varies with the size of the firm, and (c) an exemption from the emission tax for certain size firms.

[15]This is the standards and charges approach described in Chapter 2, Section 8.

increase or decrease in the oligopolistic market. This result can be contrasted with the perfect competition case in which an increase in emission taxes always causes a reduction in profits.

(ii)     Taxation effects on the industry as a whole are ambiguous. If emission taxes increase, industry profits and concentration may also increase instead of decreasing.

(iii)    If the effects of emissions on demand, and their feedback on the production of the firms, are taken into account then the 'degree of competition' in the industry may increase since strategic interactions among firms increase. Thus environmental policy may reduce the probability of collusive behavior in oligopolistic markets.

(iv)     When optimal environmental taxation is considered, firms may increase their market share and/or profits when the emission tax is increased towards its optimal level.

A duopoly in the framework of a repeated game is analysed by Damania (1996). In this game firms use the 'grim trigger strategy' to deter cheating from collusive output and are subject to an emission tax. It is shown that even when firms could avoid the cost of the emission tax by abating pollution, they may choose not to do so, but rather to restrict output. This counterintuitive result is due to the fact that the tax lowers gains from defection, thus inducing the duopolists to restrict collusive output in order to raise profits. The policy implication of this result is that if it is desirable to have firms investing in pollution abatement equipment in highly concentrated industries, then emission taxes should be sufficiently high to capture these collusive profits.

Although the above results by no means exhaust the possible impacts of emission taxes in oligopolistic industries, the complexities induced by the oligopolistic market structure provide a wide area of policy-relevant analysis, both in terms of taxation incidence and in terms of combinations among different policy instruments[16] which constitute a large area for future research in environmental economics.

## 3.4 Regulation through Tradeable Emission Permits

When the use of tradeable emission permits as a policy instrument is considered, one more market – in addition to the product market – is

---

[16]See for example Ebert (1996) for a comparison between taxes and standards under oligopoly when the regulator uses the policy instruments naively, that is by neglecting relevant information in the decision process.

introduced into the model, namely the market for emission permits. In the analysis of tradeable permits in the second chapter both these markets were assumed to be competitive. Under these assumptions the permit system can achieve the given environmental standard at a minimum cost and without any welfare losses. Furthermore the least-cost outcome does not depend on the initial allocation of permits. The introduction of market imperfections into the model implies three possible configurations regarding the two markets. There is the possibility of competitive product markets with imperfections in the permits market, oligopolistic product markets with competitive permits markets, and finally imperfections in both markets. These three possibilities are examined in the following sections.

### 3.4.1 Market power in the permit market

We consider a market of $n$ firms which are price takers in the product market, but following Hahn (1984) firms $i=2,...,n$ are price takers in the permit market, while firm 1 has market power in the sense that it can influence the market price for tradeable emission permits. A situation like this can arise in the regulation of $SO_2$ emissions in a given region. If an electric utility using coal-fired power plants operates in the region, then it is very likely that most of the emissions will be generated by the electric utility; thus the utility can acquire power in the permit market since it would claim a relatively larger share of allowable emissions.

To analyse this case the model presented in Section 8.1.2 of Chapter 2 is used. A typical firm in the competitive fringe which is given an initial permit holding $\bar{e}_i$, $i=2,...,n$ will choose abatement to minimize total costs or,

$$\min_{a_i \geq 0} C(a_i) + P^T z_i \qquad (5.20)$$

where $z_i = (e_i - a_i - \bar{e}_i) \gtreqless 0$ is the number of traded permits, with first-order conditions for interior solution:

$$C_i'(a_i^o) = P^T \qquad (5.21)$$

Thus the number of permits demanded or supplied by firm $i$ is determined by the optimal abatement choice as a function of permit price, $a_i^o = a_i^o(P^T)$, and is independent of the initial permit holdings, $\bar{e}_i$. Then the net demand for permits is determined as $z_i = z_i(P^T)$, $i=1,...,n$ with $z_i' < 0$. The firm with the market power in the permit market will choose the price that maximizes its profits (Hahn 1984). Given that the total number of permits issued by the regulator is $\bar{e}$, the permits traded by firm 1 are defined as:

$$z_1 = e_1 - a_1 - \tilde{e}_1 = \bar{e} - \sum_{i=2}^{n} z_i (P^T) \qquad (5.22)$$

Firm 1 then solves the problem

$$\min_{P^T} C_1(a_1) + P^T(e_1 - a_1 - \tilde{e}_1) \qquad (5.23)$$

$$\text{s. t. } a_1 = e_1 - \tilde{e}_1 - \bar{e} + \sum_{i=2}^{n} z_i (P^T) \qquad (5.23.1)$$

The first-order condition for this cost minimization problem is:

$$\left( C_1'(a_1^o) - P^T \right) \sum_{i=1}^{n} z_i'(P^T) + (e_1 - a_1^o - \tilde{e}_1) = 0 \qquad (5.24)$$

Condition (5.24) implies that only if the initial permit holdings of firm 1 are optimal in the sense that it is the number of permits that the firm requires in equilibrium or equivalently $\tilde{e}_1 : e_1 - a_1^o - \tilde{e}_1 = 0$, will total expenditure on abatement be equal to the cost-minimizing solution, whereby marginal abatement costs are equalized across firms according to (5.21). If this is not the case then total expenditure on abatement exceeds the cost-minimizing solution. Furthermore it can be seen from (5.24) that $P^T = P^T(\tilde{e}_1)$, and therefore the initial permit holdings of the firm with the market power affect the market for permits. Put differently the initial distribution of permits not only influences equity issues, as in the case of competitive product and permit markets, but also affects efficiency by causing deviations from the cost-minimizing solution. By totally differentiating (5.24) the following comparative static result can be obtained:

$$\frac{\partial P^T}{\partial \tilde{e}_1} = \left[ (C_1' - P^T) \sum_{i=2}^{n} z_i''(P^T) + C_1'' \left( \sum_{i=2}^{n} z_i'(P^T) \right)^2 - 2 \sum_{i=2}^{n} z_i'(P^T) \right]^{-1}$$

The above derivative is positive under appropriate concavity assumptions for the minimization problem (5.23). Thus an increase in the initial permit holdings of the firm with the market power, through a transfer of permits from the firms in the competitive fringe, will increase the price of the emission permits. As is further shown by Hahn (1984) when the initial permit holdings of the firm with the market power deviate from the equilibrium holdings then total abatement costs defined as $C_1(a_1) + \Sigma_i C_i(a_i)$ increase. In the context of the same model it has been shown recently (van Egteren and Weber 1996) that the initial distribution of permits is important in determining the level of a firm's compliance to environmental regulation.

When the firm with the market power is compliant then a redistribution of permits from the firms in the competitive fringe to the firm with the market power causes global violations to increase. When the firm with the market power is noncompliant then an increase of its initial holdings through transfers from the competitive fringe will reduce its violations. Thus the initial allocation of permits not only affects efficiency but also the enforceability of the instrument. The results found by van Egteren and Weber suggest that the initial allocation of permits can be used as an enforcement instrument.

### 3.4.2 Oligopolistic product markets

The opposite case of the one examined in the previous section is examined now. The market for permits is competitive but the product market is oligopolistic.[17] This situation can arise when tradeable emission programs seek to regulate the same pollutant which is generated by different manufacturers of different products. Thus many dischargers, which can be regarded as approximately competitive, enter the permit market, while each of the products is produced by a few producers.

It is assumed (Malueg 1990) that the emission trading program should not increase net marginal production costs relative to a command and control regulation. Using the linear demand and costs functions,

$$p = A - \sum_{i=1}^{n} q_i$$

$$c_i(q_i) = c_i q_i$$

without the symmetry assumption and disregarding abatement, the profits of firm $i$ are defined as $\pi_i = (p - c_i)q_i$ and can be written as:

$$\pi_i = \left(q_i^N\right)^2, \quad i = 1,...,n \tag{5.25}$$

where $q_i^N$ is the Cournot-Nash equilibrium value of the output defined as:

$$q_i^N = \frac{A + \sum_{j \neq i} c_j - nc_i}{n+1} \tag{5.26}$$

From (5.25) an increase in the output of the firm increases profits. Given that the emission trading program reduces costs, the condition for increased

---

[17]This section follows Malueg (1990).

profits can be defined in terms of cost changes. Taking the differential of (5.25) with respect to changes in costs and using (5.26) we obtain

$$d\pi_i = \frac{2}{(n+1)^2}\left(A + \sum_{j \neq i} c_j - nc_i\right)\left(\sum_{j \neq i} dc_j - ndc_i\right) \tag{5.27}$$

Since the second term of the product in (5.27) is positive for positive levels of output, then

$$d\pi_i > 0 \text{ if and only if } \sum_{j \neq i} dc_j - ndc_i > 0 \tag{5.28}$$

where $dc_i, dc_j \leq 0$, $i, j = 1,...,n$. If the cost reductions are the same for all firms, that is $dc_i = dc$ for all $i$, then it follows from (5.28) that $d\pi_i > 0$. If however the cost reductions are such that:

$$dc_i > \frac{n-1}{n}\frac{\sum_{j \neq i} dc_j}{n-1}$$

which means that the cost reductions for firm $i$ are sufficiently lower than the cost reductions of its rivals, then $d\pi_i < 0$ and firm $i$ will not support the trading program.

It is further shown by Malueg (1990) that total industry profits may fall as a result of the emission trading program. Total profits, $\pi$, are defined as the sum of individual profits defined in (5.25); then

$$d\pi = 2\sum_i \left(q_i^N\right)\left(dq_i^N\right) \tag{5.29}$$

If the output (and profits) of a large low-cost firm decrease while the output (and profit) of a small high-cost firm increase, then total profits in the industry will decrease. This is a result of the reshuffling of output from low-cost to high-cost firms.

Since consumer surplus increases under the emission trading program, the total effect of the program on aggregate social welfare, consumer plus producer surplus, depends on the behavior of total profits. If cost reductions are distributed evenly among firms then total profits increase and so does aggregate welfare. If, however, there is a reshuffling of output, then total profits could decrease and counterbalance the gains in consumer surplus. In this case the introduction of an emission trading program leads to a reduction in social welfare relative to command and control regulation. The source of this reduction is the inefficient redistribution of output from low-cost firms to high-cost firms because of the trading program.

The above analysis suggests that the emission trading program could reduce social welfare when the product market is oligopolistic. It has been shown recently (Sartzetakis 1997b) that the social welfare need not be reduced if the trading program is designed in a certain way. In particular this holds, with a quadratic marginal cost function, if the program replaces a command and control system, and the number of permits distributed is equal to the total allowable emissions under the command and control regulation. In this case social welfare under the emission trading program increases as compared to the command and control situation.

### 3.4.3 Oligopolistic product market and market power in the permit market

The market structure configurations examined in the previous section can be combined in the case where market power exists in both the product and the permits market. Von der Fehr (1993) identifies a possible situation in which market power can appear both in the product and the permit market, as being the electricity generation sector in the UK in which two regulated, privately-owned firms are responsible for the bulk generation of $SO_2$ emissions.

Following von der Fehr, a duopoly with firms being Cournot competitors is considered. With a fixed supply of permits the profit function for the firm can be written as:

$$\pi_i(q_i, \tilde{e}_i, q_j) = R(q_i, q_j) - c_i(q_i, \tilde{e}_i)$$
$$\tilde{e}_i + \tilde{e}_j = \overline{e}, \ i,j = 1,2, \ i \neq j \tag{5.30}$$

where as before $\tilde{e}_i$ is the number of permits initially allocated to firm $i$. It is assumed that in general $\tilde{e}_i > \tilde{e}_j$ so that firm $i$ is the largest firm. The Nash equilibrium value of the output depends on the initial allocation of permits and can be defined, after writing $\tilde{e}_j = \overline{e} - \tilde{e}_i$, as[18] $q_i^N = q_i^N(\tilde{e}_i, \overline{e})$, $q_j^N = q_j^N(\tilde{e}_i, \overline{e})$. Thus total industry profits are defined as:

$$\pi = \pi_i + \pi_j = \pi_i(q_i^N, \tilde{e}_i, q_j^N) + \pi_j(q_j^N, \overline{e} - \tilde{e}_i, q_i^N)$$

Using the envelope theorem the effect from a change in the initial

---

[18]The Cournot-Nash equilibrium values are obtained by the usual first-order conditions for interior solutions:

$$\frac{\partial \pi_i}{\partial q_i} = 0, \ i = 1,2$$

Sufficiency requires the satisfaction of the second-order conditions:

$$\frac{\partial^2 \pi_i}{\partial q_i^2} < 0, \ i = 1,2, \quad \frac{\partial^2 \pi_i}{\partial q_i^2} \frac{\partial^2 \pi_j}{\partial q_j^2} - \frac{\partial^2 \pi_i}{\partial q_i \partial q_j} \frac{\partial^2 \pi_j}{\partial q_j \partial q_i} > 0$$

allocation of permits on industry's profits is given by:

$$\frac{\partial \pi}{\partial e_i} = \frac{\partial \pi_i}{\partial e_i} - \frac{\partial \pi_j}{\partial e_i} + \frac{\partial \pi_i}{\partial q_j} \frac{\partial q_j}{\partial e_i} + \frac{\partial \pi_j}{\partial q_i} \frac{\partial q_i}{\partial e_i}$$

As shown by von der Fehr, industry profits can increase if the permits of firm $i$ increase. That is, there are gains from having a more asymmetric distribution of permits. Under product homogeneity and sub-additivity of the cost function in output, industry profits are maximized when the industry becomes a monopoly. That is, it is more profitable for the large firms to buy all the permits and become monopolists. Numerical simulations of the above model indicate that consumer surplus decreases because of this asymmetry in the market, as the large firm acquires more permits towards monopolizing the market. These losses tend to increase when the products are differentiated. The effects on aggregate welfare (consumer plus producer surplus) are ambiguous since the increased asymmetry, while having a negative effect on consumer surplus, has a positive effect on profits.

When strategic interactions are considered in the same model, and in the context of a two-stage game, where in the first stage firms compete in the permit market and in the second compete in output, it follows that firms will overinvest in emission permits if the products are strategic substitutes. If one firm has first mover advantage in the price of permits, it will overinvest in permits in order to raise their price, and subsequently raise its rivals' costs. Raising rivals' cost strategies, via the permits markets, decreases social welfare, but the initial distribution of permits can be used to ameliorate welfare losses (Sartzetakis 1997a).

In a similar analytical framework Fershtman and de Zeeuw (1996) examine a market in which two firms that compete in the product market trade emission permits. The number of permits traded and the trading terms are determined by the two firms through a bargaining processes. Fershtman and de Zeeuw show that allowing trade in the permit market improves chances for collusive agreements. This may lead to the choice of inferior production and abatement technologies, may result in lower aggregate output and higher prices and may shift production from the low-cost firm to the high-cost firm. Under these circumstances trade in the permit market is not beneficial.

The results presented in this section support the idea that once we deviate from the perfectly competitive conditions in both the product and the permit markets, the efficiency which the emission trading programs obtained under the competitive assumption does not carry over to the oligopolistic model. Thus in comparing taxes and tradeable emission permits, the advantages of the permit system associated with the fewer informational requirements relative to the tax case, must be weighed against possible welfare losses resulting from oligopolistic market distortions.

## 4    ENVIRONMENTAL INNOVATION

As discussed in Section 9 of Chapter 2, one of the most important advantages of economic-based instruments – basically emission taxes and tradeable emission permits – over command and control regulation is the incentives they provide for technological change and the introduction of environmentally-clean, or environmentally-friendly, technologies.

The issue of environmental innovation can be examined from different points of view. Alternative policy instruments, emission taxes or emission permits, can be compared regarding their effects on environmental innovation; the choice of the optimal set of instruments (optimal in the sense of achieving the socially-desirable levels of innovation and pollution) can be examined; and endogenous incentives for research and development (R&D) with respect to the introduction of environmentally-clean technologies, either of the rivalrous R&D type (patents race) or of the nonrivalrous R&D type (research joint ventures) can be analysed.[19]

The issue of comparing incentives for adopting environmentally-innovative technologies is examined by Requate (1995) in the context of a *n* firms oligopoly with two types of technology: a conventional one resulting in high pollution, and an environmentally-friendly one resulting in low pollution for given output levels. The conventional technology has a cost advantage over the innovative technology. It is shown that at the social optimum the number of firms adopting the environmentally-clean technology depend on a damage parameter that reflects the degree of the hazardousness of pollution. The more hazardous the pollution is the more firms should adopt the clean technology. Thus the social optimum is characterized by partial adoption. When taxes and permits are compared regarding their effects on the adoption process, it is shown that both instruments may lead to excess adoption or too little adoption of the clean technology, but their effects work in different directions. Taxes could cause too much adoption when little adoption is optimal, or too little adoption when complete adoption is optimal. The effects

---

[19]Since the different approaches used for the analysis of environmental innovation do not conform to the use of a unified model, the basic results for the various cases will be presented in a nontechnical way.

of a permit system are the opposite of those of taxes. It is shown, however, that permits have the advantage of not reducing social welfare, something which is possible under taxes.

Carraro and Soubeyran (1996b) compared emission taxes and innovation subsidies which correspond to a partial covering of the fixed operating costs of the environmentally-friendly technology. The comparison is carried out on the basis of whether taxes or subsidies result in higher social welfare. Using a duopoly model[20] they show that if output contraction caused by emission taxes is negligible and/or the regulator does not desire output reductions and there is no constraint on the supply of clean technologies, then the appropriate instrument is an innovation subsidy. Otherwise emission taxes could be the preferred instrument.

The impact on environmental innovation of a permit system consisting of one-year spot and future markets is examined by Laffont and Tirole (1996a,b),[21] who consider environmental innovation in the form of introducing environmentally-clean technologies as 'a form of bypassing [the cost of buying permits] that involves some long term investment'. Two types of environmental innovation are considered. The one is in the form of private investment in clean technologies, while the second form can be used by all potential polluters and thus it is a public good. It is shown that in the first case the stand-alone spot markets create excess investment in environmentally-clean technologies or equivalently excess adoption.[22] This excess adoption is mitigated by the introduction of future markets where in the first period polluters buy permits that allow them to pollute in the second period at a slightly lower price than the price in the stand-alone spot market.

The optimal regulation in the case where environmental innovation is private can take two forms. An 'overall regulation' where the regulator, through his/her policy, influences emissions, investment in environmentally-clean technologies and production, and a 'pure pollution regulation' where only emissions are regulated. The optimal regulation in the first place consists of a menu of options on pollution rights, with the purchase price of the menu being decreasing in the strike price. In the second case the regulator could include purchase of options with lower price for current permits.

When innovation is a public good there is one potential innovator. It is shown that spot markets do not provide incentives for this potential innovator

---

[20]The two firms are located in different countries.

[21]Under the 1990 US Clean Air Act Amendments these permits are tradeable on the Chicago Board of Trade.

[22]In stand alone markets the regulator sets the number of permits at the beginning of the period.

to engage in R&D for environmentally-clean technologies. Very small incentives are also provided by future markets. The government can design an incentive contract for the innovator so that the new technology is produced in the first place, then sell the licence to use the technology at a welfare maximizing-price[23] without issuing permits.

The issue of the optimal choice of environmental policy instruments in the presence of environmental innovation is examined by Katsoulacos and Xepapadeas (1996b,c). A homogeneous product oligopoly is considered where emissions per unit of output can be reduced by using environmentally-costly innovation. Positive spillovers of the knowledge developed by environmental innovation is assumed so that innovation in pollution abatement can reduce the cost of the rival firms. The optimal regulation is derived in the context of a two-stage model where in the first stage firms choose environmental R&D and in the second stage firms choose output. The scheme consists of a tax on emissions and a subsidy on environmental R&D. It is interesting to note that in the presence of R&D spillovers a subsidy is always necessary in order to achieve the socially-optimal amount of R&D.

In the cases examined above environmental innovation is undertaken as a result of environmental policy introduced exogenously by the environmental regulator. The issue of endogenous incentives for environmental innovation when political economy considerations are taken into account in oligopolistic markets is examined by Hackett (1995). A *n* firms oligopoly is considered where firms are Cournot rivals and produce two types of goods: a standard pollution-generating good and an alternative pollution-free good. Process innovation results in the reduction of the unit cost of the pollution-free good which is however still higher than the unit cost of the 'dirty' good. Firms engaged in environmental innovation can exercise influence on a regulator, in a political economy context, to undertake a policy which will internalize the external costs of emissions generated by the standard good, thus raising the cost of rival firms. If the internalization policy is actually imposed then the environmentally-clean good is produced. Regarding the generation of incentives for environmental innovation, it is shown that in a patent race context there are incentives for environmental innovation as long as there is either one winner or not too many winners. In the case of research joint ventures (RJVs), there are incentives for industry-wide, pollution-preventing RJVs; the purpose is, however, to limit the introduction of clean technologies. This is because limiting the introduction of clean technologies, through R&D cartelization, eliminates the endogenous incentives for rivalrous

---

[23]This is a Ramsey price.

R&D (patent races) which arise because the winners raise the cost of the losers.

# 6. The International Dimension of Environmental Policy

## 1 INTRODUCTION

In the analysis of environmental policy presented in the previous chapters, two assumptions were maintained. First it was assumed that emissions, or more generally environmental pollution, does not cross national boundaries. Second it was also assumed that the effects of environmental policy on international trade among countries, as well as the effects of trade policies on environmental quality in a given country, are not taken into account.

When the first assumption is relaxed we are able to analyse environmental problems that go beyond cases where pollution and its effects are concentrated in one country only, and move to cases where activities in one country create negative externalities not only in the country itself but also in other countries. Such problems include the pollution of rivers and lakes that border more than one country[1] – a transboundary pollution problem – and regional or global environmental problems, such as acid rains, ozone depletion and global warming.[2]

Acid rains relate to the emission of sulphur and nitrogen oxides which are transported by wind in the atmosphere. Chemical processes transform sulphur oxide into sulfates which are removed from the atmosphere by direct 'dry' deposition or by rains' 'wet' deposition. These depositions damage the ecosystems, mainly the forests, of countries different from those in which emissions originated.

Ozone depletion refers to the depletion of the earth's stratospheric ozone,[3]

---

[1] More than two hundred river basins are multinational, and in more than fifty countries 75 per cent of their total water areas lie in international basins. This is in addition to ocean bodies which are common access international resources (Carraro and Siniscalco 1991).

[2] For a more detailed, yet compact, description of these problems, see Tietenberg (1996) and Hanley et al. (1997).

[3] Ozone in the troposhere, which is located below the stratosphere, is a regular air pollutant that relates to health effects such as respiratory problems, and agricultural damages.

which acts as a shield for the earth by absorbing harmful infra-red radiation. Chlorofluorocarbons (CFCs), which are chemical compounds present in a large number of industrial processes – such as aerosols, home refrigerators, air conditioning – are responsible for ozone depletion.

Global warming, also referred to as the 'greenhouse problem', is associated with the accumulation in the atmosphere of the greenhouse gases (GHGs)[4] and water vapour which trap part of the earth's outbound radiation (longwave radiation), thus increasing the earth's average surface temperature. Anthropogenic emissions from the burning of fossil fuels have led to a rise in the concentration of carbon dioxide by about 25 per cent as compared to the preindustrial level. The increase in the earth's temperature is expected to produce major and potentially disastrous changes in the long run, such as a rise in the sea level, change in rainfall and wind patterns, shift in agricultural zones.[5]

When the second assumption is relaxed, that is, along with the environmental considerations, trade among countries is also considered, the analysis can be conducted on two levels. The first concentrates on local pollution problems and focuses on the effects of environmental policy on environmental quality and countries' competitiveness.[6] It has been argued for example that trade liberalization – the single European market, GATT – will result in a larger ratio of consumption of natural and environmental resources. It is also felt that in the absence of traditional trade policies, owing to trade liberalization, some countries could use lax environmental policies to improve their international competitiveness. Thus trade liberalization could create excess pollution in countries, and 'flight of capital' and loss of international market shares of countries that follow relatively tougher environmental policies. The second level of analysis considers trade policy in the context of transboundary or global pollution problems and analyses how trade policy can help to design and enforce international agreements for the protection of the environment in the presence of transboundary or global pollution problems.

The purpose of this chapter is to present economic policies relevant to

---

[4]See also Chapter 3.

[5]A common characteristic of the three problems mentioned above, but also of transboundary pollution problems in general, is that they have common or open access characteristics, since the environmental resource is used by more than one country. As is well known, in such cases outcomes related to laissez-faire are inefficient, leading to overemission of pollutants, since each country chooses its emissions by ignoring the cost imposed by its behaviour on other countries. These inefficiencies will be examined in the subsequent sections.

[6]For a survey of these issues, see Ulph (1994).

transboundary or global pollution problems, as well as to examine some aspects of the interrelationships between international trade and environmental policy.

## 2  GLOBAL POLLUTION AND ENVIRONMENTAL POLICY

As noted by Chander and Tulkens (1992), from the point of view of resource allocation, the problem associated with transboundary or global pollution belongs to the theory of the voluntary provision of public goods, or more precisely 'public bads', since global pollution satisfies the basic characteristics of a public good, namely nonrivalry in consumption and nonexcludability.

The general methodological approach in dealing with these problems[7] is to: (i) determine the laissez-faire equilibrium where countries choose their emission levels without taking into account the external costs imposed on other counties; (ii) determine a cooperative equilibrium where countries determine their emissions so that a Pareto efficient outcome is obtained; (iii) establish the inefficiency of the laissez-faire or noncooperative equilibrium compared to the cooperative case; and (iv) propose a course of action that can achieve the efficient outcome, which is the global pollution level that satisfies the Pareto criterion.

This approach is similar to the one used to deal with local pollution problems, where the inefficiency of competitive markets as compared to the social welfare optimum is established and then appropriate policy is designed to secure the welfare-maximizing outcome. This similarity would imply that, in principle, the general policy framework for correcting environmental externalities developed in the previous chapters of this book can be used as a basis for designing policies capable of dealing with global pollution problems. There is, however, one important institutional difference stemming from the 'voluntary provision' aspect of the global pollution problems. When dealing with a pollution problem which is confined within the boundaries of one nation, whatever policy is chosen by the environmental regulator can be enforced (within of course the limitations imposed by the enforcement and informational constraints discussed in previous chapters), given the legal framework of the country which describes the ways in which such policies

---

[7]See for example Mäler (1989, 1990), Hoel (1992a) and Newbery (1990).

are implemented. When, however, a global environmental problem is examined, there is not a regulator *per se* vested with the power to enforce a given policy in a number of nations. This would require the existence of some supranational authority with the legal power to enforce policies on different nations.[8] In the absence of such an authority capable of imposing and enforcing the policy, the policy needs to be agreed upon. So as noted by Carraro and Siniscalco (1991), when international environmental problems are examined, the analysis should shift from the context of government intervention – the regulation approach – to the context of negotiations between nations and international policy coordination.[9]

Negotiations among nations should lead to some international agreement specifying policies which should be adopted by countries participating in the agreement. For example the 1985 Helsinski Protocol required the signatory countries to reduce $SO_2$ emissions by 30 per cent as compared to the 1980 levels, while the Montreal Protocol, signed in 1987 and further amended in London in 1990, required a complete ban on production and consumption of certain CFCs by the year 2000.[10] The proposed European carbon tax would require EU counties to impose a tax on the carbon context of fossil fuels. Thus an international agreement should refer either to the adoption by all countries of a specific policy instrument, like an international tax on emissions or some internationally applied quota system, or to the adoption by the signatory countries of the obligation to reduce domestic emissions in a uniform or a discriminatory way by following some type of national environmental policy.[11]

A major problem however with international agreements either to adopt an internationally-designed instrument or to reduce emissions through domestic policies, is the free-riding incentives which develop because of the common access character of the environmental problem and which can seriously impede the sustainability of the agreement. It might be in a country's best interest not to participate in the agreement to reduce emissions when the rest of the countries participate, since by doing so it can reduce its

---

[8]The European Union can be regarded as such an authority. However in the EU, policies need to be agreed upon, and as discussions in recent years about the introduction of a European carbon tax reveal, agreement on environmental policies which could impose a financial burden on the member states in exchange for global environmental benefits is by no means guaranteed.
[9]For a summary of the issues related to international cooperation to protect the environment, see Barrett (1995).
[10]Further negotiations in Copenhagen moved the phase out of CFCs up to 1996.
[11]As noted by Barrett (1995) the United Nations Environmental Programme lists 132 multilateral agreements adopted before 1991 and several that were adopted afterwards.

own cost of abating pollution and enjoy the benefits from the overall pollution reduction brought about by the cooperation of the rest of the countries. If countries have strong free-riding incentives, the agreement cannot be sustained.

This situation corresponds to the well-known prisoners' dilemma. For a transboundary pollution problem involving two countries, the game is shown in the pay-off matrices (a) and (b) below.

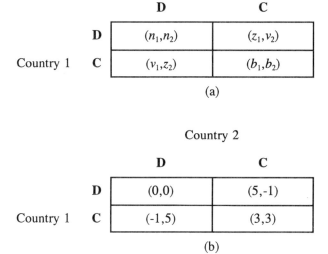

Country 2

|  | **D** | **C** |
|---|---|---|
| **D** | $(n_1, n_2)$ | $(z_1, v_2)$ |
| **C** | $(v_1, z_2)$ | $(b_1, b_2)$ |

Country 1

(a)

Country 2

|  | **D** | **C** |
|---|---|---|
| **D** | (0,0) | (5,-1) |
| **C** | (-1,5) | (3,3) |

Country 1

(b)

In these matrices D means 'defect' from the agreement to reduce emissions and C means 'cooperate' in reducing emissions. Assume that the values of net benefits (or welfare levels) corresponding to the different courses of action available to the countries are as in the pay-off matrix (b). In this game defect is the dominant strategy, since it maximizes the pay-off of each country for any strategy that the other country might follow. So the Nash equilibrium for this game is (0,0): no agreement for emission reduction can be reached or sustained in this one-shot game.

Actually in this one-shot game things can become even worse than in the noncooperative equilibrium. As shown by Hoel (1991) if one country unilaterally decides to reduce emissions, then total emissions may even increase and aggregate welfare may decrease. However, both countries would have been better off by cooperation. That is, by entering the agreement and cooperating in emissions reduction, the pay-offs for each country under cooperation are individually rational as compared to the pay-offs under mutual defection, or $(b_1,b_2) > (n_1,n_2)$. So, if the time horizon is extended in the context of an infinitely repeated game, then the folk theorem (Friedman 1989) can be invoked to show that cooperation can be sustained. Let $\pi_{it}$ be the pay-off of country $i$ at time $t$. Then the present value of the pay-off for the country using $\alpha$ as the discount factor is given by:

$$PV_i = \sum_{t=0}^{\infty} \alpha^t \pi_{it}$$

According to the folk theorem, if countries maximize the present value of their pay-off, then the cooperative solution can be sustained, for a sufficiently low discount rate, by using an appropriate trigger strategy as long as the condition $(b_1,b_2) > (n_1,n_2)$ is satisfied. Using for example the values of the pay-off matrix (b), and a discount factor equal to 0.90, cooperation results in a pay-off for each country of $3(1+0.9+0.9^2+...)=30$. Consider the following strategy: Country 1 cooperates to reduce emissions at the beginning of the horizon and continues to cooperate as long as both countries have cooperated in the past. If, however, country 2 defects then country 1 will forever resort to the policy of defection (no agreement). If country 2 follows the same strategy then both counties will have a pay-off of 30 each. If country 2 takes advantage of country 1's willingness to cooperate (reduce emissions) and cheats at the beginning of the time horizon, it will receive 5 at the beginning and zero at each subsequent time period, for a total pay-off of 5. It is clear that in the context of a repeated game with an appropriate trigger strategy, free riding can be eliminated and cooperation to reduce emissions through an international agreement can be sustained.[12] As Barrett (1991) notes, a trigger strategy can be recognized in the 1957 North Pacific Seal Treaty (Article 12).

Cooperation however cannot be sustained, even in the repeated game framework, if moving from the noncooperative equilibrium to cooperation creates gainers and losers, as can be seen in pay-off matrix (c).[13]

---

[12]Bac (1996) shows that elimination of free riding in the context of a repeated game does not hold in general if there is incomplete information regarding the countries' valuations of the agreement benefits.
[13]The pay-offs presented in this matrix are the basis for the linkage between environmental and other issues of mutual interest among countries in international agreements. The entries in matrix (c) follow Cesar (1994).

Country 2

|  |  | D | C |
|---|---|---|---|
| | **D** | (0,0) | (5,-3) |
| Country 1 | **C** | (-1,2) | (4,-1) |

(c)

Although cooperation to reduce pollution increases the joint pay-off, since $(b_1+b_2) > (n_1+n_2)$ in terms of the notation of pay-off matrix (a), cooperation is not however individually rational since country 2 is better off without the agreement. Under this situation of asymmetries among countries, extension of the time horizon cannot sustain cooperation to reduce emissions, and free riding incentives prevent international agreement unless further elaborations are made.

Thus this analysis suggests that international agreements among countries should be designed to be sustainable, that is, to overcome countries' incentives to cheat or defect from the agreement, when asymmetries require the use of side payments or issue linkage, in addition to trigger strategies, or when the repeated game framework cannot be regarded as appropriate.[14] Therefore in the subsequent sections we mainly focus on: (i) how agreements leading to international cooperation regarding global environmental problems can be formed and sustained, and (ii) how some standard environmental policy instruments can be extended to international environmental problems so that both the structure of the policy scheme and the type of the agreement necessary for the implementation of the scheme are determined.

## 3   INTERNATIONAL ENVIRONMENTAL AGREEMENTS

The basic question in the case of international environmental agreements is whether sovereign countries can voluntarily – since there is no authority to force them to cooperate – reach an agreement to protect the international

---

[14]Carraro and Siniscalco (1993a) note that for the case of global pollutant emissions such as $CO_2$ or CFCs, the repeated game framework is not particularly helpful since emission reductions involve substantial and irreversible investments, and increases in emissions as a form of trigger strategy will probably harm the triggering country. This, however, can be prevented by renegotiation proof strategies.

commons by cutting down domestic emissions.

Three main approaches have been developed in the literature regarding this issue. The first approach analyses the problem in terms of agreements of subgroups of countries, which seek to expand the agreement to reduce emissions by inducing other countries to join the agreement through self-financing welfare transfers.[15] The second analyses the problem in the context of a cooperative game with externalities and derives conditions under which a group of countries can agree to reduce emissions to a desired level in a cooperative way, and share total costs including abatement costs and environmental damages in such a way that every country is better off by cooperation.[16] The third refers to issue linkage where agreement on the environmental issue is linked to agreement on another issue in such a way that the agreement on both issues is sustainable.[17]

The above approaches to analysing environmental agreement rely on the concepts of cooperative and noncooperative games among countries (plus characteristic function approaches and the 'core' concept) and thus it is helpful to define these two concepts more precisely. A cooperative game reflects emission decisions taken together by all countries in cooperation, while a noncooperative game reflects emission decisions that satisfy the objectives of each single country itself, without the country taking into account the environmental damages caused by its emissions on the rest of the countries in the group.

## 3.1 International Agreements and Coalition Formation

We consider a group of $i=1,\ldots,n$ countries, where production activities generate pollution that crosses national boundaries and its total concentration in the environment affects the whole group.[18] Let $e_i$ be the emissions of a global pollutant, say carbon dioxide from country $i$. The concentration of the pollutant in the ambient environment of the group of countries, defined as $X=\Sigma_i e_i$, causes damages to all countries. It is assumed that the damage function in each country takes the simple linear form $m_i X$, where $m_i \geq 0$ measures marginal damages in country $i$. Following Hoel (1992b), it is

---

[15]See for example Barrett (1990, 1992, 1994a, 1995, 1997), Carraro and Siniscalco (1991, 1993a), Hoel (1992b) and Petrakis and Xepapadeas (1996).

[16]See for example Chander and Tulkens (1992, 1994, 1995).

[17]See for example Folmer et al. (1993), Cesar and de Zeeuw (1996) and Cesar (1994).

[18]The presentation in this section follows mainly Petrakis and Xepapadeas (1996). For earlier treatments of the same problem see, for example, Barrett (1991,1992), Hoel (1992b) and Carraro and Siniscalco (1993a).

further assumed that $m_1 \geq m_2 \geq ... \geq m_n$, $M = \Sigma_i m_i > 0$. Therefore, countries with a high marginal damage coefficient, $m$, are considered to suffer the most damages from environmental pollution. If $m=0$ for some country, then this country does not suffer any damages from global pollution. The benefit of each country is determined by the usual function of its emissions, $e_i$, defined as $B_i(e_i)$, $B_i(0) = 0$, $B_i'' < 0$. Thus the net benefits for country $i$ are determined by the emissions levels of all other countries' as:

$$W(e_i, e_{-i}) = B_i(e_i) - m_i X \text{ where } e_{-i} = (e_1, ..., e_{i-1}, e_{i+1}, ..., e_n)$$

In the absence of international cooperation, each country's emissions are determined as the Nash equilibrium of the noncooperative game where countries choose emissions simultaneously to maximize their net benefits. Thus the Nash equilibrium emissions level for each country is defined as the solution of the problem:

$$\max_{e_i \geq 0} B_i(e_i) - m_i X \qquad\qquad (6.1)$$

For interior solutions the noncooperative emissions level is determined as:

$$e_i^o : B_i'(e_i^o) - m_i = 0, \ i=1,...,n \qquad\qquad (6.1.1)$$

The noncooperative emissions level can be compared to the emissions level corresponding to the first-best optimum which corresponds to the cooperative game. This solution is obtained by maximizing global welfare, defined as the sum of individual countries' net benefit functions. That is, the first-best emissions level corresponds to the solution of the problem:

$$\max_{(e_1,...,e_n) \geq 0} \sum_{i=1}^{n} W(e_i, e_{-i}) = \sum_{i=1}^{n} \left[ B_i(e_i) - m_i X \right] \qquad\qquad (6.2)$$

The solution to the cooperative game can be regarded as the case in which some supranational authority would have set the emissions level for each country at the first-best optimum. These first-best emissions levels are determined as:

$$e_i^* : B_i(e_i^*) - M = 0, \ i=1,...,n \qquad\qquad (6.2.1)$$

By comparing (6.2.1) and (6.2.2) we have that $e_i^* < e_i^o$, $\forall i$, and $X^* < X^o$. This is a well-established result in the analysis of international pollution aspects;[19] emissions under cooperation fall short of the emissions corresponding to the noncooperative solution. This discrepancy can be seen

---

[19]See, for example, van der Ploeg and de Zeeuw (1992).

in Figure 6.1 below.

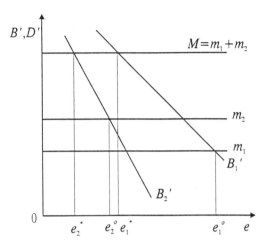

*Figure 6.1. Cooperative and noncooperative emissions*

Having defined the cooperative and the noncooperative outcomes the next step is to examine conditions under which a coalition of countries can be formed for the purpose of signing an agreement to reduce emissions compared to the noncooperative outcome. Carraro and Siniscalco (1994) suggest that two such conditions, profitability and stability, must be satisfied.

*Profitability*    Profitability is a necessary condition for the formation of a coalition. A coalition is profitable if the net benefits for the countries in the coalition exceed the net benefits of the noncooperative Nash equilibrium. Consider the case in which the formation of a coalition including all countries is considered, such that the first-best cooperative emissions are achieved. The coalition will be profitable if:

$$W_i(e_i^*, e_{-i}^*) > W_i(e_i^o, e_{-i}^o) \text{ for all } i$$

That is, each country gains from joining the coalition for the purpose of emitting at the cooperative level as compared to the noncooperative case, or put differently, joining the coalition is individually rational for all countries.[20]

---

[20]The coalition can of course be defined for a subset of countries. In this case profitability will be defined in terms of net benefits when the subset of countries cooperates, as compared to the noncooperative case.

*Stability* Although profitability is a necessary condition for the formation of a coalition, it is not however sufficient. Sufficiency requires that the profitable coalition is also stable in the sense that:

(i)     no country inside the coalition has an incentive to defect once the other countries are participating, that is, there are no free-riding incentives; and

(ii)    no country outside the coalition has an incentive to enter the coalition.[21]

In the context of the model presented above the profitability condition need not always be satisfied. That is, not all countries are better off at the first-best optimum as compared to the Nash equilibrium. Countries for which:

$$m_i < \frac{B_i(e_i^*) - B_i(e_i^o)}{X^* - X^o} \qquad (6.3)$$

will be better off under cooperation. On the other hand, countries for which the reverse holds will be worse off at the first-best optimum as compared to the noncooperative Nash equilibrium. It is clear that when individual rationality does not hold for all countries, that is, there are gainers and losers from moving to the first-best, then there will be no voluntary cooperation by all $n$ countries for the achievement of the first-best. There is, however, the possibility of improving upon the inefficient laissez-faire outcome. The methods for exploring potential improvements depend on how the countries that might agree to cooperation are determined and how their corresponding emissions levels are chosen.

One approach is to identify countries for which (6.3) holds as environmentally conscious (ENCC), and countries for which the reverse holds as less environmentally conscious (LENCC). The ENCC are indexed by $j \in J$ and the LENCC by $k \in K$. The sets $J$ and $K$ partition the set $I = \{1, \ldots, n\}$, that is, $J \cup K = I$, $J \cap K = \phi$.

Assume that the ENCC consider forming a coalition under which they will emit at the first-best optimum while the rest of the LENCC will emit at the noncooperative Nash equilibrium.[22] This coalition will be profitable if

---

[21]This stability concept corresponds to the concept of internal and external cartel stability (D'Aspremont et al. 1983).

[22]Of course the ENCC may consider an agreement on some other emission level that represents a reduction as compared to the noncooperative outcome, $\tilde{e}_j \in [e_j^*, e_j^o)$. Alternatively the ENCC can choose emission levels for themselves and the LENCC that maximize their own welfare subject to the constraint of paying transfer payments to the LENCC for moving from the

$$W_J(e_j^*, e_{-j}^*, e_1^o, ..., e_k^o) > W_J(e_j^o, e_{-j}^o, e_1^o, ..., e_k^o) \quad \forall j \in J$$

$$\text{where } e_{-j} = (e_1, ..., e_{j-1}, e_{j+1}, ..., e_J)$$

However, even if the coalition is profitable, it is by no means stable in the sense defined above, and in particular with respect to the internal stability which is a crucial characteristic. A country $j \in J$ will have an incentive to free ride and defect from the coalition if there are additional benefits from being outside the coalition and emitting at some level $\bar{e}_j \in (e_j^*, e_j^o]$, when the rest of the ENCC stay in the coalition. Formally a country $j$ will have incentive to free ride if

$$W_j(\bar{e}_j, e_{-j}^*, e_1^o, ..., e_k^o) > W_j(e_j^*, e_{-j}^*, e_1^o, ..., e_k^o)$$

Since given the structure of our model, free-riding incentives cannot be excluded, the coalition is not internally stable. Actually it is known that the size of the stable coalition, when problems of climate are analysed, depends on the values of marginal benefits and marginal costs and is likely to be small (Barrett 1991, 1995; Hoel 1992b).[23] The internal stability requirements, which might be satisfied for a small – but not the whole – group of the ENCC, can, however, be regarded as too restrictive in reality. It seems natural to consider a group of countries like the EU or the OECD as the ENCC, which can be regarded as prime candidates for forming a stable coalition of countries agreeing to emit at the first-best, since breaking of the agreement by one of these countries will not only entail possible costs in legal terms (EU legal apparatus) but also costs in terms of breaking social norms (Hoel 1994). If the ENCC commit to a stable coalition then these countries can seek ways of expanding the coalition to the LENCC.

Expansion of the coalition to the LENCC, which are the nonsignatory countries, can be obtained by transfers of resources from the ENCC to the LENCC. In order to have a credible mechanism of transfers the following conditions should be satisfied (Carraro and Siniscalco 1994):

(i)     Transfers must be self-financed. The total transfer of resources to the LENCC must not exceed the total welfare gain of the ENCC from taking the LENCC into the existing coalition.

(ii)    The stable coalition commitment must be satisfied. That is, the ENCC countries in the stable coalition which provide the transfers

---

noncooperative Nash equilibrium (Hoel 1994, Kverndokk 1994).

[23] In a recent empirical study referring to $CO_2$ emissions, Botteon and Carraro (1997) using data from five world regions, show that coalitions involving more than three countries are not stable.

must commit to cooperation.[24]

(iii)     The committed countries should try to include the maximum number of the LENCC in the coalition.

In the context of the model developed above, and given the stable coalition assumption (ii), a system of self-financed transfers exists such that all the LENCC enter the coalition and emit at the first-best cooperative solution if:

$$\left[\sum_i B_i(e_i^*) - MX^*\right] - \left[\sum_i B_i(e_i^o) - MX^o\right] \geq$$

$$\sum_k m_k\left[(X^o - X^*) - \left(e_k^o - e_k^*\right)\right]$$

(6.4)

To show this, consider the $k$th LENCC. This country will be no worse off under the first-best if it receives a transfer $t_k^o = B_k(e_k^o) - B_k(e_k^*) - m_k(X^o - X^*)$ which is equal to its losses for moving to the first-best. This transfer might not, however, be sufficient to eliminate free-riding incentives and secure the stability of the coalition, because country $k$ will have an incentive to defect once all other countries have entered the coalition and are emitting at the Nash equilibrium emission level. The gains from defection are defined as:

$$G_k = \left[B_k(e_k^o) - m_k\left(e_k^o + \sum_{i \neq k} e_i^*\right)\right] - \left[B_k(e_k^*) - m_k\sum_i e_i^*\right] \text{ or}$$

$$G_k = B_k(e_k^o) - B_k(e_k^*) - m_k(e_k^o - e_k^*)$$

(6.5)

Country $k$ will have no incentive to defect only if $t_k^o \geq G_k$. If condition (6.4) is satisfied then the sum of the benefits of the ENCC from moving to the first-best exceed the sum of potential gains from defection of the LENCC.[25] Thus the mechanism of transfers satisfies the criteria (i) to (iii) above and the coalition of the ENCC countries can be expanded to include all countries and create a grand coalition where all countries emit at the first-best optimum.[26]

This result implies that, if the benefits from moving to the first-best are sufficiently large for the ENCC, then these countries can offer sufficient

---

[24]In their empirical study, Botteon and Carraro (1997) show that transfers can be used to broaden the stable coalition even in the absence of any form of partial commitment.

[25]This is true since (6.4) can be written equivalently as:

$$\sum_j \left[B_j(e_j^*) - B_j(e_j^o) - m_j(X^* - X^o)\right] \geq \sum_k \left[B_k(e_k^o) - B_k(e_k^*) - m_k(e_k^o - e_k^*)\right] = \sum_k G_k$$

[26]This result is an extension of the results by Carraro and Siniscalco (1993a) for the case in which the participating countries are not identical.

inducement for the LENCC to form a stable coalition wherein all countries will emit at the first-best. As can be seen by (6.4), where the left-hand side is always positive, since it represents the difference in total benefits between the first-best and the noncooperative Nash equilibrium, a stable coalition can always be achieved if the marginal pollution damages of the LENCC are sufficiently small.[27]

## 3.2 Cost-Sharing and International Environmental Agreements

The main idea behind this approach is to determine a rule to share among the participating countries the aggregate costs of: (a) abating emissions, such that the first-best cooperative solution is achieved, and (b) environmental damages that correspond to the first-best, such that all countries involved are willing to participate in the agreement to attain the first-best.

Following Chander and Tulkens (1995), the objective function of a country is defined in terms of the aggregate cost of emission abatement and environmental damages:[28]

$$J_i(e_i, e_{-i}) = c_i(e_i) + D_i(X) , \quad X = \sum_{i=1}^{n} e_i$$

where $c_i(e_i)$ is a strictly decreasing and convex abatement cost function – abatement costs are reduced when more emissions are allowed – and $D_i(X)$ is the usual strictly increasing and convex damage function.

As in the previous section the Nash equilibrium of the noncooperative game is the solution of the problem:

$$\min_{e_i \geq 0} J(e_i, e_{-i})$$

The optimum is again characterized by the well-known necessary and sufficient conditions:

$$e_i^o : c_i'(e_i^o) + D_i'(X^o) = 0, \ e_i^o > 0, \ i = 1,...,n$$

---

[27]The approach used to derive conditions which ensure the stability of the coalition of all countries can be used to examine partial expansions (see Petrakis and Xepapadeas 1996). Petrakis and Xepapadeas further show that if there are enough benefits to achieve the grand coalition then the agreement can be sustained even under informational constraints that take the form of moral hazard, where only the global pollution accumulation can be observed but not individual country emissions. To sustain the agreement to emit at the first-best a truth-telling mechanism should be included in the international agreement.

[28]For the development of dynamic adjustment processes for achieving the first-best in the context of cost sharing models, see Chander and Tulkens (1992).

The first-best optimum is determined as the solution of the cooperative game:

$$\min_{(e_1,...,e_n)\geq 0} \sum_{i=1}^{n} J_i(e_i, e_{-i}) \tag{6.6}$$

with the optimum determined again as:

$$e_i^*: c_i'(e_i^*) + \sum_{i=1}^{n} D_i'(X^*) = 0, \ e_i^* > 0 \tag{6.6.1}$$

As in Section 3.2 of this chapter, it is clear that $e_i^* < e_i^o$ for all $i$. The total minimized cost of the cooperative game defined in (6.6) determines the total worth of the game as:

$$V(n) = \min_{(e_1,...,e_n)} \sum_{i=1}^{n} J_i(e_i, e_{-i}) \tag{6.7}$$

Chander and Tulkens (1995) define an imputation by a vector $y = (y_1,...,y_n)$ such that $\sum_i y_i = V(n)$. That is, the imputation is a way of sharing the total cost of abatement and environmental damages that correspond to the first-best cooperative solution.

The vector of emissions $e^* = (e_1^*,...,e_n^*)$ at the cooperative optimum determines the minimum cost for each country as $J(e_i^*, e_{-i}^*)$. Thus $\sum_i J_i(e_i^*, e_{-i}^*) = V(n)$, and the vector $(J_1(e_1^*, e_{-1}^*),...,J_n(e_n^*, e_{-n}^*))$ is an imputation where each country bears its own cost for achieving the cooperative emission levels. An imputation involving transfers or side payments among countries can be defined as:

$$y_i^P = J_i(e_i^*, e_{-i}^*) + P_i, \ \text{with} \ \sum_{i=1}^{n} P_i = 0 \tag{6.8}$$

The imputation defined by (6.8) indicates that country $i$ bears its abatement cost at the cooperative optimum plus or minus a transfer. Since the sum of transfers is zero, the imputation (6.8) defines another way of sharing among countries the cost at the cooperative optimum. The basic question is whether an imputation exists, that is whether a cost sharing rule exists, such that all countries will agree to emit at the first-best. If all countries agree then the grand coalition is formed. On the other hand if some country attempts to free ride then the coalition breaks and each country acts as a single player to minimize its costs. It can be shown (Chander and Tulkens 1995) that the imputation defined as:

$$y_i^* = J_i(e_i^* e_{-i}^*) + P_i^*, \ i = 1,...n$$

where

$$P_i^* = -\left[c_i(e_i^*) - c_i(e_i^o)\right] + \frac{D_i'}{D'}\left(\sum_{i=1}^{n} c_i(e_i^*) - \sum_{i=1}^{n} c_i(e_i^o)\right)$$

$$D' = \sum_{i=1}^{n} D_i'$$

(6.9)

provides a sharing rule among countries of the grand coalition such that no other coalition of countries with members $s \neq n$ can improve upon it, in the sense of securing a better pay-off to its members as compared to the grand coalition.[29]

This cost sharing can be regarded as a proposal to countries to share the costs of achieving the first-best. The transfers are necessary to induce countries that are not experiencing sufficiently high damages from global pollution (LENCCs in the terminology of the previous section) to bear the increased abatement costs. As seen from (6.9) the first term of the transfer covers the payment to the country to counterbalance the cost difference from abating at the first-best as compared to the noncooperative Nash equilibrium, while the second term is the payment the country makes which is proportional to the ratio of own marginal damages to the global marginal damages.[30] If $D_i' = 0$ then the country receives only a payment to cover its abatement costs for moving to the first-best. The result can be compared to the one in the previous section. In equation (6.5) if marginal environmental damages for country $k$ are zero then in order to cooperate the country should be fully compensated for the losses in benefits from moving from the noncooperative Nash equilibrium to the first-best. This observation exemplifies the fact that both approaches are in the spirit of the 'victim pays' principle rather than the 'polluter pays' principle which underlies most of the environmental policy analysis dealing with domestic or localized pollution problems.

In the present approach free riding is prevented by the threat of breaking the coalition. If a coalition of $s \neq n$ envisages free riding, the rest of the non free riders will break into singletons and try to minimize their costs individually. Since no coalition can do better than the grand coalition of all $n$ countries, the breaking of the free riders into singletons is sufficient to deter the $s$ countries from free riding.[31]

---

[29]In technical terms the coalition belongs to the core of the cooperative game with $n$ players.

[30]Chander and Tulkens (1992) propose the creation of an international agency for handling these transfers.

[31]Welsch (1993) provides a cost-sharing mechanism for a global pollution problem that is based on the benefit approach in the allocation of public goods. Determination of the cost shares according to the benefits received in each country leads to an efficient solution. An

One transboundary problem that has been analysed in a framework similar to the cost sharing approach is the acid rain problem in Northern Europe.[32] In a static framework the problem is described by a decreasing control cost function $c_i(e_i)$, for sulphur dioxide emissions $e_i$, and a damage function $D_i(X_i)$, where $X_i$ denotes acid depositions in country $i$. The transboundary character of the problem means that depositions in country $i$ are determined by emissions of other countries through a transboundary process determined by the transfer matrix $A=[a_{ij}]$, $i, j=1,...n$, where the element $a_{ij}$ denotes the portion of emissions of one ton of sulphur emitted in country $j$ that is deposited in country $i$. Given the vector of sulphur emissions $e=(e_1,...,e_n)$ and the vector of depositions $a=(a_1,...,a_n)$, depositions in country $i$ are determined as $x_i = a_i \cdot e' + b_i$,[33] while the vector of depositions in each country is determined as:

$$x' = A \cdot e' + b', \quad x' = \begin{bmatrix} x_1 \\ . \\ x_n \end{bmatrix}, \quad b' = \begin{bmatrix} b_1 \\ . \\ b_n \end{bmatrix}$$

where $b_i$ denotes depositions with natural origin.

The first-best emissions are determined as solutions of the cooperative game:

$$\min_{(e_1,...,e_n) \geq 0} \sum_{i=1}^{n} \left[ c_i(e_i) + D_i(X_i) \right]$$

$$\text{s. t. } X' = Ae' + b'$$

On the other hand the noncooperative Nash equilibrium emissions are defined as the solution of:

$$\min_{e_1 \geq 0} c_i(e_i) + D_i(X_i)$$

$$\text{s. t. } X' = Ae' + b'$$

---

implementation mechanism that can improve upon the inefficient laissez-faire is also developed. Heal (1993) considers a minimum critical coalition and examines the case in which it is not rational for each country to undertake abatement by itself, but it is rational for a group of countries to do so. In this approach the minimum critical coalition is a necessary though not a sufficient approach for a self-enforced agreement.

[32] See, for example, Mäler (1989, 1992, 1994a), Mäler and de Zeeuw (1995), Tahvonen et al. (1993), Kaitala et al. (1995) and Germain et al. (1996).

[33] Primes associated with vectors or matrices denote transposes.

In examining the European case Mäler (1994a) found that if a cooperative solution with side payments is possible then total emissions in Europe can be reduced by about 40 per cent as compared to 1984 emissions. Mäler also shows that the cooperative agreement can be sustained in a repeated game context using trigger strategies, since the numerical parameters of the problem justify the small discount rate, which is necessary for the existence of trigger strategies.

Informational problems which might arise in practice because of the need to know the emission control function and the damage function over the whole range of possible values (global knowledge), in order to apply the above-described approach, can be alleviated by introducing a dynamic process representing an emission reduction program, described by a differential equation:

$$\frac{de_i(t)}{dt} = -k\left[c_i'(e_i) + \sum_{j=1}^{n} a_{ij}D_j'(X_j)\right]$$

In the context of the process described by the differential equation, the cost and damage function need to be known only at the margin. By transforming the continuous time problem described above into a discrete time problem, Germain et al. (1996) show that for the acid rain problem involving tree regions of Finland, Russia and Estonia, the cooperative optimum with side payments can be reached at a finite number of negotiation stages.

### 3.3  Issue Linkage and International Environmental Agreements

The achievement of an international environmental agreement, either through coalition expansion or through cost-sharing rules, requires side payments to some countries, with these transfers being basically governed by the victim pays principle. As however is pointed out by Cesar and de Zeeuw (1996), while transfers are rarely observed in international environmental agreements,[34] it is more common to have an international agreement in which the agreement on the part of a country or group of countries to reduce emissions is linked to agreements among the same countries on other issues. In the London amendment of the Montreal Protocol the developing countries agreed to phase out the CFCs, but their agreement was linked to technology

---

[34]Exceptions are the 1957 North Pacific Seal Treaty in which the US and the USSR agreed to pay Canada and Japan and the 1972 agreement between France and the Netherlands in which the Netherlands agreed to pay cleaning-up costs for the river Rhine (Cesar and de Zeeuw 1996).

transfers from the developed countries.[35]

The main advantage of linking issues is that international environmental agreements can become profitable and sustainable when: (i) asymmetries among countries create gainers and losers in the move from the noncooperative to the cooperative outcome, so repeated game arguments can not be applied to sustain cooperation; and (ii) when transfers or side payments are not possible or convenient. Consider, following Cesar and de Zeeuw (1996), the game with pay-offs as shown in matrix (c). These pay-offs are depicted in Figure 6.2. In this game all outcomes in the shaded area *ODE* are individually rational and can be sustained by repeated game arguments. However, the cooperative equilibrium point is not individually rational for country 2 which loses by moving to the cooperative equilibrium. For this outcome to be sustainable side payments need to be introduced.

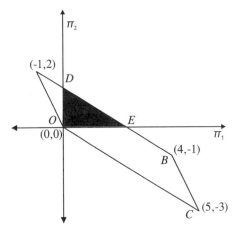

*Figure 6.2  Pay-offs of the isolated game*

The idea of issue linkage is to link the negotiations on the environmental issue (represented by the game of Figure 6.2) to another roughly equivalent issue[36] in which country 2 will be the gainer at the cooperative solution. A mirror image game can be presented in the following pay-off matrix, which can be regarded as reflecting the other issue.

---

[35]See Cesar (1994) and Cesar and de Zeeuw (1996) for more examples on issue linkage involving environmental agreements.
[36]For a definition of rough equivalence see Cesar (1994).

Country 2

|  |  | D | C |
|---|---|---|---|
|  | **D** | (0,0) | (2,-1) |
| Country 1 | **C** | (-3,5) | (-1,4) |

(d)

Assume now that the two issues are negotiated together so that the pay-offs are presented in matrix (e) and Figure 6.3.

Country 2

|  |  | **(D,D)** | **(D,C)** | **(C,D)** | **(C,C)** |
|---|---|---|---|---|---|
|  | **(D,D)** | (0,0) | (2,-1) | (5,-3) | (7,-4) |
|  | **(D,C)** | (-3,5) | (-1,4) | (2,2) | (4,1) |
| Country 1 | **(C,D)** | (-1,2) | (1,1) | (4,-1) | (6,-2) |
|  | **(C,C)** | (-4,7) | (-2,6) | (1,4) | (3,3) |

(e)

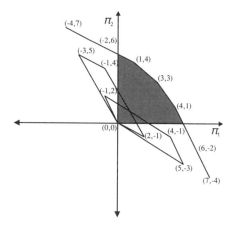

*Figure 6.3  Pay-offs of the linked games*

The cooperative outcome in the shaded area of Figure 6.3 is individually rational for both countries and can therefore be sustained by repeated game arguments. As shown by Cesar and de Zeeuw (1996) the linking of the two mirror image games makes it possible to sustain the cooperative outcomes as a subgame perfect renegotiation proof equilibrium in which the two players threaten to punish each other by defecting in both issues.[37] The above results indicate that issue linkage in the presence of asymmetric countries can increase the profitability of the agreement.

There have been attempts in the literature to link environmental agreements to other issues. Carraro and Siniscalco (1997) show for the case of symmetric countries that linking the negotiations on emission reductions to the negotiations of R&D cooperation can reduce the incentives to free ride on the environmental agreement and stabilize the agreement. For the cooperating countries R&D generates a positive externality that can be excluded from the noncooperating countries. Thus when potential free riders join the coalition they receive R&D benefits. These benefits offset losses from bearing the cost of emissions reductions. In a similar context Katsoulacos (1997) examines the linking of environmental agreements to R&D cooperation under R&D spillovers. It is shown that there are incentives for governments to agree to jointly subsidize research joint ventures between firms, making the agreement contingent on all governments choosing the cooperative emission levels. Barrett (1994c) links the achievement of an environmental agreement with trade restrictions. It is shown that an environmental agreement can be sustained if there is a credible threat of trade restrictions. The credible threat can be provided by restriction of imports to the signatory countries from the nonsignatory countries and restriction of exports from the signatory countries to the nonsignatory countries.

## 4 DYNAMIC ASPECTS OF GLOBAL POLLUTION PROBLEMS

As was explained in Chapter 3, global pollution problems such as those associated with greenhouse warming, sulphur deposition or ozone depletion, represent stock externalities and as such they should be examined in a

---

[37]The game described above is the so-called asymmetric prisoners' dilemma in which no country is stronger than the other. Sustainability of cooperation through issue linkage can also be proved in the so-called suasion game, where one country is stronger, and the weaker country has an incentive to free ride on the stronger country (Cesar and de Zeeuw 1996).

dynamic framework.

In a way similar to the static approach, the dynamic approach to the analysis of global pollution problems examines policy options when the stock characteristics of the global pollutants are fully accounted, and compares cooperative and noncooperative outcomes. When the noncooperative solution is analysed each country should choose a strategy consisting of a path of emissions $\{e_i(t)\}$. As presented in Chapter 3, Section 3.5, the information structure of the game determines the strategy space for the country in question. Following the same approach as in the third chapter, open-loop (OL) and feedback (FB) information structures are examined. In this context the infinite horizon problem corresponding to global pollution can be described in the following way.[38] The social welfare for each country $i=1,...n$ is defined as:

$$W_i(t) = \int_o^\infty e^{-rt}\left[B_i(e_i(t)) - D_i(X(t))\right]dt \tag{6.10}$$

The global pollutant accumulates in the environment according to the first-order differential equation:[39]

$$\dot{X}(t) = \sum_{i=1}^n e_i(t) - bX(t), \ X(0) = X_o \geq 0 \tag{6.11}$$

The cooperative solution is obtained by maximizing $\sum_i W_i(t)$ subject to (6.11) for $e_i \geq 0$. The current value Hamiltonian for the cooperative game is defined as:

$$H = \sum_{i=1}^n \left[B_i(e_i(t)) - D_i(X(t))\right] + \lambda(t)\left[\sum_{i=1}^n e_i(t) - bX(t)\right] \tag{6.12}$$

where $\lambda(t)$ is the shadow cost or the cooperative valuation of the global pollutant. According to the maximum principle the necessary and sufficient optimality conditions are:

$$B_i'(e_i^*(t)) \leq -\lambda(t) \text{ with equality if } e_i^*(t) > 0 \tag{6.13.1}$$

$$\dot{\lambda}(t) = (r+b)\lambda + \sum_i D_i'(X^*(t)) \tag{6.13.2}$$

---

[38]The approach here is similar to the one followed by van der Ploeg and de Zeeuw (1992). See also Hoel (1992a), Dockner and van Long (1993), Martin et al. (1993) and Xepapadeas (1995a,b).

[39]This is the simplest possible accumulation relationship used for expositional clarity. The accumulation of the global pollutant for specific cases can take more complicated forms as will be shown later on in this chapter.

$$\dot{X}(t) = \sum_i e^*(t) - bX^*(t) \qquad\qquad (6.13.3)$$

along with the usual transversality conditions at infinity.

From (6.13.1) cooperative emissions are defined as a function of the pollutant's shadow cost, or

$$e_i^*(t) = e_i^*(\lambda(t)), \text{ with } e^{*\prime}(\lambda) > 0 \qquad\qquad (6.14)$$

The MHDS determines the evolution of the global pollutant and its shadow cost and is obtained by substituting (6.14) into (6.13.2) and (6.13.3). The cooperative or first-best, long-run steady state accumulation of the pollutant and its shadow cost are determined as $(X_\infty^*, \lambda_\infty^*) : \dot{X} = \dot{\lambda} = 0$. By using the same approach as was used in Chapter 3, Section 2, it can be shown that the steady state exists, is unique and has the global saddle point property. The steady state is shown in Figure 6.4.

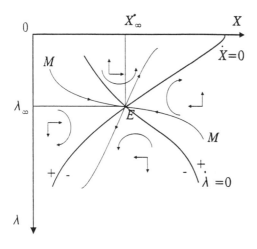

*Figure 6.4  Steady state equilibrium for global pollution*

In the noncooperative equilibrium with an OL information structure the strategy of each country with respect to emissions is a function of the initial stock of the global pollutant, or $e_i(t) = \theta_i(X_o, t)$, $i=1,...,n$. When an FB information structure is assumed, each country uses Markov strategies and emissions are defined as functions of the current stock of the global pollutant or, $e_i(t) = \theta_i(X(t), t) = \bar{e}_i - \beta X(t)$, $\beta > 0$, for all $i$, assuming again linear Markov strategies. For the open-loop Nash equilibrium (OLNE) the current value Hamiltonian, assuming a common discount rate for all countries, is defined as:

$$H^i = B_i(e_i(t)) - D_i(X(t)) + \lambda_i^{OL}\left[e_i(t) + \sum_{j \neq i} e_j^o(t) - bX(t)\right] \tag{6.15}$$

where $\lambda_i^{OL}$ is the individual country valuation, or shadow cost, of the global pollutant and $e_{-i} = (e_1^o,\dots,e_{i-1}^o, e_{i+1}^o,\dots,e_i^o)$ is the optimal response vector for the rest of the countries. The problem is similar to the one discussed in Chapter 3, Section 5. Following the same approach it can be shown that the global pollution in OLNE exceeds global pollution in the cooperative equilibrium.

For the feedback Nash equilibrium (FBNE) the current value Hamiltonian is defined as:[40]

$$H^i = B_i(e_i(t)) - D_i(X(t)) + \lambda_i^{FB}\left[e_i(t) + \sum_{j \neq i} \theta_j(X(t)) - bX(t)\right]$$

The optimality conditions imply:

$$B_i'(e_i^o(t)) \leq -\lambda_i^{FB} \text{ with equality if } e_i^o(t) > 0 \tag{6.16.1}$$

$$\dot{\lambda}_i^{FB} = (r + b + (n-1)\beta)\lambda_i^{FB} + D_i'(X^o(t)) \tag{6.16.2}$$

$$\dot{X}^o = \sum_i e_i^o(t) - bX^o(t) \tag{6.16.3}$$

Given the strong time consistency properties of the FBNE we concentrate on this solution. It can be shown, along the lines of Chapter 3, Section 5, that for linear Markov strategies, pollution at the steady state exceeds both the cooperative equilibrium and the OLNE.

This is a result similar to the one obtained in the static case, indicating the need for international cooperation to avoid excess accumulation of the global pollutant resulting from the laissez-faire solution.[41]

When we focus on linear Markov strategies the excess pollution at the steady state is a result of the differences in the valuation of the pollutant between the cooperative and the noncooperative solution. The steady state cooperative valuation is defined through (6.13.2) as:

$$\lambda_\infty^* = \frac{\sum_{i=1}^{n} D_i'}{r+b}$$

---

[40]The dynamic programming approach, with the help of the Hamilton-Bellman-Jacobi equation, is an alternative solution technique.

[41]The discussion about international environmental agreements in the static model developed in the previous section can be applied to the dynamic model by defining the countries' welfare as the present value of the flow of net benefits during the infinite time horizon.

while the individual country valuation in the FBNE is defined as:

$$\lambda_\infty^{FB} = \frac{D_i'}{r+b+(n-1)\beta}$$

Since $\beta > 0$, the above two relationships imply that $\left|\lambda_\infty^*\right| > \left|\lambda_\infty^{FB}\right|$, that is the cooperative shadow cost of the global pollutant exceeds the noncooperative shadow cost. This is due to two factors. The first is that in the noncooperative solution the two countries consider only their own marginal damages from global pollution, $D_i'$, and not aggregate marginal damages, $\Sigma_i D_i'$. The second factor relates to the linear Markov strategy. The negative slope of the function $\theta_i(X(t),t)$ implies that when a country decides to overemit it realizes that the effects of its own emissions on the accumulation of the global pollutant will be partly offset by other countries' lower emissions, as they will be responding in this way to the increase in the pollution stock. This is an added incentive to have more emissions under the linear Markov strategies. Thus noncooperative pollution levels exceed the corresponding cooperative pollution levels.[42,43]

Having provided an analytical framework for the analysis of global pollution problems in a dynamic framework, we focus now on modelling two of the most important problems of this type: global warming and acid rains.

## 4.1 Global Warming

There is a considerable body of literature dealing both with the economic and the scientific aspects of the global warming problem, which has already been described in previous sections.[44] In this section we present the building blocks

---

[42]In the OLNE $\beta = 0$, thus $\left|\lambda_\infty^*\right| > \left|\lambda_\infty^{OL}\right| > \left|\lambda_\infty^{FB}\right|$, and pollution in this case is between the cooperative and the feedback noncooperative case.

[43]The opening however of the model to an infinite horizon and the introduction of Markov perfect strategies increases the possible results. As shown by Dockner and van Long (1993), in a two-country symmetric model with quadratic benefit and damage functions, if countries follow nonlinear Markov perfect strategies, and the discount rate is sufficiently low, then the steady state first-best cooperative stock of the global pollutant can be attained by the noncooperative game. This result implies that in order to achieve the first-best optimum countries should agree only on selecting the nonlinear Markov strategy and then determine emissions that maximize their individual welfare in a noncooperative way. In this case the cooperative outcome is obtained as the solution of the noncooperative game without a need for side payments or trigger strategies.

[44]Nordhaus (1977) was the first to develop economic approaches to global warming. For concise treatment of various aspects of the problem see for example Cline (1991, 1992) and Nordhaus (1994). See also papers in the *American Economic Association Papers and Proceedings* (1982), The Global Commons I, Cost and Climatic Effects; *The Economic Journal* (1991), Policy

necessary for the construction of models describing the greenhouse problem, which can be used for policy issues.

Three main building blocks are necessary to construct an economic model describing greenhouse warming:

(i)     The benefit function from GHGs emissions,
(ii)    The cost function for reducing GHGs emissions, and
(iii)   The environmental damage function from GHGs emissions.

The benefit function can be determined by assuming that benefits from the use of combustion fuels in production activities that result in anthropogenic GHGs emissions[45] can be captured by a function which takes the form $y_i(t) = B_i(e_i(t), t)$ where $y_i$ is total product – that is GDP – produced by country $i$ at time $t$, which accounts for the benefits, and $e_i$ are GHGs or $CO_2$ equivalent emissions.[46] Hence the GHGs emissions are regarded as a generalized input in the production process. Finally $t$ is assumed to reflect technical change. In this formulation benefits from GHGs emissions are separable from damages caused by these emissions. Standard economic theory assumptions imply that:[47]

$$\frac{\partial B_i}{\partial e_i} \geq 0, \quad \frac{\partial B_i}{\partial t_i} > 0, \quad \frac{\partial^2 B_i}{\partial e_i^2} < 0, \quad \lim_{e_i \to 0} \frac{\partial B_i}{\partial e_i} + \infty$$

The cost function for reductions of GHGs reflects the abatement cost function introduced in Section 3.2 and specifies the cost to the society necessary for reducing the GHGs emissions. Weyant (1993) refers to four alternative cost concepts:

(i)     The marginal cost of the last ton of carbon emissions reduced,
(ii)    The marginal cost of emissions reductions integrated over all emissions reductions,
(iii)   The losses in GDP from emissions reductions. This concept can be determined directly from the partial derivative with respect to

Forum; *Journal of Economic Perspectives* (1993), Symposium on Global Warming; and *Resource and Energy Economics* (1993), special issue on Global Warming.

[45] As has already been noted, carbon dioxide is not the only GHG. However in the majority of the studies the focus is on $CO_2$, since it is the most important of the GHGs, contributing approximately 80 per cent to the global mean greenhouse forcing (Nordhaus 1991).

[46] This formulation is very common in theoretical models. See for example Welsch (1993), Dockner and van Long (1993) and Hoel and Isaksen (1995). The benefit function is actually a derived profit function, which can be determined as described in Chapter 2, Section 2.1.

[47] For the estimation of such a benefit function, as a long-run relationship using cointegration techniques for five groups of countries in the world, see Xepapadeas and Yiannaka (1997).

emissions of the benefit function, and

(iv)       The compensated income variation which expresses how much consumers have to be compensated in order to be as well off, after the emission reduction program has been implemented.[48]

A benefit function combining emissions and abatement costs is introduced by Kverndokk (1993).[49] Thus an income function is determined as:

$$B_i^{\,a}(e_i) = B_i(\hat{e}_i) - \frac{\lambda \hat{e}_i}{\varepsilon} \left[ \frac{\hat{e}_i - e_i}{\hat{e}_i} \right]^{\varepsilon}$$

where $\hat{e}_i$ are emissions when no attempt is made to reduce them, in the business as usual (BAU) case. On the other hand $\lambda$ denotes the shadow cost of emissions and can be regarded as a tax on emissions that results in eventual substitution of fossil fuels, and $\varepsilon$ can be interpreted as the elasticity of abatement costs.[50]

The damage function, which measures damages from GHGs emissions, is a much more complicated issue than the benefit or cost functions, since it includes a large number of uncertainties of both a scientific and an economic nature.[51] Damages relate to the impact of climate changes due to greenhouse warming. These impacts are expected to affect countries in different ways, with developing countries whose economies are more dependent on climatic conditions being more vulnerable to climate changes. However, despite these difficulties a damage function can be defined. This function essentially links the effects from the changes in the GHGs, or in the majority of the cases $CO_2$ or $CO_2$ equivalent gases, to global average temperature, and then transforms temperature changes to costs expressed in money terms. Thus a damage function can be defined as:

$$D_i = D_i(T(t), t), \quad \frac{\partial D}{\partial T} > 0$$

$$T(t) = T(X(t))$$

where $T(t)$ is the average global temperature increase above preindustrial

---

[48]The cost of stabilizing world emissions in the year 2010 to the 1990 levels has been estimated at approximately 4 per cent of the world GDP per year by the year 2100 (Weyant 1993).

[49]See also Fankhauser and Kverndokk (1996).

[50]It should be noted that the benefit function, $B_i$, implicitly determines any actual loss in GDP terms from emission reductions. This function is estimated by econometric approaches using time series data. The income function subtracts these losses directly and parameter values are used in empirical studies for calibration, of the income function.

[51]Nordhaus (1991) refers to the social and economic impact of climate change as *terra incognita*.

levels due to greenhouse warming and $X(t)$ is the anthropogenic concentration of GHGs above its preindustrial level. To determine such a damage function it is necessary to describe the relationship between GHGs emissions and climate development. To find the impact of an increase of GHGs on the climate, the temperature adjustment process should be taken into account, because the average climate responds slowly to the increase in radiative inputs. Nordhaus (1991) has suggested the following simplified two-box diffusion model:

$$\dot{T}(t) = \sigma[\lambda h(X(t)) - T(t)] \tag{6.17}$$

$$\dot{X}(t) = \beta e(t) - bX(t) \tag{6.18}$$

where $\sigma$ is a delay parameter of temperature in response to radiative increase (per year); $\lambda$ is a factor of proportionality between radiative forcing and the long-run temperature response, the value of $\lambda$ is set at 0.75 which means that an increase in the radiative forcing of $1W/m^2$ gives a long-run temperature increase of 0.75 degrees (Celsius); $h(M)$ is the increase in the radiative forcing from $CO_2$ equivalent emissions relative to the preindustrial level (measured in $W/m^2$), the $h$ function for $CO_2$ takes the form $6.3\ln(X/X_o)$, where $X_o$ is the atmospheric concentration of $CO_2$ relative to preindustrial time (Wingley 1987, IPCC-I 1990); $\beta$ is the fraction of GHGs aggregate emissions that enter the atmosphere; $e(t) = \sum_{i=1}^{n} e_i$ is aggregate emissions of GHGs by all countries, and $b$ is the rate of removal of the GHGs from the atmosphere, which reflects residence time in years. Possible values for these parameters are $\sigma = 0.025$; $\beta = 0.64$; and $b = 0.0083$ representing a residence time of 120 years (Nordhaus 1991, Hoel and Isaksen 1995).[52]

The damage function can be specified by the following functional form:[53]

$$D_i(T_i(t), t) = A_i[T(t)]^{\varrho} \exp(\theta_i t) \tag{6.19}$$

where $\varrho$ is the curvature of the damage function from the climate change with a usual value of 1.5 to allow for convexity (Cline 1992), and $\theta_i$ expresses how the monetary damage of the climatic change develops over time for a constant climate in a specific country. Cline (1992) considers this parameter as proportional to the gross domestic product. Thus the $\theta$ parameter can be defined as the growth rate of the GDP. In global studies the

---

[52]The climate model can be extended to take into account the changes in the deep ocean temperature. In this case the evolution of the temperature described by (6.17) is also a function of the deep ocean temperature relative to the preindustrial level, and one more transition equation is added to describe the evolution of the deep ocean temperature (Nordhaus and Yang 1996).

[53]See for example Hoel and Isaksen (1995) and Fankhauser and Kverndokk (1996).

value of $A$, along with a value of $\varrho = 1.5$, reflects the proportional damages in world GDP from a 3°C increase in temperature. There have been different estimates of this proportional damage ranging from 0.25 per cent (Nordhaus 1991) to 2.4 per cent (Ayres and Walter 1991). An estimate of 2 per cent suggested by Cline (1992) yields an estimate of $A = 115$ billion in 1990 dollars (Hoel and Isaksen 1995).

Solution of the differential equation (6.18) determines the concentration of the $CO_2$ equivalent emissions as a function of the emissions themselves and the rest of the parameters, or $X(t) = X(t; \Sigma_i e_i, \beta, b)$. Substituting this solution into (6.17) and solving the differential equation again, the development of the temperature increase relative to the preindustrial level is determined as a function of emissions as $T(t) = T(t; \Sigma_i e_i, \beta, b, \lambda, X_o)$.

These building blocks of the global warming model can be used to define cooperative and noncooperative solutions as described in Section 4. The cooperative solution can be used as a benchmark for comparison to the noncooperative solution and designing optimal policies. In practice different variations of this general approach have been followed.

Kverndokk (1994) defines a dynamic model and uses it to determine optimal consumption and emission paths for a group of cooperating countries that form a coalition. The model contains a production-consumption module, the damage function from $CO_2$ emissions and a climate module. The optimal solution is used to determine possible sizes of side payments to be given to other countries for emissions reductions. Fankhauser and Kverndokk (1996) use a static model to calculate and compare the cooperative (social optimum) and the noncooperative Nash equilibrium for five world regions. Nordhaus and Yang (1996) use a regional dynamic general equilibrium model (model RICE) to analyse dynamic paths for ten world regions of $CO_2$ emissions and implied carbon taxes corresponding to unregulated market equilibrium (no $CO_2$ emissions control), cooperative equilibrium, and noncooperative equilibrium. In Nordhaus and Yang's model, global warming damages and abatement costs determine a scale factor which reduces gross domestic product, produced by a Cobb-Douglas production function, in a multiplicative way.

## 4.2  Acid Rains

The problem of acid rains, also described earlier in this chapter, can be formulated in the context of a differential game. Mäler and de Zeeuw (1995) introduce the concept of the critical load of acid depositions, indicating how much deposition of acids can be received by a country before damages due to soil acidification commence.

Using the notation of Section 3.2 and following Mäler and de Zeeuw (1995), the accumulation of acid depositions in country $i=1,...,n$ is determined by the system of first-order differential equations, written in matrix notations as:

$$\dot{X}(t)=Ae'(t)-c,\ X'(0)=X_o,\ c=\begin{bmatrix} c_1 \\ . \\ c_n \end{bmatrix} \qquad (6.20)$$

where $c$ is the vector of critical loads and $A$ is the constant transportation matrix defined in Section 3.2. The problem for country $i$ is to minimize in an infinite time horizon the aggregate costs of acid abatement and damages due to depositions, or

$$\min_{\{e_i(t)\geq 0\}} J_i = \int_0^\infty e^{-rt}\left[c_i(e_i(t))+D_i(X_i(t))\right]dt,\ i=1,...,n \qquad (6.21)$$

s. t. (6.20)

Problem (6.21) is a differential game in which the first-best cooperative solution and the noncooperative solution can be defined. The cooperative solution is the solution of the problem:

$$\max_{\{(e_1(t),...,e_n(t))\geq 0\}} \sum_{i=1}^n J_i$$

s. t. (6.20)

In the noncooperative equilibrium each country solves as usual problem (6.21), subject in addition to the informational structure for the differential game. Using a quadratic function for the cost of abatement and damages, defined respectively as:

$$c_i(e_i)=\frac{1}{2}\gamma_i(e_i-\bar{e}_i),\ \gamma_i>0$$

$$D_i(X_i)=\frac{1}{2}\delta_i X_i^2,\ \delta_i>0$$

the optimality conditions can be derived for the cooperative solution and the OLNE and FBNE with linear Markov strategies. Using empirical data regarding the damage function, the transportation matrix and the critical loads, Mäler and de Zeeuw (1995) determine the different steady state equilibria for a two-country case between Great Britain and Ireland. It is shown that the cooperative outcome benefits Ireland relatively more. In the

FBNE it was found that the steady state acid deposition increases significantly as compared to the cooperative solution, indicating that cooperation will improve the situation in both countries. The less realistic OLNE results in less depositions at the steady state as compared to the FBNE, a result that confirms earlier theoretical results (van der Ploeg and de Zeeuw 1992, Hoel 1992a, Xepapadeas 1995a,b).

## 5   EMISSION TAXES AND GLOBAL POLLUTION PROBLEMS

In the previous sections the international environmental policy discussed was in the form of international agreements among countries to reduce emissions. This reduction could then be obtained through domestic policy measures. Of course another way to obtain the desired outcome of reducing the global pollutant, which is more along the lines of traditional environmental policy, is to introduce an international emission tax which would internalize the global externality.[54]

International emission taxes have been mainly proposed in the form of a carbon tax, based on the carbon content of fuels in order to control $CO_2$ emissions. An international carbon tax along with a scheme for the international redistribution of the tax receipts can be used to achieve the first-best in a Pigouvian taxation fashion (Hoel 1992a).

The international tax can be defined with the help of the model (6.10). Assume that the $n$ countries consider adopting an incentive scheme consisting of a time path $\{\tau(t)\}$ of a tax per unit of emissions for the global pollutant generated in country $i$.[55] Tax revenues are given back to all countries in proportions described by the vector $\theta(t) = (\theta_1(t),...,\theta_n(t))$, with $\sum_i \theta_i(t) = 1$. Under this scheme the flow of benefits to country $i$ can be defined, after dropping $t$ to simplify notation, as:

---

[54]There is a considerable body of literature on the carbon tax, inspired mainly by the European Commission's proposal for a carbon/energy tax to reduce $CO_2$ emissions. For information on the design of such a tax, its effectiveness and its distributional effects, see for example Pearce (1991), Nordhaus (1982), Hoel (1991, 1993, 1996), Pearson and Smith (1991), Golombek et al. (1993), Ingham et al. (1991), OECD (1992), Carraro and Siniscalco (1993b) and Porteba (1993).
[55]This approach is similar to that in Xepapadeas (1995b). If the benefit function is redefined as $B_i(f_i(x_i^P(t)))$, where $x_i^P(t)$ is the use of the polluting input at time $t$ and emissions are determined by the emission function $e_i(t) = s_i(x_i^P(t))$, then the emission tax can be readily interpreted as a tax on the polluting input, that is a carbon tax.

$$B_i(e_i) - D(X) - \tau_i e_i + \theta_i \sum_{i=1}^{n} \tau_i e_i$$

Assuming a feedback information structure and linear Markov strategies of the form $e_i = \bar{e}_i - \beta X$, $\beta > 0$, the current value Hamiltonian for each country takes the form:

$$H_i = B_i(e_i) - D_i(X) - \tau_i e_i + \theta_i \left[ \tau_i e_i + \sum_{j \neq i} \tau_j (\bar{e}_j - \beta X) \right] + $$
$$\lambda_i^{FB} \left[ e_i + \sum_{j \neq i} (\bar{e}_j - \beta X) - bX \right] \tag{6.22}$$

The optimality conditions assuming interior solutions can be written as:

$$B_i'(e_i^o) - \tau_i (1 - \theta_i) + \lambda_i^{FB} = 0 \tag{6.23.1}$$

$$\dot{\lambda}_i^{FB} = [r + b + (n-1)\beta] \lambda_i^{FB} + D_i'(X) \tag{6.23.2}$$

The tax parameter should be chosen so that the FBNE emission level defined by (6.23.1) coincides with the first-best emission levels defined by (6.13.1). This requires:

$$\lambda = \lambda_i^{FB} - \tau_i (1 - \theta_i), \text{ or } \tau_i = \frac{\zeta_i - \lambda}{1 - \theta_i} \tag{6.24}$$

where $\zeta_i$ is the parameter of the tax scheme that reflects the individual countries' valuation of pollution. In fact, as was shown in Section 4 of this chapter, the reason for overemissions is that individual countries' shadow values are less than global values $|\lambda_i^{FB}| < |\lambda|$. Therefore a tax that bridges this deviation will achieve the cooperative optimum. It should be noted that in the steady state equilibrium we obtain from (6.15.2) $\lambda_\infty^* = -\left( \sum_i D_i' \right) / (r+b)$, that is, the steady state shadow cost of the pollutant equals the present value of global marginal damages discounted at the natural rate of interest $(r+b)$. On the other hand at the noncooperative equilibrium we have $\lambda_\infty^{FB} = -D_i' / [r + b + (n-1)\beta]$. Thus the optimal tax should bridge the gap between the present value of global marginal damages and the present value, adjusted for the feedback parameter, of the individual country marginal damages. To choose the parameter of the tax scheme for any arbitrary vector $\theta = (\theta_1, ..., \theta_n)$ of reimbursement parameters, the following approach can be used. Assume that $\zeta_i = \lambda_i^{FB}$, then by (6.23.1), emissions in each country are at their first-best level. The individual countries' valuations $\lambda_i^{FB}$ are themselves functions of the parameters of the scheme and need to be approximated. After substituting (6.24) into (6.23.1), solutions of the differential system (6.11) and

(6.23.2) for the costate variable $\lambda$ will be dependent on the parameters of the scheme, as

$$\lambda_i^{FB} = \hat{\lambda}_i(t; \zeta, \theta) \qquad (6.25)$$

where $\zeta = (\zeta_1, ..., \zeta_n)$. In (6.25) substitute $\lambda_i^{FB} = \zeta_i$. The parameters for all $i$ which are fixed points of the system (6.25) will be the required country valuations. If $\zeta_n$ are chosen arbitrarily close to $\hat{\lambda}_i$, then the tax scheme will be asymptotically efficient, in the sense of securing the first-best emissions and resource use.

The second part of the definition of the incentive scheme is the determination of the reimbursement parameters. Let $W_i^*$, $W_i^o$ be country $i$'s maximum welfare at the first-best and at the FBNE respectively before the tax scheme is imposed. Countries for which $W_i^* > W_i^o$ will benefit from a move to the first-best without any tax, emission reduction is individually rational for them, while the opposite holds for $W_i^* < W_i^o$. Since the global optimum corresponds to less emissions than the noncooperative solution, countries which are likely to find themselves worse off at the cooperative solution are those for which pollution damages are not considered very important. Under the tax scheme, the net gains for the country from moving to the first-best will be:

$$NB_i = W_i^* - W_i^o - \int_0^\infty e^{-rt} \left( \tau_i e_i^* - \theta_i \sum_{i=1}^n \tau_i e_i^* \right) dt \qquad (6.26)$$

where the tax is calculated at first-best emissions. Clearly a country will be willing in principle to participate in the international tax agreement if $NB_i \geq 0$. If the net effect is negative, the country will not be willing to enter into an international tax agreement. For all countries to benefit under the scheme, there must exist a vector $\theta \geq 0$ such that $NB_i \geq 0$, and $\Sigma_i \theta_i = 1$ for all $i$. However, from (6.26), it is not clear that such a vector exists. Furthermore, even if this optimal vector can be determined, in the absence of a supranational authority capable of imposing the tax scheme on individual countries, it is not certain that every country will participate in an agreement to implement the tax scheme because of the free-riding issue. Even if the cooperative outcome is individually rational for all countries, it might be even better for any single country to behave noncooperatively and become a free rider while all the others cooperate.

Assume that a vector $\theta_i^*$ exists such that $NB(\theta_i^*) \geq 0$ for all $i$ and for at least one $i$, $NB(\theta_i^*) > 0$, with $\Sigma_i \theta_i^* = 1$, $\theta_i^* \geq 0$ for all $i$. Consider the case where a country assesses the potential benefits from breaking from the agreement to participate in the incentive scheme when the rest of the countries are participating. Denote by $N\tilde{B}_i(\tilde{e}_i, e^*_{-i})$ the net benefits for country $i$ when the country follows noncooperative emission policy outside of the agreement while the rest of the countries follow the agreed first-best (cooperative) policies. Let $G_i \equiv N\tilde{B}_i - NB_i$. If $G_i > 0$, country $i$ has an incentive to become a free rider, that is, to defect from the agreement to participate in the tax scheme once all other countries are participating. Thus country $i$ overemits as compared to the first-best optimum. Free-riding incentives will also exist under any other arbitrarily chosen reimbursement vector. Under these conditions, the coalition of all $i = 1,...,n$ countries that could agree to participate in the tax/reimbursement agreement is not stable since defection incentives exist.

Therefore although an efficient tax scheme can be determined, it might not be possible to implement the scheme through an international agreement because:

(i)     An optimal reimbursement vector does not exist. In this case, there will be countries for which $NB_i < 0$. These countries will not agree to participate in the agreement, and the coalition can not be formed.

(ii)    Even with an optimal reimbursement vector, $NB_i(\theta^*_i) \geq 0$, countries might exist which have incentives to defect from the agreement once all other countries are participating. In this case, the coalition is unstable.

The tax scheme can be implemented in the above cases, along the lines of international agreements discussed earlier in this chapter. Assume that a subset of countries which benefits from the scheme, commits to the tax agreement and gives side payments to the potential defectors to participate in the agreement. Order countries so that the $j = 1,...,J$ are committed to the tax/reimbursement/side payment scheme and the last $k = J+1,...,n$ are countries that have incentives to defect and become free riders or not to participate at all. Then if $\sum_j NB_j \geq \sum_k G_k$, the committed countries can compensate potential defectors and still be better off. The side payment scheme can be defined either for the optimal reimbursement vector $\theta^*$ or for any other arbitrarily chosen, through negotiations, reimbursement vector.

Although side payments alone could have been used to achieve the cooperative outcome directly, the use of the tax reimbursement scheme along with side payments increases the degrees of freedom in the design of international environmental policy. This might be important since it indicates a qualitative relationship between the acceptability of international taxes and transfers among countries. In a sense, this relationship could be regarded as similar to issue linkage in international negotiations discussed above. Countries could, for example, settle simultaneously the issue of joining the international tax scheme with some kind of concessions to other countries on issues already outstanding that will play the role of side payments.

Problems associated with possible inabilities to obtain complete international cooperation for reduction of global pollutants by an international tax are pointed out by Bohm (1993) for the case of reduction of $CO_2$ emissions by an international carbon tax. The action taken by a small number of cooperating countries to reduce $CO_2$ emissions would reduce fossil fuel prices, thus increasing the fossil fuel consumption of noncooperating countries.[56] There might also be further problems for the fossil fuel producing countries due to lower volume of sales and lower prices. Bohm suggests alleviating these problems by transfers from the cooperating countries to the nonsignatory countries through a new agreement. Under this agreement the nonsignatory countries would not increase their fossil fuel consumption after the price reduction. Another suggested way to reduce the supply of fossil fuel is by having the cooperating countries buy or lease fuel deposits, which would have otherwise been used for production.

Hoel (1994) considers a similar problem in a model where the cooperating countries are also fossil fuel suppliers, and the production of fossil fuels can be reduced by appropriately chosen product taxes. In this case the optimal policy mix consists of consumption and production taxes in the cooperating countries. These countries could also induce the noncooperating countries to change their consumption/production policies regarding fossil fuels by appropriately chosen transfers.

## 6   INTERNATIONAL EMISSION PERMITS

The international taxes discussed in the previous section are of course one policy instrument that can be used to deal with a global pollution problem. Although taxes have received much attention due to the debate caused by the EU proposal to introduce the carbon tax, a natural extension of the space of available instruments would be the introduction of tradeable emission permits.

The use of international tradeable emission permits as a policy instrument against greenhouse warming has been analysed by Chichilnisky et al. (1996). The main idea is that each country is given an initial endowment of permits to emit carbon dioxide, with countries being able to trade permits in a

---

[56]Welsch (1994) considers the same model in a monopolistic framework for the world fossil fuel market and shows that under price discrimination the fossil fuel price for the nonsignatory countries that do not impose the tax may increase and their consumption may decrease.

competitive permit market. As was shown in Chapter 5, when permit markets are competitive then the initial distribution of permits does not affect the efficiency properties of the solution. For the global pollution case, however, Chichilnisky et al. (1996) show that only a finite number of initially-allocated permits leads to Pareto efficient outcomes. This discrepancy can be explained as follows. In the domestic pollution problem efficiency requires equalization of marginal abatement costs with the competitive permit price. In the global case the objective is to maximize the sum of utilities of individual countries subject to the given level of allowable emissions.[57] Efficiency requires equalization of marginal abatement costs with the price of the permit. However, marginal cost equalization is efficient if marginal social valuation of consumption is equalized across countries. Therefore trading is efficient under marginal social valuation equalization, but equalization is possible only under redistribution of wealth. The initial allocation of permits affects the redistribution of wealth; therefore there is a finite number of initial allocations that leads to equalization of social valuations. Thus the initial allocation of permits affects the efficiency properties of the permit system. So, unless there is some other instrument that will take care of distributional issues, an arbitrarily chosen permit allocation does not ensure efficiency.

Of course the initial allocation of international permits, whether consistent with efficiency as described above or not, has to be determined by some principle. This is an important issue since in the international problem, as has already been discussed, there is no supranational authority to decide about the distribution of permits in the way that the environmental regulator, in the domestic case, can decide about grandfathering or auctioning the permits. Rose and Stevens (1996) discuss this issue by considering ten alternative international equity criteria.[58] They consider minimum abatement costs with initial distribution of international permits determined by these criteria. Their findings indicate that there are substantial savings in abatement costs from trading of permits as compared to emission quotas or limits. When the relative gains according to the initial distribution of permits are examined, the results indicate that gains vary among industrialized or developing countries

---

[57]The same result holds in the general case where each country tries to maximize its utility subject to the given utility level for the other countries. See Chichilnisky et al. (1996) for a formal proof of this statement.

[58]The criteria are divided into two groups: (i) allocation-based criteria that include the principles of ability to pay; sovereignty; egalitarianism; market justice; consensus, and (ii) outcome-based criteria including the horizontal equity principle; vertical equity principle; Rawlsian principle; compensation principle; and environmental principle. For details see Rose and Stevens (1993) and Rose (1992).

according to the criteria chosen for the initial allocation of permits. This indicates that some sort of international agreement, possibly involving transfers, is required in order to obtain some acceptable method of initial distribution of the international emission permits.

# 7   ENVIRONMENTAL POLICY AND INTERNATIONAL TRADE

The previous sections dealt with environmental problems associated with the transboundary or global character of pollution and the relationships that could potentially develop among countries in their attempt to mitigate these problems. Although most of the policies presented focused on direct agreements either for the regulation of emissions or for the introduction of international taxes, the possibilities of issue linkages discussed in Section 3.3 of this chapter create a direct link between environmental policy and trade issues, since the issues linked with the environmental problem will most likely have repercussions on trade among countries. This is one type of relationship between environmental policy and international trade. Another relationship is the one stemming from a direct link between international trade and environmental policy. International trade, by affecting the pattern of domestic production and consumption activities, will affect domestic emissions of the pollutant associated with these activities. Conversely environmental policy, by affecting pollution generating activities, will affect the pattern of international trade. It is on this direct relationship that we concentrate for the remainder of this chapter.

Two lines of approach have been developed in the analysis of environmental policy and international trade. The first, the traditional one, is based on the assumption that producers and consumers behave competitively and only governments may or may not influence world prices, which is the usual large or small country assumption. This approach leads to conclusions indicating that there is an incompatibility between trade liberalization and environmental protection and that tough domestic environmental policies are likely to harm the international competitiveness of a country that adopts this policy. The second line of approach is based on strategic international trade, and considers the case where producers as well as governments are allowed to act strategically.[59] This approach leads in

---

[59]This section follows Ulph (1994) who provides an excellent survey of these issues.

general to a variety of results. Depending on the assumptions made, the strategic trade approach could produce results supporting the idea of environmental dumping, or results supporting the idea that tough environmental policies might improve the international competitiveness of a country.

Baumol and Oates (1988) analyse a two-country case where a polluting commodity is produced and consumed in both countries. It is shown, without considering optimal policy issues, that a laxer environmental policy in the one country, in the sense of a policy with relatively less pollution control cost, when the other country follows a tougher policy, is expected to increase the comparative advantage of the country that follows the lax policy and encourage greater specialization in the production of the polluting commodity. In a more general context trade liberalization resulting in export expansion without appropriate control policies could increase environmental damages to the point that benefits from free trade are outweighed.

When optimal policy issues are examined, countries are assumed to seek to determine in an optimal way two basic instruments: emission taxes[60] and trade taxes.[61] Under the small country assumption with localized, not transboundary, pollution the optimal policy is to set an emission tax equal to marginal damages, and a trade tax equal to zero. Therefore the small country has the incentive to follow optimal environmental policy and not impede free trade. Actually, as pointed out by Ulph (1994), there is no need for a small country to deviate from free trade even if environmental policy is not optimal. The free trade equilibrium with optimal environmental policy can however lead to higher or lower pollution as compared to the autarchy case,[62] the final effect on welfare depending on the country's environmental preferences. In the large country case the policy consists of an optimal tariff and an emission tax equal to marginal damages. The tariff depends on the demand for net emissions, since for the large country it is beneficial to move from free trade equilibrium.

If direct trade policies are prohibited due to trade liberalization and countries are considering the use of environmental policy as a surrogate trade policy, then as shown by Ulph (1994) there is no presumption that governments will seek to adopt lax environmental policies as a means of favourably influencing their terms of trade.

---

[60]For a comparison between emission taxes and emission permits, see Ulph (1994).

[61]For a detailed presentation of these results, see Markusen (1975), Krutilla (1991), Copeland (1994) and Ulph (1994).

[62]See Rauscher (1992) and Pearce (1992).

In the transboundary pollution case and under the small country assumption the optimal tax equals the global marginal damages under free trade.[63] Under the large country assumption the trade tax differs from the optimal tariff by a factor embodying the impacts of trade taxes on world prices and emissions generated by the other polluting countries.

The results described above hold when perfectly competitive conditions are assumed in the international markets and only governments can have market power. The new trade theory and policy emerging in the 1980s relaxed the assumption of perfect competition in the international markets and introduced imperfections in the international markets (Helpman and Krugman 1989). When, however, producers have market power, this might reduce the government's incentives to exploit their market power in order to increase prices. On the other hand imperfectly competitive conditions create opportunities for the producers to increase rents. Governments could try to increase rents for their own producers; this attempt could create incentives for lax environmental policies. The incentive to introduce lax environmental policies could be made stronger by the fact that governments might not be able to use direct trade policy instruments, owing to trade liberalization.

In a framework where international markets are oligopolistic and governments act strategically in the sense that they recognize the fact that changing the domestic emission tax will affect production both at home and abroad, Kennedy (1994) shows that there are two effects influencing emission taxes in each country. A rent capture effect tends to lower emission taxes in each country as the one country tries to gain competitive advantage over the other country, and a pollution shifting effect tends to increase emission taxes, as each country raises emission taxes trying to shift the pollution generating activity to the other country.[64] The net effect on taxes of these two influences is negative indicating that under these conditions trade liberalization could provide incentives for lax environmental policies.

Strategic interactions in the context of international trade, without, however, the possibility of direct trade policy, can be further augmented by allowing producers to behave strategically in choosing their R&D expenses. In this context R&D could reduce production costs (process R&D) and/or emissions (environmental R&D). The strategic interactions arise because the

---

[63]This result is compatible with the result of the previous section given the static character of the models examining the relationship between trade and the environment. The extent to which a country will agree on the tax depends on whether the move from the noncooperative Nash equilibrium is individually rational, and the incentives to free ride.

[64]Kennedy (1994) shows that the pollution shifting effect disappears in the case of perfect transboundary pollution between the countries.

players of the game, governments and producers, do not make their choices simultaneously but in stages.[65] Thus governments act strategically by committing to policies before producers make their output or R&D decisions and producers act strategically by committing to R&D expenses before choosing output.[66]

Ulph (1996) shows that when producers act strategically there are incentives by the governments to follow lax environmental policies, and that the strategic behaviour of governments and producers are greater when the environmental policy instruments are taxes as compared to standards.

The introduction of R&D into the picture raises another issue. As indicated above, the traditional approach suggests that tough environmental policies might reduce a country's comparative advantage. Recently, however, Porter (1991) argued that strict environmental policies in the form of economic incentives can trigger innovation that may eventually improve the competitiveness in the country, outweighing the private costs imposed by environmental regulation.[67] Porter considers the competitive advantage in the dynamic context with environmental regulation improving it in the long run. Porter's thesis has received considerable attention both at the theoretical and applied policy level along with some criticism (Palmer et al. 1995, Oates et al. 1993).[68]

At the theoretical level it should be noted that if a firm is a price taker then stricter environmental regulation can not make it more profitable (Palmer et al. 1995). Thus theoretical models tend to rely on other arguments to show that strict environmental regulation could improve the competitiveness of a firm.[69] These include X-efficiency arguments under which the external shock by environmental regulation tends to reduce intra-firm inefficiencies and move the firm towards its production possibility frontier. Stricter environmental regulation may give to the firm in the home country an early mover advantage in specific international markets through innovation, thus increasing the firm's competitiveness. Strategic interactions among firms in the process of selecting R&D spending and output in the

---

[65]See Ulph (1994, 1996).

[66]As is the standard approach, the subgame perfect Nash equilibrium is obtained by solving backwards.

[67]See also Porter and van der Linde (1995) for a more detailed presentation of the argument and some empirical support from a number of case studies.

[68]See Palmer et al. (1995) for reactions of the policy making community. One point of agreement between Porter and his critics is that environmental regulation should be based on economic instruments.

[69]See Rauscher (1995) for details.

context of strategic trade policy, under strict environmental regulation, can create incentives for excess R&D and improve competitiveness in the long run. In general, however, there has been weak support for Porter's hypothesis from the theoretical models. The results indicated by Porter appear only under special circumstances.[70]

At the level of empirical analysis, Hazzila and Kopp (1990) and Jorgenson and Wilcoxen (1990) indicate that the cost of environmental protection is higher in the long run because environmental regulation can crowd out productive investment. On the other hand Jaffe et al. (1995) found little evidence to support the hypothesis that environmental regulation has a large adverse effect on competitiveness. They also provide a number of reasons why this effect is low or difficult to determine, which include data limitations in measuring the stringency of the regulation, the relatively small cost of complying with the environmental regulation and the relatively similar regulatory requirements among the large industrialized countries.

---

[70]See Rauscher (1995), Simpson and Bradford (1996), Ulph (1996) and Barrett (1994b).

# 7. Mathematical Tools in Environmental Economics

## 1  INTRODUCTION

A variety of mathematical tools were used in the earlier chapters of this book for the analysis of environmental policy. This last chapter provides a condensed presentation of these mathematical tools and concepts. It should not be regarded as a substitute for the systematic treatment of the same issues provided by the appropriate texts, but rather as a way of bringing together in the same book the environmental policy issues and the mathematical tools for analysing them.[1]

## 2  FUNDAMENTAL CONCEPTS[2]

### 2.1  Sets and Functions

A set is any collection of objects regarded as single entity. The objects of the collection are called elements or points of the set. When an element $x$ belongs to a set $X$, we write $x \in X$, while when an element does not belong to $X$ we write $y \notin X$. A set can be written either by enumeration of its elements, $X = \{x, y, z\}$, or by describing a common property $P(x)$ that its elements have, $X = \{x : x \text{ satisfies } P(x)\}$. Given two sets, $X$ and $Y$, the set $X$ is a subset of $Y$ if every element of $X$ is also an element of $Y$, in which case we write $X \subset Y$.

---

[1] It should be noted that the technical conditions which appear in this chapter, regarding mainly the structure of sets used to define functions, are not mentioned in the earlier chapters in order not to obscure the exposition by mathematical technicalities. Nevertheless it is relatively straightforward to apply these conditions to the analysed environmental policy problems.

[2] Extensive treatment of these concepts can be found in standard texts of mathematical analysis such as Apostol (1974), Kolmogorov and Fomin (1970), or in texts of mathematical economics such as Takayama (1985, 1994), Beavis and Dobbs (1990), Sydsaeter and Hammond (1994), Ostaszewski (1990), Novsek (1993) and Simon and Blume (1993).

If $X \subset Y$ and $Y \subset X$, then the two sets are equal and we write $X = Y$. If $X \subset Y$ and $X \neq Y$ then we say that $X$ is a proper subset of $Y$.

If $X$ and $Y$ are two sets, the following operations can be defined:

(i)     Union: $X \cup Y = \{x : x \in X \text{ or } x \in Y\}$

(ii)    Intersection: $X \cap Y = \{x : x \in X \text{ and } x \in Y\}$
        If the two sets have no common elements, that is, their intersection is the null set $\varnothing$, or $X \cap Y = \varnothing$, then they are called disjoint. The operations of union and intersection can be carried over to any finite or infinite collection of sets.

(iii)   Complement of $X$ relative to a universal set $Y$, $X \subset Y$:
        $X \setminus Y = \{x : x \in Y \text{ and } x \notin X\}$

An ordered pair is defined as the pair $(x,y)$ if and only if $(x,y) = (x',y') \Rightarrow x = x'$, $y = y'$. Given two sets $X, Y$, the set of all ordered pairs is called the Cartesian product, $X \otimes Y = \{(x,y) : x \in X \text{ and } y \in Y\}$.

Let $\Re$ denote the set of all real numbers. The $n$-dimensional Euclidean space, $\Re^n$, is defined as the Cartesian product $\Re^n = \Re \otimes \Re \otimes ... \otimes \Re$, $n$ times. The $n$-dimensional Euclidean space is the set of all $n$-tuples of real numbers, or $n$-dimensional points, or column vectors $x = (x_1, x_2, ..., x_n)$, such that:

$$\Re^n = \{x = (x_1, ..., x_n) : x_i \in \Re, \ i = 1, ..., n\}$$

The set of nonnegative points in the $n$-dimensional Euclidean space is defined as:   $\Re_+^n = \{x = (x_1, ..., x_n) : x_i \in \Re \text{ and } x_i \geq 0\}$.   In $\Re^n$ addition and scalar multiplication are defined as $x + y = (x_1 + y_1, ..., x_n + y_n)$, $ax = (ax_1, ... ax_n)$, $a \in \Re$. Open intervals $(a,b)$, closed intervals $[a,b]$, and half-open intervals $(a,b]$, or $[a,b)$, in the set of real numbers are defined in the usual way.

A subset $X$ of the real numbers is bounded above if a real number $a$ exists such that $x \leq a \ \forall x \in X$. If $a \in X$ then $a$ is called a maximum point of $X$. In the same way $X$ is bounded below if a number $\beta$ exists such that $x \geq \beta \ \forall x \in X$. If $\beta \in X$ then it is called a minimum point of $X$. The least upper bound of a set is its suptemum or sup$X$, while the greatest lower bound of a set is its infimum or inf$X$.

The Euclidean inner or dot product between two vectors or points $x$ and $y$ is defined as $x \cdot y = \sum_{i=1}^n x_i y_i$. The distance between two points $x$ and $y$ is defined as: $\|x - y\| = d(x,y) = \left[\sum_{i=1}^n (x_i - y_i)^2\right]^{1/2}$. For $x, y \in \Re$, $d(x,y)$ is the usual absolute value, $|x-y|$. The Euclidean space is a metric space with the Euclidean distance satisfying the following properties:

$d(x,y) \geq 0$

$d(x,y) = 0$ if and only if $x = y$

$$d(x,y)=d(y,x)$$
$$d(x,z) \leq d(x,y)+d(y,z)$$

The distance between any point $x$ and the origin $0$, is called the norm or the length of the point and is defined as $\|x\|=d(x,0)=\left[\sum_{i=1}^{n} x_i^2\right]^{1/2}$.

Let the real numbers $a_1,...,a_n$. The collection of vectors $x_1,...,x_n$ of $\Re^n$ are linearly independent if and only if the vanishing of the linear combination $a_1 x_1 + ... + a_n x_n = 0$, implies $a_1 = ... = a_n = 0$. If the linear combination vanishes and some of the real numbers are nonzero then the vectors are linearly dependent.

Given two sets $X \subset \Re$ and $Y \subset \Re$, a real valued function of one independent variable is a rule associating each member of $X$ with a single element of $Y$, or $f:X \rightarrow Y$. The set $X$ is the domain of the function and the set $f(X)=\{f(x):x \in X\}$ is called the range of the function. The graph of the function is the set $\{(x,y) \in X \otimes Y : y = f(x)\}$. If the function associates one and only one element of $X$ with a single element of $Y$, then it has a an inverse function $f^{-1}$, where $f^{-1}(y) = x \Leftrightarrow y = f(x)$.

If $X \subset \Re^n$ and $Y \subset \Re^m$, then the function $f:X \rightarrow Y$ defines a real vector valued function or a system of functions, with each coordinate function defined as $y^j = f^j(x_1,...x_n)$, $j = 1,...,m$. If $m=1$ then we have a real valued function of $n$ independent variables.

A set $X \subset \Re^n$ is convex if it contains the line segment connecting any two of its points. More formally the set $X$ is convex if for any $x_1, x_2 \in X$ we have:

$$ax_1 + (1-a)x_2 \in X, \ a \in [0,1]$$

Let $a \in \Re^n$, $a \neq 0$, $c \in \Re$, then the hyperplane generated by $a$ and $c$ is the set defined as $H = \{x \in \Re^n : a x = c\}$. The sets $\{x \in \Re^n : a x \geq c\}$ and $\{x \in \Re^n : a x \leq c\}$ are called the half-space above and below the hyperplane $H$ respectively. Hyperplanes and half-spaces are convex sets.

## 2.2 Linear Algebra

### 2.2.1 Matrices
A matrix is an array of real numbers. The elements of the $i$th row and the $j$th column are denoted by $a_{ij}$ and the matrix $A$ can be denoted as $A = [a_{ij}]$, $i=1,...,n$ and $j=1,...,m$. The order of the matrix is $(n$x$m)$, and if $n=m$ the matrix is called square. The identity matrix is a square matrix with ones on the principal diagonal and zeros elsewhere, or $I = [\delta_{ij}]$, $\delta_{ij}=1$ if $i=j$, $\delta_{ij}=0$ if $i \neq j$. Addition and scalar multiplication are defined as $A + B = [a_{ij} + b_{ij}]$, and $\alpha A = [\alpha a_{ij}]$. The product of an $(n$x$m)$ matrix with an $(m$x$k)$ matrix is an $(n$x$k)$ matrix, $C=AB$, with the $ij$ element defined as

$\sum_{p=1}^{m} a_{ip} b_{pj}$. For the definition of the product $AB$, the number of the columns of $A$ should be equal to the number of the rows of $B$. In general $AB \neq BA$ even if both products are defined.

The transpose of a matrix is defined by interchanging the rows and the columns of the matrix and is denoted by $A'$. If $A = A'$ the matrix is called symmetric.

The row (column) rank of a matrix of order $(n \times m)$ is equal to the maximum number of linearly independent row (column) vectors of the matrix. The row rank equals the column rank. The rank is denoted by $r(A)$ and it holds that $r(A) \leq \min (n, m)$.

The determinant of a square matrix is a real number associated with the matrix and denoted by $|A|$, or det$A$. It holds that $|I| = 1$, $|A| = |A'|$, and that $|AB| = |BA|$. The $\{ij\}$ principal minor of a matrix $A$ is the determinant resulting from deleting the $i$th row and the $j$th column of $A$, and is usually denoted by $M_{ij}$. The cofactor of a matrix is defined as $C_{ij} = (-1)^{i+j} M_{ij}$. The determinant of an $(n \times n)$ matrix can be evaluated by expanding along any row or column as:

$$|A| = \sum_{i=1}^{n} a_{ij} C_{ij}, \ j = 1, \ldots, n \ \text{ or } \ |A| = \sum_{j=1}^{n} a_{ij} C_{ij}, \ i = 1, \ldots, n$$

A square matrix is called nonsingular or invertible if a matrix $B$ exists such that $AB = BA = I$. Matrix $B$ — when it exists — is unique, is denoted by $A^{-1}$ and is called the inverse of $A$. The inverse of a matrix $A$ can be computed as:

$$A^{-1} = \frac{(C_{ij})'}{|A|} = \frac{((-1)^{i+j} M_{ij})'}{|A|}$$

where $C_{ij}$ is the matrix of cofactors and its transpose is called the adjoint matrix.

The rank of a matrix can be determined by the order of the largest nonvanishing determinant that can be defined from the matrix. If $A$ is of order $(n \times n)$ and $r(A) = n$, then this means that $|A| \neq 0$. If $r(A) < n$ then $|A| = 0$. The rank of a nonsingular $(n \times n)$ matrix is $n$, while if the matrix is singular, $r(A) < n$, and $|A| = 0$.

### 2.2.2 Systems of linear equations

A system of $m$ linear equations in $n$ unknowns is defined as:

$$a_{11}x_1 + a_{12}x_2 + \ldots + a_{1n}x_n = b_1$$
$$a_{21}x_1 + a_{22}x_1 + \ldots + a_{2n}x_1 = b_2$$

$$\ldots$$

$$a_{m1}x_1 + a_{m2}x_1 + \ldots + a_{mn}x_1 = b_m$$

or in matrix notation

$$Ax = b$$

where $A = [a_{ij}]$, $i = 1,\ldots,m$, $j = 1,\ldots,n$ is the matrix of coefficients, $x$ is a ($n$x1) column vector of unknowns and $b$ is ($m$x1) vector of constants.

Existence and uniqueness of solutions for linear systems can be analysed by using the augmented matrix $(A \mid b)$ defined by adding the column vector of constants to the matrix of coefficients. A solution to the system of linear equations exists if and only if $r(A) = r(A \mid b)$. The solution, if it exists, is unique if and only if $r(A) = r(A \mid b) = n$. If $r(A) = r(A \mid b) = \rho < n$, the solution is nonunique and $n - \rho$ unknowns can be chosen arbitrarily.

Assume that the matrix $A$ of order ($n$x$n$) is nonsingular and its rank is $n$. Then there is a unique solution obtained as $x = A^{-1}b$. The solution can also be obtained by Cramer's rule as:

$$x_j = \frac{|A_j|}{|A|}$$

where $|A_j|$ is the determinant obtained by replacing the $j$th column of the coefficient matrix $A$ with the column vector $b$ of the coefficients.

A system of linear equations is called homogeneous if the vector of constants is zero or $Ax = 0$. A homogeneous system always has the trivial solution $x = 0$. The homogeneous system has more solutions in addition to the trivial one if $r(A) = \rho < n$ in which case $n - \rho$ unknowns can be chosen arbitrarily.

### 2.2.3 Characteristic roots and vectors

Assume that $a$ is an ($n$x$n$) matrix, then the characteristic value problem consists of finding a nonzero vector $x \in \Re^n$ and a scalar $\lambda \in \Re$ such that:

$$Ax = \lambda x, \ x \neq 0 \tag{7.1}$$

The vector $x$ is called the characteristic vector or the eigenvector, while the scalar $\lambda$ is called the characteristic root or the eigenroot. Equation (7.1) can be written as:

$$(A - \lambda I)x = 0 \tag{7.2}$$

In order for the homogeneous system (7.2) to have a nontrivial solution $x \neq 0$, it is necessary for the matrix $(A - \lambda x)$ to be singular, in which case

$$|A - \lambda I| = 0 \tag{7.3}$$

Condition (7.3) defines the characteristic equation of matrix $A$. The characteristic equation is a polynomial in $\lambda$. The solution of the characteristic equation consists of $n$ characteristic roots, $\lambda_1, ..., \lambda_n$, which are not necessarily real or distinct. If the matrix $A = [a_{ij}]$ is of order (2x2), that is $i, j = 1, 2$, then the characteristic equation is defined as $\lambda^2 - \gamma_1 \lambda + \gamma_2 = 0$, where $\gamma_1 = (a_{11} + a_{22})$ and $\gamma_2 = a_{11}a_{22} - a_{12}a_{21}$. Given the discriminant of the characteristic equation, there could be two real distinct roots, one real double root, imaginary roots or complex conjugate roots. For two real distinct roots, the characteristic vector is determined as the solution of the system $(A - \lambda_i I)x^i = 0$, $i = 1, 2$. Since the coefficient matrix $(A - \lambda_i I)$ is singular there is an infinite number of solutions (characteristic vectors) for each root. The unique solution can be obtained by normalizing the characteristic vectors to have unit length or $\left[(x_1^i)^2 + (x_2^i)^2\right]^{1/2} = 1$, $i = 1, 2$.

Given a square matrix $A$, its trace is the sum of the elements on the principal diagonal or $\operatorname{tr}(A) = \sum_{i=1}^{n} a_{ii}$. If $\lambda_1, ..., \lambda_n$ are the eigenvalues of $A$ then $\operatorname{tr}(A) = \sum_{i=1}^{n} \lambda_i$, and $|A| = \lambda_1 \cdot \lambda_2 \cdot ... \cdot \lambda_n$. If the matrix $A$ is symmetric then all its characteristic roots are real numbers.

### 2.2.4 Quadratic forms

Let $A$ be a square symmetric matrix of order $(nxn)$ and $x \in \mathfrak{R}^n$ a column vector. The quadratic form of $A$ is defined as:[3]

$$Q_A(x) = x'Ax = \sum_{i=1}^{n} \sum_{j=1}^{n} a_{ij}x_{ij}$$

The quadratic form $Q_A(x)$ and the associated matrix $A$ are said to be:

(i)     Positive definite, if $Q_A(x) > 0$ for all $x \neq 0$.
(ii)    Negative definite, if $Q_A(x) < 0$ for all $x \neq 0$.
(iii)   Positive semidefinite, if $Q_A(x) \geq 0$ for all $x \neq 0$.
(iv)    Negative semidefinite, if $Q_A(x) \leq 0$ for all $x \neq 0$.

The quadratic form $Q_A(x)$ is:

---

[3]Matrix $A$ need not be symmetric. If in fact it is not symmetric then new elements $b_{ij} = (1/2)[a_{ij} + a_{ji}]$ can be defined. The matrix $B = [b_{ij}] = (1/2)[A + A']$ is a symmetric matrix and $Q_A(x) = x'Ax = Q_B(x) = x'Bx$. Thus the theory of the quadratic forms can be developed with references to symmetric matrices.

(i)      Positive definite if and only if all the characteristic roots[4] of $A$ are positive.

(ii)     Negative definite if and only if all the characteristic roots of $A$ are negative.

(iii)    Positive semidefinite if and only if all the characteristic roots of $A$ are nonnegative and at least one is zero.

(iv)    Negative semidefinite if and only if all the characteristic roots of $A$ are nonpositive and at least one is zero.

The following determinant test is useful in checking the sign definiteness of matrix $A$. Let the symmetric matrix

$$A = \begin{bmatrix} a_{11} & a_{12} & \cdots & a_{1n} \\ a_{21} & a_{22} & \cdots & a_{2n} \\ \cdot & \cdot & \cdot & \cdot \\ a_{n1} & a_{n2} & \cdots & a_{nn} \end{bmatrix}, \quad a_{ij} = a_{ji}, \; i \neq j$$

The leading principal minors of the matrix is the sequence of determinants $D_1, D_2, \ldots, D_k$ where

$$D_k = \begin{vmatrix} a_{11} & a_{12} & \cdots & a_{1k} \\ a_{21} & a_{22} & \cdots & a_{2k} \\ \cdot & \cdot & \cdot & \cdot \\ a_{k1} & a_{k2} & \cdots & a_{kk} \end{vmatrix}, \quad k = 1, 2, \ldots, n$$

The $k$th order leading principal minor $D_k$ of the matrix $A$ is the determinant of the $(k \times k)$ matrix consisting of the first $k$ rows and columns of $A$. The $k$th order principal minor of $A$, denoted by $\tilde{D}_k$, is the $k$th order principal minor of the matrix $P'AP$, where $P$ is a permutation matrix.[5] Then the following result can be stated.

(i)      The matrix $A$ is positive definite if and only if:
         $D_1 > 0, D_2 > 0, \ldots, D_n > 0$.

(ii)     The matrix $A$ is negative definite if and only if:
         $D_1 < 0, D_2 > 0, \ldots, (-1)^n D_n > 0$.

(iii)    The matrix $A$ is positive semidefinite if and only if:

---

[4]Since $A$ is symmetric all the characteristic roots are real.

[5]A permutation matrix is a square matrix for which each column and each column contains a one, while all the other elements are zero. There are $n! = n(n-1)(n-2)\ldots(2)(1)$ permutation matrices of order $n$; one of them is the identity matrix.

$$\tilde{D}_1 \geq 0, \ \tilde{D}_2 \geq 0, \ \dots , \tilde{D}_n \geq 0.$$

(iv)    The matrix $A$ is negative semidefinite if and only if:

$$\tilde{D}_1 \leq 0, \ \tilde{D}_2 \geq 0, \ \dots ,(-1)^n \tilde{D}_n \geq 0.$$

In cases (iii) and (iv), $\tilde{D}_k$ means all the possible principal minors of order $k=1,2,\dots,n$.

## 2.3 Elements of Point Set Topology

Let $x \in \mathfrak{R}^n$ and let $\varepsilon$ be a positive real number. The set of points $B_\varepsilon(x) = \{x' \in \mathfrak{R}^n : \|x' - x\| < \varepsilon\}$, is called an open ball ($n$-dimensional ball) around $x$. The open ball is also called $\varepsilon$-neighbourhood of $x$ and is denoted by $N_\varepsilon(x)$.

Let $A \subset \mathfrak{R}^n$ and $x \in A$, the point $x$ is an interior point of $A$ if an $\varepsilon > 0$ exists such that $B_\varepsilon(x) \in A$ The set of all interior points of $A$ is called the interior of $A$ and is denoted by int$A$. The set $A$ is open if all its points are interior points. Let $A \subset \mathfrak{R}^n$ and $\mathfrak{R}^n \setminus A$ its complement. The set $A$ is closed if its complement is an open set. The union of any finite or infinite collection of open sets is an open set. The intersection of any finite collection of open sets is an open set. The sets $\varnothing$ and $\mathfrak{R}^n$ are both open and closed sets.

A point $x$ is a boundary point of a set $A \subset \mathfrak{R}^n$ if each open ball around $x$ contains points of $A$ as well as points not in $A$ (in $\mathfrak{R}^n \setminus A$). The set of all boundary points of $A$ is called the boundary of $A$. Set $A$ is closed if it contains all its boundary points.

A set $A \subset \mathfrak{R}^n$ is bounded if a real number $r$ exists such that $\|x\| < r$ for all $x$ in $A$. A set $A \subset \mathfrak{R}^n$ is compact if it is closed and bounded relative to $\mathfrak{R}^n$.

A sequence in $\mathfrak{R}^n$ is a function from the positive integers to vectors $x \in \mathfrak{R}^n$ and is denoted by $x^m$, $m=1,2,\dots$ . The sequence $x^m$ converges to $x_o \in \mathfrak{R}^n$ and we write $\lim_{m \to \infty} x^m = x_o$, or $x^m \to x_o$ as $m \to \infty$, if for every $\varepsilon > 0$ there is an integer $M_\varepsilon$ such that $d(x^m, x_o) < \varepsilon$ whenever $m > M_\varepsilon$, where $d(x^m, x_o)$ is the Euclidean distance between $x^m$ and $x_o$. The point $x_o$ is called the limit of the sequence. Intuitive convergence means that as the limit is approached the terms of the sequence become close to each other. A set is closed if every convergent sequence in the set converges to a point of the set.

A function $f:X \to \mathfrak{R}^m$, $X \subset \mathfrak{R}^n$ converges to a point $y^o \in \mathfrak{R}^m$ as $x$ approaches $x_o$ in $\mathfrak{R}^n$ if for every $\varepsilon > 0$, a $\delta > 0$ exists such that $d(x, x_o) < \delta$ implies $d(f(x), y^o) < \varepsilon$ and we write $\lim_{x \to x_o} f(x) = y^o$ or $f(x) \to y^o$ an $x \to x_o$. This means that $f(x)$ can approach arbitrary close $y^o$ if $x$ comes sufficiently close to $x^o$.

A function $f:X \to \mathfrak{R}$, $X \subset \mathfrak{R}^n$ is continuous at the point $x_o \in X$ if $\lim_{x \to x_o} f(x) = f(x_o)$. The function $f$ is continuous in $X$ if it is continuous at every point in $X$. The function $f:X\to\Re^m$, $X\subset\Re^n$ is continuous if every coordinate function $f_m$ is continuous. Intuitively a function is discontinuous at a point if its value 'jumps' at the point.

Let $f:X\to\Re$, $X\subset\Re^n$ be a continuous function defined in a compact set $X$. Then $f$ achieves a maximum and a minimum in $X$. That is, points $x^*$ and $x^{**}$ exist such that $f(x^{**})\le f(x)\le f(x^*)$ for all $x\in X$ (Weierstrass theorem).

## 2.4 Fixed Point Theorem

Fixed point theorems are used in economics to establish the solution of systems of equations expressing equilibrium conditions. There are a number of fixed point theorems.[6] The most well-known is Brower's fixed point theorem which can be stated as follows.

Let $X$ be a nonempty compact and convex subset of $\Re^n$ and let $f:X\to X$ be a continuous function from $X$ to itself. Then there is at least one point $x_o\in X$ that is mapped through $f$ on itself or $x_o=f(x_o)$. The point $x_o$ is a fixed point for the function $f$. Brower's fixed point theorem is illustrated in Figure 7.1 for the case of a function of one independent variable defined in the closed interval $[0,1]$.

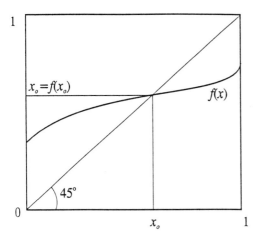

*Figure 7.1. Brower's fixed point theorem*

Thus $x\in[0,1]$ and $f(x)\in[0,1]$. The fixed point theorem says that the graph

[6] See Mas-Colell et al. (1995, mathematical supplement).

of any continuous function from $[0,1]$ to itself must cross the $45°$ line at least once. The point of intersection defines the fixed point of the function.

## 2.5 Differentiability

Given a function $f:X\rightarrow X$, $X\in\Re$, the derivative of the function at an interior point $x^o\in\Re$ is given by:

$$\frac{df(x^o)}{dx} = \lim_{h\rightarrow 0}\frac{f(x^o+h)-f(x^o)}{h}$$

if the limit exists. The derivative is also denoted by $f'(x_o)$. If the derivative exists then the function is called differentiable at $x^o$.

Given a function $f:X\rightarrow X$, $x\in\Re^n$, the derivative of $f$ at an interior point $x^o\in X$ is given by an $n$-dimensional vector $a=(a_1,a_2,...,a_n)$ that depends in general on $x^o$ such that

$$\lim_{\|h\|\rightarrow 0}\frac{f(x^o+h)-f(x^o)-a\cdot h}{\|h\|}=0$$

if the limit exists, where $a\cdot h = \sum_{i=1}^n a_i h_i$ is the differential of $f$ at $x^o$. If the derivative exists when the function is differentiable at $x^o$. Let $e_i$ be an $n$-dimensional vector with the $i$th coordinate equal to 1 and all the others equal to zero. The partial derivative of the function $f$ with respect to $x_i$ at the interior point $x^o=(x_1^o,x_2^o,...,x_n^o)$ is given by $a_i\in\Re$, which in general depends on $x^o$ such that

$$\lim_{h\rightarrow 0}\frac{f(x^o+he_i)-f(x^o)-a_i h}{h}=0,\ h\in\Re$$

if the limit exists. The partial derivative is denoted by:

$$f_i(x^o),\ \text{or}\ \frac{\partial f(x^o)}{\partial x_i},\ f_{x_i}(x^o)$$

If a function $f(x)$ is differentiable at a point $x^o$, then it has partial derivatives with respect to all its coordinate variables. The vector of partial derivatives $(a_1,...,a_n)$ is called the gradient vector and is denoted by:

$$\nabla f(x^o)=\left(\frac{\partial f(x^o)}{\partial x_1},...,\frac{\partial f(x^o)}{\partial x_n}\right)$$

A function is differentiable if it is differentiable for every point in its domain. If the partial derivatives of the function are continuous then the function is continuously differentiable. Given the gradient vector the differential of a function $y=f(x)$ at $x^o$ can be written as:

$$dy = \sum_{i=1}^{n} \frac{\partial f(x^{o})}{\partial x_i} dx_i$$

Given a vector valued function $f:X \to \Re^m$, $X \subset \Re^n$, with each coordinate function being differentiable at an interior point $x^o$ of $X$, then the Jacobian matrix is defined as the $(mxn)$ matrix where each row is the gradient vector of the corresponding coordinate function.

$$J = \left[ \frac{\partial f^j(x^o)}{\partial x_i} \right], \, j=1,...,m, \, i=1,...,n$$

Given a continuously differentiable function $f(x)$ defined on $X \subset \Re^n$, the second-order partial derivatives at a point $x^o$ can be obtained by differentiating the partial derivatives as:

$$\frac{\partial^2 f(x^o)}{\partial x_i \partial x_j} = \frac{\partial^2 f(x^o)}{\partial x_j \partial x_i}, \, i,j=1,...,n$$

The second-order partial derivatives are also denoted as $f_{ij}(x^o)$. If the second-order partial derivatives exist, then the function is called twice differentiable. The matrix of all second-order partial derivatives is a symmetric matrix called the Hessian matrix:

$$H = \begin{bmatrix} \frac{\partial^2 f(x^o)}{\partial x_1^2} & \cdots & \frac{\partial^2 f(x^o)}{\partial x_1 \partial x_n} \\ . & . & . \\ \frac{\partial^2 f(x^o)}{\partial x_n \partial x_1} & \cdots & \frac{\partial^2 f(x^o)}{\partial x_n^2} \end{bmatrix}, \quad \frac{\partial^2 f(x^o)}{\partial x_i \partial x_j} = \frac{\partial^2 f(x^o)}{\partial x_j \partial x_i}, \, i \neq j$$

Let $g: \Re^n \to \Re^m$ and $f: \Re^m \to \Re^k$ be differentiable functions. The composite function $f(g(.))$ is also differentiable. Consider the point $x \in \Re^n$. The chain rule or composite rule function allows us to determine the $(kxn)$ matrix of partial derivatives $D = \left[ \partial f^j(x)/\partial x_i \right] j=1,...,k$, $i=1,...,n$, by multiplying the Jacobian matrix of $f$ with the Jacobian matrix of $g$, or $D = J^f \cdot J^g$.

## 2.6 The Implicit Function Theorem

Consider the following system of equations depending on $n$ endogenous variables $x = (x_1,...,x_n)$, $x \in X \subset \Re^n$ and $m$ parameters or exogenous variables $a = (a_1,...a_n)$, $a \in A \subset \Re^m$, defined as:

$$F^1(x_1,\dots,x_n;a_1,\dots,a_m)=0$$

$$\dots \tag{7.4}$$

$$F^n(x_1,\dots,x_n;a_1,\dots,a_m)=0$$

The implicit function theorem provides sufficient conditions for solving the system (7.4) for the endogenous variables $x$ as functions of the exogenous variables $a$ in the neighbourhood of a point $(x^o,a^o)$ which satisfy $F^k(x^o,a^o)=0$, $k=1,\dots,n$. Consider the open neighbourhoods $X'\subset X$ and $A'\subset A$ of $x^o$ and $a^o$ respectively. The system of equations (7.4) can be solved locally for $x$ as functions of $a$ in the neighbourhood of $(x^o,a^o)$ if there exist $n$ uniquely determined implicit functions $x_i=f^i(a_1,\dots,a_m)$ with $f^i:A'\rightarrow X'$ such that $F^i(x_1(a),\dots,x_n(a);a)=0$, $\forall a\in A'$, $i=1,\dots,n$ and $x_i=f^i(a^o)$.

*Implicit function theorem*    Assume that the equations of system (7.4) are continuously differentiable in $X\otimes A\subset \Re^{n+m}$ and let a point $(x^o,a^o)$ that satisfies (7.4). If the Jacobian matrix of (7.4) with respect to the endogenous variables evaluated at this point is nonsingular, or

$$J=\begin{bmatrix} F_1^1(x^o,a^o) & \dots & F_n^1(x^o,a^o) \\ . & . & . \\ F_1^n(x^o,a^o) & \dots & F_n^n(x^o,a^o) \end{bmatrix} \text{ with } |J|\neq 0,$$

then the system can be solved locally at $(x^o,a^o)$ as described above and define implicitly differentiable functions $f^i:A'\rightarrow X'$.

The effects on $x$ from changes of $a$ at the neighbourhood of $(x^o,a^o)$ are given by differentiating the system of the implicitly defined functions. These effects are in turn determined as solutions of the linear system:

$$\frac{\partial F^1}{\partial x_1}\left(\frac{\partial x_1^o}{\partial a_j}\right)+\dots+\frac{\partial F^1}{\partial x_n}\left(\frac{\partial x_n^o}{\partial a_j}\right)=-\frac{\partial F^1}{\partial a_j}$$

$$. \qquad . \qquad . \tag{7.5}$$

$$\frac{\partial F^n}{\partial x_1}\left(\frac{\partial x_1^o}{\partial a_j}\right)+\dots+\frac{\partial F^n}{\partial x_n}\left(\frac{\partial x_n^o}{\partial a_j}\right)=-\frac{\partial F^n}{\partial a_j}$$

for all $j=1,\dots,m$.

System (7.5) has a unique solution, since $|J|\neq 0$, for the unknown partial derivatives $\partial x_i/\partial a_j$, $i=1,\dots,n$ and $j=1,\dots m$, which can be obtained for example by the Cramer rule:

$$\frac{\partial x_i^{\,o}}{\partial a_j} = \frac{|J_j|}{|J|}, \quad i=1,...,n \text{ for every } j=1,...,m \qquad (7.5.\text{a})$$

To the extent that system (7.4) describes an economic equilibrium for given values of the exogenous parameters the derivatives (7.5.a) are the comparative static derivatives reflecting the response of the equilibrium values of the endogenous variables to small changes in the values of the exogenous variables at the neighbourhood of the equilibrium. If $n=m=1$, that is there is one endogenous and one exogenous variable, the derivative (7.5.a) is reduced to:

$$\frac{dx^{\,o}}{da} = -\frac{\partial F(x^{\,o};a^{\,o})/\partial a}{\partial F(x^{\,o};a^{\,o})/\partial x}$$

### 2.7 Contour Sets and Homogeneous Functions

Consider the function $f:X\to\Re$ with $X\subset\Re_+$. The contour or level set of the function is defined as the set of points $\{x\in\Re_+:f(x)=c\}$ for some constant $c$. The set of contours obtained as the constant varies is the contour map. The upper contour set of $f$ is defined as $\{x\in\Re_+:f(x)\geq c\}$. The lower contour set is defined in an analogous way. The contour map and the upper contour set of a function of two independent variables is shown in Figure 7.2.

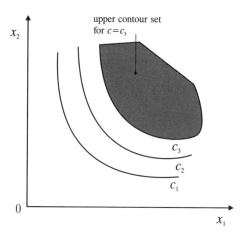

*Figure 7.2. Contour sets*

The function $f(x)$ defined in $X\subset\Re_+^n$ is homogeneous of degree $p$ where

$(p = \dots -1, 0, 1, \dots)$ if for every $\lambda > 0$ we have:

$$f(\lambda x_1, \dots, \lambda x_n) = \lambda^p f(x_1, \dots, x_n)$$

If $f$ is homogenous of degree $p = 1$ and we take $x_1 > 0$ then the function can be written as:

$$f\left(1, \frac{x_2}{x_1}, \dots, \frac{x_n}{x_1}\right) = \frac{1}{x_1} f(x_1, \dots, x_n)$$

If $f$ is homogeneous of degree $p$ and differentiable then its partial derivatives are homogeneous of degree $p-1$.

If $f$ is homogeneous of degree $p$ and differentiable then for every $x \in X$ it holds (Euler's theorem) that:

$$\sum_{i=1}^{n} \frac{\partial f(x)}{\partial x_i} x_i = pf(x)$$

## 2.8 Concave and Homogeneous Functions

Let the function $f : X \rightarrow \mathfrak{R}$, $X \subset \mathfrak{R}^n$, $X$ convex. The function is concave if

$$f(ax + (1-a)x') \geq af(x) + (1-a)f(x'), \; \forall x, x' \in X \text{ and } a \in [0,1]$$

If the inequality is strict for all $x' \neq x$ and $a \in (0,1)$, then $f$ is a strictly concave function. A strictly concave function of one variable is shown in Figure 7.3a.

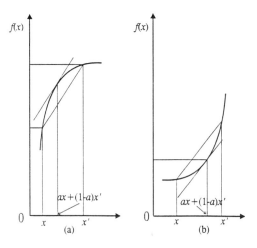

*Figure 7.3. Strictly concave and convex functions*

The function $f$ as defined above is convex if

$$f(ax+(1-a)x') \le af(x)+(1-a)f(x'), \quad \forall x, x' \in X \text{ and } a \in [0,1]$$

A strictly convex function is defined in a way similar to the strictly concave function. A strictly convex function is shown in Figure 7.3b. Every strictly concave (convex ) function is also concave (convex). If $f$ is (strictly) concave then $-f$ is (strictly) convex. A linear function is simultaneously concave and convex. A function cannot be simultaneously strictly concave and strictly convex.

Let $f_i(x)$, $i=1,...,n$ be concave functions defined in a convex set $X \subset \Re^n$. Then the function $f(x)$ defined as $\Sigma_i a_i f_i(x)$, $a_i \in \Re_+$ is also a concave function in $X$.

If a function $f$ is concave then the upper contour sets $\{x \in X : f(x) \ge c\}$ are convex sets for any real $c$. If a function is convex the lower contour sets defined as $\{x \in X : f(x) \le c\}$ are convex sets.

A continuously differentiable function $f : X \to \Re$, $X \subset \Re^n$ is concave if and only if

$$f(x)-f(x^o) \le \sum_{i=1}^{n} \frac{\partial f(x^o)}{\partial x_i}(x_i-x_i^o) \quad \forall x \in X$$

A continuously differentiable function $f : X \to \Re$, $X \subset \Re^n$ is convex if and only if

$$f(x)-f(x^o) \ge \sum_{i=1}^{n} \frac{\partial f(x^o)}{\partial x_i}(x_i-x_i^o) \quad \forall x \in X$$

The function $f$ is strictly concave if the inequality is strict for all $x \in X$ and $x \ne x^o$. The above concavity condition for a differentiable function of one independent variable is shown in Figure 7.3a. Strict concavity implies that any tangent to the graph of the function lies above the graph of the function.

If a function is twice continuously differentiable in its domain then conditions for concavity convexity can be defined in terms of the sign definiteness of its Hessian matrix $H$. Let $H_1$, $H_2,...,H_n$ denote the leading principal minors of $H$ and $\tilde{H}_1$, $\tilde{H}_2,...,\tilde{H}_n$ the principal minors of $H$. Then the following can be stated (Takayama 1985):

(i)     The function $f$ is concave in its domain $X$ if and only if $H$ is negative semidefinite for all $x \in X$. Or equivalently if and only if $\tilde{H}_1 \le 0$, $\tilde{H}_2 \ge 0,...,(-1)^n \tilde{H}_n \ge 0$.

(ii)    The function $f$ is strictly concave in its domain $X$ if and only if $H$ is negative definite for all $x \in X$. Or equivalently if and only if $H_1 < 0$, $H_2 > 0,...,(-1)^n H_n > 0$.

(iii)      The function $f$ is convex in its domain $X$ if and only if $H$ is positive semidefinite for all $x \in X$. Or equivalently if and only if $\tilde{H}_1 \geq 0$, $\tilde{H}_2 \geq 0,..., \tilde{H}_n \geq 0$.

(iv)      The function $f$ is strictly convex in its domain $X$ if and only if $H$ is positive definite for all $x \in X$. Or equivalently if and only if $H_1 > 0$, $H_2 > 0,...,H_n > 0$.

A class of functions with similar properties to concave and convex functions are the quasi-concave, quasi-convex functions.[7]

A function $f : X \rightarrow \Re$, $X \subset \Re^n$, $X$ convex, is called quasi-concave if

$$f(x) \geq f(x') \Rightarrow f(ax + (1-a)x') \geq f(x'), \ \forall x, x' \in X \text{ and } a \in [0,1] \quad (7.6)$$

or equivalently

$$f(ax + (1-a)x') \geq \min\{f(x), f(x')\} \quad (7.6.a)$$

If the inequality is strict in the second part of (7.6) or in (7.6.a) for all $x' \neq x$ and $a \in (0,1)$, then $f$ is a strictly quasi-concave function. A strictly quasi-concave function is shown in Figure 7.4a.

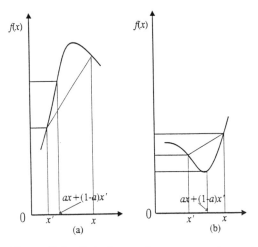

*Figure 7.4. Strictly quasi-concave and quasi-convex functions*

The function $f$ as defined above is quasi-convex if

$$f(x) \geq f(x') \Rightarrow f(ax + (1-a)x') \leq f(x), \ \forall x, x' \in X \text{ and } a \in [0,1]$$

or equivalently

---

[7]For definitions of more concavity kinds, see Takayama (1994).

$$f(ax + (1-a)x') \le \max\{f(x), f(x')\} \tag{7.6.b}$$

A strictly quasi-convex function is defined in a way similar to the strictly quasi-concave function. A strictly quasi-convex function is shown in Figure 7.4b. The function $f$ is quasi-concave if its upper contour sets are convex sets and quasi-convex if its lower contour sets are convex sets.

Let $f$ be a twice differentiable function defined on a convex set $X \subset \Re^n$, and define the bordered Hessian as:

$$\bar{H} = \begin{bmatrix} 0 & f_1 & f_2 & \cdots & f_n \\ f_1 & f_{11} & f_{12} & \cdots & f_{1n} \\ f_2 & f_{21} & f_{22} & \cdots & f_{2n} \\ \cdot & \cdot & \cdot & \cdot & \cdot \\ f_n & f_{n1} & f_{n2} & \cdots & f_{nn} \end{bmatrix}$$

Let $B_k$ be the $(k+1)th$ order leading principal minor of $\bar{H}$, or

$$B_k = \begin{vmatrix} 0 & f_1 & \cdots & f_k \\ f_1 & f_{11} & \cdots & f_{1k} \\ \cdot & \cdot & \cdot & \cdot \\ f_k & f_{k1} & \cdots & f_{kk} \end{vmatrix}, \quad k = 1,\ldots,n$$

Then the following results can be stated (Takayama 1985):

(i)     If $f$ is quasi-concave then
        $B_2 \ge 0, B_3 \le 0, \ldots, (-1)^n B_n \ge 0, \forall x \ge 0$.

(ii)    If $B_1 < 0, B_2 > 0, B_3 < 0, \ldots, (-1)^n B_n > 0, \forall x \in X$, then $f$ is strictly quasi-concave.

## 3   STATIC OPTIMIZATION[8]

Static optimization or optimization in finite dimensional spaces examines the problem of choosing values for variables $x_1, x_2, \ldots, x_n$, called instruments or

---

[8]For a detailed analysis of static optimization in economic problems, see for example Intriligator (1971), Takayama (1985, 1994), Chiang (1984), Dixit (1990), Beavis and Dobbs (1990), Sydsaeter and Hammond (1994).

control variables, so as to maximize a given function $f$ called the objective function which reflects the objective of the problem. The instruments are denoted by a column vector $x \in \mathfrak{R}^n$. The instrument vector is feasible if it satisfies all the constraints of the problem. The set of all feasible vectors defines the opportunity or feasible set, $X \subset \mathfrak{R}^n$. In the unconstrained optimization case the opportunity set is $\mathfrak{R}^n$.

Let $f: \mathfrak{R}^n \to \mathfrak{R}$, then the optimization problem can be stated as:

$$\max_{x} f(x) \text{ subject to } x \in X \subset \mathfrak{R}^n$$

The maximization of $f$ is equivalent to the minimization of $-f$ and vice versa, thus only maximization or minimization problems need to be considered and not both.

The different types of maxima for the function $f: \mathfrak{R}^n \to \mathfrak{R}$, can be classified as follows:

(i)    The function achieves a global maximum at a point $x^* \in \mathfrak{R}^n$, which is called a maximizer if $f(x^*) \geq f(x)$ for all $x \in \mathfrak{R}^n$. If $f(x^*) > f(x)$ for all $x \in \mathfrak{R}^n$, $x \neq x^*$, then the function achieves a strict (or strong or unique) global maximum.

(ii)   The function achieves a local maximum at a point $x^* \in \mathfrak{R}^n$, which is called a local maximizer if $f(x^*) \geq f(x)$ for all $x \in N_\varepsilon(x^*) \cap \mathfrak{R}^n$. If $f(x^*) > f(x)$ for all $x \in N_\varepsilon(x^*) \cap \mathfrak{R}^n$, $x \neq x^*$, then the function achieves a strict (or strong or unique) local maximum.

Clearly global and local minima can be defined in an analogous way. We shall call a maximum or a minimum an extremum. The following result relates global maxima with the concavity of a function.

Let $f: X \to \mathfrak{R}$, $X \subset \mathfrak{R}^n$ be a concave or quasi-concave function defined on the convex set X. Then any local maximum of $f$ in X is also a global maximum of $f$ over X. A global maximum of a strictly concave or strictly quasi-concave function over a convex set is unique.

## 3.1 Unconstrained Optimization

The unconstrained optimization problem consists of choosing instruments $x \in X$ where X could be the entire $\mathfrak{R}^n$, or an open subset of $\mathfrak{R}^n$ to maximize (or minimize) a twice continuously differentiable function $f: X \to \mathfrak{R}$. Thus the maximization problem can be stated as:

$$\max_{x} f(x), \ x \in X$$

The following conditions characterize the extrema of the function:

(i) *First-order necessary conditions* (FOC)   If $f(x)$ has a local extremum at $x^*$ then

$$\frac{\partial f(x^*)}{\partial x_i} = 0, \; i = 1, ..., n$$

The point $x^*$ that satisfies the first-order conditions is called a critical or stationary point.

(ii) *Second-order sufficient conditions* (SOC)   If the FOC are satisfied for $x^*$ and the Hessian matrix of $f$ evaluated at the same point is negative definite, then $f(x)$ achieves a local maximum at $x^*$. If the Hessian matrix of $f$ evaluated at the point $x^*$ is positive definite, then $f(x)$ achieves a local minimum at $x^*$.

Second-order conditions are related to the concavity or convexity of the objective function in the neighbourhood of the stationary point. They can be dispensed with if the objective function is known to be concave or convex.

Let $f:X \to \Re^n$ be a differentiable and concave function defined in the open convex set $X \subset \Re^n$. The function achieves a global maximum at $x^*$ if and only if

$$\frac{\partial f(x^*)}{\partial x_i} = 0, \; i = 1, ..., n$$

If $f$ is strictly concave then $f$ achieves a unique global maximum at $x^*$, that is the stationary point $x^*$ is a unique global maximizer. Therefore the concavity of the objective function implies that the FOC are necessary and sufficient for a global maximum. In an analogous way if $f$ is convex then the stationary point that satisfies the FOC is a global minimizer.

## 3.2 Constrained Optimization

Constrained optimization problems can be divided into problems with equality constraints or classical programming problems and problems with inequality constraints or nonlinear programming problems, with linear programming being a special case of the latter category.

### 3.2.1 Equality constraints
The problem of maximizing an objective function $f(x)$ under $m$ equality constraints can be written as:

$$\max_{x} f(x_1,...,x_n)$$

$$\text{s. t. } g^{1}(x_1,...,x_n)=b_1 \qquad\qquad (7.7)$$

$$\cdots$$

$$g^{m}(x_1,...,x_n)=b_m$$

where the functions $f$ and $g^1,...,g^m$ are defined on $\mathfrak{R}^n$ or on some open subset $X \subset \mathfrak{R}^n$ and $n \geq m$. The feasible set for problem (7.7) is the set of points $x \in \mathfrak{R}^n$ that satisfy the constraints of the problem or $\{x \in \mathfrak{R}^n : g^j(x) = b_j, \ j=1,...,m\}$.

To solve problem (7.7) a new set of variables $\lambda = (\lambda_1,...,\lambda_n)$ called Langrangean multipliers is associated with the constraints and the Lagrangean function is defined as:

$$\mathcal{L}(x,\lambda)=f(x_1,...,x_n)+\sum_{j=1}^{m} \lambda_j\left[b_j-g^j(x_1,...,x_n)\right] \qquad (7.8)$$

The solution of the problem can be characterized in terms of first-order necessary and second-order sufficient conditions.

(i)  *First-order necessary conditions*  If $x^*$ solves (is a local maximizer) problem (7.7) and if the rank condition that the Jacobian matrix of the constraint functions $\left[\partial g^j(x^*)/\partial x_i\right]$ has rank $m$, then unique Lagrangean multipliers $\lambda = (\lambda_1,...,\lambda_m)$ exist, such that:

$$\frac{\partial \mathcal{L}(x^*,\lambda)}{\partial x_i} = \frac{\partial f(x^*)}{\partial x_i} - \sum_{j=1}^{m} \lambda_j \frac{\partial g^j(x^*)}{\partial x_i} = 0, \ i=1,...,n \qquad (7.9.1)$$

$$\frac{\partial \mathcal{L}(x^*,\lambda)}{\partial \lambda_i} = b_j - g^j(x^*) = 0, \ j=1,...,m \qquad (7.9.2)$$

The $(n+m)$ variables $(x_1^*,...,x_n^*; \lambda_1,...,\lambda_m)$ can be obtained as solutions of the system of $(n+m)$ equations (7.9.1) and (7.9.2).

For the case of $n=2$, $m=1$, the solution of the problem is determined by the well-known tangency of the contours of the objective function with the constraint curve as shown in Figure 7.5.

Conditions (7.9.1) and (7.9.2) are, however, only necessary and determine basically the stationary point $(x^*,\lambda)$ of the Lagrangean function. The characterization of the point requires sufficient conditions.

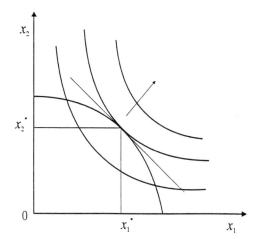

*Figure 7.5. Equality constraint optimization with two variables*

(iia)    *Global sufficient conditions*    Assume that $f$ and the $g$s are twice continuously differentiable functions in an open subset $X \subset \mathfrak{R}^n$. If $(x^*, \lambda)$ is a stationary point of the Lagrangean function (7.8), that is, it satisfies the FOC (7.9.1) and (7.9.2) then:

•If the Lagrangean function is concave in $x$, then $x^*$ is a local maximizer of problem (7.7).

•If the Lagrangean function is convex in $x$, then $x^*$ is a local minimizer.

The Lagrangean function is concave if $f$ is concave and $\lambda g(x)$ is convex or $g(x)$ is linear. The Lagrangean function is convex if $f$ is convex and $\lambda g(x)$ is concave or $g(x)$ is linear.

(iib)    *Local sufficient conditions*    Define the border Hessian matrix at the point $(x^*, \lambda)$, as

$$\bar{H} = \begin{bmatrix} 0 & | & J_g \\ - & - & - \\ J_g' & | & H_{xx}^{\mathcal{L}} \end{bmatrix}$$

where $J_g$ is the ($m$x$n$) Jacobian matrix of the constraint functions and

$$H_{xx}^{\mathcal{L}} = \left[ \frac{\partial^2 f}{\partial x_i \partial x_s} - \sum_{j=1}^{m} \lambda_j \frac{\partial^2 g^j}{\partial x_i \partial x_s} \right], \quad i,s = 1,...,n$$

is the Hessian matrix of the Lagrangean function with respect to $x$.
Assume that $(x^*, \lambda)$ satisfies the FOC (7.9.1) and (7.9.2) and consider the last $(n\text{-}m)$ leading principal minors of $H$. The first of these principal minors will have order $(2m+1) \times (2m+1)$, while the last will be $|H|$ itself. Then,
  • If the leading principal minors alternate in sign, with the sign of the first being that of $(-1)^{m+1}$, then $x^*$ is a local maximizer.
  • If the leading principal minors all have the same sign, that of $(-1)^m$, then $x^*$ is a local minimizer.

### 3.2.2 Inequality constraints: Nonlinear programming
The general nonlinear problem can be stated as:

$$\max_{x} f(x_1, \dots, x_n)$$

$$\text{s. t. } g^1(x_1, \dots, x_n) \leq b_1$$

$$\dots \tag{7.10}$$

$$g^m(x_1, \dots, x_n) \leq b_m$$

$$x_1, x_2, \dots, x_n \geq 0$$

Problem (7.10) is a nonlinear programming problem where both cases $n \geq m$ and $n \leq m$ are possible. All functions are defined on $\Re^n$ or some open subset of $\Re^n$, furthermore the feasible set is defined as:

$$F = \{x \in \Re^n : g^j(x) \leq b_j, x_i \geq 0, j = 1, \dots, m, \ i = 1, \dots, n\}$$

Minimization problems can be handled by multiplying the objective function by $(-1)$ and changing the inequality constraints to $g(x) \geq b$.

Considering only the nonnegativity constraints in problem (7.10), the problem can be defined as:

$$\max_{x \geq 0} f(x_1, \dots, x_n) \tag{7.11}$$

In problem (7.11) the maximizer vector $x^*$ can contain both zero and nonzero elements. If $x_i^* = 0$ for some $i$ the solution is called a boundary solution, while if $x_i^* > 0$ for some $i$, the solution is called an interior solution.

Assume that $f$ is a differentiable and concave function. The function achieves a global maximum at $x^* > 0$, if and only if

$$\frac{\partial f(x^*)}{\partial x_i} \leq 0, \ \frac{\partial f(x^*)}{\partial x_i} x^* = 0, \ x_i^* \geq 0, \ i = 1, \dots, n \tag{7.12.1}$$

or equivalently

$$\frac{\partial f(x^*)}{\partial x_i} \leq 0, \text{ with equality if } x_i^* > 0, \ i = 1, \dots, n \tag{7.12.2}$$

Conditions (7.12.1) or (7.12.2) are therefore necessary and sufficient first-order conditions for problem (7.11).

Considering now the whole problem (7.10), the Lagrangean function is introduced again along with Lagrangean multipliers $\lambda = (\lambda_1, ..., \lambda_n)$ associated with each inequality constraint, as

$$\mathcal{L}(x, \lambda) = f(x) + \sum_{j=1}^{m} \lambda_j \left[ b_j - g^j(x) \right]$$ (7.13)

*Kuhn-Tucker necessary conditions* If $x^*$ solves the nonlinear problem (7.10) and if a constraint qualification holds, then there are unique Lagrangean multipliers $(\lambda_1, ..., \lambda_m) \in \mathfrak{R}_+^m$, such that:

$$\frac{\partial \mathcal{L}(x^*, \lambda)}{\partial x_i} \leq 0 \text{ with equality if } x_i^* > 0, \; i = 1, ..., n$$ (7.14.1)

$$\lambda_j \left[ b_j - g^j(x^*) \right] = 0, \; \lambda_j \geq 0 (= 0 \text{ if } g^j(x^*) < b_j), \; j = 1, ..., m$$ (7.14.2)

If the constraint is not binding at the solution, then the corresponding Lagrangean multiplier is zero. On the other hand if $\lambda_j > 0$ at the solution, the corresponding constraint is binding. A nonlinear problem is depicted in Figure 7.6.

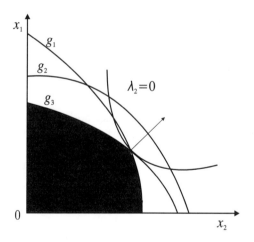

*Figure 7.6. A nonlinear problem*

*The constraint qualification* The constraint qualification ensures that the feasible set does not contain cusps. The constraint qualification for problem (7.10) is satisfied if any one of the following conditions are satisfied (Arrow-

Hurwicz-Uzawa):

(i)     $g^j(x)$ are linear functions, $j=1,\ldots,m$.

(ii)    $g^j(x)$ are convex functions and a $x^o \in F$ exists such that $g^j(x^o) < b_j$, $j=1,\ldots,m$ (Slater condition).

(iii)   The feasible set $F$ is convex, has a nonempty interior and $g_x^j(x^*) \neq 0 \ \forall j \in B$, where $B$ is the set of binding constraints at the solution.

(iv)    The rank condition, as defined for the case of optimization under equality constraints, is satisfied for the binding constraints.

*Kuhn-Tucker sufficient conditions*     Consider the problem (7.10) and assume that: (a) $f$ is a concave function, (b) the $g$s are convex functions, (c) both Lagrangean multipliers $(\lambda_1,\ldots,\lambda_j)$ and a feasible vector $x^*$ exist such that the Kuhn-Tucker conditions (7.14.1) and (7.14.2) are satisfied, then $x^*$ solves the problem (7.10).

If in addition to (a) and (b) the constraint qualification is satisfied then the Kuhn-Tucker conditions are necessary and sufficient for the maximum.

*Arrow and Enthoven sufficient conditions* (*quasi-concave programming*)
Consider again problem (7.10) and assume that:

(i)     $f$ is a quasi-concave function

(ii)    the $g$s are quasi-convex for $x \geq 0$

(iii)   Lagrangean multipliers $\lambda$ and a point $x^*$ exist, satisfying the Kuhn-Tucker conditions (7.14.1) and (7.14.2)

(iv)    One of the following conditions is satisfied

    (a)   $f_{x_i}(x^*) < 0$ for at least one variable $x_i$

    (b)   $f_{x_i}(x^*) > 0$ for some variable that can take positive values without violating the constraints. This variable is called the relevant variable

    (c)   $\nabla f(x^*) \neq 0$ and $f(x)$ is twice differentiable in the neighbourhood of $x^*$

    (d)   the function $f$ is concave

Then $x^*$ solves problem (7.10).

If, in addition to (a), (b) and (d), the constraint qualification is satisfied, then the Kuhn-Tucker conditions are necessary and sufficient for the maximum.

### 3.2.3 Inequality constraints: Linear programming

The general linear programming problem can be stated in matrix notation as:

$$\max_{x \geq 0} c \cdot x$$
$$\text{s. t. } Ax \leq b \tag{7.15}$$

where $A = [a_{ij}]$, $i = 1, \ldots, m$, $j = 1, \ldots, n$ is a matrix of coefficients and $c \in \Re^n$, $x \in \Re^n$, $b \in \Re^m$.

Problem (7.15) can be associated with a minimization problem called the dual problem, with (7.15) being called the primal problem. The dual problem is defined as:

$$\min_{y \geq 0} b' \cdot y$$
$$\text{s. t. } A'y \geq c', y \in \Re^m \tag{7.16}$$

The duality theorem of linear programming states that if $x^*$ is the solution to the primal problem and $y^*$ is the solution to the dual problem, then $cx^* = by^*$. That is, the maximum value attainable in the primal problem is equal to the minimum value attainable in the dual problem.

### 3.3 Comparative Statics

In the static optimization problems discussed above the objective and the constraint functions in general depend on some exogenous variables or parameters. Thus the optimal instrument choice will depend on these parameters. Changes in the parameters values will in general affect the optimal choices. The objective of comparative statics is to determine the effects from changes in the values of the exogenous variables on the optimal instrument choices.

*Unconstrained problems*    Consider the problem

$$\max_{x \in \Re^n} f(x, a), \ a = (a_1, \ldots, a_k) \in A \subset \Re^k \tag{7.17}$$

where $a$ is the vector of exogenous variables or parameters.

Assume that $f$ is twice differentiable, that $x^*$ is a maximizer for a given $a^o \in A$, that second-order conditions for a strong local maximum are satisfied, and that $x^*(a^o)$ is a differentiable function in the neighbourhood of $a^o$. The effects from a variation of the exogenous variables in the neighbourhood of $a^o$, on the optimal choice of $x^*$, are given by the partial derivatives $[\partial x_i^*/\partial a_s]$, $i = 1, \ldots, n$, $s = 1, \ldots, k$. They are determined by the solutions of the linear system:

$$
\begin{bmatrix} f_{11} & \cdots & f_{in} \\ \cdot & \cdot & \cdot \\ f_{nl} & \cdots & f_{nn} \end{bmatrix}
\begin{bmatrix} \dfrac{\partial x_1^*}{\partial a_s} \\ \cdots \\ \dfrac{\partial x_n^*}{\partial a_s} \end{bmatrix}
=
\begin{bmatrix} -f_{1a_s} \\ \cdots \\ -f_{na_s} \end{bmatrix} , \quad s=1,\ldots,k
$$

where all derivatives are evaluated at the $(x^*,\, a^o)$.

*Constrained problems*   Consider the problem:

$$\max_{x} f(x,a)$$

s. t. $g^1(x,a)=b_1$

$$\cdots \tag{7.18}$$

$$g^m(x,a)=b_m$$

$$x\in X\subset\Re^n,\; a\in A\subset\Re^k,\; m<n$$

Assume that $f$ and the $g$s are twice differentiable, that $x^*$ is a maximizer for a given $a^o\in A$, that second-order conditions for a constrained local maximum are satisfied, and that $x^*(a^o)$ is a differentiable function in the neighbourhood of $a^o$. The effects from a variation of the exogenous variables in the neighbourhood of $a^o$, on the optimal choice of $x^*$ and the Lagrangean multipliers $\lambda_j$, are given in a way similar to the unconstrained problem by the partial derivatives $[\partial x_i^*/\partial a_s]$, $[\partial \lambda_j/\partial a_s]$, $i=1,\ldots,n$, $j=1,\ldots,m$, $s=1,\ldots,k$. They are determined by the solutions of the linear system:

$$
\begin{bmatrix} 0 & | & J_g \\ -\; -\; - \\ J_g' & | & H_{xx}^{\mathscr{L}} \end{bmatrix}
\begin{bmatrix} \dfrac{\partial \lambda}{\partial a_s} \\ - \\ \dfrac{\partial x^*}{\partial a_s} \end{bmatrix}
=
\begin{bmatrix} \dfrac{-\partial g}{\partial a_s} \\ - \\ -\partial^2 \mathscr{L} \\ \partial x \partial a_s \end{bmatrix} , \quad s=1,\ldots,k
$$

where $\partial\lambda/\partial a_s$, $\partial g/\partial a_s$ are $(m\mathrm{x}1)$ column vectors and $\partial x^*/\partial a_s$, $\partial^2\mathscr{L}/\partial x\partial a_s$ are $(n\mathrm{x}1)$ column vectors of partial derivatives.

## 3.4 Envelope Results

Envelope results follow from the envelope theorem that examines the effects from variations of the exogenous variables on the optimal (maximized) value of the objective function.

*Unconstrained problem*     Define the optimal value function or simply value function $v(a)$ to be the maximized value attained by $f$ at the solution of problem (7.17) and assume that the value function is differentiable in the neighbourhood of $a^o \in A$. Then $v(a) = f(x^*(a), a)$.

The envelope theorem states that the effects on the value function from a change in the exogenous variables in the neighbourhood of $a^o$ are determined as:

$$\frac{\partial v(a^o)}{\partial a_s} = \frac{\partial f(x^*(a^o), a^o)}{\partial a_s}, \quad s = 1, ..., k$$

*Constrained problem*   Consider problem (7.18) and assume again that $v(a)$ is differentiable in the neighbourhood of $a^o \in A$, and that $\lambda_1, ..., \lambda_m$ are Lagrangean multipliers corresponding to the maximizer $x^*(a)$. Then the envelope theorem states that:

$$\frac{\partial v(a^o)}{\partial a_s} = \frac{\partial \mathcal{L}(x^*(a), \lambda(a), a)}{\partial a_s} =$$

$$\frac{\partial f(x^*(a), a)}{\partial a_s} - \sum_{j=1}^{m} \lambda_j(a) \frac{\partial g^j(x^*(a), a)}{\partial a_s}, \quad s = 1, ..., k$$

The same result can be obtained for the nonlinear programming problem (7.10) assuming $(x^*, \lambda) > 0$.

The following results refer to the concavity of the optimal value function (Beavis and Dobbs 1990). In all cases the objective function $f$ and the constraint functions $g$ are defined in an open subset of $\mathfrak{R}^n$, while the exogenous variables belong to a subset $A \subset \mathfrak{R}^k$.

(i)     Consider the problem $\max_x f(x, a)$, s. t. $g^j(x, a) \leq b_j, j = 1, ..., m$. If $f$ is concave and the $g$s are convex jointly in $x$ and $a$, then $v(a)$ is a concave function.

(ii)    Consider the problem $\max_x f(x, a)$, s. t. $g^j(x) \geq 0, j = 1, ..., m$. If $f$ is convex in $a$ then $v(a)$ is a convex function.

(iii)   Consider the problem $\max_x f(x)$, s. t. $g^j(x) \leq b_j, j = 1, ..., m$. If $f$ is concave and the $g$s are convex then $v(b)$ a concave function.

### 3.4.1 Interpretation of Lagrangean multipliers

Consider either the classical programming problem (7.7) or the nonlinear programming problem (7.10). Then the maximizer $x^*$ and the Lagrangean multipliers at the solution are functions of the vector of the constraint constants, or $x^*(b)$, $\lambda(b)$. The value function is defined as $v(b)=f(x^*(b))$, then by the envelope theorem:

$$\frac{\partial v(b)}{\partial b_j} = \frac{\partial \mathcal{L}(x^*(b), \lambda(b))}{\partial b_j} = \lambda_j(b), \ j=1,...,m$$

Therefore the $j$th Lagrangean multiplier expresses the marginal change of the optimal value function with respect to a change in the $j$th constraint constant. If the constraint constant as usual in economics reflects resource availability, then the Lagrangean multiplier reflects the shadow value or the opportunity cost of the resource.

## 4    DIFFERENTIAL EQUATIONS AND DYNAMICAL SYSTEMS[9]

### 4.1  Differential Equations

An ordinary differential equation can be informally defined as an equation involving derivatives of functions of one independent variable which in most cases is taken to represent time. The $n$th order differential equation can be written as:

$$\frac{dx^n(t)}{dt} = f\left(x(t), \frac{dx(t)}{dt}, \frac{dx^2(t)}{dt}, ..., \frac{dx^{n-1}(t)}{dt}, t\right) \tag{7.19}$$

If $x \in \mathfrak{R}^n$ then (7.19) represents a system of $n$ differential equations. In the following we examine only systems of first-order differential equations which can be formally defined as follows:[10]

Let $t$ in an open subset $T \subset \mathfrak{R}$, with $t$ interpreted as time and

---

[9]For more detailed analysis of these issues with special reference to economic problems, see for example Chiang (1984), Takayama (1985,1994), Beavis and Dobbs (1990), Brock and Malliaris (1989), Leonard and van Long (1992), Sydsaeter and Hammond (1994).

[10]An $n$th order differential equation can be transformed to a system of $n$ first-order differential equations.

$D = T \otimes \Re^n \subset \Re^{n+1}$, be a connected set.[11]. Let $f : D \to \Re^n$ be a continuous vector valued function. The system of $n$ first-order differential equations can be written as:

$$\dot{x}_i(t) = f^i(x_1(t), \dots, x_n(t), t), \ i = 1, \dots, n, \ \dot{x} \equiv \frac{dx}{dt} \qquad (7.20)$$

or in vector notations as $\dot{x}(t) = f(x(t), t)$.

When $f$ does not explicitly depend on time, $\dot{x}(t) = f(x(t))$, then the system is called autonomous. The system $\dot{x}(t) = Ax(t) + u(t)$, where $A = [a_{ij}]$, $i, j = 1, \dots, n$ is a matrix of constant coefficients and $u(t)$ is a control function is called a linear system with constant coefficients. If $u(t) \equiv 0$, the system is called homogeneous.

A continuously differentiable vector valued function $\phi(t)$ defined in an open interval $(t_1, t_2) \in T$, with range in $\Re^n$, is a solution of the system (7.20) if $\dot{\phi}(t) = f(\phi(t), t)$. Let $(t_o, x^o) \in D : x(t_o) = x^o$, the point $(t_o, x^o)$ is an initial condition and the initial value problem consists of finding a solution $\phi(t) : \phi(t_o) = x_o$. The solution of the initial value problem is denoted as $\phi(x^o, t_o; t)$.

The system of differential equations can be regarded as defining implicitly the state function $F : D \to \Re^n$ of a dynamical system, where $F(x, t)$ is the state of the system at time $t$, if the system was at state $x^o$ at $t = 0$.

### 4.1.1 Solutions

Before discussing the solution of a system of differential equations, the existence and the uniqueness of the solution should be established along with some further qualifications characterizing the solution.

*Existence of solution*   If the coordinate functions $f^i$, $i = 1, \dots, n$ are continuous in $D$ and furthermore they satisfy a Lipschitz condition which states that for any two $x^1$, $x^2$ a positive constant $L$ exists such that:

$$\| f^i(x^1, t) - f^i(x^2, t) \| \leq L \| x^1 - x^2 \|, \ i = 1, \dots, n$$

then a solution to the system (7.20) with initial condition $(t_o, x^o)$ exists and it is unique. If the $f$s are differentiable and have bounded derivatives then the Lipschitz condition is satisfied.

The existence of a solution as defined above is basically guaranteed in the neighbourhood of $(t_o, x^o)$. In most economic models, however, there is a need to consider the solution in an extended time interval, possibly $(-\infty, +\infty)$. Assume that the $f$s are continuous and that $D = \Re^{n+1}$, and assume further that

---

[11]A set is connected if it can be expressed as a union of two disjoint sets.

two continuous functions of time $a(t)$, and $b(t)$ exist, such that $\|f(x(t),t)\| \leq a(t) \|x(t)\| + b(t)$. Then a solution to the system (7.20) with initial condition $(t_o, x^o)$ exists in $(-\infty, +\infty)$. The global existence implies that the solution can continue to the left and to the right in the neighbourhood of $t_o$.

*Dependence on initial values and parameters*    Consider the initial value problem $\dot{x} = f(x,t,z)$, $x(t_o) = x^o$, where $z \in Z \subset \Re^k$ is a vector of exogenous variables or parameters. Assume that the coordinate functions $f^i$ are continuous in a closed and compact domain $D' \subset \Re^{n+k+1}$ and all partial derivatives of $f$s with respect to $x$ and $z$ exist and are continuous in $D'$. Then the solution $\phi(x^o, z, t_o; t)$ to the initial value problem is a continuous function of $(x^o, z, t_o, t)$ and its derivatives with respect to $x^o$, and $z$ exist.

*Solutions for linear systems*    Consider the homogeneous linear system with constant coefficients:

$$\dot{x} = Ax \tag{7.21}$$

The solution of (7.20) can be written as:

$$\phi(t) = Be^{\Lambda t}c \tag{7.22}$$

where $B$ is the matrix of the characteristic vectors of $A$ and $e^{\Lambda t}$ is the diagonal matrix

$$e^{\Lambda t} = \begin{bmatrix} e^{\lambda_1 t} & 0 & \cdots & 0 \\ 0 & e^{\lambda_2 t} & \cdots & 0 \\ \cdot & & \cdot & \cdot \\ 0 & 0 & \cdots & e^{\lambda_n t} \end{bmatrix}$$

where $\lambda_i$ is the $i$th characteristic root of matrix $A$, and $c$ is a column vector of constants. Given the initial condition $(t_o, x^o)$ for $t_o = 0$, then $x^o = Bc$ and $c = B^{-1}x^o$. Then the solution of the initial value problem becomes:

$$\phi(x^o, t_o = 0; t) = Be^{\Lambda t}B^{-1}x^o \tag{7.23}$$

If the nonhomogeneous system $\dot{x} = Ax + b$ is considered then its solution is the sum of the solution of the homogeneous part (7.22) plus a particular solution $\psi(t)$ of the nonhomogeneous system. The particular solution can be obtained by considering any constant solution with $\dot{x} = 0$. In this case $\psi(t) = -A^{-1}b$. Thus the solution of the nonhomogeneous system is:

$$\phi(t) = Be^{\Lambda t}c - A^{-1}b \tag{7.24}$$

For any initial condition $(x^o, t_o = 0)$, the solution to the initial value problem is obtained by setting $c = B^{-1}x^o + B^{-1}A^{-1}b$.

## 4.2 Equilibrium

Consider the autonomous system $\dot{x} = f(x)$, and the corresponding initial value problem with initial condition $(t_o, x^o)$, and assume that the conditions for existence, uniqueness and continuous dependence of the solution are satisfied.

An equilibrium point or critical point or rest point of the system is a point $x^*$ such that $f(x^*) = 0$, or equivalently a point $x^*: \dot{x} = 0$. An equilibrium point is isolated if there is no other equilibrium point in its neighbourhood. Let $\phi(x^o, t_o; t)$ be the solution of the initial value problem that at $t = t_o$ passes through the initial point $x^o$, and let $x^*$ be an equilibrium point. The stability of the equilibrium point is defined with respect to the initial conditions, and the following stability concepts are commonly used:

(i)    The equilibrium point $x^*$ is stable in the Liapunov sense if the solution $\phi(x^o, t_o; t)$ with $x^o$ 'close' to the equilibrium point remains in the neighbourhood of $x^*$ for all $t \geq 0$. Or more precisely if for any $\epsilon > 0$, a $\delta > 0$ exists, such that if $\|x^o - x^*\| < \delta$ then $\|\phi(x^o, t_o; t) - x^*\| \leq \epsilon$, $\forall t \geq t_o$.

(ii)   The equilibrium point is asymptotically stable if it is Liapunov stable and furthermore $\phi(x^o, t_o; t) \to x^*$ as $t \to \infty$.

(iii)  The equilibrium point is globally asymptotically stable if it is asymptotically stable and $x^o$ need not be 'close' to $x^*$. To put it differently the solution converges to the equilibrium point for any initial value in the domain of $f$ and not just for initial values in the neighbourhood of $x^*$.

The concept of asymptotic stability is very important in economics since it relates directly to the steady state long-run equilibrium. An equilibrium point is unstable if it not stable.

### 4.2.1 Stability of linear systems
Consider the linear system with constant coefficients $\dot{x} = Ax + b$. The equilibrium point is defined as $x^*: \dot{x} = 0$ or $x^* = -A^{-1}b$. The equilibrium point is globally asymptotically stable if and only if the real parts of the characteristic roots of $A$ are negative.[12] Matrix $A$ is then called a stable

---

[12] A necessary and sufficient condition for all the real parts of the characteristic roots to be negative is provided by the Ruth-Hurwitz condition. See for example Takayama (1985).

matrix.

A real matrix $A$, $(n \times n)$, is stable:

(i)      If and only if a symmetric positive definite matrix $B$ exists such that $BA + A'B$ is negative definite.

(ii)     If $A$ is symmetric and negative definite.

A trajectory passing through the initial point $x^o$ is a set of points defined as $\{\phi(x^o, t_o; t) : t \in \mathfrak{R}\}$. The analysis of the structure of trajectories in the neighbourhood of the equilibrium point can be analysed in the plane for $n=2$.

Consider the linear system $\dot{x} = Ax$, $x \in \mathfrak{R}^2$, in which the origin is the equilibrium point. The characteristic roots of A can be written (see section 2.2.3 of this chapter) as $\lambda_{1,2} = (1/2)(\text{tr}(A) \pm \sqrt{\Delta})$, where $\Delta = [\text{tr}(A)]^2 - 4|A|$. The different kinds of equilibrium corresponding to the possible values of the two characteristic roots are shown in Table 7.1 and Figure 7.7.

*Table 7.1  Classification of equilibrium*

| Characteristic root[a] | tr($A$), $\|A\|$, $\Delta$ | Type of equilibrium |
|---|---|---|
| $\lambda_1 = \lambda_2 = \lambda > 0$ | tr($A$)>0, $\|A\|$>0, $\Delta$=0 | Unstable proper node |
| $\lambda_1 = \lambda_2 = \lambda < 0$ | tr($A$)<0, $\|A\|$>0, $\Delta$=0 | Stable proper node |
| $\lambda_1 \neq \lambda_2$, $\lambda_1, \lambda_2 > 0$ (a) | tr($A$)>0, $\|A\|$>0, $\Delta$>0 | Unstable improper node |
| $\lambda_1 \neq \lambda_2$, $\lambda_1, \lambda_2 < 0$ (b) | tr($A$)<0, $\|A\|$>0, $\Delta$>0 | Stable improper node |
| $\lambda_1 > 0, \lambda_2 < 0$ (c) | $\|A\|$<0 | Saddle point |
| $\lambda_1, \lambda_2$ complex positive real parts (d) | tr($A$)>0, $\Delta$<0 | Unstable focus |
| $\lambda_1, \lambda_2$ complex negative real parts (e) | tr($A$)<0, $\Delta$<0 | Stable focus |
| $\lambda_1, \lambda_2$ complex zero real parts (f) | tr($A$)=0, $\Delta$<0 | Centre |

[a]Letters in parentheses in the Characteristic root column refer to parts of Figure 7.7.

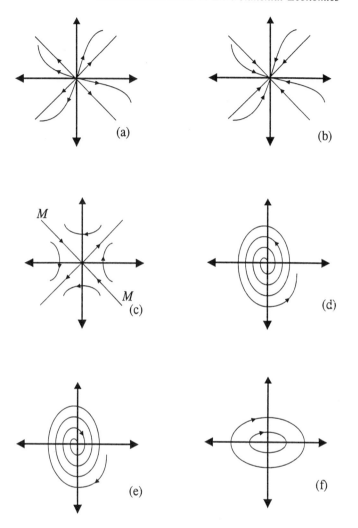

*Figure 7.7. Classification of equilibrium*

Of special interest in economics is the saddle point equilibrium occurring when one of the characteristic roots is positive while the other is negative. In this case the general solution of the homogeneous system is:

$$\phi_i(t) = b_i^1 c_i e^{\lambda_1 t} + b_i^2 c_i e^{\lambda_2 t} \qquad (7.25)$$

where $b_i' = (b_i^1, b_i^2)$, $i = 1,2$ are characteristic vectors associated with each characteristic root and $c_i$ are constants.[13]. In a saddle point equilibrium the system converges towards equilibrium only along the trajectory *MM* (Fig. 7.7c), which is called the stable arm of equilibrium. The stable arm is a special case of a one-dimensional manifold that appears in saddle point equilibrium.[14] In the general case of a system of $n$ differential equations, if the matrix $A$ has $m$ eigenvalues with negative real parts and $n-m$ eigenvalues with positive real parts, then an $m$-dimensional stable manifold exists such that any solution starting on this manifold at $t=0$ converges to the equilibrium point as $t\to\infty$. Furthermore any solution starting near the equilibrium point but not on the stable manifold does not converge to equilibrium.

### 4.2.2 Stability of nonlinear systems: Qualitative analysis
The stability of nonlinear systems can be examined using two methods: the linearization method and the Liapunov direct method.

*Linearization method*   Consider the following system of nonlinear differential equations:

$$\dot{x}(t)=f(x(t)), \ f:\Re^n\to\Re^n$$

and assume that $x^*$ is an equilibrium. By taking the first-order Taylor expansion around the equilibrium point, the linearized system can be obtained as:[15]

$$\dot{x}(t)=A(x(t)-x^*), \ A=\left[\frac{\partial f^i(x^*)}{\partial x_j}\right], \ i,j=1,...,n$$

Thus $A$ is the Jacobian matrix of the system evaluated at the equilibrium point. If the equilibrium point in the linear approximation is globally stable, then it is locally stable at the original nonlinear system. The converse however is not necessarily true. Nonlinear systems can, however, exhibit a behaviour which cannot be exhibited by a linear system. This is the behaviour of limit cycles. A limit cycle is a closed curve or orbit surrounding an isolated equilibrium point. The system can spiral towards or away from the

---

[13]By normalizing the characteristic vectors so that $b_1^1=b_1^2=1$, we have the following relationships: $b_2^1=(\lambda_1-a_{11})/a_{12}$, $b_2^2=(\lambda_2-a_{11})/a_{12}$.

[14]If $U$ and $V$ are open subsets of $\Re^n$, a differentiable function $f:U\to V$ with a differentiable inverse is called a diffeomorphism. A set $M\subset\Re^n$ is called an $m$-dimensional manifold if for every point $x\in M$, there exists an open set $U$ containing $x$, an open set $V\subset\Re^n$ and a diffeomorphism $f:U\to V$ such that $f(U\cap M)=V\cap(\Re^m\otimes\{0\})=\{y\in V:y^{m+1}=...=y^n=0\}$.

[15]Higher order derivatives of the Taylor expansion are assumed to tend to zero in the neighbourhood of the equilibrium point.

limit cycle. This limit cycle is the only closed orbit in the neighbourhood of the equilibrium in contrast to linear systems where more than a closed orbit appears in the cases of centres.[16]

*Liapunov direct method* The Liapunov method can be used to analyse the global stability of nonlinear systems. Consider again the autonomous system defined above and assume that a Liapunov function, $V(x_1-x_1^*,...,x_n-x_n^*)$, exists with the following properties:

(i) $V>0$ if $x_i-x^* \neq 0$ for at least one $i=1,...,n$, and $V=0$ if and only if $x_i-x_i^*=0 \ \forall i$.

(ii) $V \to +\infty$ as $\|x-x^*\| \to +\infty$.

(iii) For the trajectory derivative defined as:

$$\frac{dV}{dt} \equiv \dot{V}(t) = \sum_{i=1}^{n} \frac{\partial V}{\partial (x_i-x_i^*)} \frac{d(x_i-x_i^*)}{dt} \quad \text{it holds that:}$$

$$\dot{V}(x(t)) < 0 \ \text{if} \ x_i-x_i^* \neq 0, \text{ for at least one } i.$$

$$\dot{V}(x(t)) = 0 \ \text{if} \ x_i-x_i^* = 0 \ \forall i.$$

Then $x^*$ is globally stable. In various applications the Euclidean distance $\|x-x^*\|$ or the modified Euclidean distance $\|a(x-x^*)\|$ has been used as a Liapunov function.[17]

Systems of nonlinear differential equations on the plane can be analysed with the help of phase diagrams. Consider the nonlinear system on the plane $\dot{x}_1=f^1(x_1,x_2)$, $\dot{x}_2=f^2(x_1,x_2)$. The phase diagram analysis can be carried out as follows (Fig 7.8):

(i) Define the isocines as the locus of the points on the plane such that $\dot{x}_1=f^1(x_1,x_2)=0$, $\dot{x}_2=f^2(x_1,x_2)=0$. The slope of the isocines will then be defined as $-(f_1^1/f_2^1)$, $-(f_1^2/f_2^2)$. Their intersection defines the equilibrium point.

(ii) Define the direction of motion for points on the plane that do not lie on the isocines and assume that a point exists such that $(x_1^a,x_2^a)$: $\dot{x}_{1a}=f^1(x_1^a,x_2^a)>0$, $\dot{x}_{2a}=f^2(x_1^a,x_2^a)<0$. Then the direction of motion is indicated by the arrows. The direction of motion can be determined in all regions and trajectories can be drawn in the

---

[16]Conditions for ruling out limit cycles are provided by the theorem of Poincare and Bendixson (see Hirsch and Smale 1974).

[17]See Brock and Malliaris (1989) for various global stability results based on the Liapunov method.

following way. Consider point $x^a$ and take the total differential of $f^1$ for fixed $x_2^a$. Then $dx_{1a} = f_1^1(x_1^a, x_2^a)dx_1^a \gtrless 0$ as $f_1^1 \gtrless 0$, by fixing $x_1^a$ we have for $f^2$, that $dx_{2a} = f_2^2(x_1^a, x_2^a)dx_1^a \gtrless 0$ as $f_2^2 \gtrless 0$. Thus the qualitative direction of motion can be determined from the signs of the partial derivatives of the system.

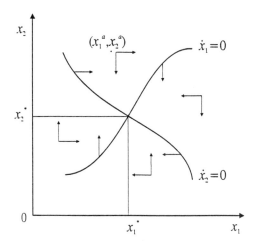

*Figure 7.8. Phase diagram analysis*

## 5    DYNAMIC OPTIMIZATION

Dynamic optimization problems[18] are characterized by an objective function and constraints which are not separable across time, that is they can depend on the history of the problem or the rate of change with respect to time of the state of the problem.

Consider the problem of finding functions $x(t)$ that maximize (or minimize) the following form:

$$I[x] = \int_{t_o}^{t_1} f_o[t, x(t), \dot{x}(t)]dt, \quad \dot{x}(t) = \frac{dx(t)}{dt} \tag{7.25}$$

---

[18]Detailed analysis of dynamic optimization methods with spacial focus in economics can be found in Kamien and Schwartz (1982), Arrow and Kurz 1970), Seierstad and Sydsaeter (1987), Takayama (1985, 1994), Lambert (1985), Carlson et al. (1991), Dixit (1990), Intriligator (1971), Leonard and van Long (1992), Beavis and Dobbs (1990). For a detailed mathematical treatment of dynamic optimization problems see for example Cesari (1983).

where $x(t) = (x_1(t),...,x_n(t)) \in \mathfrak{R}^n$, with $t \in [t_o,t_1] \in \mathfrak{R}$ usually interpreted as time, is a vector-valued continuously differentiable function of time $x:[t_o,t_1] \to \mathfrak{R}^n$, which is called a state variable, or trajectory. The coordinate functions of $x(t)$ are called state variables. The trajectory for the state variable is also denoted as $\{x(t)\}_{t=t_o}^{t=t_1}$ or $\{x(t)\}$. Let $X[t_o,t_1]$ be a collection of functions $x(t)$ on $[t_o,t_1]$. The basic difference between the static optimization problems of Section 3 and problem (7.25) is that in the static optimization, the objective was to choose a vector in the finite dimensional $\mathfrak{R}^n$, or equivalently $n$ numbers, to maximize an objective function, while in the dynamic optimization the function is chosen from $X[t_o,t_1]$ which is an infinite dimensional space.[19] The function $I[x]$ from $X$ into $\mathfrak{R}$ is called a functional with $f_o$ being a real-valued function defined on $\mathfrak{R}^{1+2n}$ or some appropriate subset.

Consider the trajectory $x$ and its graph defined as the set $\Gamma = \{(t,x(t)): t \in [t_1,t_2]\}$, $\Gamma \subset \mathfrak{R}^{n+1}$. The $\delta$ neighborhood of $\Gamma$ is the set of all trajectories $(t,x) \subset \mathfrak{R}^{n+1}$ at a distance less than or equal to $\delta$ from $\Gamma$. Let $x$ and $y$ be two trajectories. The distance between the two trajectories $x$ and $y$ is defined as $d(x,y) = \sup[\,|y(t)-x(t)|,\ t \in [t_o,t_1]]$.

A trajectory $x^* \in X$ is said to give a global maximum to the functional $I[x]$, and we say that $x^*$ is an optimal trajectory if $I[x^*] \geq I[y]$ for all $y \in X$. The functional is said to achieve a global maximum at $x^*$. The global maximum is unique if $I[x^*] > I[y]$ for all $y \in X$.

The functional achieves a local maximum at $x^*$ if $I[x^*] \geq I[y]$ for $y$ sufficiently close to $x^*$, with closeness defined as above in terms of distances between trajectories. Global and local minima can be defined in an analogous way.

The fundamental characteristic of an optimal trajectory is expressed by the principle of optimality. Given the problem (7.25) with initial time $t_o$ and terminal time $t_1$, introduce the restrictions that $(t,x(t)) \in A \subset \mathfrak{R}^{n+1}$, $t \in [t_o,t_1]$ and the boundary conditions $(t_o,x(t_o),t_1,x(t_1)) \in B$. All the continuous functions that belong to $A$ and satisfy the boundary condition are the class of all admissible trajectories.

*Principle of Optimality*   Let $\Omega$ be the class of all admissible trajectories for problem (7.25) and let $x^*(t)$ be the optimal trajectory as defined above in $\Omega$. Let $y^o$ denote any subarc of the curve $x^*$, as shown in Figure 7.9, and let $\Omega_o$ be the class of all admissible trajectories $y(t)$, $t \in [a,b]$, with initial conditions and terminal conditions the same as $y^o$. That is

---

[19]See Takayama (1985) for a description of infinite dimensional spaces.

$\bar{y}(a) = y^o(a)$, $\bar{y}(b) = y^o(b)$. Then $y^o$ is an optimal trajectory for problem (7.25) in $\Omega_o$. In other words a truncated part of an optimal trajectory is itself optimal for the time interval corresponding to the truncated part.

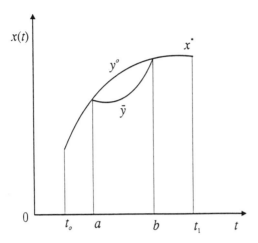

*Figure 7.9  The principle of optimality*

Problem (7.25), with the appropriate restrictions on the state variables and the boundary conditions, is referred to as the Lagrange problem of calculus of variations. A dynamic optimization problem with extensive applications in economics is the Lagrange problem of optimal control or simply optimal control problem.

The optimal control problem consists of finding functions $u(t) = (u_1, ..., u_m) \in \Re^m$, $t \in [t_o, t_1] \in \Re$, which are called control variables, from a set of functions $U$ in order to maximize or minimize an objective functional.

The optimal control problem for the maximization case can be defined as:

$$\max I[x,u] = \int_{t_o}^{t_1} f_o(x(t), u(t), t) dt \tag{7.26}$$

subject to

$$\dot{x}_i = f_i(x(t), u(t), t), \; i = 1, ..., n, \; t \in [t_o, t_1] \tag{7.26.1}$$

the boundary conditions

$$(t_o, x(t_o), t_1, x(t_1)) \in B \tag{7.26.2}$$

the constraints

$$(t,x(t)) \in A, \quad t \in [t_o,t_1] \tag{7.26.3}$$

$$u(t) \in U(t,x(t)) \tag{7.26.4}$$

Constraints (7.26.1) is a system of differential equations describing the motion of the system called transition equations or equations of motion. Initial and possibly terminal conditions for these equations are given by (7.26.2). Through the equations of motion the trajectories of the state variables are described for any given control by the solution of the system (7.26.1). Constraints (7.26.3) describe constraints on the state variables, while constraints (7.26.4) describe the control space or the restraint set which may depend on $t$ and $x$.

The optimal control problem is called the Bolza problem of optimal control if the problem is to maximize (or minimize)

$$I[x,u] = g(x(t_o),x(t_1),t_o,t_1) + \int_{t_o}^{t_1} f_o(x(t),u(t),t)\,dt \tag{7.27}$$

subject to (7.26.1) to (7.26.4), where $g$ is a real-valued function defined on $B$. Related to the problem of Bolza is the Meyer problem of optimal control where the objective is to maximize (or minimize)

$$I[x,u] = g(x(t_o),x(t_1),t_o,t_1) \tag{7.28}$$

subject to (7.26.1) to (7.26.4).

The optimal control problems of Lagrange, Bolza and Meyer can be shown to be theoretically equivalent. Furthermore problems of the calculus of variations can be written as Lagrange problems of optimal control.

## 5.1 Calculus of Variations

Consider the problem of calculus of variations:

$$\max_{\{x(t)\}} \int_{t_o}^{t_1} f_o(x(t),\dot{x}(t),t)\,dt, \quad x(t) = (x_1,...,x_n) \tag{7.29}$$

s. t. $x(t_o) = x_o$ fixed, $(t,x(t)) \in A$ $\tag{7.29.1}$

$\quad x_i(t_1) = x_i^1$ fixed, $i=1,...,l$ $\tag{7.29.2}$

$\quad x_i(t_1) \geq x_i^1, \quad i=l+1,...,h$ $\tag{7.29.3}$

$\quad x_i(t_1)$ free, $i=h+1,...,n$ $\tag{7.29.4}$

*Euler equation* (First order necessary conditions)    If $x^*(t)$ is a trajectory that solves problem (7.29) in the fixed time interval $[t_o, t_1]$, then it satisfies the Euler equation

$$\frac{\partial f_o}{\partial x_i} - \frac{d}{dt}\left(\frac{\partial f_o}{\partial \dot{x}_i}\right) = 0, \ i = 1,...,n \tag{7.30}$$

and the transversality conditions

$$x_i^*(t_1) = x_i^1, \ i = 1,...,l \tag{7.30.1}$$

$$\left.\frac{\partial f_o}{\partial \dot{x}_i}\right|_{t=t_1} \leq 0 \ (=0 \ \text{if} \ x_i^*(t_1) > x_i^1), \ i = l+1,...,h \tag{7.30.2}$$

$$\left.\frac{\partial f_o}{\partial \dot{x}_i}\right|_{t=t_1} = 0, \ i = h+1,...,n \tag{7.30.3}$$

If $f_o$ is concave in $x(t)$ and $\dot{x}(t)$, then the Euler conditions are necessary and sufficient for the solution of the problem. If $f_o$ does not depend explicitly on $t$, that is the problem is autonomous, as is usual in economics, then assuming that $\partial f_o / \partial x \neq 0$, the Euler equation can be simplified to:

$$f_o - \dot{x}_i \left(\frac{\partial f_o}{\partial \dot{x}_i}\right) = c, \ c \ \text{constant} \ \forall i \ \text{and} \ x = x^* \tag{7.31}$$

## 5.2  Optimal Control

### 5.2.1  Unconstrained optimal control
Consider the following optimal control problem

$$\max_{\{u(t)\}} \int_{t_o}^{t_1} f_o(x(t), u(t), t)dt, \ x(t) = (x_1,...,x_n), \ u(t) = (u_1,...,u_m) \tag{7.32}$$

s. t. $\dot{x}_i = f_i(x(t), u(t), t), \ i = 1,...,n, \ (t, x(t)) \in A$  (7.32.1)

$\qquad x(t_o) = x_o$ fixed  (7.32.2)

$\qquad x_i(t_1) = x_i^1$ fixed, $i = 1,...,l$  (7.32.3)

$\qquad x_i(t_1) \geq x_i^1, \ i = l+1,...,h$  (7.32.4)

$\qquad x_i(t_1)$ free, $i = h+1,...,n$  (7.32.5)

$\qquad u \in U \subset \Re^m$

The Pontryagin maximum principle, or simply maximum principle, provides necessary conditions for the solution of problem (7.32).

If $u^*(t)$ is a piecewise continuous control[20] in the fixed time interval $[t_o,t_1]$ that solves problem (7.32) and $x^*(t)$ is the associated optimal trajectory or optimal path for the state variables, then there exist a constant $p_o$ and a continuous and piecewise continuously differentiable vector valued function $p(t) = (p_1(t),...,p_n(t))$ from $[t_o,t_1]$ to $\mathfrak{R}^n$, such that:

$$(p_o, p_1(t),...,p_n(t)) \neq 0 \tag{7.33.1}$$

$u^*(t)$ maximizes the Hamiltonian function for $u \in U$ defined as

$$H(x(t),u(t),p(t),t) = p_o f_o(x,u,t) + \sum_{i=1}^{n} p_i f_i(x,u,t) \tag{7.33.2}$$

that is

$$H(x^*(t),u^*(t),p(t),t) \geq H(x^*(t),u(t),p(t),t) \quad \forall u \in U \tag{7.33.3}$$

Except at the points of discontinuity of $u^*(t)$, $\{x^*(t), p(t)\}$ solves the Hamiltonian system

$$\dot{p}_i(t) = -\frac{\partial H^*}{\partial x_i}, \quad H^* = H(x^*(t),u^*(t),t) \tag{7.33.4a}$$

$$\dot{x}_i(t) = \frac{\partial H^*}{\partial p_i} \tag{7.33.4b}$$

$$p_o = 0 \text{ or } p_o = 1$$

The following transversality conditions are also satisfied

$$p_i(t_1) \text{ no conditions}, \ i = 1,...,l \tag{7.33.5}$$

$$p_i(t_1) \geq 0 \ (=0 \text{ if } x^*(t_1) > x_i^1), \ i = l+1,...,h \tag{7.33.6}$$

$$p_i(t) = 0, \ i = h+1,..., n \tag{7.33.7}$$

In the economic applications $p_o$ is taken to be one.

For interior solutions condition (7.33.3) implies the usual first-order conditions

$$\frac{\partial H^*}{\partial u_j} = 0, \ j = 1,...,m \tag{7.33.8}$$

---

[20] A function is piecewise continuous in its domain if it is continuous except for a finite number of discontinuities.

with a concave Hamiltonian in $u$ the sufficient conditions are also satisfied.

The variables $p$ are called costate or auxiliary variables while the Hamiltonian system (7.33.4a) and (7.33.4b) is sometimes called the auxiliary system.

The first-order conditions can be solved to determine the optimal control as a function of the state and the costate variables

$$u_j^* = u_j(x(t), p(t), t), \ j = 1, ..., m$$

Substituting the solutions for the optimal controls into the Hamiltonian system, the following system of first-order differential equations is obtained:

$$\dot{p}_i = p_i(x(t), p(t), t), \ i = 1, ..., n$$

$$\dot{x}_i = f_i(x(t), p(t), t)$$

The solution of this system with boundary conditions determined by the initial conditions and the transversality conditions determines the optimal path or optimal trajectory for the state variables, and the paths for the costate variables. Along the optimal trajectory it holds that $dH^*/dt = \partial H^*/\partial t$.

The optimality conditions of the maximum principle are necessary conditions. Second-order sufficient conditions can be stated as follows.

*Mangasarian sufficient conditions*    Let $\{x^*(t), u^*(t)\}$ be an admissible pair of trajectories for problem (7.32). If auxiliary variables $(p_1(t), ..., p_n(t))$ exist with $p_o = 1$, such that the conditions of the maximum principle are satisfied and $H(x, u, p, t)$ is concave in $(x, u)$ for all $t$, then $\{x^*(t), u^*(t)\}$ solve problem (7.32). If the Hamiltonian is strictly concave then a unique solution to the problem exists.

*Arrow sufficient conditions*    Let $\{x^*(t), u^*(t)\}$ be an admissible solution to the problem (7.32) and assume that auxiliary variables $p(t)$, $p_o$ exist such that the conditions of the maximum principle are satisfied. Define the maximized Hamiltonian

$$H^o(x, p, t) = \max_{u \in U} H(x, u, p, t)$$

If $H^o$ is concave in $x$ for all $t$, then $\{x^*(t), u^*(t)\}$ solve problem (7.32). If $H^o$ is strictly concave then the solution is unique.

*Current value Hamiltonians*    Consider the problem (7.32) with $f_o$ replaced by $e^{-\delta t} f_o$, where $\delta > 0$ is a discount rate. This is a very common case in economics where maximization is defined in present value terms. With $p_o = 1$

the current value Hamiltonian is defined as:

$$H_c(x,u,\lambda,t) = f_o(x,u,t) + \sum_{i=1}^{n} \lambda_i(t) f_i(x,u,t)$$

The conditions of the maximum principle – (7.33.1) to (7.33.7) – remain the same with $p_i(t)$ substituted by $\lambda_i(t)$, $i=1,...,n$ and (7.33.4a) replaced by

$$\dot{\lambda}_i(t) = \delta\lambda_i(t) - \frac{\partial H_c^*}{\partial x_i}, \quad i=1,...,n \qquad (7.33.4c)$$

*Interpretation of the costate variables*  Consider the maximum value function for problem (7.32) with terminal conditions $x_i(t_i) = x_i^1$, defined as

$$v(x_o, x^1, t_o, t_1) = \max_{\{u(t)\}} \int_{t_o}^{t_1} f_o(x,u,t) dt$$

Then it can be shown that for all $i$,

$$\frac{\partial v}{\partial x_{oi}} = p_i(t_o)$$

$$\frac{\partial v}{\partial x_i^1} = p_i(t_1)$$

Thus the costate variable can be interpreted as the dynamic shadow value, or the opportunity cost of the state variable $x_i$ at the initial and terminal state. The result can be generalized to any time $\theta$. Then $p_i(\theta)$ is the dynamic shadow value of the state variable at any instant of time in the given time horizon.

*Open final time problems*  In problem (7.32) both initial and terminal time are fixed. There are however problems where the optimal time is open and should be chosen optimally. In this case the necessary conditions for the maximum principle are the same as (7.32) with one additional condition. If $t_1^* \in (t_o, \infty)$ is the optimal final time, then

$$H(x^*(t_1^*), u^*(t_1^*), p(t_1^*), t_1^*) = 0 \qquad (7.33.9)$$

Condition (7.33.9) can be used to determine the optimal final time.

**5.2.2  Infinite horizon optimal control**

The infinite horizon optimal control problem can be stated for $t_o = 0$ as:

$$\max_{\{u(t)\}} \int_0^\infty e^{-\delta t} f_o(x(t), u(t)) dt, \; \delta > 0 \tag{7.34}$$

$$\text{s. t. } \dot{x}_i = f_i(x(t), u(t)), \; x(0) = x_o \text{ fixed} \tag{7.34.1}$$

$$x \in A, \; u \in U$$

Problem (7.34) is an autonomous optimal control problem, since the $f$ functions do not explicitly depend on time, which is a case very often encountered in economic models. For this problem a usual optimality criterion is that of the overtaking optimality which can be defined as follows:[21] Let

$$I_T[x_o, u] = \int_0^T e^{-\delta t} f_o(x(t), u(t)) dt$$

where $u(t)$ is an admissible control for problem (7.34). Let also the trajectory $\{x^*(t), u^*(t)\}$, with $x(0) = x_o$. The trajectory $x^*(t)$ generated by $u^*(t)$ is overtaking optimal if

$$\lim_{T \to \infty} \inf \{I_T[x_o, u^*] - I_T[x_o, u]\} \geq 0, \; \text{for } u \in U$$

Assuming interior solutions for the optimal control $u$, necessary conditions for problem (7.34) can be set out as follows.

If the trajectory $\{x^*(t), u^*(t)\}$, with $x(0) = x_o$ solves problem (7.34), then $u^*(t)$ maximizes the current value Hamiltonian defined, with $\lambda_o = 1$, as

$$H(x, u, \lambda) = f_o(x, u) + \sum_{i=1}^n \lambda_i f_i(x, u) \tag{7.35.1}$$

$$\text{or } \frac{\partial H^*}{\partial u} = 0, \; H^* = H(x^*, u^*, \lambda), \; u^* = u(x^*, \lambda) \tag{7.35.2}$$

The triplet $\{x^*(t), u^*(t), \lambda(t)\}$ solves the modified Hamiltonian dynamic system (MHDS)

$$\dot{\lambda}_i = \delta \lambda - \frac{\partial H^*}{\partial x_i} \tag{7.35.3}$$

$$\dot{x}_i = \frac{\partial H^*}{\partial \lambda_i} = f_i(x^*, u^*) \tag{7.35.4}$$

The Arrow type transversality conditions at infinity are satisfied, or

$$\lim_{t \to \infty} e^{-\delta t} \lambda_i(t) \geq 0, \; \lim_{t \to \infty} e^{-\delta t} \lambda_i(t) x_i(t) = 0 \tag{7.35.5}$$

---

[21]For other definitions of optimality especially for nonautonomous, nondiscounted problems, see for example Carlson et al. (1991).

Sufficient conditions are the same as in the finite time horizon case, with the addition of the transversality condition (7.35.5).

A characteristic of autonomous infinite horizon control problems is that they can describe a long-run steady state equilibrium or a critical point for the MHDS. The long-run equilibrium is defined as the point $(x_\infty^*, \lambda_\infty)$ such that $\dot{x} = \dot{\lambda} = 0$, or

$$0 = \delta\lambda - \frac{\partial H_\infty^*}{\partial x_i}, \quad H_\infty^* = H\left(x_\infty^*, u_\infty^*, \lambda_\infty\right), \quad u_\infty^* = u^*(x_\infty^*, \lambda_\infty) \qquad (7.36.1)$$

$$0 = f_i(x_\infty^*, u_\infty^*) \qquad (7.36.2)$$

In general the MHDS is a nonlinear system of $2n$ differential equations with initial conditions $x(0) = x_o$ and finite $\lambda_\infty$ as indicated by the transversality conditions. The existence,[22] uniqueness and stability of equilibrium can be analysed by using standard methods applied to dynamical systems.

Of special interest in economic problems are the stability properties of the steady state equilibrium. In the undiscounted case, $\delta = 0$, it can be shown that the equilibrium point has the saddle point property. That is an n-dimensional manifold exists such that for any initial state, $x_o$, an initial value for the costate variables $\lambda_o$ exists, such that the solution of the Hamiltonian dynamic system converges to the equilibrium point. When the discounted case is considered, an additional curvature condition on the Hamiltonian function should be imposed to ensure stability of the MHDS in the saddle point sense.

Stability conditions for the case of $\delta > 0$ can be described as follows.[23] Let $\phi(x_o, \lambda_o; t)$ be a solution of the MHDS. The solution will be called bounded if it belongs to a compact set. The equilibrium point $(x_\infty^*, \lambda_\infty)$ is said to be globally asymptotically stable (GAS) for all bounded solutions if for all initial conditions $(x_o, \lambda_o)$ such that $\phi(x_o, \lambda_o; t)$ is bounded, it holds that

$$\phi(x_o, \lambda_o; t) \rightarrow (x_\infty^*, \lambda_\infty), \text{ as } t \rightarrow \infty$$

Assume that the equilibrium point $(x_\infty^*, \lambda_\infty)$ is isolated and define the curvature matrix

---

[22]The existence of the steady state equilibrium in optimal control problems can be shown, in addition to the general methods for finding solutions for nonlinear systems, by using the solution of the so called implicit programming problem (Feinstein and Luenberger 1981).

[23]For a detailed analysis of stability conditions, in addition to those presented here, see Brock and Malliaris (1989) and the references cited there.

$$Q = \begin{bmatrix} H_{xx} & -\dfrac{\delta}{2}I \\ -\dfrac{\delta}{2}I & -H_{\lambda\lambda} \end{bmatrix}$$

where $I$ is an $(nxn)$ identity matrix. If $Q$, evaluated at the equilibrium point, is negative definite then all bounded solutions of the MHDS converge to the equilibrium point as $t \to \infty$. Thus, the equilibrium point has the global saddle point property and the stable manifold is globally asymptotically stable.

### 5.2.3 Constrained optimal control

Optimal control problems can be analysed under general inequality constraints involving the control and the state variables. When both the control and the state variables are involved in the constraint, the constraint is called mixed; when only state variables are included the constraint is called a pure state constraint.[24] A control problem with mixed inequality constraints can be defined using problem (7.32) as:

$$\max_{\{u(t)\}} \int_{t_o}^{t_1} f_o(x(t),u(t),t)dt \tag{7.37}$$

$$\text{s. t. } \dot{x}(t) = f_i(x(t),u(t),t),\ x(t_o) = x_o \text{ fixed} \tag{7.37.1}$$

$$h_k(x(t),u(t),t) \le b_k,\ k = 1,...,K \tag{7.37.2}$$

$$x_i(t_1) = x_i^1 \text{ fixed},\ i = 1,...,l \tag{7.37.3}$$

$$x_i(t_1) \ge x_i^1,\ i = l+1,...,h \tag{7.37.4}$$

$$x_i(t_1) \text{ free},\ i = h+1,...,n \tag{7.37.5}$$

$$u \in U \subset \Re^m$$

It is assumed that all the functions involved have continuous partial derivatives with respect to the state and the control variables. Introduce the Hamiltonian and the Lagrangean functions

---

[24] For more general formulation of constraints, including integral constraints and control parameters following the work of Hestenes, see Takayama (1985). In this section only mixed constraints are examined. For an extensive analysis of pure state constraints as well as of combined mixed and pure state constraints, see Seierstad and Sydsaeter (1987).

$$H(x,u,p,t) = f_o(x,u,t) + \sum_{i=1}^{n} p_i f_i(x,u,t) \tag{7.38}$$

$$\mathcal{L}(x,u,p,\mu,t) = H(x,u,p,t) + \sum_{k=1}^{K} \mu_k \left[ b_k - h_k(x,u,t) \right] \tag{7.39}$$

Necessary conditions for problem (7.37) can be stated as follows:

Let $u^*(t)$ solve problem (7.37) and let $x^*(t)$ be the associated optimal trajectory for the state variables. Assume that for any $t \in [t_o, t_1]$ and $\{x^*(t), u^*(t)\}$ the constraint functions $h$ satisfy the constrained qualification as defined in Section 3.2.2. Then there exist a constant $p_o$ and a continuous and piecewise continuously differentiable vector valued function $p(t) = (p_1(t), ..., p_n(t))$ from $[t_o, t_1]$ to $\mathfrak{R}^n$, and piecewise continuous Lagrangean multipliers such that for all $t \in [t_o, t_1]$:

$$p_o = 0, \text{ or } p_o = 1, \ (p_o, p_1(t), ..., p_n(t)) \neq 0 \tag{7.40.1}$$

$u^*(t)$ maximizes the Hamiltonian function (7.38) for $u \in U$ subject to the constraints $h_k(x^*, u^*, t) \leq b_k$, $k = 1, ..., K$, or

$$\frac{\partial \mathcal{L}^*}{\partial u_j} = 0, \ j = 1, ..., m, \text{ where } \mathcal{L}^* = \mathcal{L}(x^*, u^*, p, \mu, t) \tag{7.40.2}$$

$$\mu_k(t) \left[ b_k - h_k(x^*, u^*, t) \right] = 0, \ m_k \geq 0, \ k = 1, ..., K$$
$$\text{or } m_k \geq 0 \left[ = 0 \text{ if } h_k(x^*, u^*, t) < b_k \right] \tag{7.40.3}$$

Except at the points of discontinuity of $u^*(t)$, $\{x^*(t), p(t)\}$ solves the Hamiltonian system

$$\dot{p}_i(t) = -\frac{\partial \mathcal{L}^*}{\partial x_i} \tag{7.40.4a}$$

$$\dot{x}_i(t) = \frac{\partial \mathcal{L}^*}{\partial p_i} \tag{7.40.4b}$$

The transversality conditions (7.33.5) to (7.33.7) are also satisfied. If nonnegativity constraints on the controls are imposed, as is usual in economic problems, then (7.40.2) is replaced by

$$\frac{\partial \mathcal{L}^*}{\partial u_j} \leq 0, \text{ with equality if } u_j^* > 0, \ j = 1, ..., m \tag{7.40.5}$$

If there is an infinite horizon control problem with constant discount rate

$\delta > 0$, then the necessary conditions are defined in terms of the current value Hamiltonian and Lagrangean functions, in which case (7.40.4a) is replaced by

$$\dot{\lambda}_i(t) = \delta\lambda(t) - \frac{\partial \mathcal{L}^*}{\partial x_i}, \quad i = 1,...,n \tag{7.40.6}$$

Furthermore the Arrow type transversality conditions at infinity should be satisfied.

In the mixed constraint case the Arrow type transversality conditions remain valid with the additional requirement that the set $\{x : \text{for some } u, h_k(x,u,t) \le b_k\}$ be a convex set.

### 5.2.4 Envelope results

There is a dynamic analog of the static envelope theorem which can be used to determine the effects of a change in a parameter of an optimal control problem on the entire optimal path.[25] Consider the optimal control problem

$$\max_{\{u(t)\}} \int_{t_o}^{t_1} f_o(x(t),u(t), a,t)dt \tag{7.41}$$

s. t. $\dot{x}_i(t) = f_i(x(t),u(t), a,t), \quad i = 1,...,n, \; x(t_o) = x_o$ fixed $\tag{7.41.1}$

$$h_k(x(t),u(t), a,t) = 0, \; k = 1,...,K \tag{7.41.2}$$

$$g_s(x(t),u(t), a,t) \ge 0, \; s = 1,...,S \tag{7.41.3}$$

where $a \in \mathfrak{R}^r$ is a vector of fixed parameters.

Define the Lagrangean function as

$$\mathcal{L} = f_o(x,u,a,t) + \sum_{i=1}^{n} p_i f_i(x,u,a,t) + \sum_{k=1}^{K} \lambda_k h_k(x,u,a,t)$$

$$+ \sum_{s=1}^{S} \mu_s g_s(x,u,a,t) \tag{7.42}$$

where the Hamiltonian function is defined as

$$H = f_o(x,u,a,t) + \sum_{i=1}^{n} p_i f_i(x,u,a,t)$$

Assume further that all the functions are twice continuously differentiable, that the set of feasible controls is compact and convex and satisfies the

---

[25]For a detailed exposition of the dynamic envelope theorem, see Caputo (1990a,b), LaFrance and Barney (1991). This section follows LaFrance and Barney.

constraint qualification, and that the optimal paths for the state and the costate variables, which are functions of the vector of parameters $a$, are unique, and define the optimal value function as

$$J^*(a) = \int_{t_o}^{t_1} f_o(x^*(a,t), u^*(a,t), a, t) dt$$

It holds that

$$\frac{\partial J^*(a)}{\partial a} = \int_{t_o}^{t_1} \frac{\partial \mathcal{L}^*}{\partial a} dt$$

where $\mathcal{L}^* = \mathcal{L}(x^*(a,t), u^*(a,t), p(a,t), \lambda(a,t), \mu(a,t), a, t)$. Furthermore if $f_o$ is convex in $a$ and the $f_i, h_j, g_s$ are independent of $a$, then $J^*(a)$ is convex in $a$.

# 6   DIFFERENTIAL GAMES

A differential game can be defined as a situation of conflict where players choose strategies over time.[26] In addition to the characteristics of an optimal control problem, a number of new concepts are introduced in a differential game. In contrast to an optimal control problem, in a differential game there is more than one decision maker (player). There is a set of players indexed by $I = 1,...,N$ and characterized by the index set $N_p = \{1,...,N\}$. For each player $I \in N_p$, a control space exists, $U^I$, whose elements $u^I(t)$, $t \in [t_o, t_1]$ are the control variables for each player $I$. The transition equations for the differential game describing the state of the game at each point in time depend on the control variables of all players. Thus they can be written as

$$\dot{x}_i(t) = f_i(x(t), u^1(t),...,u^N(t)), \ x(t) \in \Re^n, \ x(t_o) = x_o \ \text{fixed}$$

$$u^I(t) = \left(u_1^I(t),...,u_m^I(t)\right), \ I = 1,...,N \tag{7.43}$$

The strategy for each player is a function $u^I(t) = \theta^I(x,t)$. The set of strategies for player $I$ is its strategy space.

Crucial to the structure of the differential game is the specification of the information about the state of the game gained and recalled by each player at each point in time $t \in [t_o, t_1]$. There are a number of possible information structures for a differential game (Basar and Olsder 1982), only two of which

---

[26]See Intriligator (1971) for an introduction to the differential game concept, and Basar and Olsder (1982) for a detailed analysis.

are examined here.

The differential game is said to have an open-loop informational structure if the players follow open-loop strategies:

$$u^I(t) = \theta^I(x_o, t) \tag{7.44.1}$$

The differential game is said to have feedback informational structure if the players follow feedback strategies:

$$u^I(t) = \theta^I(x(t), t) \tag{7.44.2}$$

Given the above definitions a differential game is defined as:

$$\max_{\{u(t)\}} J^I = \int_{t_o}^{t_1} f_o(x(t), u^1(t), \dots, u^N(t)) dt \tag{7.45}$$

subject to (7.43) with the players' strategies defined by (7.44.1) or (7.44.2).

In the differential game (7.45), the open-loop Nash equilibrium is defined as the *n*-tuple of open-loop strategies $(u^{1*}, \dots, u^{N*})$ satisfying

$$J^I(u^{1*}, \dots, u^{N*}) \geq J^I(u^{1*}, \dots, u^{I-1*}, u^I, u^{I+1*}, \dots, u^{N*}) \tag{7.46}$$

A feedback Nash equilibrium is an *n*-tuple of feedback strategies that satisfies conditions (7.46) for every possible $(t_o, x_o)$. From the above definitions it follows that the open-loop Nash equilibrium is not subgame perfect, while a feedback equilibrium is subgame perfect.

Consider problem (7.45). If $u^{I*}(t) = \theta^I(x_o, t)$, $I = 1, \dots, N$ provides an open-loop Nash equilibrium and $x^*(t)$ is the associated optimal trajectory for the state variables, then costate variables $p^I(t) \in \Re^n$, $I = 1, \dots, N$ exist such that $u^{*I}(t)$, $I = 1, \dots, N$ maximizes the Hamiltonian function

$$H^I(x, u^1, \dots, u^N, t) = f_o^I(x, u^1, \dots, u^N, t)$$

$$+ \sum_{i=1}^{n} p_i^I f_i(x, u^1, \dots, u^N, t) \tag{7.47.1}$$

$u^{*I}(t)$, $x^*(t)$, $p^I(t)$ solve the system of differential equations

$$\dot{p}_i^I(t) = -\frac{\partial H^{I*}}{\partial x_i}, \quad i = 1, \dots, n, \ I = 1, \dots, N \tag{7.47.2}$$

where     $H^{I*} = H^I(x^*, u^{1*}, \dots, u^{N*})$, $u^{*I} = u^I(x^*, p)$

$$\dot{x}_i(t) = f_i(x^*, u^{1*}, \dots, u^{N*}) \tag{7.47.3}$$

The transversality conditions depend on the type of terminal conditions, on the state variables and can be determined as in (7.33.5) to (7.33.7).

If $u^{I*}(t) = \theta^I(x(t), t)$, $I = 1,...,N$ provides a feedback Nash equilibrium and $x^*(t)$ is the associated optimal trajectory for the state variables, then costate variables $p^I(t) \in \Re^n$, $I = 1,...,N$ exist such that $u^{*I}(t)$, $I = 1,...,N$ maximizes the Hamiltonian function

$$H^I(x,\theta^1,...,\theta^{I-1}, u^I, \theta^{I+1},..., \theta^N, t) = f_o^I(x, \theta^1,..., u^I,..., \theta^N, t)$$

$$+ \sum_{i=1}^{n} p_i^I f_i(x, \theta^1,..., u^I,..., \theta^N, t)$$

(7.48.1)

$u^{*I}(t)$, $x^*(t)$, $p^I(t)$ solve the system of differential equations

$$\dot{p}_i^I(t) = -\frac{\partial H^{I*}}{\partial x_i}, \quad i = 1,...,n, \ I = 1,...,N$$

(7.48.2)

where
$$H^{I*} = H^I(x^*, \theta^{1*},..., \theta^{I-1*}, u^{I*}, \theta^{I+1*},..., \theta^{N*}, t)$$

$$\dot{x}_i(t) = f_i(x^*, u^{1*},..., u^{N*})$$

(7.48.3)

The transversality conditions can be defined as before.

Infinite horizon differential games can be analysed by introducing a current value Hamiltonian and using the conditions of the maximum principle as defined above.

# 7  STOCHASTIC CONTROL

The analysis turns now to the case in which the transition equation of the optimal control problem is a stochastic differential equation.[27] A stochastic differential equation of the Itô type is defined as:

$$dx(t) = f(x,(t),t)dt + \sigma(x(t),t)dz(t), \ x(0) = x_o$$

(7.49)

In (7.49), $x(t)$ is a real-valued stochastic process, $f$ and $\sigma$ are real-valued functions defined in a given time interval, and $z(t)$ is a Wiener process.[28] A stochastic process $x(t)$ is the solution of (7.49) for $t \in [t_o, t_1]$ if the functions $f$ and $\sigma$ are such that:

---

[27]The exposition follows Malliaris and Brock (1982) where more detailed definitions can be found. For a detailed analysis of stochastic differential equations, see Gard (1988).

[28]A Wiener process or Brownian motion process is a stochastic process $\{z(t), t \in [0, \infty)\}$ whose increments are normally distributed with zero mean and unit variance.

$$\int_{t_o}^{t_1} |f(x(t),t|\,dt < \infty \quad \text{and} \quad \int_{t_o}^{t_1} |\sigma(x(t),t|^2\,dt < \infty$$

and $x(t)$ satisfies the stochastic integral equation

$$x(t) = x_o + \int_o^t f(x(s),s)\,ds + \int_o^t \sigma(x(s),s)\,ds$$

Let $u(t,x)$ be a continuous nonrandom real-valued function defined in $[0,T] \times \Re$ with continuous partial derivatives $u_t, u_x, u_{xx}$. Assume that $\{x(t)\}$ is a stochastic process for which

$$dx(t) = f(t)\,dt + \sigma(t)\,dz(t)$$

Let $y(t) = u(t,x(t))$, then the differential of $y(t)$ on $[0,T]$ is given by

$$dy(t) = \left[ u_t(t,x(t)) + u_x(t,x(t))f(t) + \frac{1}{2} u_{xx}(t,x(t))\sigma^2(t) \right] dt$$
$$+ u_x(t,x(t))\sigma(t)\,dz(t)$$

The above result is known as Itô's lemma.

A stochastic control problem requires the maximization of the expected value of a functional subject to a transition equation described by a stochastic differential equation. The problem can be stated for the autonomous case as:

$$J(x(t),t_o,t_1) = \max_{\{u(t)\}} \mathcal{E}_{t_o} \int_{t_o}^{t_1} f_o(x(t),u(t))\,dt \qquad (7.50)$$

s. t. $dx(t) = f(x(t),u(t))dt + \sigma(x(t),u(t))dz(t),\; x(0) = x_o$ fixed $\qquad (7.50.1)$

$\qquad\qquad x(t_1) = x_1$ fixed $\qquad (7.50.2)$

For this problem the Hamilton-Jacobi-Bellman equation is defined as:

$$-J_t = \max_u \left[ f_o(x(t),u(t)) + J_x f(x(t),u(t)) + \frac{1}{2} J_{xx}\sigma^2(x(t),u(t)) \right]$$

where subscripts indicate partial derivatives. The costate variable for the maximum principle is then defined as:

$$p = J_x, \quad p_x = \frac{\partial p}{\partial x} = J_{xx}$$

Let $u^*(t)$ solve problem (7.50) and let $x^*(t)$ be the associated state trajectory, then costate variables $p(t)$ exist such that $u^*(t)$ maximizes the Hamiltonian function:

$$H\left(x,u,p,\frac{\partial p}{\partial x}\right) = f_o(x,u) + pf(x,u) + \frac{1}{2}\sigma^2\frac{\partial p}{\partial x} \qquad (7.51.1)$$

$u^*(t)$, $x^*(t)$, $p(t)$ solve the system of stochastic differential equations (stochastic Hamiltonian system)

$$dp = -\frac{\partial H^*}{\partial x} dt + \sigma(x^*, u^*)\frac{\partial p}{\partial x} dz, \quad H^* = H\left(x^*, u^*, p, \frac{\partial p}{\partial x}\right) \qquad (7.51.2)$$

$$dx = f(x^*, u^*) dt \qquad (7.51.3)$$

The transversality condition holds

$$p(t_1) = 0 \qquad (7.51.4)$$

The above conditions are the stochastic maximum principle, which can be extended to cover cases with discounting, or

$$J(x, t_o, t_1) = \max_{\{u(t)\}} \mathscr{E}_{t_o} \int_{t_o}^{t_1} e^{-\delta t} f_o(x, u) dt$$

s.t. (7.50.1) and (7.50.2)

Write

$$W(x(t), t_o, t_1) = e^{\delta t} J(x(t), t_o, t_1)$$

then the Hamilton-Jacobi-Bellman equation is defined as

$$\delta W = \max_{u} \left[ f_o(x, u) + W_x f(x, u) + \frac{1}{2}\sigma^2(x, u)W_{xx} \right]$$

By introducing the current value Hamiltonian, the necessary condition of the stochastic maximum principle remains the same, except for (7.51.2) which is replaced by

$$dp = \left(\delta p - \frac{\partial H^*}{\partial x}\right) dt + \sigma(x^*, u^*)\frac{\partial p}{\partial x} dz$$

The stochastic control problem can be further generalized to multi-dimensional cases, to problems involving constraints on the control, and to infinite horizon problems. In the latter case, the notion of stability and steady state distributions are introduced (Brock and Magill 1979).

# Bibliography

Adar, Z. and J.M. Griffin (1976), 'Uncertainty and the Choice of Pollution Control Instruments', *Journal of Environmental Economics and Management*, **3** (3), 178–88.

*American Economic Association Papers and Proceedings* (1982), 'The Global Commons I, Cost and Climatic Effects'.

Apostol, T.M. (1974), *Mathematical Analysis*, Second Edition, Reading, Mass.: Addison-Wesley Publishing Company.

Arrow, K.J. and M. Kurz (1970), *Public Investment, the Rate of Return, and Optimal Fiscal Policy,* Baltimore: Johns Hopkins University Press for Resources for the Future.

Atkinson, S.E and T.H. Tietenberg (1982), 'The Empirical Properties of Two Classes of Designs for Transferable Discharge Permit Markets', *Journal of Environmental Economics and Management*, **9**, 101–21.

Atkinson, S.E and T.H. Tietenberg (1984), 'Approaches for Reaching Ambient Standards in Non-Attainment Areas: Financial Burden and Efficiency Considerations', *Land Economics*, **60**, 148–59.

Atkinson, S.E and T.H. Tietenberg (1991), 'Market Failure in Incentive-Based Regulation: The Case of Emission Trading', *Journal of Environmental Economics and Management*, **21** (1), 17–31.

Ayres, R.U. and J. Walter (1991), 'The Greenhouse Effect: Damages, Costs and Abatement', *Environmental and Resource Economics*, **1**, 237–70.

Bac, M. (1996), 'Incomplete Information and Incentives to Free Ride on International Environmental Resources', *Journal of Environmental Economics and Management*, **30**, 301–15.

Barbier, E.B. (1996), 'Endogenous Growth and Natural Resource Scarcity', University of York, Discussion Papers in Environmental Economics and Environmental Management, Number 9601.

Barnett, A.H. (1980), 'The Pigouvian Tax Rule under Monopoly', *American Economic Review*, **70**, 1037–41.

Barrett, S. (1990), 'The Problem of Global Environmental Protection', *Oxford Review of Economic Policy*, **6** (1), 168–79.

Barrett, S. (1991), 'The Paradox of International Environmental Agreements', mimeo, London Business School.

Barrett, S. (1992), 'International Environmental Agreements as Games', in R. Pethig (ed.), *Conflicts and Cooperation in Managing Environmental Resources*, Berlin: Springer-Verlag, 18–33.

Barrett, S. (1994a), 'Self-Enforcing International Environmental Agreements', *Oxford Economics Papers*, **46**, 878–94.

Barrett, S. (1994b), 'Strategic Environmental Policy and International Trade', *Journal of Public Economics*, **54**, 325–38.

Barrett, S. (1994c), 'Trade Restrictions in International Environmental Agreements', CSERGE Working Paper GEC 94–13.

Barrett, S. (1995), 'Toward a Theory of International Environmental Cooperation', Fondazione ENI Enrico Mattei Discussion Paper 60.95, Milan.

Barrett, S. (1997), 'Heterogeneous International Environmental Agreements', in C. Carraro (ed.), *International Environmental Negotiations*, Aldershot: Edward Elgar, forthcoming.

Basar, T. (1989), 'Time Consistency and Robustness of Equilibria in Non-cooperative Dynamic Games', in F. van der Ploeg and A.J. de Zeeuw (eds), *Dynamic Policy Games in Economics*, Amsterdam: North-Holland.

Basar, T. and G.J. Olsder (1982), *Dynamic Non-cooperative Game Theory*, New York: Academic Press.

Baumol, W.J. (1964), 'External Economies and Second-Order Optimality Conditions', *American Economic Review*, **54**, 358–72.

Baumol, W.J. (1972), 'On Taxation and the Control of Externalities', *American Economic Review*, **62**, 307–22.

Baumol, W.J. and D.F. Bradford (1972), 'Detrimental Externalities and Non-Convexity of the Production Set', *Economica*, **39**, 160–76.

Baumol, W.J. and W.E. Oates (1971), 'The Use of Standards and Prices for Protection of the Environment', *Scandinavian Journal of Economics*, **73**, 42–54.

Baumol, W.J. and W.E. Oates (1988), *The Theory of Environmental Policy*, Second Edition, Cambridge: Cambridge University Press.

Beavis, B. and I.M. Dobbs (1990), *Optimization and Stability Theory for Economic Analysis*, Cambridge: Cambridge University Press.

Becker, R.A. (1982), 'Intergenerational Equity: The Capital-Environment Trade-Off', *Journal of Environmental Economics and Management*, **9**, 165–85.

Beltratti, A. (1992), 'Endogenous Growth with Fixed Factors of Production', Fondazione Eni Enrico Mattei Discussion Paper 16.92, Milan.

Beltratti, A. (1996), *Sustainability of Growth: Reflections on Economic Models*, Dordrecht: Kluwer Academic Publishers.

Beltratti, A., G. Chichilnisky and G. Heal (1993), 'Sustainable Growth and the Green Golden Rule', Fondazione Eni Enrico Mattei Discussion Paper 61.93, Milan.

Besanko, D. (1987), 'Performance versus Design Standards in the Regulation of Pollution', *Journal of Public Economics*, **34**, 19–44.

Bohm, P. (1981), *Deposit-Refund Systems: Theory and Applications to Environmental, Conservation, and Consumer Policy*, Baltimore: Johns Hopkins University Press for Resources for the Future.

Bohm, P. (1993), 'Incomplete International Cooperation to Reduce $CO_2$ Emissions: Alternative Policies', *Journal of Environmental Economics and Management*, **24**, 258–71.

Bohm, P. and C.S. Russell (1985), 'Comparative Analysis of Alternative Policy Instruments', in A.V. Kneese and J.L. Sweeney (eds), *Handbook of Natural Resource and Energy Economics*, Volume I, Amsterdam: North-Holland, pp. 395–460.

Botteon, M. and C. Carraro (1997), 'Burden-Sharing and Coalition Stability in Environmental Negotiations with Asymmetric Countries', in C. Carraro (ed.), *International Environmental Negotiations*, Aldershot: Edward Elgar, forthcoming.

Bovenberg, L.A. (1995), 'Environmental Policy, Distortionary Labor Taxation and Employment: Pollution Taxation and the Double Dividend', Fondazione ENI Enrico Mattei Discussion Paper 38.95, Milan.

Bovenberg, L.A. and L. Goulder (1996), 'Optimal Environmental Taxation in the Presence of Other Taxes: General Equilibrium Analysis', *American Economic Review*, **86** (4), 985–1000.

Bovenberg, L.A. and R.A. de Mooij (1994), 'Environmental Levies and Distortionary Taxation', *American Economic Review*, **94** (4), 1085–89.

Bovenberg, A.L. and S. Smulders (1995), 'Environmental Quality and Pollution-Augmenting Technological Change in a Two-Sector Endogenous Growth Model, *Journal of Public Economics*, **57**, 369–91.

Bovenberg, L.A. and F. van der Ploeg (1994), 'Environmental Policy, Public Finance and the Labour Market in a Second-Best World', *Journal of Public Economics*, **55** (3), 349–90.

Bovenberg, L.A. and F. van der Ploeg (1996), 'Optimal Taxation, Public Goods and Environmental Policy with Involuntary Unemployment', *Journal of Public Economics*, **62**, 59–83.

Boyd, J. and D.E. Ingberman (1994), 'Extending Liability: Should the Sins of the Producer Be Revisited upon Others?', Resources for the Future Discussion Paper, Washington.

Boyer, M. and J.-J. Laffont (1996), 'Environmental Protection, Producer

Insolvency and Lender Liability', in A. Xepapadeas (ed.), *Economic Policy for the Environment and Natural Resources: Techniques for the Management and Control of Pollution,* Edward Elgar.

Braden, J.B. and C.D. Kolstad (eds) (1991), *Measuring the Demand for Environmental Quality,* Amsterdam: North-Holland.

Braden, J. and K. Segerson (1993), 'Information Problems in the Design of Nonpoint-Source Pollution Policy', in C. Russell and J Shogren (eds), *Theory, Modeling, and Experience in the Management of Nonpoint-Source Pollution,* Boston: Kluwer Academic Publishers, 1–35.

Brock, W.A. (1977), 'A Polluted Golden Age', in V.L. Smith (ed.), *Economics of Natural and Environmental Resources,* New York: Gordon & Breach.

Brock, W.A. and D.S. Evans (1985), 'The Economics of Regulatory Tiering', *Rand Journal of Economics,* **16,** 398–409.

Brock, W.A. and M.J.P. Magill (1979), 'Dynamics under Uncertainty', *Econometrica,* **47** (4), 843–68.

Brock, W.A. and A.G. Malliaris (1989), *Differential Equations, Stability and Chaos in Dynamic Economics,* Amsterdam: North-Holland.

Brock, W.A. and J. Scheinkman (1976), 'The Global Asymptotic Stability of Optimal Control Systems with Applications to the Theory of Economic Growth', *Journal of Economic Growth Theory,* **12,** 164-90.

Brundtland Commission (1987), World Commission on Environment and Development, *Our Common Future,* Oxford: Oxford University Press.

Buchanan, J.M. (1969), 'External Diseconomies, Corrective Taxes and Market Structure', *American Economic Review,* **59,** 174–7.

Burrows, P. (1979), 'Pigouvian Taxes, Polluter Subsidies, Regulation, and the Size of a Polluting Industry', *Canadian Journal of Economics,* **12,** 494–501.

Cabe, R. and J. Herriges (1992), 'The Regulation of Nonpoint Sources of Pollution under Imperfect and Asymmetric Information', *Journal of Environmental Economics and Management,* **22,** 134–46.

Caputo, M.R. (1990a), 'Comparative Dynamics via Envelope Method in Variational Calculus', *Review of Economic Studies,* **57,** 689–97.

Caputo, M.R. (1990b), 'How to Do Comparative Dynamics on the Back of an Envelope in Optimal Control Theory', *Journal of Economic Dynamics and Control,* **14,** 655–83.

Carlson, D.A., A.B. Haurie and A. Leizarowitz (1991), *Infinite Horizon Optimal Control,* Second Edition, Berlin: Springer-Verlag.

Carraro, C., M. Galeolti and M. Gallo (1996), 'Environmental Taxation and Unemployment: Some Evidence of the Double Dividend Hypothesis in

Europe', *Journal of Public Economics*, **62**, 141–81.

Carraro, C., Y. Katsoulacos and A. Xepapadeas (eds) (1996), *Environmental Policy and Market Structure*, Dordrecht: Kluwer Academic Publishers.

Carraro, C. and D. Siniscalco (1991), 'The International Protection of the Environment: Voluntary Agreements among Sovereign Countries', in P. Dasgupta, K.-G. Mäler and A. Vercelli (eds), *The Protection of Trans-National Commons*, Oxford: Clarendon.

Carraro, C. and D. Siniscalco (1993a), 'Strategies for the International Protection of the Environment', *Journal of Public Economics*, **52**, 309–28.

Carraro, C. and D. Siniscalco (eds) (1993b), *The Carbon Tax: An Economic Assessment*, Dordrecht: Kluwer Academic Publishers.

Carraro, C. and D. Siniscalco (1994), 'International Coordination of Environmental Policies and Stability of Global Environmental Agreements', Fondazione ENI Enrico Mattei Discussion Paper 57.94, Milan, to appear in L. Bovenberg and G. Cnossen (eds), *Public Economics and the Environment in an Imperfect World*, Dordrecht: Kluwer Academic Publishers.

Carraro, C. and D. Siniscalco (1996), 'Voluntary Agreements in Environmental Policy', in A. Xepapadeas (ed.), *Environmental Policy for the Environment and Natural Resources*, Cheltenham, U.K.: Edward Elgar.

Carraro, C. and D. Siniscalco (1997), 'R&D Cooperation and the Stability of International Environmental Agreements', in C. Carraro (ed.), *International Environmental Negotiations*, Aldershot: Edward Elgar, forthcoming.

Carraro, C. and D. Soubeyran (1996a), 'Environmental Feedbacks and Optimal Taxation in Oligopoly', in A. Xepapadeas (ed.), *Economic Policy for the Environment and Natural Resources*, Cheltenham, UK: Edward Elgar Publishing, 30–58.

Carraro, C. and A. Soubeyran (1996b), 'Environmental Policy and the Choice of Production Technology', in C. Carraro, Y. Katsoulacos and A. Xepapadeas (eds), *Environmental Policy and Market Structure*, Dordrecht: Kluwer Academic Publishers, 151–80.

Carraro, C. and A. Soubeyran (1996c), 'Environmental Taxation, Market Share, and Profits in Oligopoly', in C. Carraro, Y. Katsoulacos and A. Xepapadeas (eds), *Environmental Policy and Market Structure*, Dordrecht: Kluwer Academic Publishers, 23–44.

Cason, T.N. and C.R. Plott (1996), 'EPA's New Emissions Trading Mechanism: A Laboratory Evaluation', *Journal of Environmental Economics and Management*, **30**, 133–60.

Cass, D. and K. Shell (1976), 'The Structure and Stability of Competitive Dynamical Systems', *Journal of Economic Theory*, **12**, 31–70.

Cesar, H. (1994), 'Control and Game Models of the Greenhouse Effect', in *Lecture Notes in Economics and Mathematical Systems*, Vol. 416, Berlin: Springer-Verlag.

Cesar, H. and A. de Zeeuw (1996), 'Issue Linkage in Global Environmental Problems', in A. Xepapadeas (ed.), *Economic Policy for the Environment and Natural Resources: Techniques for the Management and Control of Pollution*, Aldershot: Edward Elgar, 158–73.

Cesari, L. (1983), *Optimization – Theory and Applications*, New York: Springer-Verlag.

Chander, P. and H. Tulkens (1992), 'Theoretical Foundations of Negotiations and Cost Sharing in Externalities', Mimeo, CORE and Indian Statistical Institute.

Chander, P. and H. Tulkens (1994), 'The Core of an Economy with Multilateral Environmental Externalities', CORE Discussion Paper.

Chander, P. and H. Tulkens (1995), 'A Core-Theoretic Solution for the Design of Cooperative Agreements in Transfrontier Pollution', *International Tax and Public Finance*, **2**, 279–93.

Chiang, A.C. (1984), *Fundamental Methods of Mathematical Analysis*, Third Edition, New York: McGraw-Hill Book Company.

Chichilnisky, G. (1993), 'What Is Sustainable Development?', paper presented at the 1993 workshop of the Stanford Institute for Theoretical Economics.

Chichilnisky, G., G. Heal and D. Starrett (1996), 'International Emission Permits: Equity and Efficiency', Annual Congress of ASSA, San Francisco.

Cline, W. (1991), 'Scientific Basis for the Greenhouse Effect', *The Economic Journal*, **101**, 904–19.

Cline, W. (1992), *The Economics of Global Warming*, Washington, D.C.: Institute for International Economics.

Coase, R.H. (1960), 'The Problem of Social Cost', *Journal of Law and Economics*, **3**, 1–44.

Conrad, K. and J. Wang (1993), 'The Effect of Emission Taxes and Abatement Subsidies on Market Structure', *International Journal of Industrial Organization*, **11**, 499–518.

Copeland, B.R. (1994), 'International Trade and the Environment: Policy Reform in a Polluted Small Open Economy', *Journal of Environmental Economics and Management*, **26**, 44–65.

Crocker, T.D. (1966), 'The Structuring of Atmospheric Pollution Control

Systems', in H. Wolozin (ed.), *The Economics of Air Pollution*, New York: W.W. Norton.

Cropper, M. and W.E. Oates (1992), 'Environmental Economics: A Survey', *Journal of Economic Literature*, **30**, 675–740.

Dales, J.H. (1968), 'Land, Water, and Ownership', *Canadian Journal of Economics*, **1** (4), 791–804.

Daly, H.E. and J.B. Cobb, Jr (1989), *For the Common Good: Redirecting the Economy toward Community, the Environment and a Sustainable Future*, Boston: Beacon Press.

Damania, D. (1996), 'Pollution Taxes and Pollution Abatement in an Oligopoly Supergame', *Journal of Environmental Economics and Management*, **30**, 323–36.

d'Arge, R.C. and K.C. Kogiku (1973), 'Economic Growth and the Environment', *Review of Economic Studies*, **40**, 61–77.

Dasgupta, P.S. (1982), *Control of Resources*, Oxford: Basil Blackwell.

Dasgupta, P.S. and G.M. Heal (1979), *Economic Theory and Exhaustible Resources*, Oxford: James Nisbet and Co., Ltd. and Cambridge University Press.

Dasgupta, P.S. and K.-G. Mäler (1991), 'The Environment and Emerging Development Issues', Proceedings of the World Bank Annual Conference on Development Economics 1990, The International Bank for Reconstruction and Development/The World Bank.

D'Aspremont, C., A. Jacquemin, J. Gabszewics and J. Weymark (1983), 'On the Stability of Collusive Price Leadership', *Canadian Journal of Economics*, **16**, 17–25.

de Bruyn, S., J. van den Bergh and H. Opschoor (1995), 'Environmental Kuznets Curve and the Alleged De-linking of Environmental Pressure from Environmental Growth', paper presented at the 6th Annual Conference of the European Association of Environmental and Resource Economists, Umea, Sweden.

DeCoursey, D. (1985), 'Mathematical Models for Nonpoint Pollution Control', *Journal of Soil and Water Conservation*, **40**, 408–13.

Dinar, A. and D. Zilberman (eds) (1991), *The Economics and Management of Water and Drainage in Agriculture*, Boston: Kluwer Academic Publishers.

Dixit, A.K. (1990), *Optimization in Economic Theory*, Second Edition, New York: Oxford University Press.

Dockner, E. and N. Van Long (1993), 'International Pollution Control: Cooperative versus Noncooperative Strategies', *Journal of Environmental Economics and Management*, **25**, 13–29.

Dosi, C. and M. Moretto (1992), 'Non Point Source Pollution, Maintenance Policy and the Choice of Time Profile for Environmental Fees', Fondazione Eni Enrico Mattei Discussion Paper 2.92, Milan.

Dosi, C. and M. Moretto (1994), 'Non Point Source Externalities and Polluter's Site Quality Standards under Incomplete Information', in C. Dosi and T. Tomasi (eds), *Nonpoint Source Pollution Regulation: Issues and Analysis*, Dordrecht: Kluwer Academic Publishers, 107–36.

Downing, P.B. and L.J. White (1986), 'Innovation in Pollution Control', *Journal of Environmental Economics and Management*, **13**, 18–27.

Ebert, U. (1991/2), 'Pigouvian Tax and Market Structure', *Finanz Archiv*, **49**, 154–66.

Ebert, U. (1992), 'On the Effect of Effluent Fees under Oligopoly: Comparative Static Analysis', Discussion Paper V-82–91, University of Oldenburg, Institute of Economics.

Ebert, U. (1996), 'Naive Use of Environmental Instruments', in C. Carraro, Y. Katsoulacos and A. Xepapadeas (eds), *Environmental Policy and Market Structure*, Dordrecht: Kluwer Academic Publishers, 45–64.

*The Economic Journal* (1991), 'Policy Forum', **101**, 904–48.

Elbasha, E.H. and T.L. Roe (1996), 'On Endogenous Growth: The Implications of Environmental Externalities', *Journal of Environmental Economics and Management*, **31** (2), 240–68.

Environmental Protection Agency (EPA) (1992), *The United States Experience with Economic Incentives to Control Environmental Pollution*.

Fankhauser, S. and S. Kverndokk (1996), 'The Global Warming Game – Simulations of a $CO_2$-Reduction Agreement', *Resource and Energy Economics*, **18**, 83–102.

Farzin, Y.H. (1996), 'Optimal Pricing of Environmental and Natural Resource Use with Stock Externalities', *Journal of Public Economics*, **62**, 31–57.

Feinstein, C.D. and D.J. Luenberger (1981), 'Analysis of Asymptotic Behavior of Optimal Control Trajectories: The Implicit Programming Problem', *SIAM Journal of Control and Optimization*, **19**, 561–85.

Fershtman, C. (1987), 'Identification of Classes of Differential Games for Which the Open Loop Is a Degenerate Feedback Nash Equilibrium', *Journal of Optimization Theory and Applications*, **55** (2), 217–31.

Fershtman, C. and A. de Zeeuw (1996), 'Tradeable Emission Permits in Oligopoly', CentER Discussion Paper No. 9630.

Fershtman, C. and S. Nitzan (1991), 'Dynamic Voluntary Provision of Public Goods', *European Economic Review*, **35**, 1057–67.

Fisher, A.C. (1981), *Resource and Environmental Economics*, Cambridge:

Cambridge University Press.

Folmer, H., P. van Mouche and S. Ragland (1993), 'Interconnected Games and International Environmental Problems', *Environmental and Resource Economics*, **3**, 313–35.

Forster, B.A. (1973), 'Optimal Capital Accumulation in a Polluted Environment', *Southern Economic Journal*, **39**, 544–7.

Forster, B.A. (1975), 'Optimal Pollution Control with a Nonconstant Exponential Rate of Decay', *Journal of Environmental Economics and Management*, **2**, 1–6.

Freeman, A.M. (1985), 'Methods for Assessing the Benefits of Environmental Programs', in A.V. Kneese and J.L. Sweeney (eds), *Handbook of Natural Resource and Energy Economics*, Volume I, Amsterdam: North-Holland, pp. 223–70.

Friedman, J.W. (1989), *Game Theory with Applications to Economics*, New York: Oxford University Press.

Gard, T.C. (1988), *Introduction to Stochastic Differential Equations*, New York: Marcel Dekker, Inc.

Germain, M., P. Toint and H. Tulkens (1996), 'International Negotiations on Acid Rains in Northern Europe: A Discrete Time Iterative Process', in A. Xepapadeas (ed.), *Economic Policy for the Environment and Natural Resources: Techniques for the Management and Control of Pollution*, Aldershot: Edward Elgar, 217–36.

Golombek, R., C. Hagem and M. Hoel (1993), 'The Design of a Carbon Tax in an Incomplete International Climate Agreement', in C. Carraro (ed.), *Trade, Innovation, Environment*, Dordrecht: Kluwer Academic Publishers.

Goulder, L. (1995a), 'Effects of Carbon Taxes in an Economy with Prior Tax Distortions: An Intertemporal General Equilibrium Analysis', *Journal of Environmental Economics and Management*, **29** (3), 271–97.

Goulder, L. (1995b), 'Environmental Taxation and Double Dividend: A Reader's Guide', *International Tax and Public Finance*, **2** (2), 157–83.

Gradus, R. and S. Smulders (1993), 'The Trade-off between Environmental Care and Long-term Growth – Pollution in Three Prototype Growth Models', *Journal of Economics*, **58** (1), 25–51.

Griffin, R. and D. Bromley (1982), 'Agricultural Runoff as a Nonpoint Externality', *American Journal of Agricultural Economics*, **64**, 547–52.

Grossman, G.M. and E. Helpman (1991), *Innovation and Growth*, Cambridge, Mass.: The MIT Press.

Grossman, G.M. and A.B. Krueger (1993), 'Environmental Impacts of a North American Free Trade Agreement', in P. Garber (ed.), *The U.S.-*

*Mexico Free Trade Agreement*, Cambridge, Mass.: The MIT Press.

Grossman, G.M. and A.B. Krueger (1995), 'Economic Growth and the Environment', *The Quarterly Journal of Economics*, May, 353–77.

Gruver, G.W. (1976), 'Optimal Investment in Pollution Control Capital in a Neoclassical Growth Context', *Journal of Environmental Economics and Management*, **3**, 165–77.

Guesnerie, R. and J.-J. Laffont (1984), 'A Complete Solution to a Class of Principal–Agent Problems with an Application to the Control of a Self-Managed Firm', *Journal of Public Economics*, **25**, 329–69.

Hackett, S.C. (1995), 'Pollution-Controlling Innovations in Oligopolistic Industries: Some Comparisons between Patent Races and Research Joint Ventures', *Journal of Environmental Economics and Management*, **29**, 339–56.

Hahn, R.W. (1984), 'Market Power and Transferable Property Rights', *Quarterly Journal of Economics*, **99**, 753–65.

Hahn, R.W. (1989), 'Economic Prescription for Environmental Problems: How the Patient Followed the Doctor's Orders', *Journal of Economic Perspectives*, **3** (2), 95–114.

Hahn, R.W. and R.N. Stavins (1992), 'Economic Incentives for Environmental Protection: Integrating Theory and Practice', *American Economic Review*, **82** (2), 464–8.

Hanley, N., J.F. Shogren and B. White (1997), *Environmental Economics in Theory and Practice*, London: Macmillan Press Ltd.

Harford, J.D. (1978), 'Firm Behavior under Imperfectly Enforceable Pollution Standards and Taxes', *Journal of Environmental Economics and Management*, **5** (1), 26–43.

Harford, J.D. (1987), 'Self-Reporting of Pollution and the Firm's Behavior under Imperfectly Enforceable Regulation', *Journal of Environmental Economics and Management*, **14**, 293–303.

Hartl, R.F. and P.M. Kort (1994), 'Optimal Input Substitution of a Firm Facing Environmental Constraint', University of Magdeburg Working Paper No. 5.

Hartl, R.F. and P.M. Kort (1996), 'Marketable Permits in a Stochastic Dynamic Model of the Firm,' *Journal of Optimization Theory and Applications*, **89** (1), 129–55.

Hartwick, J.M. (1977), 'Intergenerational Equity and the Investing of Rents from Exhaustible Resources', *American Economic Review*, **66**, 972–4.

Hartwick, J.M. (1989), *Non-renewable Resources. Extraction Programs and Markets*, London: Harwood Academic Publishers.

Hartwick, J.M. (1990), 'Natural Resources, National Accounting and

Economic Depreciation', *Journal of Public Economics,* **43**, 291–304.

Hazzila, M. and R.J. Kopp (1990), 'Social Cost of Environmental Quality Regulations: A General Equilibrium Analysis', *Journal of Political Economy*, **98**, 853–73.

Heal, G.M. (1982), 'The Use of Common Property Resources', in V.K. Smith and J.V. Krutilla (eds), *Explorations in Natural Resource Economics*, Baltimore: Johns Hopkins University Press.

Heal, G.M. (1993), 'Formation of International Environmental Agreements', in C. Carraro (ed.), *Trade, Innovation, Environment*, Dordrecht: Kluwer Academic Publishers.

Heal, G.M. (1995), 'Interpreting Sustainability', Fondazione Eni Enrico Mattei Discussion Paper 1.95, Milan.

Helfland, G.E. and J. Rubin (1994), 'Spreading versus Concentrating Damages: Environmental Policy in the Presence of Nonconvexities', *Journal of Environmental Economics and Management*, **27** (1), 84–91.

Helpman, E. and P. Krugman (1989), *Trade Policy and Market Structure*, Cambridge, Mass.: MIT Press.

Herriges, J., R. Govindasamy and J. Shogren (1994), 'Budget-Balancing Incentive Mechanisms', *Journal of Environmental Economics and Management*, **27**, 275–85.

Hettige, H., R.E.B. Lucas and D. Wheeler (1992), 'The Toxic Intensity of Industrial Production: Global Patterns, Trends, and Trade Policy', *AEA Papers and Proceedings*, **82** (2), 478–81.

Hirsch, M.W. and S. Smale (1974), *Differential Equations, Dynamical Systems and Linear Algebra*, New York: Academic Press.

Hoel, M. (1991), 'Global Environmental Problems: The Effects of Unilateral Actions Taken by One Country', *Journal of Environmental Economics and Management*, **20**, 55–70.

Hoel, M. (1992a), 'Emission Taxes in a Dynamic International Game of $CO_2$ Emissions', in R. Pethig (ed.), *Conflicts and Cooperation in Managing Environmental Resources*, Berlin: Springer-Verlag.

Hoel, M. (1992b), 'International Environmental Conventions: The Case of Uniform Reduction of Emissions', *Environmental and Resource Economics*, **2**, 141–60.

Hoel, M. (1993), 'Stabilizing $CO_2$ Emissions in Europe: Individual Stabilization vs. Harmonization of Carbon Taxes', in C. Carraro and D. Siniscalco (eds), *The Carbon Tax: An Economic Assessment*, Dordrecht: Kluwer Academic Publishers.

Hoel, M. (1994), 'Efficient Climate Policy in the Presence of Free Riders', *Journal of Environmental Economics and Management*, **27**, 259–74.

Hoel, M. (1996), 'Should a Carbon Tax Be Differentiated across Sectors?', *Journal of Public Economics*, **59**, 17–32.

Hoel, M. and I. Isaksen (1995), 'The Environmental Costs of Greenhouse Gas Emissions', *Annals of the International Society of Dynamics Games*, 2.

Holmstrom, B. (1982), 'Moral Hazard in Teams', *Bell Journal of Economics*, **13**, 323–40.

Howe, C.W. (1994), 'Taxes versus Tradeable Discharge Permits: A Review in the Light of the US and European Experience', *Environmental and Resource Economics*, **4**, 151–69.

Ingham, A., J. Maw and A. Ulph (1991), 'Empirical Measures of Carbon Taxes', *Oxford Review of Economic Policy*, **7**, 99–122.

Intriligator, M.D. (1971), *Mathematical Optimization and Economic Theory*, Englewood Cliffs, N.J.: Prentice-Hall, Inc.

IPCC-1 (1990), '*Scientific Assessment of Climate Change*, Report prepared for IPCC by Working Group I, World Meteorological Organization and United States Environmental Program.

Jaffe, A.B., S.R. Peterson, P.R. Portney and R.N. Stavins (1995), 'Environmental Regulation and the Competitiveness of U.S. Manufacturing: What Does the Evidence Tell Us?', *Journal of Economic Literature*, **33**, 132–63.

Jaffe, A.B. and R.N. Stavins (1995), 'Dynamic Incentives of Environmental Regulations: The Effects of Alternative Policy Instruments on Technology Diffusion', *Journal of Environmental Economics and Management*, **29** (3), S43–S63.

Jorgenson, D.W. and P.J. Wilcoxen (1990), 'Environmental Regulation and U.S. Economic Growth', *RAND Journal of Economics*, **21** (2), 314–40.

*Journal of Economic Perspectives* (1993), 'Symposium on Global Warming', **7**, 3–86.

*Journal of Economic Perspectives* (1994), Special issue, **8** (1),

*Journal of Environmental Economics and Management* (1990), Special issue on 'The Social Discount Rate', **18** (2), part 2.

*Journal of Political Economy* (1990), Special issue on 'Development', **98** (5), part 2.

Kaitala, V., K.-G. Mäler and H. Tulkens (1995) 'The Acid Rain Game as a Resource Allocation Process with Application to Negotiations between Finland, Russia and Estonia', *The Scandinavian Journal of Economics*, **97**, 325–44.

Kamien, M.I. and N.L. Schwartz (1982), 'The Role of Common Property Resources in Optimal Planning Models with Exhaustible Resources', in

V.K. Smith and J.V. Krutilla (eds), *Explorations in Natural Resource Economics*, Baltimore: Johns Hopkins University Press.

Katsoulacos, Y. (1997), 'R&D Spillovers, Cooperation, Subsidies and International Agreements', in C. Carraro (ed.), *International Environmental Negotiations*, Aldershot: Edward Elgar, forthcoming.

Katsoulacos, Y. and A. Xepapadeas (1995), 'Environmental Policy under Oligopoly with Endogenous Market Structure', *Scandinavian Journal of Economics*, **97**, 411–20.

Katsoulacos, Y. and A. Xepapadeas (1996a), 'Emission Taxes and Market Structure', in C. Carraro, Y. Katsoulacos and A. Xepapadeas (eds), *Environmental Policy and Market Structure*, Dordrecht: Kluwer Academic Publishers, 3–22.

Katsoulacos, Y. and A. Xepapadeas (1996b), 'Environmental Innovation, Spillovers and Optimal Policy Rules', in C. Carraro, Y. Katsoulacos and A. Xepapadeas (eds), *Environmental Policy and Market Structure*, Dordrecht: Kluwer Academic Publishers, 143–50.

Katsoulacos, Y. and A. Xepapadeas (1996c), 'Environmental R&D, Spillovers and Optimal Policy Schemes under Oligopoly', in A. Xepapadeas (ed.), *Environmental Policy for the Environment and Natural Resources*, Cheltenham, U.K.: Edward Elgar, 59–79.

Keeler, A.G. (1991), 'Noncompliant Firms in Transferable Discharge Permit Markets: Some Extensions', *Journal of Environmental Economics and Management*, **21** (2), 180–89.

Keeler, E., M. Spence and R. Zeckhauser (1971), 'The Optimal Control of Pollution', *Journal of Economic Theory*, **4**, 19–34.

Kennedy, P.W. (1994), 'Equilibrium Pollution Taxes in Open Economies with Imperfect Competition', *Journal of Environmental Economics and Management*, **27**, 49–63.

Ko, I.-D., H.E. Lapan and T. Sandler (1992), 'Controlling Stock Externalities: Flexible versus Inflexible Pigovian Corrections', *European Economic Review*, **36** (6), 1263–76.

Kohn, R.E. (1994), 'Do We Need the Entry–Exit Condition on Polluting Firms?', *Journal of Environmental Economics and Management*, **27** (1), 92–7.

Kolstad, C.D. (1987), 'Uniformity versus Differentiation in Regulating Externalities', *Journal of Environmental Economics and Management*, **14**, 386–99.

Kolstad, C.D., T.S. Ulen and G.V. Johnson (1990), '*Ex Post* Liability for Harm vs. *Ex Ante* Safety Regulation: Substitutes or Complements?', *American Economic Review*, **80** (4), 888–901.

Kolmogorov, A.N. and S.V. Fomin (1970), *Introductory Real Analysis*, New York: Dover Publications, Inc.

Kort, P.M. (1995), 'The Effects of Marketable Pollution Permits on the Firm's Optimal Investment Policies', *Central European Journal for Operations Research and Economics*, **3**, 139–55.

Krupnick, A.J., W.E. Oates and Van de Verg (1983), 'On Marketable Air Pollution Permits: The Case for a System of Pollution Offsets', *Journal of Environmental Economics and Management*, **10**, 233–47.

Krutilla, K. (1991), 'Environmental Regulation in an Open Economy', *Journal of Environmental Economics and Management*, **20**, 127–42.

Kverndokk, S. (1993), 'Global $CO_2$ Agreements: A Cost-Effective Approach', *The Energy Journal*, **14**, 91–112.

Kverndokk, S. (1994), 'Coalitions and Side Payments in International $CO_2$ Treaties', in E.C. van Ierland (ed.), *International Environmental Economics: Theories and Applications for Climate Change, Acidification and International Trade*, Amsterdam: North-Holland, Elsevier Science Publishers.

Laffont, J.-J. (1989), *The Economics of Uncertainty and Information*, Cambridge, Mass.: MIT Press.

Laffont, J.-J. (1994a), 'The New Economics of Regulation Ten Years After', *Econometrica*, **62**, 507–37.

Laffont, J.-J. (1994b), 'Regulation of Pollution with Asymmetric Information', in C. Dosi and T. Tomasi (eds), *Nonpoint Source Pollution Regulation: Issues and Analysis*, Dordrecht: Kluwer Academic Publishers, 39–66.

Laffont, J.-J. (1995), 'Regulation, Moral Hazard and Insurance of Environmental Risks', *Journal of Public Economics*, **58**, 319–36.

Laffont, J.-J. and J. Tirole (1993), *A Theory of Incentives and Procurement in Regulation*, Cambridge, Mass.: MIT Press.

Laffont, J.-J. and J. Tirole (1996a), 'Pollution Permits and Compliance Strategies', *Journal of Public Economics*, **62**, 85–125.

Laffont, J.-J. and J. Tirole (1996b), 'Pollution Permits and Environmental Innovation', *Journal of Public Economics*, **62**, 127–40.

LaFrance, J.T. and L.D. Barney (1991), 'The Envelope Theorem in Dynamic Optimization', *Journal of Economic Dynamics and Control*, **15**, 355–85.

Lambert, P.J. (1985), *Advanced Mathematics for Economists: Static and Dynamic Optimization*, Oxford: Blackwell.

Leonard, D. and N. van Long (1992), *Optimal Control Theory and Static Optimization in Economics*, Cambridge: Cambridge University Press.

Levin, D. (1985), 'Taxation within Cournot Oligopoly', *Journal of Public Economics*, **27**, 281–90.

Lichtenberg, E. and D. Zilberman (1988), 'Efficient Regulation of Environmental Health Risks', *Quarterly Journal of Economics*, **103**, 167–78.

Lipton, D., J. Poterba, J. Sachs and L. Summers (1982), 'Multiple Shooting on Rational Expectations Models', *Econometrica*, **50** (5), 1329–33.

Lucas, R.E., Jr (1988), 'On the Mechanics of Economic Development', *Journal of Monetary Economics*, **22** (1), 3–42.

Lyon, R.M. (1982), 'Auctions and Alternative Procedures for Allocating Pollution Rights', *Land Economics*, **58** (1), 16–32.

Mäler, K.-G. (1974), *Environmental Economics: A Theoretical Inquiry*, Baltimore: Johns Hopkins University Press.

Mäler, K.-G. (1989), 'The Acid Rain Game', in H. Folmer and E. C. van Ierland (eds), *Valuation Methods and Policy Making in Environmental Economics*, Amsterdam: Elsevier Science Publishers, 231–52.

Mäler, K.-G. (1990), 'International Environmental Problems', *Oxford Review of Economic Policy*, **6**, 80–108.

Mäler, K.-G. (1991), 'National Accounts and Environmental Resources', *Environmental and Resource Economics*, **1**, 1–15.

Mäler, K.-G. (1992), 'Critical Loads and International Environmental Cooperation', in R. Pethig (ed.), *Conflicts and Cooperation in Managing Environmental Resources*, Berlin: Springer-Verlag.

Mäler, K.-G. (1994a), 'Acid Rain in Europe: A Dynamic Perspective on the Use of Economic Incentives', in E.C. van Ierland (ed.), *International Environmental Economics. Developments in Environmental Economics*, Amsterdam: Elsevier Science Publishers, 351–72.

Mäler, K.-G. (1994b), 'Economic Growth and the Environment', in L.L. Pasinetti and R.M. Solow (eds), *Economic Growth and the Structure of Long-Term Development*, New York: St Martin's Press.

Mäler, K.-G and A. de Zeeuw (1995), 'Critical Loads in Games and Transboundary Pollution Control', Fondazione ENI Enrico Mattei Discussion Paper 7.95, Milan.

Malik, A.S. (1990), 'Markets for Pollution Control when Firms are Noncompliant', *Journal of Environmental Economics and Management*, **18**, 97–106.

Malliaris, A.G. and W.A. Brock (1982), *Stochastic Methods in Economics and Finance*, Amsterdam: North-Holland.

Malueg, D.A. (1989), 'Emission Credit Trading and the Incentive to Adopt New Pollution Abatement Technology', *Journal of Environmental*

*Economics and Management*, **16** (1), 52–7.

Malueg, D.A. (1990), 'Welfare Consequences of Emission Credit Trading Programs', *Journal of Environmental Economics and Management*, **18** (1), 66–77.

Mankiw, N.G. and M.D. Whinston (1986), 'Free-Entry and Social Inefficiency', *Rand Journal of Economics*, **17**, 48–58.

Markusen, J.R. (1975), 'International Externalities and Optimal Tax Structures', *Journal of International Economics*, **5**, 15–29.

Martin, W.E., R.H. Patrick and B. Tolwinski (1993), 'A Dynamic Game of a Transboundary Pollutant with Asymmetric Players', *Journal of Environmental Economics and Management*, **25**, 1–12.

Mas-Colell, A., M.D. Whinston and G.R. Green (1995), *Microeconomic Theory*, New York: Oxford University Press.

McGartland, A.M. and W.E. Oates (1985), 'Marketable Permit for the Prevention of Environmental Deterioration', *Journal of Environmental Economics and Management*, **12**, 207–28.

Meran, G. and U. Schwalbe (1987), 'Pollution Control and Collective Penalties', *Journal of Institutional Theoretical Economics*, **143**, 616–29.

Michel, P. (1993), 'Pollution and Growth towards the Ecological Paradise', Fondazione Eni Enrico Mattei Discussion Paper 80.93, Milan.

Michel, P. and G. Rotillon (1992), 'Pollution's Disutility and Endogenous Growth', Mimeo, Université Paris I.

Milliman, S.R. and R. Prince (1989), 'Firm Incentives to Promote Technological Change in Pollution Control', *Journal of Environmental Economics and Management*, **17** (3), 247–65.

Misiolek, S.W. (1980), 'Effluent Taxation in Monopoly Markets', *Journal of Environmental Economics and Management*, **7**, 103–107.

Misiolek, S.W. (1988), 'Pollution Control through Price Incentives: The Role of Rent Seeking Costs in Monopoly Markets', *Journal of Environmental Economics and Management*, **15**, 1–8.

Montgomery, W.D. (1972), 'Markets in Licenses and Efficient Pollution Control Programs', *Journal of Economic Theory*, **5**, 395–418.

Musu, I. (1995), 'Traditional Dynamics to Optimal Sustainable Growth', Fondazione Eni Enrico Mattei Discussion Paper 50.95, Milan.

Newbery, D. (1990), 'Acid Rain', *Economic Journal*, **5**, 297–346.

Nordhaus, W.D. (1977), 'Strategies for the Control of Carbon Dioxide', Cowles Foundation Discussion Paper 443.

Nordhaus, W.D. (1982), 'How Fast Should We Craze the Global Commons?', *American Economic Association Papers and Proceedings*, **72**, 242–6.

Nordhaus, W.D. (1991), 'To Slow or Not to Slow: The Economics of the Greenhouse Effect', *Economic Journal*, **101**, 920–37.

Nordhaus, W.D. (1994), 'Reflections on the Concept of Sustainable Economic Growth', in L.L. Pasinetti and R.M. Solow (eds), *Economic Growth and the Structure of Long-Term Development*, New York: St Martin's Press.

Nordhaus, W.D. and Z. Yang (1996), 'A Regional Dynamic General-Equilibrium Model of Alternative Climate-Change Strategies', *American Economic Review*, **86**, 741–65.

Novshek, W. (1993), *Mathematics for Economists*, New York: Academic Press.

Oates, W.E. (1991), 'Pollution Charges as a Source of Public Revenues', Resources for the Future Discussion Paper QE92-05 RFF, Washington, D.C.

Oates, W.E., K. Palmer and P.R. Portney (1993), 'Environmental Regulation and International Competitiveness: Thinking about the Porter Hypothesis', Resources for the Future Discussion Paper 94-02.

Oates, W.E. and D.L. Strassmann (1984), 'Effluent Fees and Market Structure', *Journal of Public Economics*, **24**, 29–46.

OECD (1989), *Economic Instruments for Environmental Protection*, Paris, OECD.

OECD (1991), *Environmental Policy: How to Apply Economic Instruments*, Paris, OECD.

OECD (1992), *Climate Change: Designing an Practical Tax System*, Paris, OECD.

OECD (1994a), *Applying Economic Instruments to Environmental Policies in OECD and Dynamic Non-Member Economies*, Paris, OECD.

OECD (1994b), *Managing the Environment: The Role of Economic Instruments*, Paris, OECD.

Ostaszewski, A. (1990), *Advanced Mathematical Methods*, Cambridge: Cambridge University Press.

Palmer, K., W.E. Oates and P.R. Portney (1995), 'Tightening Environmental Standards: The Benefit-Cost or the No-Cost Paradigm?', *Journal of Economic Perspectives*, **9**, 119–32.

Parry, I.W.H. (1995), 'Pollution Taxes and Revenue Recycling', *Journal of Environmental Economics and Management*, **29** (3), S64–S79.

Pearce, D.W. (1991), 'The Role of Carbon Taxes in Adjusting to Global Warming', *Economic Journal*, **101**, 938–48.

Pearce, D.W. (1992), 'Should the GATT be Reformed for Environmental Reasons?', CSERGE Working Paper GEC 92–06.

Pearce, D.W., E. Barbier and A. Markandya (1990), *Sustainable Development: Economics and Environment in the Third World*, Worcester, UK: Edward Elgar.

Pearce, D. W. and R.K. Turner (1990), *Economics of Natural Resources and the Environment*, Baltimore: The Johns Hopkins University Press.

Pearson, M. and S. Smith (1991), 'The European Carbon Tax: An Assessment of the European Commission's Proposal', The Institute for Fiscal Studies, London.

Pethig, R. (1993), 'Ecological Dynamics and the Valuation of Environmental Change', manuscript, University of Siegen.

Petrakis, E. and A. Xepapadeas (1996), 'Environmental Consciousness and Moral Hazard in International Agreements to Protect the Environment', *Journal of Public Economics*, **60**, 95–110.

Pezzey, J. (1992), 'Some Interactions between Environmental Policy and Public Finance', Working Paper, University of Bristol.

Pezzey, J. (1995), 'Sustainable Development, Intergenerational Equity and Environmental Policy', University College London Discussion Papers in Economics, No. 95-01.

Pigou, A.C. (1938), *The Economics of Welfare*, Fourth Edition, London: Macmillan and Co.

Pitchford, R. (1995), 'How Liable Should a Lender Be? The Case of Judgement-Proof Owner-Managed Firms', *American Economic Review*, **85**, 1171–86.

Plourde, C.G. (1972), 'A Model of Waste Accumulation and Disposal', *Canadian Journal of Economics*, **5** (1), 119–25.

Plourde, G. and D. Yeung (1989), 'A Model of Industrial Pollution in a Stochastic Environment', *Journal of Environmental Economics and Management*, **16**, 97–105.

Porter, M. (1991), 'America's Green Strategy', *Scientific American*, **264**, 168.

Porter, M. and C. van der Linde (1995), 'Towards a New Conception of the Environment–Competitiveness Relationship', *Journal of Economic Perspectives*, **9**, 97–118.

Poterba, J.M. (1993), 'Global Warming: A Public Finance Perspective', *Journal of Economic Perspectives*, **7** (4), 47–63.

Provencher, B. and O. Burt (1993), 'The Externalities Associated with the Common Property Exploitation of Groundwater', *Journal of Environmental Economics and Management*, **24** (2), 139–58.

*Quarterly Journal of Economics* (1991), Special issue on 'Economic Growth', **106** (2).

Rasmusen, E. (1987), 'Moral Hazard in Risk-Averse Teams', *RAND Journal of Economics*, **18**, 428–35.

Rauscher, M. (1992), 'Economic Integration and the Environment: Effect on Members and Non-Members', *Environmental and Resource Economics*, **2**, 221–36.

Rauscher, M. (1995), 'Strategic Environmental Policy in Oligopolistic Markets', Fondazione ENI Enrico Mattei Discussion Paper 65.95, Milan.

Rawls, J. (1971), *A Theory of Justice*, Massachusetts: Harvard University Press.

Rebello, S. (1991), 'Long Run Policy Analysis and Long Run Growth', *Journal of Political Economy*, **99** (3), 500–21.

Repetto, R. (1987), 'The Policy Implications of Non-Convex Environmental Damages: A Smog Control Case Study', *Journal of Environmental Economics and Management*, **14**, 13–29.

Repetto, R., R.C. Dower, R. Jenkins and J. Geoghagan (1992), 'Green Fees: How a Tax Shift Can Work for the Environment', World Resources Institute, Washington, D.C.

Requate, T. (1992), 'Pollution Control under Imperfect Competition: Asymmetric Bertrand Duopoly with Linear Technologies', University of Bielefeld, Institute of Mathematical Economics Working Paper No. 216.

Requate, T. (1995), 'Incentives to Adopt New Technologies under Different Pollution-Control Policies', *International Tax and Public Finance*, **2**, 295–317.

*Resource and Energy Economics* (1993), 'Global Warming' (special issue), **15**.

Rivera-Batiz, L. and P. Romer (1991), 'Economic Integration and Endogenous Growth', *Quarterly Journal of Economics*, **106**, 531–56.

Roberts, M.J. and M. Spence (1976), 'Effluent Charges and Licenses under Uncertainty', *Journal of Public Economics*, **5**, 193–208.

Romer, P.M. (1986), 'Increasing Returns and Long-Run Growth', *Journal of Political Economy*, **94** (5), 1002–37.

Romer, P.M. (1987), 'Growth Based on Increasing Returns Due to Specialization', *American Economic Review*, **77** (2), 56–62.

Romer, P.M. (1990), 'Endogenous Technological Change', *Journal of Political Economy*, **98**, S71–S102.

Romer, P.M. (1994), 'New Goods, Old Theory and the Welfare Costs of Trade Restrictions', *Journal of Development Economics*, **43** (1).

Rose, A. (1992), 'Equity Considerations of Tradeable Carbon Entitlements', in S. Barrett et al. (eds), *Tradeable Carbon Emission Entitlements*, Geneva: UNCTAD.

Rose, A. and B. Stevens (1993), 'The Efficiency and Equity of Marketable Permits for CO$_2$ Emissions', *Resource and Energy Economics*, **15**, 117–46.

Rose, A. and B. Stevens (1996), 'Equity Aspects of the Marketable Permits Approach to Global Warming Policy', paper presented at the Sixth Annual Conference of the European Association of Environmental and Resource Economists, Lisbon, Portugal, June 1996.

Rose-Ackerman, S. (1973), 'Effluent Charges: A Critique', *Canadian Journal of Economics*, **6**, 512–28.

Russell, C.S., W. Harrington and W.J. Vaughan (1986), *Enforcing Pollution Control Laws*, Washington, D.C.: Resources for the Future.

Sartzetakis, E. (1997a), 'Raising Rivals' Costs Strategies via Emission Permits Markets', *Review of Industrial Organization*, forthcoming.

Sartzetakis, E. (1997b), 'Tradeable Emission Permits Regulations in the Presence of Imperfectly Competitive Product Markets: Welfare Implications', *Environmental and Resource Economics*, forthcoming.

Segerson, K. (1988), 'Uncertainty and Incentives for Nonpoint Pollution Control', *Journal of Environmental Economics and Management*, **15**, 87–98.

Segerson, K. (1993), 'Liability Transfers: An Economic Assessment of Buyer and Lender Liability', *Journal of Environmental Economics and Management*, **25** (1), S46–S63.

Seierstad, A. and K. Sydsaeter (1987), *Optimal Control Theory with Economic Applications*, Amsterdam: North-Holland.

Selden, T.M. and D. Song (1994), 'Environmental Quality and Development: Is There a Kuznets Curve for Air Pollution Emissions?', *Journal of Environmental Economics and Management*, **27** (2), 147–62.

Selden, T.M. and D. Song (1995), 'Neoclassical Growth, the J Curve for Abatement, and the Inverted U Curve for Pollution', *Journal of Environmental Economics and Management*, **29** (2), 162–8.

Sen, A. (1988), 'The Concept of Development', in H. Chenery and T.N. Srinivasan (eds), *Handbook of Economic Development*, Vol. 1, Amsterdam: North-Holland.

Seskin, E.P., R.J. Anderson and R.O. Reid (1983), 'An Empirical Analysis of Economic Strategies for Controlling Air Pollution', *Journal of Environmental Economics and Management*, **10**, 112–24.

Shah, A. and B. Larsen (1992), 'Carbon Taxes, the Greenhouse Effect and Developing Countries,' World Bank Policy Research Working Paper 957, The World Bank, Washington, D.C.

Shavell, S. (1984), 'A Model of the Optimal Use of Liability and Safety Regulation', *Rand Journal of Economics*, **15**, 271–80.

Shogren, J., J. Herriges and R. Govindasamy (1993), 'Limits to Environmental Bonds', *Ecological Economics*, **8**, 109–33.

Shortle, J. and D.G. Abler (1994), 'Incentives for Nonpoint Pollution Control', in C. Dosi and T. Tomasi (eds), *Nonpoint Source Pollution Regulation: Issues and Analysis*, Dordrecht: Kluwer Academic Publishers, 137–49.

Shortle, J. and J. Dunn (1986), 'The Relative Efficiency of Agricultural Source Water Pollution Control Policies', *American Journal of Agricultural Economics*, **68**, 668–77.

Siebert, H. (1985), 'Spatial Aspects of Environmental Economics', in A.V. Kneese and J.L. Sweeney (eds), *Handbook of Natural Resource and Energy Economics*, Volume I, Amsterdam: North-Holland, pp. 125–64.

Siebert, H. (1992), *Economics of the Environment,* Third Edition, Berlin: Springer-Verlag.

Simon, C.P. and L. Blume (1993), *Mathematics for Economists*, New York: Norton.

Simpson, R.D. and R.L. Bradford III (1996), 'Taxing Variable Cost: Environmental Regulation in Industrial Policy', *Journal of Environmental Economics and Management*, **30**, 282–300.

Solow, R. (1956), 'A Contribution to the Theory of Economic Growth', *Quarterly Journal of Economics*, **70**, 65–94.

Solow, R. (1957), 'Technical Change and the Aggregate Function', *Review of Economics and Statistics*, **39**, 312–20.

Solow, R. (1974), 'Intergenerational Equity and Exhaustible Resources', *Review of Economic Studies*, Symposium on the Economics of Exhaustible Resources, 29–45.

Solow, R. (1986), 'On the Intergenerational Allocation of Natural Resources', *Scandinavian Journal of Economics*, **88** (1), 141–9.

Solow, R. (1992). *An Almost Practical Step toward Sustainability*, Washington, D.C.: Resources for the Future.

Spence, A.M. (1976), 'Production Differentiation and Welfare', *American Economic Review*, **66**, 407–14.

Spulber, D.F. (1985), 'Effluent Regulation and Long-run Optimality', *Journal of Environmental Economics and Management*, **12**, 103–16.

Spulber, D.F. (1988), 'Optimal Environmental Regulation under Asymmetric Information', *Journal of Public Economics*, **35**, 163–81.

Starrett, D.A. (1972), 'Fundamental Nonconvexities in the Theory of Externalities', *Journal of Economic Theory*, **4**, 180–99.

Stavins, R.N. (1995), 'Transaction Costs and Tradeable Permits', *Journal of Environmental Economics and Management*, **29**, 133–48.

Stavins, R.N. (1996), 'Correlated Uncertainty and Policy Instrument Choice', *Journal of Environmental Economics and Management*, **30**, 218–33.

Sydsaeter, K. and P.J. Hammond (1994), *Mathematics for Economic Analysis*, Prentice-Hall, Inc.

Tahvonen, O. V. Kaitala and M. Pohjola (1993), 'A Finnish-Soviet Acid Rain Game: Noncooperative Equilibria, Cost Efficiency, and Sulfur Agreements', *Journal of Environmental Economics and Management*, **24**, 87–99.

Tahvonen, O. and Kuuluvainen (1993), 'Economic Growth, Pollution, and Renewable Resources', *Journal of Environmental Economics and Management*, **24** (2), 101–18.

Tahvonen, O. and S. Salo (1996), 'Nonconvexities in Optimal Pollution Accumulation', *Journal of Environmental Economics and Management*, **31** (2), 160–77.

Tahvonen, O. and C. Withagen (1996), 'Optimality of Irreversible Pollution Accumulation', *Journal of Economic Dynamics and Control*, **20**, 1775–95.

Takayama, A. (1985), *Mathematical Economics,* Second Edition, Cambridge: Cambridge University Press.

Takayama, A. (1994), *Analytical Methods in Economics*, New York: Harvester Wheatsheaf.

Terkla, D. (1984), 'The Efficiency Value of Effluent Tax Revenues', *Journal of Environmental Economics and Management*, **11**, 107–25.

Thomas, A. (1995), 'Regulation of Pollution under Asymmetric Information: The Case of Industrial Wastewater Treatment Activity', *Journal of Environmental Economics and Management*, **28**, 357–73.

Tietenberg, T.H. (1978), 'Spatially Differentiated Air Pollutant Emission Charges: An Economic and Legal Analysis', *Land Economics*, **54**, 265–77.

Tietenberg, T.H. (1980), 'Transferable Discharge Permits and the Control of Stationary Source Air Pollution: A Survey and Synthesis', *Land Economics*, **56**, 391–416.

Tietenberg, T.H. (1985), *Emissions Trading: An Exercise in Reforming Pollution Policy*, Washington, D.C.: Resources for the Future.

Tietenberg, T.H. (1995), 'Tradeable Permits for Pollution Control when Emission Location Matters: What Have We Learned?', *Environmental and Resource Economics*, **5**, 95–113.

Tietenberg, T.H. (1996), *Environmental and Natural Resource Economics*, Fourth Edition, HarperCollins College Publishers.

Ulph, A. (1994), 'Environmental Policy and International Trade - A Survey of Recent Economic Analysis', Fondazione ENI Enrico Mattei Discussion

Paper 53.94, Milan.

Ulph, A. (1996), 'Environmental Policy and International Trade when Governments and Producers Act Strategically', *Journal of Environmental Economics and Management*, **30**, 265–81.

van der Ploeg, F. and A.J. de Zeeuw (1992), 'International Aspects of Pollution Control', *Environmental and Resource Economics*, **2**, 117–39.

van der Ploeg, F. and C. Withagen (1991), 'Pollution Control and the Ramsey Problem', *Environmental and Resource Economics*, **1**, 215–36.

van Egteren, H. and M. Weber (1996), 'Marketable Permits, Market Power, and Cheating', *Journal of Environmental Economics and Management*, **30**, 161–73.

Varian, H.R. (1981), 'Dynamical Systems with Applications to Economics', in K.J. Arrow and M.D. Intriligator (eds), *Handbook of Mathematical Economics*, Vol. I, Amsterdam: North-Holland.

Vatn, A., L.R. Bakken, M. A. Bleken, P. Botterweg, H. Lundeby, E. Romstad, P.K. Rorstad and A. Vold (1996), 'Policies for Reduced Nutrient Losses and Erosion from Norwegian Agriculture', *Norwegian Journal of Agricultural Sciences*, Supplement No. 23.

von der Fehr, N.-H.M (1993), 'Tradeable Emission Rights and Strategic Interaction', *Environmental and Resource Economics*, **3**, 129–51.

Weaver, R.D (1996), 'Prosocial Behavior: Private Contributions to Agriculture's Impact on the Environment', *Land Economics*, **72**, 231–47.

Weaver, R.D., J.K. Harper and W.J. Gillmeister (1996), 'Efficacy of Standards vs. Incentives for Managing the Environmental Impacts of Agriculture', *Journal of Environmental Economics and Management*, **46**, 173–88.

Weaver, R.D. and A. Thomas (1996), 'Regulation of Nonpoint Source Pollution with Factor Augmentation of Polluting Inputs', paper presented at the 7th Annual Conference of the European Association of Environmental and Resource Economics, Lisbon, Portugal, June 1996.

Weitzman, M.L. (1974), 'Prices *vs.* Quantities', *Review of Economic Studies,* **41**, 477–91.

Weitzman, M. (1976), 'On the Welfare Significance of National Product in a Dynamic Economy', *Quarterly Journal of Economics*, **90**.

Weitzman, M. (1994), 'On the 'Environmental' Discount Rate', *Journal of Environmental Economics and Management*, **26** (3), 200–209.

Welsch, H. (1993) 'An Equilibrium Framework for Global Pollution Problems', *Journal of Environmental Economics and Management*, **25**, S64–S79.

Welsch, H. (1994), 'Incomplete International Cooperation to Reduce $CO_2$

Emissions: The Case of Price Discrimination', *Journal of Environmental Economics and Management*, **27**, 254–8.

Weyant, J.P. (1993), 'Costs of Reducing Global Carbon Emissions', *Journal of Economic Perspectives*, **7**, 27–46.

Wingley, T.M.L. (1987), 'Relative Contributions of Different Trace Gasses to the Greenhouse Problem', *Climate Monitor*, **16**, 14–20.

World Bank (1992), *World Development Report 1992: Development and the Environment*, New York: Oxford University Press.

Xepapadeas, A. (1991), 'Environmental Policy under Imperfect Information: Incentives and Moral Hazard', *Journal of Environmental Economics and Management*, **20**, 113–26.

Xepapadeas, A. (1992a), 'Environmental Policy, Adjustment Costs, and Behavior of the Firm', *Journal of Environmental Economics and Management*, **23** (3), 258–75.

Xepapadeas, A. (1992b), 'Environmental Policy Design and Dynamic Nonpoint-Source Pollution', *Journal of Environmental Economics and Management*, **23** (1), 22–39.

Xepapadeas, A. (1992c), 'Optimal Taxes for Pollution Regulation: Dynamic, Spatial and Stochastic Characteristics', *Natural Resource Modelling*, **6**, 139–70.

Xepapadeas, A. (1994), 'Controlling Environmental Externalities: Observability and Optimal Policy Rules', in C. Dosi and T. Tomasi (eds), *Nonpoint Source Pollution Regulation: Issues and Analysis*, Dordrecht: Kluwer Academic Publishers, 67–86.

Xepapadeas, A. (1995a), 'Induced Technical Change and International Agreements', *Resource and Energy Economics*, **17**, 1–23.

Xepapadeas, A. (1995b), 'Managing the International Commons: Resource Use and Pollution Control', *Environmental and Resource Economics*, **5**, 375–91.

Xepapadeas, A. (1995c), 'Observability and Choice of Instrument Mix in the Control of Externalities', *Journal of Public Economics*, **56**, 485–98.

Xepapadeas, A. (1996a), 'Managing Common-Access Resources under Production Externalities', in A. Xepapadeas (ed.), *Environmental Policy for the Environment and Natural Resources*, Cheltenham, U.K.: Edward Elgar.

Xepapadeas, A. (1996b), 'Quantity and Quality Management of Groundwater: An Application to Irrigated Agriculture in Iraklion, Crete', *Environmental Modeling and Assessment*, **1**, 25–35.

Xepapadeas, A. (1997a), 'Economic Development and Environmental Traps', *Structural Change and Economic Dynamics*, forthcoming.

Xepapadeas, A. (1997b), 'Non-Point Source Pollution Control', in J. van den Bergh (ed.), *The Handbook of Environmental and Resource Economics*, Edward Elgar Publishers.

Xepapadeas, A. (1997c), 'Regulation of Mineral Emissions under Asymmetric Information', in E. Romstad, J. Simonsen and A. Vatn (eds), *Controlling Mineral Emissions in European Agriculture: Economics, Policies and the Environment*, Wallingfor, U.K.: CAB Publishers.

Xepapadeas, A. and E. Amri (1997), 'Some Empirical Indications of the Relationship between Environmental Quality and Economic Development' *Environmental and Resource Economics*, **6**, 1-14.

Xepapadeas, A. and A. Yiannaka (1997), 'Measuring Benefits and Damages from Carbon Dioxide Emissions and International Agreements to Slow Down Greenhouse Warming', in C. Carraro (ed.), *International Environmental Negotiations*, Aldershot: Edward Elgar.

# Index